CND

Hamish Henderson: A Biography

Volume 2: *Poetry Becomes People*

Hamish and Felicity (Katzel) Henderson in Dublin, 1961 (KH).

HAMISH HENDERSON

A BIOGRAPHY

Volume 2 *Poetry Becomes People* (1952–2002)

TIMOTHY NEAT

Polygon

First published in Great Britain in 2009 by
Polygon, an imprint of Birlinn Ltd

West Newington House
10 Newington Road
Edinburgh
EH9 1QS

www.birlinn.co.uk

ISBN: 978 1 84697 063 4

The publishers gratefully acknowledge subsidy from the Scottish Arts Council
towards the publication of this book

Scottish
Arts Council

British Library Cataloguing-in-Publication Data
A catalogue record for this book is available on request from the British Library

Typeset by Hewer Text UK Ltd, Edinburgh
Printed and bound in Britain by MPG Books, Bodmin, Cornwall

To

Robin Smart of Dunkeld

Christopher James Neat of Vancouver Island

Carmen Marubini Neat, Great Nonna Kate (1918–2009)

and

Hamish's Scotland

as in the story and in the song

Above all they are very shallow people who take everything literal. A man's life of any worth is a continual allegory – and very few eyes can see the mystery of his life . . . a life like the scriptures, figurative.

John Keats

Contents

Preface

In February 1949 the historian E.P. Thompson wrote to congratulate Hamish on the publication of his *Elegies for the Dead in Cyrenaica.*

> I greet you with humility, *compagno*, for you are that rare man, a poet. You have achieved poems out of our dead century . . . You must remain a poet. Remember always who you are writing for: the people of Glasgow, of Halifax, of Dublin . . . You, more than any poet I know, are an instrument through which thousands of others can become articulate. And you must not forget that your songs and ballads . . . are quite as important as your Elegies.

Hamish took this advice very seriously, partly because it coincided with his own deep instincts, and within a couple of years he had become a professional folklorist determined to 'sing' a new, post-Calvinist Scotland into being. He encountered opposition but for the next fifty years determinedly went out amongst the folk, broadcasting and reaping, and, long before his death on 8 March 2002, at the age of eighty-two, Hamish had become, as W.H. Auden wrote of Sigmund Freud, 'a whole climate of opinion'.

The London BBC News made no mention of Hamish's passing but, to the surprise of many, Scotland's new Parliament paid homage to Hamish with an hour-long tribute (the only person so honoured in the Parliament's history). He was applauded as a great humanitarian, an internationalist, a peace campaigner, a man of the people, a poet who, like Shakespeare, put a mirror up to nature and the nation that he loved. Hamish's song 'The Flyting o' Life and Daith' gives poetic force to the clash of the kind of opposites to which he dedicated his great energies:

> Quo life, the warld is mine.
> The floo'ers and trees, they're a' my ain.
> I am the day, and the sunshine
> Quo life, the warld is mine.

Quo daith, the warld is mine.
        Your lugs are deef, your een are blin
Your floo'ers maun dwine in my bitter win
        Quo daith , the warld is mine.

Quo Life the warld is mine.
        I hae saft wins, an healin rain,
Apples I hae, an breid an wine
        Quo life, the warld is mine . . .[1]

Shortly after E.P. Thompson wrote the letter quoted above, Hamish began working on a long poem, 'Freedom becomes People'. Outlining the structure of his poem, Hamish noted that the Christ story is the archetypal life-story of the artist–hero, 'a truth-loving poet in an authoritarian climate which adores only lies'. His heroes Antonio Gramsci, John MacLean, Nelson Mandela (and Che Guevara) all suffered forms of similar martyrdom. Here are some of Hamish's early jottings:

Memories of the undone
On narrow shoulder lean their atrocious weight.
The ideal poetry of the world beyond appearance reveals itself
in a flash from time to time.

There is power, power
        Wonderworking power
In the blood of the Lord
        There is power.

When the old hear me
        talk of death – or say the word themselves –
                for a minute they are lost.
                        incompetent to deal with it –
                                and say knowing for sometime.

The madonna of the roads
                the sacred traveller.

        To think is to think long on all the horror:
                Histories saturnalia.[2]

---

1 HH, 'The Flyting o' Life and Daith', published in *Hamish Henderson: Collected Poems and Songs* (Curly Snake 2000).

2 HH, unpublished notes, Henderson archive.

Pagan, Christian, rational, ecstatic – there we have Hamish in an acorn cup. Initially he entitled his poem 'The Cell', then 'Christus'[3] but settled finally on Heine's inspired words, 'Freedom becomes People'. His friend Duncan Glen then adapted the phrase as the rubric 'Poetry becomes People' to describe the totality of Hamish's highly original cultural/political vision. It brilliantly encapsulates the organic nature, the oceanic scale of Hamish's cultural ambition, his wish to nurture life – individual, collective, biological, historical and ecological. I am proud to make Duncan's words the title of this volume.

In a society that still accepts it as normal that the British taxpayer should pay for Prince Andrew to fly to St Andrews for a round of golf it is not surprising that the death of a man like Hamish is not considered national news. In years to come, however, when our obsequious subservience to royalty is recognised as offensive, the songs and poems that Hamish made and championed will still bring beauty and truth to the minds of men and women 'with a thought or two to rub together', as Hamish liked to say.

* * *

Readers will find that Volume 2 of this biography moves more slowly than Volume 1. The intensity of Hamish's youthful focus gradually softened and widened as the years passed and others began to share his burdens and joys. By his mid thirties his personal artistic creativity was waning but with his appointment as a folk studies researcher at the School of Scottish Studies at the University of Edinburgh (in 1952) he gained a public platform that enabled him to make Scotland the stage for fifty years of Prospero-like experiments. Hamish made himself champion of Scotland's rich oral traditions at the very moment when the new media were also beginning to challenge the tyranny of institutionalised literacy. Any lingering desire Hamish retained for fame as 'a published poet' was extinguished as he took personal responsibility for 'the word' and music of his people in a new multimedia, multicultural world.

His stance as a folklorist was philosophical, cultural and political: he saw no division between the artistic power of the written and the unwritten word, the authorial voice and folk tradition, the witty one-liner and the wisdom of the ages. He recognised that the vernacular culture of Scotland was a vast

---

3 It is no accident that many of Hamish's poems explore Christian themes: 'Ballad of the Twelve Stations of my Youth', 'Patmos', 'The Salamander', 'Lament for the Son'. He believed in a practical Christian socialism and whilst determined to enjoy his time on earth he was propelled by the idea of service to his brother man. The title of *Elegies for the Dead in Cyrenaica* owes more than a little to the fact that it was Simon of Cyrene who gave Christ practical help when He fell beneath the weight of His Cross.

reservoir of energies and traditions that should be celebrated and broadcast worldwide. He felt passionately that poetry must be reconnected to its origin in song and the direct life of its audience, the tribe.

Through his work for the School of Scottish Studies Hamish quickly gained a reputation as an exemplary professional scholar but refused to be conscribed by self-referential academic norms. He saw the field of folklore as a great open space – a university – for the study of everything concerning people. He had a matchless ear for the deeps of Scots culture, a faultless eye for authenticity of performance, quality and honesty of mind. For him folk studies were a revolutionary force: a well, not at the world's end but 'here and now'. He was a romantic but knew his history and always sought practical objectives. As Byron foresaw the means by which he might bring freedom (and genius) back to the Greek people, so Hamish believed he could nurture new freedoms and spread new concepts of genius, in Scotland. In 1938 he wrote of the Gorbals:

> Alone and alonie
> I climb Balmano Street. The haggard houses
> Spew out their wizened, withered aged children
> On to the dirty stone . . . So howl ye ships from Clyde![4]

Fifty years later, in his last poem, 'Under the Earth I Go' (completed in 1991), he paints a very different picture:

> . . . Change elegy into hymn, remake it –
> Don't fail again. Like the potent
> Sap in these branches, once bare, and now brimming
> With routh of green leavery,
> Remake it, and renew . . .[5]

Hamish was a legendary talker, a drinker whom many – in life and since his death – dismiss as a maudlin haverer or revolutionary hard man. But, to those with ears to hear, Hamish in full flow raised spirits and horizons as few individuals do: his listeners felt impelled to address their better selves and the faultlines in their societies. Apparently haphazard bar conversations became fulcrums of tens of thousands of adventures, projects and relationships. The story of the loaves and fishes exists in imaginations only, but what a story and what an idea.

Today, perhaps surprisingly, few of Hamish's many friends remember much of what he actually said. It was the ambience he created, the joys he liberated, the conviviality he engendered, the moral certitudes generated

4 HH, From 'Journey to a Kingdom', published in *Hamish Henderson: Collected Poems and Songs* (Curly Snake 2000).

5 Published in the *Collected Poems*.

that remain indelibly – mysteriously – comprehended. And beyond that, of course, the poems, the songs, the letters, the articles, the translations exist; and his deeds live as historical facts.

As age limited his powers, Hamish gloried in 'the art of compotation'; the passing round of drinks became a kind of baptismal immersion, a Celtic vanishing act, in which song, stories and enquiry became vehicles for a kind of public love-making in which the sensation of being alive became a transcendent reality. A filigree of possibilities, a page in the Book of Kells, would be turned. The moment is, the living is. Hamish knew drink to be a two-headed monster: like 'the twin dragons, Life and Death, / Joustin thegither under the Maypole'.[6] But for him *uisge beatha*[7] was a reality and symbol of something great – beyond measure or price. MacDiarmid had touched on the essence of this very Scottish phenomenon in the 1930s, and dull would he be of soul who presumes such an essence mere alcohol.

> In Scotland in the Gaidhealtachd there's a golden wine,
> A wine that demands so deliberate a pause,
> In order to detect its hidden peculiarities
> And subtle exquisiteness of flavour, that to drink it
> Is really more a moral than a physical delight.
> There is a deliciousness in it that eludes analysis
> And like everything else that is superlatively good
> Is better appreciated by the memory
> Than by present consciousness . . .
>
> . . . Through what else can Scotland recover its poise
> Save, as very Hope, this golden wine yet?[8]

In the eighteenth century Burns wrote that 'Whisky and Liberty gang thegither' and Hamish, with even greater determination, cocked a snook at the propriety that has hardened so many hearts in Scotland across the ages. Research exercises often take strange forms – within universities and without – and Hamish consciously used Sandy Bell's bar as a crucible in which Scots steel might become earth again. He sought a Blakean New Jerusalem where, 'Tomorrow, songs / Will flow free again, and new voices / Be borne on the carrying stream.'[9] As the history of modern Ireland proves, 'good craik' can be the springboard not just to great literary achievements but also to full stomachs, political change and human

6 From 'Under the Earth I Go', published in the *Collected Poems*.

7 *Uisge beatha*: water of life (whisky).

8 Hugh MacDiarmid, 'A Golden Wine in the Gaidhealtachd', in *The Complete Poems of Hugh MacDiarmid* (Martin Brian and O'Keeffe 1978).

9 From 'Under the Earth I Go', published in the *Collected Poems*.

fulfilment based on national freedom. Perhaps Hamish Henderson's 'folk revival' will thus be no small thing but as his friend John Berger wrote shortly after their first meeting:

> . . . the force
> of what lives us,
> outliving the mountain.[10]

10 From John Berger, *And Our Faces, My Heart, Brief As Photos* (Bloomsbury 2005).

Acknowledgements

In completing this biography a huge thank you to Katzel Henderson and her family for their continued loyal support of this project: their archive, encouragement and factual advice have been invaluable. Intellectually and creatively, Hamish's old friends Eck Finlay (editor of *The Armstrong Nose* and *Alias MacAlias*), Raymond Ross (editor of *Cencrastus* and *Hamish Henderson: Collected Poems and Songs*), Joy Hendry (editor of *Chapman*), have all given me outstanding assistance for which I extend deep thanks. Others who have given inspired support include Andrew Ward, Margaret Bennett, Alison McMorland, Geordie McIntyre, Pino Mereu, Lorn Macintyre, David Craig, Ray Burnett, Sue Finlay, Freddie Freeman, Dolina MacLennan, Sheila Stewart, George Gunn, Maurice Fleming, Jean Redpath, Deirdre MacMahon, Nicholas Johnson, John Frew, Adam McNaughtan, Maggie Mackay and staff at the School of Scottish Studies, Jean Redpath, Hilary Lyall, William Neill, Eddie Linden (editor of *Aquarius*), Lesley Lendrum, Ian Olson, Hayden Murphy, Alastair Campbell of the Tolbooth, Stirling, Howard Glasser of New York, Donald Smith of the Scottish Storytelling Centre. Also Eddie McGuire, Gerry Mangan, Jim MacGregor, Andrew Hood, David Arthur, John Brookes, Elisabetta Cozzi, Nora Albert, Danny Cooper, Derrick Chishom, Richard Carr, Angus Calder, Duncan Glen, Douglas Eadie, Ruth Frame, Jamie Macdonald Reid, Alasdair Gray, Willie and Val Gillies, Dick Greenhaus, Martin Green, Verna Gillis, the Hawkes family at Dry Drayton, Jim Gilchrist, Ian Kerr, David Ross, Michael Law, Paddy O'Neill, Jo Miller, Ed Miller, Paddy Bort, Rasjid A.J. Arthur, Stewart McLennan, Allan MacDonald, Ewan McVicar, Tony Morrow, Cathlin Macauley, Norman MacLean, Gordon Stewart, Willie MacPhee, Alec John Williamson, Peg MacPhee, Mary Morgan, Jean Mohr, J.P. McGroarty, Graham Noble, Mitchell Library, Niall O'Murchadha, Des O'Rourke, Marie MacArthur and Bob Pegg, Ross Roy, Esther Hovey, Stanley Robertson, Ian Russell, Carla Sassi, Heather Scott, Paul Scott, Ian Spring, Deidre Grieve, Tilda Swinton, Marian Sugden, Dorothy Thompson, Pete Shepheard, Elspeth Smellie, Mary Tucker, Ian Thompson, Sheena Wellington, Carmen Wright, Stephanie Wolfe Murray, George Philp, John Purser, John Dubarry, Audrey Canning of Glasgow Caledonian University, Les Wilson,

Donald Meek, Edward J. Cowan, Arnott Wilson, Michael Law, Paddy O'Neill, Arthur Thompson, Iain and Neil MacDonald, Tom McCulloch of Tomatin Distillery, and John Berger. Amongst the givers in kind I especially thank Ross Carstairs for suppling three loads of logs, a brace of mallard, five of pheasant and twelve of pigeon; John and Janet Cameron for supplying venison and eggs; Richard Turner for buying mushrooms; the Health Food Shop St Andrews and Alison Bachelor for buying honey; Dougie Storrier for mending the roof; and the little boy in Little Glenshee who stopped with his mother to call out, at a distance, 'thank you for looking after the bees'. Such things count for much in a harsh climate. Also a huge thank you to Mairi Sutherland, my editor, whose work has been to the point, inspiring and comradely; to Alastair Clark for his excellent advice; to Neville Moir and Jim Hutcheson for their good-humoured and loyal support of this project over many years. Finally, I extend posthumous thanks to Stuart MacGregor, whose novels *The Myrtle and Ivy* and *The Sinner* provided me with first-hand testimony as to what Hamish's Edinburgh was like – in the heady days of the fifties and sixties – before I met him myself.

Illustration credits. I am very grateful to the many people whose photographs and artwork appear in this biography. I thank them all, in particular the artists Andrew Ward and Brad Graves, and the photographers Jean Mohr and Tricia Malley. Photographers are acknowledged in the plate captions, with their names given in full. Initials indicate the collection from which the photograph comes, coded as follows: Katzel Henderson (KH), Timothy Neat (TN), Willie MacPhee (WM), Maurice Fleming (MF), Alec John Williamson (AJW), Arthur Elliot (AE), Eddie McGuire (EM), Davie Adams (DA), Dolina MacLennan (DM), Ruth Frame (RF), Aly Bain (AB).

Publisher's Acknowledgements

The author and the publishers would also like to thank the following for permission to publish quoted material:

STAN AWBREY: extract from letter to the Manchester Guardian, published by permission of Glamorgan Record Office; JOE CORRIE: extract from letter to Hamish Henderson, 3 April 1959, published by permission of Morag Corrie; LAWRENCE DALY: extract from letter to Hamish Henderson, 26 January 1960, published by permission of Mrs Renee Daly; MAIRGHREAD ELLIS: extract from letter of condolence to Mrs Henderson, 2002, published by permission of Dr Mairghread Ellis; PAT GERBER: extract from letter to Tim Neat, 1992, published by permission of Cyril Gerber; DUNCAN GLEN: review of 'The Freedom Come a' Ye' from *Inter Arts*, Volume 1, No. 7 (October 1988), reprinted by permission of Margaret Glen; BRUCE JACKSON: extract from Gershon Legman obituary, 1999, published by permission of Bruce Jackson; ARNOLD KETTLE: extract from letter to Hamish Henderson, published by permission of Martin Kettle; GERSHON LEGMAN: extracts from letters to Hamish Henderson, published by permission of Judith Legman; TOM LEONARD: extract from letter to Hamish Henderson, 1984, published by permission of Tom Leonard; HUGH MACDIARMID: extracts from poetry, and letter from *New & Selected Letters*, edited by Alan Riach (Carcanet Press, 2001), reproduced by permission of Carcanet Press; SORLEY MACLEAN: extracts from Hugh MacDiarmid funeral oration, and poetry from *From Wood to Ridge: Collected Poems in Gaelic and English* (Carcanet Press, 1989), reproduced by permission of Carcanet Press; JAMES MACMILLAN: extracts from letter to Hamish Henderson, 1 October 1987, and interview given to the Sunday Telegraph, 5 January 2003, reproduced by permission of James MacMillan; JOHN MCGRATH: extract from letter to Hamish Henderson, March 1972, published by permission of Casarotto Ramsay & Associates; NAOMI MITCHISON: extract from letter to Hamish Henderson, 1964, published by permission of David Higham Associates; SEAN O'BOYLE extracts from letters to Hamish Henderson, published by permission of Colm J. Boyle; SANDY PATON: extract from letter to Hamish Henderson, 20 July 1960, published by permission of Caroline Paton; JOHN PREBBLE: extracts from letters, published by permission of Curtis Brown

Group Ltd; JOHN PURSER: extract from letter to Hamish Henderson, 12 April, 1992, published by permission of John Purser; PETE SEEGER: unpublished letters to Hamish Henderson, published by permission of Pete Seeger; ZETTA SINCLAIR: extracts from letters to Hamish Henderson, published by permission of Isla St Clair; DUNCAN WILLIAMSON: quote, and recollections recounted to Hamish Henderson, published by permission of Linda Williamson; LINDA WILLIAMSON: letters and memorabilia, published by permission of Linda Williamson; WORKERS MUSIC ASSOCIATION: letter to Hamish Henderson, published by permission of WMA.

ONE

The School of Scottish Studies

The dumb boy is looking for a voice
is looking for poetry.

HH[1]

The School of Scottish Studies, formally established at the University of Edinburgh in January 1952, became the fulcrum of Hamish Henderson's life for the next fifty years. It was created as a research department dedicated 'to the study and conservation of the folk culture of Scotland'. As a teenager Hamish thrilled to Yeats's statement: 'through the theatre the mob becomes a nation': now he felt empowered to use Scots song and 'the School' as the means by which he would see Scotland become a nation again.

Hamish's vocation as a song collector went back to his childhood in Glenshee, and the scrapbook he assembled as a ten-year-old in Somerset includes this cutting from the *Weekend Scotsman*: 'Old Scots Songs – Need for a Compilation':

> Dear Sir, I was very pleased to see that last week you printed two good old Scots songs. Many years ago the 'Weekly Scotsman' was instrumental in reviving and printing some of our fine old songs, copies of which I still have, which are cut out from the 'Weekly Club'. It is a pity we could not find someone to do for Scottish songs what Mrs Kennedy Fraser did for the songs of the Hebrides. I herewith enclose you a copy of an old song, 'Auld Jock Tamsin', which I have failed to find in print, so I have written it out from memory. The words are by James Ballantyne, who is also the author of 'Ilka blade o' grass keeps its ain drop o' dew'. I had the music from 'Auld Jock Tamsin' but I 'tint' it lango . . . David Ross

'Auld Jock Tamsin' was a favourite song in the Henderson house, and Hamish appears to have taken Ross's letter as a call-to-arms: he would be a poet, a song collector, a nation-builder. What Kennedy-Fraser had done for Gaelic song in the Hebrides, he would do for Scotland as a whole but

1 HH, unpublished lines, Henderson archive.

he determined that he would do what she had done and a great deal more.[2] Hamish understood folksong to be an aspect of 'collective wellbeing' and a political force. Elevation of the Scots folk tradition was an integral part of the grand plans he laid for himself as a schoolboy at Dulwich. In the College magazine, *The Alleynian*, he writes of his 'Glenshee Assembly', an imagined bardic parliament dedicated to peace and Scotland's future renewal. This fictitious Assembly might be described as becoming 'a reality' with the foundation of the School of Scottish Studies. On 29 November 1951 in high excitement Hamish wrote to his Cambridge friend Marian Sugden:

> From 1 January I shall be on a three-month tour of the north financed by the School of Scottish Studies, Edin. University, collecting ballads and finding singers, God's own job – and hospitality money provided. The truth is the university people were so impressed by Lomax's achievements (the amount of fine singing we collected in a short time clear bowled 'em over) that they've disregarded my suspect politics at long last and given me a job . . . *'Mica male!'* About time too. The 'hospitality money' means that I'm entitled to put down as expenses the occasional drop of the immortal cratur for adding the edge to fiddle tune or song. And sae at last this bonnie cat / He had a stroke o' luck.[3]

Since his expulsion from Italy in October 1950, Hamish had lived close to the breadline, and letters from his friend the communist zoologist Mervyn Plunkett affirm his hardships. On 12 December 1951 Plunkett writes: 'Queenie Moncrieff tells us you were down a few weeks ago and seemed depressed . . . We've speculated from time to time as to what you are existing on as no doubt the Gramsci earnings have been used long since . . .' Three months later, however, he writes from Uganda in brotherly glee:

> Well, here I am deep in the heart of darkest Africa and a gey lang step frae Auld Reekie . . . The people are maybe a wee bit browner than at home, but the women are buxom strapping wenches and many a one you'll see sporting a Kanzu of Macrae or Wallace or Sinclair plaid . . . Queenie says you sound happy – which you damned well should be seeing that you've got *The Job just made for you.*

---

2 The arranging done by Marjory Kennedy-Fraser has been frowned upon by many Gaels and folklorists because of her 'artification of folksong' but, in her time, she did valuable work and her place in the history of Scottish folk scholarship (and the University of Edinburgh) is assured. In her autobiography *A Life of Song* (Oxford University Press 1921) she writes: 'Folk-song has come into its own in late years. The University of Edinburgh has set its mark on the place assigned to such racial lore by conferring on me the honorary degree of Doctor of Music.'

3 All extracts from letters written to Hamish, and copies of letters written by Hamish, are from the Henderson archive.

Hamish's formal letter of appointment is dated 13 December 1951 and came from Professor Sidney Newman (Reid Professor of Music at the University of Edinburgh).

> Dear Mr Henderson . . . This letter is confirmation of a commission to work on behalf of Edinburgh University collecting ballads folk-songs and folklore material in Aberdeenshire and Banffshire during the three months from 1 January to 31 March 1952 . . . recording Willie Matheson of King Edward and Mr Strachan of Crichie. The terms which I am authorised to offer are a fee of £35 a month . . . With £45 available for expenses, with the exception of board and lodging the main foreseeable expenses will be your travel by bus or bicycle, the charging of batteries and hospitality required by your singers.

The foundations of the School of Scottish Studies (SSS) had been laid in 1949 when the University of Edinburgh set up an advisory board on 'Postgraduate Scottish Studies' under the chairmanship of Angus McIntosh, Forbes Professor of English Language and General Linguistics.[4] In January 1951 Calum Maclean was 'seconded' from the Irish Folklore Commission to become the first Gaelic Folklore Research Fellow at Edinburgh. That summer, Hamish (and Calum Maclean), working with the American collector Alan Lomax, made remarkable field recordings which affirmed the necessity that a 'School' be established – even if only temporarily – and in January 1952 Calum Maclean, Dr Francis Collinson and Hamish began work. All were employed on short-term contracts and Hamish's appointment, in particular, stimulated questions. The Gaelic scholar John MacInnes, for instance, reports that other candidates – like William Montgomerie (a teacher, collector, scholar and poet from Dundee) – had strong supporters but Hamish had no wish to argue and quickly disappeared into the snows of Aberdeenshire.

On 29 January Professor Newman writes, 'Dear Hamish . . . I was delighted to have your long and informative letter . . . The quality of Matheson's voice is coming out remarkably well . . . Your work is very satisfactory . . .' On 15 March he was even more encouraging: 'I congratulate you on some very satisfactory recording and of course the material recovered is excellent and of very great interest . . . Will you go on till mid April?' Ten days later, he notes Hamish's contact with descendants of the earlier collector Gavin Greig and adds, 'I hope you are successful in getting a recording and an eye-witness account of the "Horseman's

---

4 McIntosh, who had arrived at the university the previous year, was the catalyst in the creation of the School, making through his friendship with John Lorne Campbell and his wife Margaret Fay Shaw the contacts in Ireland and Sweden which were crucial to its formation.

Word" ceremony that you are after . . . I will be coming up for a visit 2–5 April . . . Tell Willie that we all *very* much enjoy what we have heard so far of his songs *and* his singing.' In addition to his own vast repertoire of songs, Willie Matheson had contacts, and Hamish made use of them:

> Yesterday I had rare luck, because a travelling salesman called John Keith turned up at Willie's and sold him a couple of 'doctor' flannel vests. This salesman was a lineal descendant of the 'packmen', who in the old days used to carry news and ballads around – as well as sell their wares. Fortunately, John Keith was a very intelligent variety of the species, conscious of his own identity and the social order – so I recorded from him a fascinating description of his role and that of the packman, old and new. And the recording ends with a bit of authentic sales patter in braid Scots.[5]

Hamish never set bounds around what he was doing; everything was grist to his mill. Many of his best contacts were people whom other professional folk collectors had previously avoided. Hamish later spoke proudly of 'brushing shoulders with contemporary ancestors who not only embodied a vanishing way of life but who were creatively inspiring – to me!' After jotting down a series of 'surreal prophecies' Hamish outlined the plot of an 'International Thriller' he would write when his research contract expired.

> Influenced by G.K. Chesterton (realism and fantasy): A Commissioner of Police – *Theophraste Layuet* – a Parisian – in the Catacombs discovers that, in a former life, he was *Cartouche*, a renowned robber (character based on James MacPherson the early C18th Highlander – hanged at Banff). *Theo* applies for help from – *Messier Eliphes de Skint-Elme de Taillebourg de la Nox* – the mage. *Cartouche* relives his torture and death: boot and red hot irons – *Theo's* hair turns white (a la Norman Douglas in 'South Wind') . . . I am entering the radiant darkness of death.[6]

This death reference is probably to the subterranean world of the Horseman's Word, Hamish's first major anthropological discovery. The Horseman's Word was the name given to an ancient society of horsemen, ploughmen, farrowers and blacksmiths centred on north-east Scotland. Hamish saw the society as the continuance of a primordial horse-cult adapted to nineteenth-century agricultural practices. Rights and rituals were jealously guarded, and the Brotherhood was a depository of ancient lore of great veterinary and literary interest. Knowledge of horses and horsemanship was passed on by word of mouth and in secret rituals:

---

5 HH, unpublished notes, Henderson archive.
6 HH, unpublished notes, Henderson archive.

apprentices were inducted, oaths taken, poetry recited, songs sung. In charge was the High Horseman and, as Hamish relates, 'the black airts very much part of the process'. Membership was male but certain activities echoed those used at witches' covens. The language was frequently grand and druidic, many of the songs were wilfully bawdy, some of the rituals deliberately brutal. No previous folklorist had attended these ceremonies. As Hamish later recounted, 'it was as if I had stumbled into a Mau-Mau camp and been recognised as the brother of Jomo Kenyatta! Punishment for the betrayal of secrets was as severe as amongst the Masons. So, naturally, we all got on very well.' Hamish never claimed that his discoveries were totally original – a number of north-east journalists had written, tentatively, about the society – but he told me:

> I knew I had entered a Cave of Gold. I felt like Homer wandering through the smoking ruins of Troy might have felt, or that boy – looking up at those cloud-like rocks that roof the cave at Altamira and seeing bulls! Going out in the moonlight to those black byres to find men parading in calfskins and blind-folded boys suspended from hooks was mind-blowing. In the lantern-light, the horsemen looked as if they had just ridden in from the steppe. Here was theatre of a high order.[7]

When Hamish's field work was reviewed by Professor Newman and David Abercrombie in the summer of 1952, he told them not only that the tradition of Scots balladry was alive and well but that a new generation was still developing the tradition.

> They believed that we were completing a final 'vacuum clean' of a dying tradition! I sensed that they were going to say 'thank you – and good night!' So, I was not slow in telling them 'our work is only beginning!' They knew about Gavin Greig.[8] They knew about Dr Carpenter.[9] They had been persuaded that some gleaning needed doing but neither had any real idea that this rich, vibrant, bounding cultural phenomenon was still developing. So, I told them about

7 HH, conversation with TN. By 1955 Hamish had been initiated 'a made horseman' and was bound by certain rules of silence so he decided to keep some of his recordings of oaths and bawdy under wraps in the School of Scottish Studies. These were songs 'wi' the wee thread o' blue'. As the years passed, he spoke more openly.

8 Gavin Greig (1856–1914), folksong collector, jointly responsible with the Rev. J. B. Duncan for *The Greig–Duncan Folk Song Collection* of over 3,000 songs and tunes.

9 J. M. Carpenter, *Folk Songs of Old New England*, ed. E. H. Linscott (Macmillan 1939).

> this boy of seventeen [Arthur Argo: Greig's great-grandson] who was singing these old songs – as though he meant every word – and making new songs! . . . Well, it was marvellous to see the faces of these professors expand into grins. They then went back to convince their advisory panels that our work had to continue – that the School should expand its work. This meant that the Folk Revival, that Arthur personified, also got a very helpful leg-up.[10]

Most weekends Hamish caught the train back to Edinburgh, and his tales of the Aberdeenshire horse-cults quickly aroused tumescent interest. Bobby Watt (the veterinary student soon to be charged with conspiracy and membership of the Scottish Republican Army – see Volume 1) was greatly inspired, as was the poet Helen B. Cruickshank, with whom Hamish often enjoyed bed and breakfast. Coming from Montrose, she was fascinated by Hamish's 'Doric Discoveries'. She had recently retired from the Scottish Office and lodged in her mother's commodious house, 'Dinnieduff', making it Scotland's number one literary salon. On 31 January 1952 she wrote:

> Dear Hamish, I'm sorry I hadn't time to put a note in with your washing, but I was darning that darned sark till 1.30am, and slept in so long next morning . . . I have broken my word, I swore I would never, never mend your sarks, and I did it – the first – and most probably the last I shall ever mend! So consider yourself honoured. But for Heaven's sake don't wear them so dirty again. I had to scrub and scrub to get the dirt out of the collar. And still it wasn't clean – and I don't have a boiler. Enough of sarks!

That Scotland's leading woman poet should take such pride in playing Martha to the homeless Hamish is salutary: she recognised him as Scotland's latest champion and would scrub for him. Twenty years earlier she had given intellectual succour to James Leslie Mitchell (Lewis Grassic Gibbon), author of *Sunset Song* and *Spartacus*, and Cruickshank encouraged Hamish similarly as a peace activist and revolutionary as well as a poet and collector. Proud as a mother, she writes on 12 March 1952:

> Dear Hamish, I had tea with Flora yesterday and told her about the 'Horseman's Word'. It was news to her of a very fascinating order . . . I wonder if there's any *survival* in the rites which initiate *curlers*. Look into it, my lad! A lot of these queer ceremonies have queer origins . . . Your Aberdeen article had a nice reflection in 'Scotsman's Log' . . . I've been busy, do no literary work here – except my usual boosting of others . . .

---

10 HH, unpublished notes, Henderson archive.

A much younger woman inspired by Hamish's Horseman researches was the anthropologist Dr Una MacLean (wife to John Mackintosh MP and later to Sir Bernard Crick):

> Dear Hamish, The cult that you describe has so much in common with initiation ceremonies into animal cults in many parts of the world, notably in West Africa, that it would seem a clear remnant of indigenous paganism. The habit of using 'The Devil' in current ceremonies is a result of the extent, and limitations, of Christian influence (and shows official religion being super-imposed upon the immemorial cults) . . . It is very common for a group of men whose lives and fortunes are closely bound up with a particular animal to identify with the animal and deify the creature whom they serve and who serves them. I think the 'trade union' aspect is secondary . . . I don't think you need worry about its date of origin (C18th?) – it must have carried over from something much earlier . . . How very exciting if traces of similar ceremonies relating to oxen could be found . . . But the Horseman's Word should not be confused with the 'Witch Cult' so called. These animal cults are male only – relating to the life which the men live *apart* from the women. Witches, on the other hand, are the essence of women – as seen and feared by the men. (I have met old men in Africa who have told me 'The Witches are our mothers'.) . . . It is also probably no coincidence that when the North East coast took on Christianity it adopted a particular apostolic form – the 'Closed Brethren' and all that. It may *not* be without significance that the part of Scotland where pagan traces lasted so long took up a form of Christianity very different from the general – stricter, more ritualistic and more emotional in expression.[11]

Hamish always saw his collecting as a 'collective activity', and Una MacLean's mention of 'an ox cult' encouraged him to look into the work of the Aberdeenshire collector Peter Buchan (1790–1854), who wrote about the 'self-identification between men and animals in the North East of Scotland' and had courted ridicule by arguing for 'the sanctity of the cart horse'. His pamphlet *Cogent Proofs: That Brutes have Souls* explores 'the animality of sex'. Hamish found this extremely interesting and much later, in the 1980s, he encouraged one of his best students, Ian Spring, to make Peter Buchan's *The Secret Songs of Silence* the subject of his PhD thesis. In his search for an ox cult, Hamish unearthed a medieval *Pleugh Sang*, written down in the seventeenth century and in the *Forbes Cantus*. It appears to document a ceremony that combined an ox sacrifice, a fertility blessing, the recitation of feudal loyalties and the performance

11 Letter to HH, 1952.

of a Scots Mummers Play. Like the Horseman's Word, this *Pleugh Sang* awaits transformation into modern, very druidic opera.

My hearty service to you, my Lord . . .
Here is an ox into your plough,
It is right so, ye say the sooth,
And he no longer may be drawn
But he be led . . . Suppose you brod him
While he die – Hey, douna, douna, douna die . . .

As I was bound on with ane wicker!
For to deliver me – behead the old ox –
And I trip-free – as he be dead . . .
And bring with me my fair fresh oxe
With all that belonges to the plough –
Hey douna, douna, douna, hey . . .[12]

When Hamish's three-month contract was renewed he spent the summer of 1952 archiving his material whilst the administrative structure of the School was set in place by Secretary–Archivist Stewart Sanderson. These structures remained fluid for some time, and Helen Cruickshank's second letter (above) may hold a clue as to why: she mentions that Hamish's work had 'had a nice reflection in "Scotsman's Log"' (the *Scotsman* diary column). This reference may be entirely innocuous but Cruickshank was a committed radical who maintained a lifelong friendship with the Scots patriot–activist Wendy Wood (a woman of continuing interest to British Intelligence) and, as pointed out in Volume 1 of this biography, the author of 'A Scotsman's Log' (Wilfred Taylor) acted as an MI5/MI6 recruiter at the University of Edinburgh. Consequently Cruickshank may have been alerting Hamish to the fact that MI5 was maintaining an interest in his activities. If this was so, a question arises: was Hamish's appointment to the School of Scottish Studies also influenced by the interests or the demands of MI5?

The University of Edinburgh has had a long relationship with the British Intelligence Services and it seems improbable that Hamish would have been given a university appointment without 'a nod' of approval from MI5. If such a nod was given – in relation to the appointment of the most dangerous leftwing nationalist in Scottish politics – the inference must be that 'field folk collecting' was seen as a means of diverting and controlling Hamish's revolutionary energies. A parallel can be drawn with the decision to employ Robert Burns as a Dumfriesshire Exciseman when the War with Revolutionary France broke out in 1793.

---

12 Traditional: typed text in Henderson archive; also quoted in John Purser, *Scotland's Music* (Mainstream 2007).

Why Edinburgh as the location for the School?[13] Hamish himself had suggested Aberdeen as the best choice. Glasgow had musical, cultural and political claims. But, to the chagrin of many, it was Edinburgh that was chosen and it may not be coincidental that four of the professors associated with the School had worked with British Intelligence during the war. Professor Angus McIntosh (English Language) served at Bletchley Park, David Abercrombie (Phonetics) in North Africa, Stuart Piggott (Archaeology) in India, whilst David Talbot Rice (Fine Art) was a Byzantine specialist with a Russian wife. And when the School's fifth anniversary was celebrated in January 1957, surprisingly, the guest speaker was Wilfred Taylor. If secret interventions were going on, Hamish was delighted to ignore them and grasp the great opportunity he had been offered with both hands. He recognised that, whilst his short-term political objectives might be compromised, in the long run, his newfound freedom to champion the Scots folk tradition could only serve his ambitions for the Scots people. If Brer Rabbit outwitted Brer Fox by getting himself flung 'into the briar patch', why should he not do something similar and escape to the hills – Scot free?

If Hamish's appointment initiated controversy outside the School, the appointment of Stewart Forson Sanderson as Secretary–Archivist at the School stimulated controversy within the School. Although his post was full-time and all the school's researchers were responsible to him, he lacked formal folklore qualifications. Sanderson was born in Nyasaland in 1924. After attending George Watson's College and three years' service in the Royal Naval Volunteer Reserve (1943–46) he studied English and gained a first-class degree at the University of Edinburgh in 1951. Following a brief spell in Florence he came back to Scotland to take charge of the School of Scottish Studies, at the age of twenty-seven. His great interest was in English literature, though he subsequently engaged with Scottish folklore; Hamish took an immediate dislike to a man whom he later described as 'imperious, supercilious and authoritarian'. When the employment of a full-time Director was recommended, Hamish and Calum Maclean felt strongly that an established folklore scholar should be sought. In April 1957, they wrote to the University Principal, Sir Edward Appleton:

> Dear Principal, The first years of the School's academic existence have revealed certain definite weaknesses which are the direct result of the lack of an authoritive and scholarly direction. It is vital to the future of the School that the situation obtaining in the past should

---

13 Angus McIntosh had the vision that folklore and linguistic collecting and study go hand in hand. He was largely responsible for the creation of the Linguistic Surveys of Scotland (Gaelic and Scots) as well as the School of Scottish Studies, with initial assistance from The Carnegie Trust.

> not be perpetuated. We all agree that we would work to better purpose under the leadership of a man with recognised scholastic attainments. No capacity for administration can compensate for the absence of such qualifications. Every foreign archive we have seen is led by a scholar . . . We would welcome the appointment of an international scholar even on a short term basis, for we are confident that a native successor will eventually be found.

Later that year, Basil Megaw, an Ulsterman who had been director of the Manx Museum, was appointed, and Stewart Sanderson left in 1960 to take up a post at the University of Leeds.

One cause of conflict between Hamish and Sanderson concerned the field recordings collected. Sanderson saw the School as a library–museum dedicated to the preservation of selected material available only to *bona fide* academic researchers. Hamish wanted almost everything recorded to be preserved and made as widely available as possible. Things came to a head when Sanderson circulated staff with a demand that once tapes had been 'transcribed' they should be wiped and reused, as was the practice at the Irish Folklore Commission. For Hamish and Calum this was sacrilege. They believed their tapes contained 'unique voices that must be preserved and made available to generations unborn'. They saw the School as much more than a library/archive: they wanted it to be a workshop, a meeting place, an engine house for new developments. The Folk Revival was already a living reality, and Hamish believed that the School had a crucial role to play in ensuring that it would grow on authentic foundations: 'It was the traditional singers and musicians – whom we were capturing on tape – who embodied that authenticity.'

Stewart Sanderson had no easy job. His researchers were strong-minded individualists, and universities regularly experience problems with 'new subjects' and anyone who thinks outside the box. It has been argued that it was Sanderson's firm hand on the tiller that gained the School its international reputation but both Hamish and Calum suffered recurrent 'dark nights of the soul' during his tenure. In the late 1950s things went from bad to worse when Calum was diagnosed with cancer and needed helpers to carry his recorders. Hamish controlled his anger and frustrations with difficulty and found respite in extended field trips 'that brought in the harvest of five thousand years'. After one confrontation, Hamish noted a statement that Sanderson had assumed was a *coup de grâce*: '<u>We</u> created your post – and you needed it!' Why did Sanderson use the word 'we'? Why did Hamish underline it?

Despite these teething problems, the School quickly made a name for itself. In many ways it became a 'school' in the art-historical sense of the word. And just as an apparently backward group of realist painters had created the School of Barbizon – to stimulate Impressionism, Post-impressionism and triumphant Modernism – so the 'backwoods' folklorists at the School of Scottish Studies set in train artistic changes of worldwide significance. Amongst Hamish's colleagues, the work of Calum Maclean and Francis Collinson merits particular mention. Calum Maclean was a native Gaelic speaker. Born on the island of Raasay in 1916, he became a boarder at Portree High School on Skye before moving to Edinburgh to read Celtic. In 1939 he took up a postgraduate scholarship in Dublin and remained in Ireland throughout the Second World War. After years of splendid work in Connaught, for the Irish Folklore Commission (IFC), Maclean returned to Scotland in 1946 as IFC researcher in the Hebrides. It was there he met Hamish and their close friendship began. In Benbecula alone, within three months, Calum recorded 165 'unknown folklore items', including the longest oral story ever recorded in Scotland, *Alasdair mac a' Cheir*. Calum was a character: small, elfin and quixotic and, in Hamish's words, 'a bastion of courage, moral integrity and greatness of soul'.[14]

As scholars and friends Hamish and Calum were very much a twosome and they would sometimes 'put on a show' for foreign scholars – at a ceilidh or in Sandy Bell's bar – singing in English, Gaelic, Swedish, Italian, Scots before returning to Gaelic and declaring: 'Gaelic song has the beatings of them all!' It is their work and personalities that created the ethos that made the School famous. Following Calum's death on his adopted home, South Uist in 1960, Hamish wrote this tribute:

> Calum stood in the midst of a tradition, he was part-bearer as well as a collector (in the great Scottish tradition) and conscious of those who had gone before – John Francis Campbell of Islay, Hector MacLean, Alexander Carmichael, Ewan MacLachlan, John Lorne Campbell – yet in the end he can be seen to have excelled them all. His research papers were not numerous: he addressed the urgency of the task before him at a particular moment. He got down and announced, to the world, that which others must analyse and now take up.

Calum's death stimulated his brother, Sorley, to write an elegy that stands as one of the great poems of Scotland and an affirmation of the values of the Gaidhealtachd:

> . . . There is many a poor man in Scotland
> whose spirit and name you raised:
> you lifted the humble
> whom the age put aside.
> They gave you more
> than they would give the others
> since you gave them the zeal

14 HH, unpublished notes, Henderson archive.

that was a fire beneath your kindness.
They sensed the vehemence
that was gentle in your ways,
they understood the heavy depths of your humanity
when your fun was at its lightest . . .[15]

Hamish's second close colleague at the School of Scottish Studies was Francis Collinson, an Edinburgh musicologist with an intellectual cast of mind and a classical, very British reserve. The music of the ballads was his speciality and his interests complemented Hamish's. Collinson was an exact and productive academic, a composer and collector: Hamish was a wordsmith with a phenomenal memory for people, places and songs, at his best in the field. Collinson would become author of several major scholarly books (*The Traditional and National Music of Scotland* and *The Bagpipe* – to which Hamish made contributions) but Hamish himself was never to write a book of prose scholarship. Academic productivity can create its own problems, however, as it did in what Hamish described as 'the tragic case of Sylvia Douglas Gordon'. Sylvia was a grand-daughter of Gordon of Khartoum. She was brought up in London but became a doughty bearer of balladry from north-east Scotland. In 1945 she heard Collinson on the BBC and wrote to him from her smallholding in Derbyshire. She was less than 5 feet tall but 'descended from the Gordons of Wardhouse and Kildrummie – where my people have kept the pass for centuries – and Lord Glenbervie of County Clare'. Her repertoire was huge but in the seven years before the School was established, Collinson visited her only once and recorded nothing. In 1953 Sylvia visited Edinburgh, met Hamish, and Collinson began to record her repertoire for the School. Returning to Derbyshire she writes:

> Dear Mr Collinson, I have now made a list of ballads I remember singing and there are, at present, nearly a hundred . . .They are for the archives of our lovely Scotland, and, after what you told me about not knowing anyone else who has them, I am keener than ever to help you. It would be little short of tragic if I were to peg out and take these lovely melodies with me and they should be lost for ever.[16]

Unfortunately, another seven years (punctuated by numerous heartbreaking letters) passed before arrangements for a new recording session was made. In August 1960 Sylvia informed Collinson that having dug 'both words and music from ancient memory' her own daughter had deliberately destroyed all her notes and writings:

---

15 Sorley MacLean, *Spring Tide and Neap Tide: Selected Poems 1932–1972* (Canongate 1977).

16 Letter from Sylvia Douglas Gordon to Dr Francis Collinson, 1953.

> I told you my system for raking these old things up – I must have a start – whether it be words or music – once I get that – bit by bit more comes. I do not know where I get these old ballads, if it is my own childhood memory, or ancestral memory, or my dear father getting through to me – probably a bit of all three – I am a Spiritualist you know . . . Yes, I do know the 'Heir of Lynne', and also the 'Elfin Knight' but I shall have to dig my brains to find the tunes.

Finally, in May 1962, this seventeen-year correspondence ends – with this letter from Collinson to Hamish: 'Dear Hamish, you will be sorry to hear that my letter to Miss Douglas Gordon suggesting our visit to her this month has been returned to me by the Post Office – marked "deceased". A long series of frustrations and other pressures of work prevented me from getting back to see her – and so ends a pious hope! We are fortunate to get the half dozen or so tunes from her, as they are all good, and vain regrets will do us no good! Francis Collinson.'

This lost opportunity gives poignancy to Hamish's description of his attempts to record the oral riches of the Perthshire Travellers as 'like holding a tin can under the Niagara Falls!' It also shows why Hamish 'dropped everything' to harvest the repertoires of *his* singers – as if there were no tomorrow. If this meant the end of his own poetry, so be it. He would record as much as possible, as soon as possible. With limited skills and meagre resources this sometimes resulted in technically flawed recordings, but during his first ten years at the School he collected tens of thousands of songs, stories, rhymes, riddles, interviews and musical recordings from hundreds of people. Most of these recordings have been available in the SSS archive for sixty years. Many are now also available on the web and all are now the focus of a major digitising project. In a real sense Hamish got 'the singers of Scotland' to create a musical group-self-portrait, not just of themselves but of their nation. His tapes sometimes sound like the rough or damp houses within which they were recorded but – like many a good painter's rough sketches – these recordings have soul, vivacity, spontaneity and a poetry that make them a unique national treasure.

Largely as a consequence of his loyalty to the School, to his singers and the idea of Scotland that they represented, Hamish wrote no serious poetry (or songs) between 1952 and 1958. His literary enemies have argued that in reality his muse had left him and that drink was already taking its toll: that folk collecting and advocacy of the 'genius' of the folk was merely an excuse for personal failure. That Hamish hit a 'creative block' at this time is undeniable but, with his career as a political activist still in full flow, he was working like two men most of the time, and the idea that no artist is allowed to change the nature and focus of their activities seems wilfully destructive. Of course many were quietly pleased to see the 'big man' struggling. A secretary in the School recalls Stewart

Sanderson describing Hamish as 'a poet out of commission'. Such criticism hurt, but Hamish's ambitions as a poet had always stretched beyond named authorship of slim volumes of verse. Poetry, for him, was the ultimate expression of man's humanity to man, a calling that demanded a national address. Consequently he saw his work within the School as a God-given chance to get Scotland to sing again: in doing that, he believed, the nation would sing itself back into being. Naturally, however, 'the idea of poetry' gnawed at him lifelong, as this letter to E.P. Thompson, written in 1980, makes clear:

> As you know your judgement means a great deal to me . . . Ever since the publication of the Elegies I have been trying to complete a new long poem on a very different theme – communism and liberty, a period in which communism has got bogged down in a morass of corruption and contradiction. Time goes by and I get no forrader. Now I begin to see a way out – I can leave a petrified forest of Stalinist axioms behind for ever . . . Who I wonder knows that since the last Stalinist years I've felt my power gone completely . . . I have of course published some of these poems – but what has been published so far is not the whole truth: as Wittgenstein said, 'Silence is sometimes not only a virtue – it is a necessity.'

More excuses? Or does Hamish, here, seek to take unto himself the kind of guilt the world likes to thrust on Stalin? Did the exposure of Stalin as a paranoid mass murderer shock him into silence and creative self-hatred? I think not, or at least only partially, because the year of Stalin's death, 1953, was also the year in which Hamish discovered the Aberdeen Traveller Jeannie Robertson, whom Alan Lomax was soon describing as the greatest ballad singer in the world. At the very moment when the Soviet experiment was being brought to its knees, Hamish was saved from despair by the appearance of a singer who embodied sublime beauty and human resilience beyond measure. With Jeannie unearthed, Hamish knew that the School stood on foundations of rock. Here was genius. Here was Scotland incarnate. Here was a woman and a dispossessed people for whom he would lay down his life. What was *his* poetry compared with this reality? Here was a muse for the whole Scots people. To have turned his back on Jeannie – to write private verses – would have been 'pure sodomy of soul' as Burns put it.

Within days of first recording Jeannie Robertson, Hamish took her to Edinburgh to sing at the People's Festival.[17] Recordings of her songs were soon winging their way to Alan Lomax in New York, to Ewan

17 The Edinburgh People's Festivals 1951–4 subsequently blossomed into the Fringe: see Volume 1 of this biography.

MacColl in London, to Douglas and Peter Kennedy at the English Folk Dance and Song Society. World folk culture had a new heroine, the Scots Folk Revival the most exemplary of measures, and Hamish was in love. Shortly after receiving his first University of Edinburgh cheque, Hamish had noted:

> No one can interest me in 'fine' writing as such. Any fool poet can write well if he happens to have talent – but the poets who love have a much larger problem, not only to write well, but to express once again – after a lapse of several centuries, the *whole* world, and this impinges not on one individual but on the collective.[18]

18 HH, unpublished notes, Henderson archive.

TWO

Jeannie Robertson

The beliefs of the wanderers, millennial mankind, and what might be described as old Europe, survived only in undercurrents, as tumultuous streams in far-flung places, as with good reason the firm foundations of civilisation were set down and wilful savagery replaced the savage heart.

Claude Lévi Strauss[1]

Hamish described his 'discovery' of the ballad singer Jeannie Robertson as 'the most important, single achievement of my life – the thing of which I am most proud'. Such a statement, made in public, forced his audience to address their own value systems. When Hamish first met Jeannie in Aberdeen in July 1953 she was an unknown 'tinker woman'; a decade later the *Scottish Daily Express* was trumpeting her:

> Jeannie Robertson is hailed in America as the world's leading ballad-singer. She has appeared with Maria Callas, sung in London's Festival Hall and been asked to visit Moscow . . . Yet she is almost unknown in Scotland . . . Mrs Robertson who learned many of her ballads from her mother said: 'I have a second sight. I am descended from the Stewarts and Robertsons, the travelling clans of Scotland. Second sight sometimes allows me to recall ballads I had forgotten existed. Once I dreamed I was in a large hall singing a strange ballad. When I wakened it was still with me – and I sang it later at London's Festival Hall . . .' Hamish Henderson said yesterday: 'Jeannie is perhaps the most amazing woman in Scotland. I can regularly and always go away with something new. Even if the School of Scottish Studies had done nothing but discover her they would have accomplished something great.'[2]

In 1941, in *Poetry and Prophecy*, the archaeologist N.K. Chadwick had written that 'among the early Celtic peoples the inculcations of poetic inspiration and the mantic art were developed and elaborated to a degree for which we know no parallel'. Hamish presented Jeannie

---

1 Quoted in Leonard Schlain, *The Alphabet and the Goddess* (Allen Lane 1998).
2 *Scottish Daily Express*, 29 August 1963.

as evidence that tradition continued, and folk specialists lined up to acknowledge Jeannie's importance: Alan Lomax described her as 'a monumental figure of the world's folksong'; A.L. Lloyd described her as 'a singer sweet and heroic'. Hamish himself always honoured Jeannie as more than a singer: she was a tradition bearer, an artist, a seer, a living representative of the kind of society that Chadwick presumed had disappeared. In this context Hamish's reasons for asking Jeannie to join the rally in the Edinburgh Meadows in July 1954 – to salute the release from prison of 'the Four Conspirators' (see Volume 1 of this biography) – takes on new meaning.

In old age, MacDiarmid described Langholm, the town of his birth, as his 'touchstone in all creative matters'. For Hamish, the Perthshire of his childhood would always remain important but, once he had met Jeannie, she became his touchstone. It was only after Jeannie had said 'Hamish, I can see you've lost yer hert to that lassie' that Hamish felt impelled to marry his young German sweetheart, Katzel Schmidt. He had 'dandled' Katzel for three years; it was Jeannie who set the seal. Psychoanalysts may explain Hamish's love (and deference) to Jeannie as the remnant of a mother-fixation – and there is truth in the suggestion – but Hamish saw Jeannie as part of a bigger picture; she embodied Scotland and the poetry of the ages. No one listened with greater attention than Hamish to her utterances:

> My Ballads? I learned them from my mother. I never learned them from books – some had been on paper – they were never learned off a paper. That's certain. But they went from mouth to mouth in their day – the old songs – as my mother said to me. I said to her one day, 'how did you come to learn your songs?' 'Well lassie,' she says 'I learned my songs the same way,' she says 'as you're learning them' she says 'from me'. I learned them off my mother. The ballads – they're not only good tunes, they *are* good tunes, and they're lovely words. The words couldnae be bonnier. I'm singing a story when I sing a big ballad – and most of them is really history. When I'm singing the song, tae tell you the God's truth, I picture it – just as it wis really happening.[3]

As a singer, Hamish believed Jeannie had all the essential attributes – feeling, range, aesthetic sensibility, historical authenticity, stage presence and a commanding individual personality. She, like his mother, 'liked to talk for victory' and he was soon using her as a flagship for his own cultural ambitions. Hamish's didactic (and political) use of Jeannie has caused some academics to lodge Svengalian accusations. One question concerns the ultra slow and extremely dramatic style of Jeannie's ballad

3 HH, unpublished notes, Henderson archive.

delivery. Did Hamish nurture Jeannie's grand style? The title of the biography *Jeannie Robertson, Emergent Singer, Transformative Voice*, by James Porter and Herschel Gower (Tuckwell Press 1995), seems to hint that external interventions 'transformed' her style.[4] There is an institutional assumption that truth (and power) resides in institutional hands, that professional academics are the guardians of the Temple of Truth, and the very idea that poets and tinkers might pursue their own ends is anathema. Hamish in his relationship with Jeannie, as in everything else, put life, art, beauty, pleasure and human wellbeing ahead of the demands of institutional authority or academic niceties. For him 'the sang was the thing'. Neither Hamish nor Jeannie saw themselves as the servants of archivists, the subjects of bureaucratic collation, the objects of questionnaires: they were human beings, artists. As friends they roped themselves together – rather as Braque and Picasso had roped themselves on the rock-face of Cubism – and who a century later looks at the ropes? Luck and history seem to have been on their side. Jeannie reminisced:

> I looked young for my age – an' the very first thing in the morning I was decked up tae the ninety nines. They used to cry me the Lady o' the Lake, and that's the God's truth. I likit mysel' aye looin' nice.[5]

Jeannie's early years had been shaped by poverty and social exclusion but, like many Travellers, she had style, a sense of her own worth, natural beauty and the thorax of a diva. She also had since childhood had girlish dreams that a man – like Hamish – would one day arrive to transform her pumpkin existence into the golden carriage of her imaginings. And as she walked the roads of Aberdeenshire humping packs with her mother, 'up the Dee and doon the Don', expectation long lightened her step. In adulthood she worked as an Aberdeen fish filleter. Shortly before meeting Hamish her only son died of what Hamish called 'the disease of poverty'. Traveller life was the stuff of ballads:

---

4 Gower, however, was a great admirer of Hamish and dedicated the book to him. In February 1996, he wrote from Dallas, Texas: 'Dear Hamish, it was kind of you to telephone and wonderful to hear your voice strong and clear across a wintry sea. What a joy to have a few words again . . . I hope the Jeannie tome will find friends in Scotland, especially at the SSS. It was forty years ago that you sent me to Jeannie and nearly thirty since Jim [Porter] and I started work . . . publishers turned us down, we got discouraged, other projects intervened, cuts had to be made . . . then along came Peter Mullen who convinced the American Folklore Society to sponsor the book . . . in spite of its recognisable flaws and omissions, the caravan finally got on the road . . . Tell me, is there a proper marker at Jeannie's grave? If not, it's time we got one . . . How I love you all.'

5 Unpublished notes, Henderson archive.

So Hamish comes up – an' the knock comes to the door – an' there's this great big man in a beautiful Highland dress. O, he was beautifully dressed that day, real military-lookin' he wis. I said, 'I'm too tired to think aboot singing' . . . but Hamish wis nae easy tae put awa'. I wadna put him awa', mind ye. God forgive me, I niver put naebody awa' frae my door in my life – let him be rich or poor. So I says, 'If you like, you can come back at night.'[6]

Hamish recounted his introduction to Jeannie many times and, whilst it differs slightly from Jeannie's, it retained a consistency that suggests abiding honesty. Perhaps the most interesting recollection is in a letter to Jack Niles (then folklore professor at the University of Berkeley), written in the early 1980s.

> The discovery of Jeannie Robertson in 1953 was the culmination of my hopes. I had felt in my bones, that in the North East, which had given so much balladry to Scotland and the world in the past, that there must be somebody there yet who was not only a great tradition bearer but a great personality as well . . . The immediate chain of events was this. In 1952 I did a recording tour in the region of Echt and Ythanside in Aberdeenshire. I was eating my lunch in the clubhouse of the community centre in Fyvie when a lad came in – a rich Traveller. I invited him over: I loved having a crack. We talked about what I was doing. He asked, 'Did you ever record in Aberdeen itself?' 'Yes,' I said, 'but not much.' 'Well,' he said 'you should go to the Castlegate on a market day – the folk there will give you all the information you need.'
>
> And the next year I was there in the Castlegate on a market day and I wandered among the stalls – they were Travelling people mostly, tinkers. I went from place to place talking about songs and asking. Eventually I began to get a list of names in my notebook . . . So it was Jeannie Higgins . . . She got one, two, three, four ticks in my book . . . 'Oh you ought to go hear Jeannie Higgins.' So that evening I knocked at her door at Causewayend, her wee house. And there was Jeannie standing there. She'd been cleaning and had a turban thing upon her head, and an apron. To me, a stranger at her door, her attitude seemed to be, 'Go away, we've got one. Come back next year.' I didn't want the door to be shut so I began to sing a verse of 'The Battle of Harlaw' – and a great smile spread across her big face. 'Come away in,' she said 'and I'll show you the right way of it!' She sat me down in a wooden chair in this very small room, fixed me with her big black eyes, and began singing. Immediately, I had a

6 HH, unpublished notes, Henderson archive.

> fantastic feeling, a sort of *Nunc Dimittis* feeling – Good Lord, this is it. And by God she was a wonderful singer. So I just sat there and let the tide roll over me. She gave me a cup of tea. And I asked her if I could come back. Come back with my tape recorder – she wasn't too keen – 'Tonight?' But I couldn't wait and she agreed; and after a hurried trip back to my lodgings in Maberly Street I returned to Causewayend and we recorded into the night.

'After that,' Hamish liked to say, 'neither I nor the world were ever quite the same again.' Some will see such a statement as absurd conceit but others as a precursor of the idea of 'chaos theory': that the beat of a butterfly's wing in the Amazonian rain-forest can engender forces that become hurricanes in the Caribbean. If that is so, why should not Hamish – and Jeannie's voice – set in motion even greater events? Hamish himself had no doubts about Jeannie's powers:

> Jeannie could dignify and ennoble even the most tawdry and fustian of Grub Street Broadsides . . . Belonging to the semi-nomadic travelling clans of Scotland she inherited traditional techniques of ballad composition and singing that were still very much alive – partly because of historical non-literacy amongst the Travellers. What seems to be true is that the magnificence – and I use the word without reserve or self-consciousness – the magnificence of the best of her Scottish ballads springs from a curious, and perhaps unique, collaboration, over the centuries between the non-literate ballad tradition (of the Travellers) and the individual creative efforts of sophisticated literary characters (like Scott and Hogg) who were close, if not to the tinkers, to the rural springs of Scots folk culture. As singers the Travellers have great confidence and authority . . . Scots songs are evidently full of heart and reality. They are not written for the stage. They were the slow growth of intense passion, simple tastes, and a heroic state of society. Love, mirth, patriotism were not the ornament but the inspiration of these songs. They are full of personal narrative, steaming hopes and fears, bounding joy in music, absolute disregard of prettiness.[7]

Jeannie was born Regina Christina Robertson on 17 April 1908, the youngest of five children. Her mother was Maria Stewart. Her father, Donald Robertson, served fifteen years in the army before returning to Aberdeen – to marry and resume the Traveller life. His army pension promised the family basic security but, nine months after Jeannie's birth, Donald Robertson died of typhoid. Maria Stewart then took up with Jimmy Higgins (the children of any Traveller woman found on the road

7 HH, unpublished notes, Henderson archive.

without a man were taken into care), and a new family, nine strong, came into being. In 1914 Jimmy Higgins volunteered for the army, and Maria moved with her seven children to a small house just a mile from where Hamish would be born, in Blairgowrie. Jeannie describes her mother:

> She was a very strong woman – a bonny fechter! She was known as 'The Terror of the North'. One week after the birth of her youngest child she won a bare-fist battle on the market-stance at Alford. She told me, 'Well, lassie, I was never afeard of nae woman in my life. I wis a wee bit windy – but I wudnae show it – my bad-temper wouldn't let me show it! She fought a clean fight – and I fought a clean fight wi' her – and that woman had bonnie hands, that was scientifically learned, but I had what she didnae: I had a terrible strength, wi' naething but the power o' bad temper!'[8]

Traveller life in the early twentieth century remained a mixture of hunter–gatherer wandering, the Celtic heroic, the pastoral idyllic and the American West (with the Travellers in the role of the American Indians!). They were a historical anachronism and widely persecuted. It was their artistry and sense of history that enabled them to maintain their fantastic lifestyle as a proudly borne addiction. Like a strolling player, Hamish joined the band determined to make immortal theatre of the life around him.

> The Travellers have inherited, and created, a folk culture of unequalled richness and diversity. Moving between the Gaidhealtachd and the Lowlands they picked up, synthesised and cultivated the oral and musical traditions of not just the two major forces in Scots tradition and culture (Highland and Lowland) but also numerous regional cultures. In addition, they continued to hold their own culture – based on their particular racial identity and ancient nomadic lifestyle – with unrivalled loyalty. Of this Traveller culture (which takes in the tradition of the settled Scots, and goes beyond it) Jeannie is the acknowledged Champion and Queen. She is a singer of amazing versatilities and power who turns every item she performs – classic ballad, children's rhyme, white paternoster, ribald gallimaufry – into a work of finished folk art. She is also a gifted storyteller with a huge repertoire. Her memory is exceptional and she is a mine of information about the older Scotland, its customs, beliefs and heroic legends. In her house, ceilidhs were living, growing, cultural happenings – pipes, song, story, dance and joy o' the cratur![9]

8 Unpublished notes, Henderson archive.
9 HH, unpublished lecture notes, Henderson archive.

Having made Jeannie the star of the Third Edinburgh People's Festival Ceilidh in 1953, Hamish sent her on to London to be recorded by both Alan Lomax and Ewan MacColl. Lomax arranged for her to make an appearance on BBC television but she went down with peritonitis. He then 'nursed her like a baby' before taking her 'voice' back to America where, from the autumn of that year, it began making its impact. Jeannie's relationship with Ewan MacColl was less straightforward. MacColl certainly helped launch Jeannie's career in England, but also appears to have helped himself to numerous of her songs. Hamish's shock at the way in which she was used is evident in a letter to the American folklorist Ken Goldstein in 1962. 'Dear Ken, . . . My Jatsus, ye cowes and gowans! No doubt you will recollect how MacColl "collected" from Jeannie in 1953, kidded her he'd soon be getting her a US record, sang her songs, on his own US LP – and from that day to this, he has never, I repeat NEVER sent her as much as a 5/- postal order.' Hamish's general thinking about the problems engendered by the clash between 'the realities' of traditional folksong and the 'market forces' of modern life is neatly codified in notes made in the mid sixties:

> The electronic revolution has made possible the recording of the *real* sound of 'Folk and Primitive Music': it did what no collector had ever been in a position to do before. What I deprecate about the possibilities the new technology has given us is the *instant* use of field recordings for re-singing by professional singers who do not take the time to assimilate the material. The 'natural' singers in a lively tradition like that of the Scottish Travellers inherited their songs the organic way, sometimes from a multiplicity of sources; their versions represent the artistic achievement of an entire culture (like plain song in the medieval church). What I am against can be best illustrated by what happened to the earliest tape-recorded versions of Jeannie Robertson's songs when they were sent to Ewan MacColl, with an understanding that they were to be used on a Riverside record. Instead of using the original recordings (or re-recording Jeannie), MacColl used them as a basis for the instant re-singing, on Riverside Records, of his *own* versions – and I can assure you that some of these highly histrionic and mannered re-singings belong to a real old Hadleybury Chamber of Horrors. So little time had Ewan taken to acquainting himself with the background of the songs that in the notes to one record, Jeannie is referred to as 'Jeannie Robertson of Dundee'![10]

Another 'authority' who embraced the Jeannie phenomenon circumspectly was Alexander Keith, the farmer, writer and ballad historian whom

10 HH, unpublished lecture notes, Henderson archive.

Hamish had first met in 1937. Once Hamish had Jeannie on tape he was desperate to 'show the author of *Last Leaves* that something marvellous was stirring in the undergrowth!'

> Keith had this sense that the old singers were the best and – they were dead – that there were no singers of the quality he had recorded and written about left – so, I wanted to let him listen to Jeannie . . . His face was a study, and he freely agreed I had a winner, adding, 'but of course, these tinkers are not exactly what you'd call folk'. 'Well' I said, 'Alexander Keith – they seem like folk to me!' Though, I did know what he meant.[11]

Keith's question as to whether Jeannie actually counts as 'a Scots folk singer' raises another question. Did Hamish really 'discover' Jeannie Robertson? A number of tape recordings of Jeannie were made in the late 1940s, by Hamish's friend William Montgomerie. These recordings are today part of the Montgomerie Archive in the collection of the folk scholar and singer Dr Margaret Bennett. They await serious analysis but their existence certainly raises questions about Hamish's claim to have 'discovered Jeannie'. Whether Montgomerie played them, or spoke about them, to Hamish before his first visit to Jeannie in 1953 is unknown. Hamish never denied Montgomerie's role in Jeannie's life story but always maintained his claim of 'discovery'. Was Hamish's claim justified?

A claim of first-ness would be dishonest, but this was never Hamish's claim. Montgomerie recorded Jeannie as a tradition bearer with a good repertoire of songs but then moved on. Hamish recorded her and broadcast her songs to the world as an artist worthy of the world's attention. He did this as a poet and as a folklorist with the authority of the University of Edinburgh behind him. Cultural advances, like scientific advances, frequently depend on evolutionary leaps and, just as it was Columbus who signalled the step-change in the history of the Americas, so it was Hamish who brought Jeannie Robertson on to the Scottish and international stages. Hamish's claims therefore appear substantial and honest. Montgomerie, to his credit, never sought to bad-mouth Hamish or talked down *his* 'discovery'.[12] One reason why Hamish, perhaps over-desperately, wanted Jeannie to be *his* was that he liked to see her as having 'come to him', almost mystically, to fulfil what he saw as his life's purpose. She embodied 'the seer' he had foreseen, as a boy, in his poem 'Fellow Traveller', written in the mid 1930s and published in *The Ingleton Raconteur* (the magazine of the Clapham orphanage in which Hamish spent some of his childhood).

---

11 HH, unpublished notes, Henderson archive.

12 Montgomerie discussed the issue with me in the early 1980s at a meeting of the Dundee Art Society.

. . . Fired by the ballad's lilt, with goal I searched
In ancient screed, yet treasured by our priests
And fancied a tale like to the minstrel's lay
Promising great reward to him who sought
The distant cavern of one Kenneth Begh,
An aged mighty seer, born in the days
When Seamus Ian slew the Picts, and yet
Alive! – I tarried not but seized my staff
And spear, and started on my pilgrimage –

. . . Advancing to my side, the stranger said:
'Continue not thy journey, foolish youth –
All is a dream, deceiving fantasy
Arising from thy restless foolish brain.
Go back! Thou searchest for thy seer in vain.
There is no seer, enchantment, in the world
Can e'er restore the mountain glory more!
This land is drear and waste and nevermore
Can be aught else but hideous wilderness;
And only I remain to wail the past,
The dauntless spirit of the Celtic race!'

And with those awesome words, the demon wraithe
Vanished, as melt the wisps of mountain mists.
Yet ever in my ears there rang anew
The plaintive, haunting ballad, which seemed now
To double its appeal and wistfulness . . .
. . . with reverent steps the cavern I approached
And whispered: 'Holy seer: thy wait is o'er!
The gods have willed a pilgrim youth to come
To beg thy magic aid to make anew
The glory of the kingdom Angus ruled'.
I entered then the cave and knelt to wait
The longed for charmed answer of the seer . . .

By the spring of 1954, Hamish had begun sending young singers and folklorists to Aberdeen to meet Jeannie, hear her sing and 'learn their craft at the feet of a master'. Their responses were invariably positive. In May 1957 the American folklorist Herschel Gower writes:

> Dear Hamish, I owe all this to you . . . The L.P. from Riverside arrived today, *Songs of a Scots Tinker Lady* and is now being played through for a second time on my phonograph. It is positively superb . . . Your song subjects and your style of singing will never get old in the face of time and will stand up as art as long as

> people tell stories and sing songs . . . I have finished my 'book' on the Scottish ballads – part of what I say is this: 'When Jeannie Robertson of Aberdeen sings "My Son David", her own conviction behind every word of the text and every phrase of the music, one readily experiences Coleridge's willing suspension of disbelief. By the time she has told you the story in song, you will accept this ballad as a "true ballad", however much the researchers may attempt to persuade you against the historical validity. We feel the full force of the singer's conviction behind the singer's belief. That conviction is a product of many years of assurance – her parents' convictions, the beliefs of the whole community, and even the "certain knowledge" of a whole race.'

Much of Gower's thinking here is coloured by Hamish's belief that Jeannie was custodian of 'special powers' and Hamish delighted in letting his many friends in on the secret. For example, when Stuart MacGregor, in the postscript to his last novel, *The Sinner*, writes about a woman with special gifts, Jeannie Robertson looms up:

> I had stumbled on a simple woman whose powers of perception mocked the most modern techniques of science . . . she described all manner of local cults and beliefs which bore reference to my wider reading. Slowly and patiently her counsel healed my sickness; slowly and painfully my dead spirit revived, and my yearning for the Beyond returned. One night she was explaining to me how communication with the dead must be spontaneous and unforced . . .[13]

By sending people to Jeannie, Hamish believed he was conjoining links in chains of great spiritual importance to humanity. One man who was greatly impressed was John E.W. Wells, an assistant chemist from Dagenham, Essex. On 28 August 1957 Wells wrote the first letter in a sustained correspondence:

> Dear Hamish – I would like to thank you for giving me information that led to most satisfactory holiday of my life. I think Scottish people are wonderful – though the only part of Scotland that I saw was that which lay between Maberley House and 21 Causewayend – I'd come to Scotland not to see it but to hear it!
>
> You asked for any impressions I got. I'll give them truthfully. Jeannie is a great singer of the old songs. Her style of singing sounded strange; the long drawn-out phrases, and complete indifference to

13 Stuart MacGregor, *The Sinner* (Calder and Boyars 1973).

> any feeling of 'strict-tempo', reminded me more of Flamenco singers than English ones (her style of singing is completely alien to that of the English folksinger); also her unusual insistence on standing to sing, and singing with her eyes open took me rather by surprise. Unlike her English counterparts she seems quite capable of singing the tune without the words (and vice versa). I found she was quite conscious of 'grace notes', and could diddle a tune with or without them . . . her repertoire is truly amazing . . .
>
> She has a great deal of trust in you; when in doubt about a contract, she always says, 'Wait till I've seen Hamish, he'll tell them!' . . . To tell you the truth, I'm so taken by the music I've heard in the north – I've almost decided to come and live there . . . maybe I could assist the School and yourself by going to work in Aberdeen . . .

John Wells was an amateur folklorist of high consequence and his comments are clear evidence of the impact Hamish's work at the School of Scottish Studies was exerting worldwide by the late fifties.

Two better-known Jeannie Robertson enthusiasts were Norman and Janey Buchan.[14] The Buchans were bowled over by Jeannie's contribution to the 1953 People's Festival and she was soon a regular visitor to the folk club at Rutherglen Academy where Norman taught English. She also visited Allan Glen's school in Glasgow (where Morris Blythman[15] taught French) and became a regular at the Glasgow Folk Clubs. Within a few years Jeannie was a one-woman folk institution and her early Scottish followers included Robin Hall, Jimmie Macgregor, Andy Hunter, Jean Redpath, Matt McGinn, and Ray and Archie Fisher. On 25 March 1960 Jeanie wrote to tell Hamish about a concert at Glasgow University which the Buchans had organised:

> I did very well indeed at the university – you may be hearing about it. Sir Hector and his wife was there – they had to leave at 3.30pm. But, I can tell you, I was treated like a queen. It is true the Queen could not have been looked after any better . . . They were all overcome and thunderstruck . . . Janey and Norman were very well pleased. They were with me . . . Believe it or not, I had to get a poultice put on my chest and throat the night before I went on. My chest closed and my throat went hoarse – but I doctored myself all night – just sheer determination. I got my voice back and my throat went clear . . . It was a great experience and instead of giving me £10, they gave me £15.15.

---

14 Norman Buchan MP and his wife Janey were folksong enthusiasts. Norman compiled the book *101 Scottish Songs* (Collins 1962).

15 Morris Blythman wrote poetry under the pseudonym Thurso Berwick (see Volume 1 of this biography).

Norman Buchan sent Hamish his own account, as Jeannie had anticipated:

> Professors Orr, Peter Alexander and George Pryde jointly hosted the lecture and brought along their honours students. Several other members of the Senate and many of the staff attended, as did the Principal and Lady Hetherington . . . Jeannie sang magnificently and the whole thing was a triumph for her . . . Robin Orr said, 'She has provided us with an afternoon, which, as a musician, I can only describe as enchantment' . . . Two days before we had Jeannie singing at the Folksong Club – about 200 odd and again a triumph for Jeannie – she received a rapturous welcome . . . It was, for me, a high-water mark in activity in this field and despite what has happened between us, I felt I could not let it pass without letting you know about it.

The previous year Jeannie gained Equity Membership. She informed Hamish, 'I am Jeannie Robertson 36541 – L/8707 – British Actor' and she, briefly, envisioned her career taking off in a big way. Her second US LP did well and in 1961 she received royalties of $700.00. Consequently, Hamish's friend Ken Goldstein began organising a major singing tour sponsored by American Youth Hostels, the USA Folk Song Committee, the University of Chicago Folklore Department, North Western University and Studs Terkel at Radio Station WFMT. For some reason, Jeannie's husband, Donald Higgins, got cold feet and refused to allow her to go. Instead, Hamish took her to London where they made a joint appearance at the Mermaid Theatre in a production entitled *Homage to the Unknown Poet.* It was master-minded by the Oxford poet John Wain who, knowing of Hamish's commitment to the Anti-Nuclear Movement, ordered him 'to concentrate on his War Elegies and leave his Anti-Nuclear and Anti-Monarchical songs outside on the street – where they belonged'.[16] Mrs Vaughan Williams was more polite, inviting both Jeannie and Hamish to lunch at 69 Gloucester Crescent, and telling Jeannie, 'my husband would have been thrilled to meet you'. The enthusiasm Jeannie inspired can be judged by this letter from Burlington Willes, of Drinda, California (1964).

> Dear Mr Henderson, My wife and I believe Jeannie Robertson has one of the most beautiful voices known today. No superlative is sufficient to describe this magnificent Scottish folk singer . . . My wife and I would very much like to fly to Scotland *expressly* to see and hear Mrs Robertson in person. Does she have a singing concert schedule?

---

16 HH conversation with TN.

Hamish got everyone moving and on 6 November Burlington Willes wrote back:

> You have no idea how thrilled my wife and I were to receive your kind letter this morning. Indeed, we never thought we might actually *see* and *hear* Jeannie Robertson. This is much beyond our remotest expectations . . . Since I am a teacher our first opportunity to fly to Scotland would be after June 16. Please accept our most humble gratitude for discovering Jeannie Robertson – her music has given us great comfort and joy.

One high point in the Hamish/Jeannie relationship was the lecture they gave, jointly, to delegates at a meeting of the British Association for the Advancement of Science, in Aberdeen, in 1963.The lecture was entitled 'Scots Folk-Song Today', and Jeannie 'illustrated' Hamish's points one by one in song. The lecture was published in *Folklore 75* (1964) and mentions the proximity of Jeannie's house to King's College Library, where the Gavin Greig ballad manuscripts are preserved. Hamish had no wish to confine Jeannie to her own huge repertoire; he treated her as an artist keen to expand and enrich her song-bank. (In 1968 Hamish became a leading member of a committee established to oversee publication of the Greig–Duncan collection, in eight splendid volumes.)

Surprisingly, the one institution that proved itself resistant to Jeannie Robertson, both as a singer and a personality, was the Scottish BBC. During the mid fifties recordings of her songs were broadcast as part of just two or three programmes. In November 1960 she featured prominently in a half-hour schools broadcast but Hamish's hope that this marked a breakthrough was confounded by Education Controller David Butts. A series of testy letters were exchanged and in May 1963 Hamish wrote rather forlornly:

> What you say about me and the children's response to Jeannie's songs and singing style does not really surprise me. When there is so little broadcasting of ethnic folksong on BBC Scotland and so much intensive plugging of 'pop and skiffle' by the pop-taste makers it is obvious that the style of ethnic first-raters like Jeannie will seem 'out of this world'

Hamish knew that 'taste' needs to be cultivated and he believed that the BBC was not doing its duty. Feeling himself out of kilter with the age, he notes:

> Values:
> as old fashioned
> as the hills of Jerusalem.

> . . . 'I believe': sung in oozy obsequious non-belief
> by some horrible group on Radio Scotland –
> suddenly questions the whole meaning of existence.[17]

On completing War and Peace, Tolstoy wrote: 'A work cannot be a success unless one loves its governing idea, and the idea I loved in *War and Peace* was the people'.[18] Hamish was propelled by a similar love and, for him, the submerged mass of Scots folk culture, like the subordinated masses of Old Russia, was a great reservoir of possibilities that the BBC should give voice to – like a collective Tolstoy. His ongoing battle to this end opens the next chapter.

---

17 HH, unpublished notes, Henderson archive.

18 Henri Troyat, *Tolstoy: A Biography* (Doubleday 1967).

THREE

Shenanigans at the Scottish BBC

To arrive at what one really believes, one must speak through lips different from one's own.

Oscar Wilde[1]

From childhood, by instinct and training, Hamish was a BBC enthusiast. At the orphanage, Ingleton House, in London, he documented his pleasure at listening to the young Alistair Cooke's seminal programmes *I Hear America Singing*. Each January, he listened to the *Burns Nicht* broadcast before 'reviewing it' in his diary. And in the Western Desert, the sound of Big Ben – booming out over the sand – before the evening's *Nine O'Clock News*, always struck deep emotional chords. By the time his *Ballads of World War II* were published in 1947, however, his enthusiasm had waned, as his introduction to the ballads makes clear:

> The balladry of World War II developed in conditions quite unlike those of previous wars. It grew up under the shadow of – and often in virtual conflict with – the official or commercial radio of the combatant nations. The state radio in times of war does not encourage dissidence from the straight patriotic line. It regards most expressions of the human reaction to soldiering as a drag on the national war effort. Accordingly it does not allot a great deal of time to the genuine Army ballad . . . Of course the state radio was wrong about the Army ballad, as about nearly everything else.[2]

Perversely, the BBC seems to have become more, rather than less, censorious when the war ended. Reithian propriety was replaced by an obsession with anti-Communist rectitude. For example, after publication of Hamish's *Elegies for the Dead in Cyrenaica* in 1948, the Scottish BBC did not broadcast any of the poems; nor were they discussed or reviewed. Things were marginally better in London, as Hamish's letter to his friend Phil Stein makes clear (18 March 1948): 'As you can well imagine, there's an eloquent anti-Henderson faction in the London BBC which will probably quell my broadcast of the Elegies for political reasons. However,

---

1 Oscar Wilde, 'The Critic as Artist'.

2 *Ballads of World War II* (Lili Marleen Club, Glasgow, 1947).

I've one powerful ally in Louis MacNeice – who's brought up his big guns on the side of the angels.' Subsequently the *Elegies* were presented in what proved to be a dramatic Third Programme production. This further increased Hamish's anger at his treatment in Scotland. For various reasons it was the poet and broadcaster Maurice Lindsay on whom he vented his anger: 'He seemed to be never off the airwaves!' Following a Lindsay broadcast on 'Fingal and Cuchulainn', Hamish penned this accusatory letter (to an unknown recipient):

> . . . My gorge rose at it – this programme was bad, quite obscenely bad. The airwaves have become a happy-hunting ground for mediocrities and marionettes. In fact anyone who is a constant listener will agree with me – the more scatological the mediocrity the better chance he has of an absolute free run on the Scottish Home Service . . . There is something grievously wrong with Scottish broadcasting and it is my settled opinion that no country in Europe – not even Iceland – is worse served by its broadcasters than Scotland. The St Andrews day broadcast in 1948 was unspeakably foul and mawkish. 'The White Rose', by Dunnett, was degrading to listen to – full of clichés and comfortably installed panjandrums . . . The BBC, as is well kent, is one of the few means by which a writer who writes to create art, not homilies or propaganda, can earn an honest penny . . . But the controllers, here, work hard to ensure that such writers get not even a crumb from the table . . . The BBC is not doing its job. What does it offer any writer of quality? I'll tell you what it does! It does what it did with the 'Elegies for the Dead in Cyrenaica', it turns them down – and the very next day . . . they were awarded the Somerset Maugham Award . . . My exclusion is not, I think, a case of accent – but why insist on presenters like Nigel Tranter who has an 'obsession with the articulation of an adenoidal sheep'! The BBC in Scotland should, long ago, have attempted to popularise an accepted Scots canon of spoken English based on the purist English spoken in the United Kingdom, Invernessian.

Hamish's mention of 'Dunnett' refers to the writer and broadcaster Alastair Dunnett, whose brother Robert also makes several appearances in Hamish's notebooks. They seem to have acted together to sour Hamish's chances at the BBC. He notes:

> One evening in 1947 I was in the Cafe Royal in Edinburgh, standing talking with Sydney Goodsir Smith, Peter Westwater and others, when Robert Dunnett (whom I did not know) joined the group. I referred to my poems when someone asked what I was doing. Robert Dunnett interrupted, 'What does it matter whether you finish them

> or not?' I said it mattered to me. He asked who the devil I was. I asked him whether he had ever heard of courtesy. He said he didn't give a damn about courtesy. I answered that it was clear that he knew nothing of the world north of the Clyde or Tay. He then indicated towards others standing round – people from the Edinburgh BBC mostly – and asked me if I knew them? I didn't know them . . . On 13 November 1952 I saw him come into the Abbotsford, in Edinburgh. He came in very drunk – wagging his finger at me – and he accused me of telling him he knew nothing about the war in Africa . . . Then he became very friendly in a maudlin way and told me that he was 'on my side', then went to the lavvy. When he came back he was frankly hostile. Said, 'You're living in the wrong era – now we're going to get you Henderson. Goody, goody, gum-drops!' It was closing time, so I helped him out of the pub and down into Princes Street, where he hailed a taxi. He asked me to get in. I said I lived very near and it wasn't worth it. He answered: 'I've kept your name off the radio up till now – so get in this taxi – or else!' I shut the door on him and went off.

From 1946 till 1970 the Fraserburgh-born poet George Bruce worked at the Scottish BBC and played a leading role in shaping the tone and content of its cultural broadcasting. He had a fine mind and a commanding personality, he was a member of the Scots literary establishment and got on well with MacDiarmid. Over twenty years his correspondence with Hamish, however, shows their relationship to have been difficult, particularly with regard to Hamish's proposals for programmes about Scottish folksong. In February 1953 (the month the EIIR letterbox was blown up – see Volume 1 of this biography) Bruce writes: 'Dear Hamish, I was not successful with a proposal for a programme about Folk Song . . . Another similar proposal had been on the table for some considerable time before, against Herbert Wiseman's name [Scottish BBC Head of Music]. It will be a long time before your one is considered.' On 17 February Hamish wrote to the *Scotsman*.

> Sir – When I referred to the tape-recordings of Scots folksongs housed in the archives of the School of Scottish Studies as a 'reference library', I certainly did not mean to imply that this was their only function . . . It would be a great irony if your readers assumed that I did not want my recordings of Scots folksongs to be broadcast. On the contrary, I believe that the broadcasting of them would be an event of great cultural significance in Scotland. The decision as to whether or not they should be broadcast, however, does not rest with me. It rests, I need hardly say with the BBC and with the SSS, which owns the tapes. It is possible that either one or both of these organisations will oppose the broadcasting of the great traditional

songs which I have collected, but I consider it very unlikely. These songs lie near the heart of the older Scottish tradition; they are beyond doubt the genuine article as preserved and sung by people to whom it is still a living part of reality. As for the quality of performance it has been described by individuals well qualified to judge – for example, Professor STM Newman, Dr Herbert Wiseman, and Mr William Montgomerie . . . as exceedingly high.

One of the functions of a university is surely to inspire the people. And what is the function of a broadcasting system if it is not to entertain the people (and provide them *viva voce* with some stimulating food for thought)? I cannot imagine a project in which these various aims and functions could be more happily combined than in the broadcasting of genuine Scots folksong to the Scottish people. The singers, I might add, are all for it: they fail to see why second rate performances and battered 'lyric gems' should monopolise the airwaves for ever . . . Even when announcing the tunes in programmes of Scottish dance music – our broadcasters usually pronounce the Scots words as if they were speaking a foreign language for which they feel a slight distaste . . . 'The Muckin o Geordie's Byre' referred to as the 'The Meukin of Jawdie's Beye-a' – the most gruesome bloodbath of vowels that ever savaged a living language!

What is the solution? The BBC has a great opportunity. If it rose to the occasion it could arrest the process of wholesale anglicisation, and give fresh dignity and currency, not only to Gaelic and Lallans, but also to the traditional Scots-English of an older generation: an infinitely more pleasing speech, may I say, than the usual run of announcers' English. What is needed is an accepted standard of Scots-English pronunciation – not a hard and fast standard, but a flexible line which would permit, and indeed encourage, deviations to Highland and Lowland. If we could get provisional agreement on the need for this – and the correspondence in your columns shows that there is a widespread feeling in favour of such a move – we would shortly find, I think, that other parts of the English-speaking world would increasingly come to accept it as a standard. (I am particularly thinking of the Northern English of Tyne, Humber and Tees, who would certainly prefer Scots-English to the Hampstead-Surbiton variety.)

The Italians say that the best Italian is *lingua toscana in bocca romana* (the Tuscan speech on Roman lips). Could we not have a shot at proving that the best English is *lingua inglese in bocca scozzese?* It may be objected that we would have difficulty in agreeing on a standard. I do not think there are any formidable obstacles.

> Use might well be made of the tape recordings in the Archives of the SSS of Edinburgh University, which are not only an incomparable treasure house of the folksong of our country, as preserved by real folksingers, but also a linguistic reference library of the first importance.

The following day, two of Hamish's friends, J.K. Annand and Thurso Berwick (Morris Blythman), wrote similar letters to the BBC, to Edinburgh University and the *Scotsman* in an orchestrated attempt to secure the future of the School and its work. Annand asked 'that a structure, between the BBC and the University of Edinburgh, be created to ensure that the folksong and music collected by Mr. Henderson should be disseminated so that it continues *to live*'. This idea, so important for the Scots Folk Revival that Hamish was now promoting, is developed in these notes of his:

> The study of folklore is an exceedingly important human study, a humanistic discipline of tremendous value. Human beings, societies, communities need to understand themselves – and their neighbours . . . Nothing can be called folksong that has not been submitted to the moulding process of oral transmission. Here, Scotland has much to show – because of its *lettered* tradition – yet all folksong is part of an international dynamic – like the folk-tales . . . Why are Scotland and, in modern times, America pre-eminent in the rich tradition of balladry? One reason is that while in England the ballad long ago became entertainment for the lower orders, in Scotland it continued to delight the whole population. Another is that many Scots emigrated to the Southern and the Western states where the American ballad-tradition is strongest. Look at the names of the singers.

Hamish was determined that the unique heritage of Scotland's traditional singers should be passed on – both within families and to a new generation of 'revival singers'. When one of his first discoveries – Jessie Murray, the Buckie fishwife, who had thrilled her audience at the first People's Ceilidh Festivals in 1951 – died suddenly, Hamish tried to get her voice heard and memory honoured on the BBC. On 5 March 1953 Bruce wrote to confirm that Hamish could make 'a nine minute contribution with recordings of songs by Jessie' in the April edition of *Scottish Life and Letters*. But on 26 March Bruce wrote to announce that this item had been cancelled because a member of the family had written to say that a public tribute to Mrs Murray would be inappropriate (Buckie was a centre of fundamentalist Christianity). As if this was not disappointing enough, Bruce rubbed salt in Hamish's wounds by ending his letter: 'you will recollect that Stewart Sanderson especially requested us to obtain first the singer's permission . . . I am therefore substituting another talk for your appreciation'.

George Bruce's justification for giving 'traditional singers' such minimal air time was the same as that used by the Education Controller, 'that Scots listeners were not ready for such voices'. Bruce was a fine poet but also a Reithian Calvinist who strongly opposed Hamish's libertarian views. On 25 July 1953 Hamish writes:

> I find in George Bruce the false humility of the Presbyterian elder – the Scottish dominie quality – is the Calvinist hypocrisy carried to fantastic heights of cynicism and brutality . . . All leaderships are collective but some are more collective than others.[3]

A month earlier Hamish's first 'folk broadcast' – a pilot – had gone drastically wrong: whilst on air a series of technical problems erupted. The *Glasgow Herald* followed up with a damning review. On 23 June Hamish wrote to Phil Stein outlining his 'suspicions' that the problems encountered had been planned:

> Dear Phil . . . the Glasgow Herald reviewer *is likely* to object to real people singing their own songs, and to prefer the professional performer *who can cloud the issue*. It is a surprise to me – that after two People's Festivals – that *you* should fall in with his ideas. However, as I have pointed out two years running at the People's Festivals; the essence of Folksong is *its direct contact* with reality, its organic link with the work of loom, factory and field. Against this reality the radio lays down its daily barrage (turned on in your home, as in countless others, almost as soon as you get up. It gives you the time, I admit – but it also captures the first objective!). And what is the first objective of this barrage? Its aim – the aim indeed, of all commercial and commercialised music – is to debauch the listener, and induce in him a state of mind in which he actually prefers the second-hand to the first-hand. There are London suburbs today into which the radio flows from morning to midnight, and where *the natural singing man* is regarded as a sort of monstrosity. Luckily our Scotland is a little tougher. To throw down the gauntlet against the universal debauching of song and culture, is of course a concrete political act. And it is very correct and fitting that the 'Glasgow Herald' reviewer should object to working class people singing on the air the songs they have created. If a 'Glasgow Herald' reviewer had praised the work of the People's Festival ceilidh or the 'music of the people' (instead of ignoring one and slighting the other) I would have been seriously worried . . . This was, of course, the first programme of Folksong sung by natural singers which the Scottish BBC has ever put on.

3 Unpublished notes, Henderson archive.

> The reviewer's comment that I was 'ill at ease with my script' gives me a certain grim amusement. Owing to the loss of ten minutes, due to a 'technical hitch', I had to rewrite and compress my entire script whilst the programme was actually going on. If I had been at ease under these circumstances, it would have been a bloody miracle! . . . The sad truth is that the balls-up at the start dealt the whole programme a blow in the solar plexus. It is not impossible that this was due to the activities of certain nice gentlemen in the BBC who don't like me and what I'm doing, and who maybe have friends among the engineers in the Glasgow control room. As for my own political position and views, I feel these are better manifested by deeds than words, and even justifiably bitter words are not out of place in this connection . . . Believe me, Phil, I saw through them then, and I see through x, y and z at the present moment. Just wait and keep your eyes open.[4]

In the autumn of 1953, however, Bruce gave Hamish another bite at the cherry by asking him to present a selection of his 'folk discoveries' as part of one of the monthly *Scottish Life and Letters* programmes. One listener was a Morayshire molecatcher named John MacDonald and on 3 November he wrote to Hamish:

> Some of the so-called ballad singers we get on some of the radio programmes are too stagefied (excuse the word). I prefer them like old Jimmy MacBeath . . . I have a great many songs . . . I am also a comedian. I have for years been presenting concerts as 'The Orra Chiel' and 'Auld Donal the Hieland Man'. Some of my favourite old songs are 'The Rovin Ploughboy' – I like the air and the words: also 'The Haughs o' Cromdale' and 'The Banks and Braes o' Dunphail'. This was composed by the late Jamie MacQueen of Forres. He had the privilege to play on the old Highland Railway to amuse the

4 Hamish's interpretation of events at the Scottish BBC, in the 1950s, are strongly contradicted by Dr Ian Olson of Aberdeen. Olson's father was a sound engineer with the BBC and a close colleague of Bruce's at the time. (His account is part of a correspondence with TN between 2002 and 2006.) Dr Olson is an authority on North-East folksong, now retired from the University of Aberdeen. One of his letters reads, 'the BBC . . . warned him [Hamish] that too much reliance on Jeannie Robertson {who was by no means universally admired – "bawls like a bull" was a typical comment} would be a kiss of death. Hamish paid no attention and his programmes bombed with the public and had to be taken off . . . furthermore, MacDiarmid and others launched a continuing and longstanding public onslaught on Hamish and his promotion of "the boring doggerel of analphabetic and ineducable farm-labourers, tinkers and the like" and "unlettered ballad singers yowling like so many cats in the moonlight".'

> passengers, he was a grand fiddler. My daughter has a fine voice and sings a few songs along with me . . . I give concerts in aid of Aberlour orphanage, I will be very pleased to see you anytime and if I come across any old singers I will take a note.

In fact John MacDonald had first made contact with Hamish in 1952 following an article by Hamish in *The Northern Scot*. MacDonald wrote a letter and a thirty-year friendship began: 'About a week ago going round my mole-traps I had a surprise when a jet black owl flew out of a tree. It was the first black owl I have seen, although many years ago on Dortnachan Hills above Carrbridge I saw a black hare. Several people saw it but I never heard of it being caught or shot.' Hamish was soon using 'John MacDonald the Singing Molecatcher' as both a 'talent spotter' and informant. In January 1954 MacDonald writes:

> Dear Hamish – I have been going all out to get new songs – most of them that have come in I already have but one came in today from a Mr MacPherson of Canada. He composed it himself. It has become popular in Canada . . . I am now collecting old gramophone records of former melodeon players as I am afraid they are becoming extinct. I once met the late James Brown, Champion of the World . . . The late F. Cameron, who took London by storm with his melodeon playing, was a great friend of mine. He had his right arm shot off in the 1914 war – and that ended his playing.

Hamish had to wait two years before he got another invitation to broadcast but when it came he was full of boyish enthusiasm and wrote to his old primary teacher, Miss Peterkin, demanding she listen. On 26 September 1955 Miss Peterkin wrote back:

> Dear Hamish – How delighted I was to receive your letter! I recognized your handwriting on the envelope and felt sure it was to herald a visit from you . . . You can be assured of a great welcome, Hamish, and though you will find us considerably aged we still keep our interest in and love for youth and you are dear to us . . . We are wondering if your voice will be heard in the broadcast . . . Yes, I shall certainly write to the BBC . . . Your mother I knew and loved and also your dear grandmother who used to read stories of Scottish history to you when you were still very young. She had a great love for you – and I used to visit her frequently when of course any conversation was about you.

Before the broadcast went out, George Bruce informed Hamish that he had had to edit out one of the songs selected: 'Jeannie Robertson's Thornbush is more for the pub parlour, or the Third Programme, than the pleasant domesticity of Scottish homes. For her song I have substituted Jimmy MacBeath singing Nicky Tams.' Even on the rare occasions when he was allowed air-time, Hamish found his message so 'denatured' that he began testing other channels of communication. Evidence of this comes in a diary kept by a secretary at the School of Scottish Studies.

> *4 Dec. 1956:* Hamish and James Ross were in Kilmarnock last Thursday with TPU [SSS car] and a recording machine. On Friday the Scottish Nationalists did a pirate broadcast from Kilmarnock; (Hamish and James were in Glasgow with tinkers on the run from the police and wouldn't give them an alibi probably). On Saturday someone – probably the Daily Mail – rang up Hamish and I said he was not in Kilmarnock, but in Dumbarton . . . Now Hamish has the wind up. He has gone off to record in Kintyre.

It was exactly 170 years since Burns had published his 'Kilmarnock edition' of *Poems Chiefly in the Scottish Dialect* and Hamish knew that if he wanted his voice heard, he would have to act and risk his life – as Burns (and Blake) had risked theirs. Unlike Burns he had no Masonic Lodge to support him but he had friends, as this letter to Tony Anthony[5] (written thirty years later) makes clear.

> Dear Tony – your letter made me realize how much I've forgotten – or maybe never knew – about that awkward but productive period in the early 50s . . . My over-riding wish, as you know, was to get the old songs sung again, in something like the old style, and the opposition I encountered – which was real enough – was overcome eventually, though it took rather longer than I envisaged. However I have the liveliest memories of gratitude to people like Sidney Newman and David Abercrombie who *did* support me. And Calum, of course, above all . . . As for broadcasting, I hoped to use it as a collecting tool, in much the same way as Gavin Greig had used his column in the 'Buchanie' to collect songs – but that idea didn't appeal to the craturs in power.

Hamish was a natural radio broadcaster; he loved to talk and saw radio and television as natural allies to oral tradition and the spontaneous word. He felt himself close to the Scots population and believed that broadcasting works best when 'a speaker is talking to an audience that knows and responds to the speaker – an audience that has a group (or national) identity. The written word can be referred to – the spoken word needs to have relevance or it is dissipated in air or individual minds in which it

5 Dr Tony J. Anthony was a colleague in the Phonetics Department at the University of Edinburgh.

never gels . . . The language of the great songs is a subject in itself, hitherto virtually unexplored. In Aberdeenshire (the county that has yielded more ballads than any other) the singers of the "muckle sangs" do not use the local dialect of Scots, rich and vigorous as it is; they use a pure and dignified braid Scots that probably descends from the metropolitan language of the old Scottish Kingdom.'[6]

Hamish believed the BBC should function culturally rather as the Scots Court had functioned before 1603: as an open-house where the best was expected and the best sanctioned. When Jeannie's second American LP was released (in 1962) he let George Bruce know:

> Quite a number of Gaelic singers like Flora MacNeil have recently been given 15 or 20 minute recitals of unaccompanied song. In spite of her worldwide fame, and in spite of the fact that she has been known to the BBC since 1953, Jeannie Robertson has never been asked to give a similar recital. Don't you think it high time she did?

When two months passed and nothing happened, Hamish wrote again. By 20 May he felt himself being toyed with and wrote Bruce a letter that gathers anger by the line:

> Dear George, Thank you for your letter. I just write to say its contents were not unexpected. Indeed if I had opened it and found that the Scottish BBC had decided to do half an hour of sound radio from the School's Scots recordings it would have been my biggest surprise since the announcement that Hess had landed in Scotland by parachute . . . You are quite right to be against a 9 or 10 minute programme of snippets and illustrations. What a gormless solution! Better no programme at all than the parading of emasculated gobbets of song, salvaging the results of a plastic bomb outrage at Queen Street Station, no Sir![7]

In 1968, with Jeannie's sixtieth birthday approaching, Hamish wrote to Bruce suggesting a half-hour programme to honour the occasion. There was no response. On 27 January he wrote to Bruce's senior colleague, David Dorward:

> I find it difficult to understand the extraordinary neglect of Jeannie Robertson by the BBC in Scotland. She is now nearly sixty . . . If she

6 HH, unpublished notes, Henderson archive.

7 Queen Street is one of the rail stations in Glasgow but also the street address of the BBC's Edinburgh offices. Hamish lets Bruce know that he believes him a quisling (like Rudolph Hess, about whom Hamish had written a poem in May 1941) and his reference to 'a plastic bomb' was clearly designed to shock.

> were to die in the next twelve months the SSS would (I presume), very soon after, receive news of a 'commemorative programme' . . . Why is it, do you think, that so many of the Scots fear excellence, and only let it find its voice when it is dead? These thoughts are prompted, needless to say, by the Burns orgy now once more in full blast . . . Do try to get Jeannie a half-hour programme, exhibiting the wide range of her gifts and her repertoire, tragic, elegiac, and ribald.

At last the BBC made positive noises and on 1 February Hamish wrote to Bruce, 'Dear George, I am exceedingly glad that there seems to be the possibility of a half hour programme about Jeannie . . . I think it would be a mistake though to hang it on the fact of Jeannie's coming sixtieth birthday – Jeanie is still a magnificent singer, and her voice shows no signs of letting her down. Why not just call it a programme in her honour.' However, when a fortnight passed and he heard nothing more, Hamish became confrontational (9 February 1968):

> Dear George . . . I have been going through a lot of old correspondence, cuttings, reviews etc., going back to just after WWII, and you'll believe me when I say it has not been an altogether pleasing experience. About the egregious series of boorish rebuffs I personally have received from the BBC I need say little, for you know well enough about them. What seems to be really disgraceful, and a scandal of the first order, is the neglect of the outstanding traditional singers such as Jeannie Robertson. Even good young singers like Jean Redpath, whom I tried to get on sound radio in 1958, have had to wait years – in her case almost a decade – before appearing on the Scottish BBC . . .
>
> Visiting singers . . . often refer to the debased taste of the Scottish Folk Clubs, and the extraordinary contrast between the achievement of such singers as Jeannie and the crude vulgar commercialism of these clubs . . . An examination of the record leaves one in no doubt whatsoever that the prime guilty party in all this is the Scottish BBC. Enjoying an opportunity seldom given to any single identifiable organisation it has neglected the good and genuine with a quite astonishing consistency, and has actively promoted the inferior, glamorised and phoney . . . For these reasons I have taken the decision never to appear personally on the Scottish BBC unless and until folksingers of Jeannie's capability and reputation receive from the BBC the respect and patronage to which they are entitled. The BBC public in Scotland will certainly not miss me, for it has hardly ever heard my voice. I do not expect this decision to have any effect on the BBC's policy with regard to the unheard traditional singers, but

> nevertheless I make it for the record. The singers themselves can hardly be worse treated than they are at present . . . I find myself bound therefore – although with genuine regret – to turn down your suggestion of a short talk on McGonagall, to whose memory I feel the warmest and most sympathetic attachment.

This broadside encouraged Bruce to be conciliatory. On 21 February he writes,

> Dear Hamish, I am very sorry you feel you cannot take part in 'Scottish Life and Letters' on account of your feeling against the BBC as a whole. My efforts may have appeared slight to you but I assure you I appreciate your desire for promotion of the best in traditional Scottish popular culture . . . I take your point that we may not do enough for our heritage of folk song in Scotland, and though this is not my field, I shall raise this issue again.

Hamish notes in his diary: 'The attitude of the Scottish BBC to the arts is like Frank Harris's use of women. A professed solicitude and an actual cannibalism.' Meantime, Norman Buchan (now a Minister in Harold Wilson's Labour Government) had been networking and on 3 May 1968 Hamish received this excited letter from Jeannie:

> Just a note to Let you know I Received a Letter today from White Hall No 10, Downing street, London. Harold Wilson prime Minister stating that I am getting the MBE . . . No doubt I will have to go before the Queen . . . They will write and Let Me know. I think it will Be on her Birthday.

This news encouraged Hamish to ask Dr Nicolaisen (acting head of the School of Scottish Studies[8]) to write to Alasdair Milne, Head of BBC Scotland, to 'demand' a half-hour programme 'in honour of Jeannie's Honour!' This letter finally did the trick and on 21 May, Milne wrote to Nicolaisen: 'I have discussed this with colleagues and Mr Watson Forbes, the Head of Music for Scotland, is arranging for his staff in Aberdeen to prepare a special programme on Mrs Higgins.' This programme was subsequently written and produced by Hamish's friend Arthur Argo, under the direction of James Hunter, and broadcast on 10 June 1968. It featured Hamish, Ray Fisher and Pete Seeger, and James Hunter was soon making a name for himself as the leader of a new generation of Scots broadcasters. In 1970 George Bruce took early retirement and left the BBC to become the first Scottish Arts Council Fellow in Creative Writing (at the University of Glasgow).

8 Basil Megaw had taken early retirement on health grounds.

In December 1968 Jeannie received her MBE from the Queen at Buckingham Palace. Afterwards Norman Buchan took her to the Palace of Westminster for a reception. After that she sang nationwide on *Tonight with Dave Allen* and returned to Scotland with a cheque for £119.60.

The following year James Hunter invited Hamish to write and present a one-hour documentary-drama about the Highland tinker-freebooter James MacPherson (hanged at Banff in 1711). Hamish entitled his programme *The Magnificent Outlaw*. It was planned to be a major production. On 7 July 1970 Hunter wrote to Hamish: 'I will put through a contract to yourself for reading and writing the script . . . Remember you have the full BBC resources behind you, i.e. court effects, fights, acoustics of courtrooms etc. I am trying to fix up, as you mentioned, Roddy McMillan to play the part of MacPherson – I do not want to do a usual half-hearted Scottish type documentary on this one.' The programme when broadcast was much praised, Hunter writing: 'Dear Hamish, A note of sincere thanks to you for your very excellent script for *The Magnificent Outlaw*. I hope you enjoyed the playback on radio and that we can collaborate on more such documentaries in future.'

Despite the success of this broadcast, this first big commission came fifteen years too late and, far from marking the start of a promising radio career, this programme – in reality – marked an end. No new contracts came Hamish's way and as the years passed it became increasingly clear that frustration and sustained drinking had taken their toll. If MI5 did decide, in 1951, to snuff out Hamish's revolutionary ardour by exhausting him in the impossible task of harvesting 'the Scots folk tradition' it failed miserably, but his powers to sustain intellectual concentration on major personal projects were now evidently impaired.

For all his energy, courage and intellectual resilience Hamish was easily hurt and vulnerable to attacks on his character, his art, his personal integrity. As early as 1948, E.P. Thompson had seen 'that there are in the *Elegies* occasional indications of lack of confidence'. By the 1970s that artistic confidence had almost gone. Despite the support of friends, two decades of sustained 'institutional bombardment' had dammed the poetry that once flooded from him. But – like his mother – Hamish retained 'a heart that would sink a battleship' and, increasingly, people across Scotland were now taking up his banners.

FOUR

Folk Stories: The Stewarts of Blair

Early societies lived in an eternal present – including the dead who were remembered and thus existed within the same reality as the living . . . As hunters and gatherers, later as breeders and herders, mankind wandered the earth and experienced life: with farming came settlement, surplus and craftsmanship – great benefits ensue but they are accompanied by experiential and spiritual loss. No longer is the prime satisfaction to live but people live (and organise) to obtain satisfaction: Nature and civilisation become tools.[1]

By the mid twentieth century, oral storytelling, in public, had become the poor relation of the Western folk arts. Stories need time. Institutional education demands literacy, and reading had become a private practice that conditioned people to see storytelling as inefficient and primitive. During the 1950s the School of Scottish Studies began nurturing a fight-back against the ossification of storytelling – Calum Maclean concentrated on the Gaidhealtachd, Hamish on the Travelling People. Both men had a predilection for song but saw the revival of storytelling as a crucial part of the Folk Revival. Today, public storytelling is once again a reality in Western societies.

This revival owes something to the nature of radio and television but the intervention of folklorists like Hamish – who looked back to move forwards – was crucial. It was amongst Scotland's Travellers that Hamish found many of the best storytellers, jokers, riddlers and rhymesters. Their separate, wandering lifestyle, their hours by the fireside, had maintained traditions in which both the teller and the tales were believed. Most Traveller storytellers were non-literate. The Travellers had a taboo against books. Books were clutter-lumber and symbols of the legal controls that kept them subservient outsiders. Stories were possessions, frameworks to live by.

As early as the summer of 1952, the London publishers B.T. Batsford Ltd invited Hamish to collect and edit a book of Scottish folktales. In

1 Emilios Bouratinos, 'Consciousness and the Snare of Civilisation – A Reappraisal of Human Evolution', *Network Review: Journal of the Scientific and Medical Network*, no. 72, April 2000.

March 1953 Sam Carr suggested that the book be 'of perhaps 80,000 words?'. By the autumn Hamish had collected a host of stories from Jeannie Robertson and, over the next two years, many more from the Stewarts of Blairgowrie. The Batsford book, however, was never to materialise. Did 'bizziness' and the discipline of editorship frustrate Hamish? Was the lack of a secretarial assistant his problem? Did he succumb to the Travellers' 'druidic' inhibition against the written word? Yes is probably the answer to all these questions.

Certainly Hamish was disturbed by his inability to get the wonderful material the School was gathering made publicly available, but he justified his lack of 'publications' on two fronts. First, he knew that the modern world was not short of books, publishers or bookshops, whereas Scotland's traditional storytellers were few and far between, and dying every year. Second, the oral tradition was an *Oral* Art and, in the short term, he believed it far more important to meet, honour and record the storytellers than to see selections of their stories edited, printed and for sale in bookshops. Thus he took a bold cultural decision: he would record, support and nurture his source tellers, as storytellers, not as authors. He believed it important that these oral stories should remain oral experiences until a new generation had absorbed their magic and their art as storytellers. Printed books were common as grass but Ossianic tales, handed down by word-of-mouth in the nuclear age, were 'gey thin on the groon'. By frustrating his publishers, Hamish glorified the cultural continuum that makes the Celtic heritage part of European Modernism:[2]

> My commitment was to the oral tradition. The choices were – success at my desk or failure in the berry-fields. I chose the dreels o' Blairgowrie – and life with the Stewarts.[3]

The dramatic circumstances that led Hamish to the great Stewart clan based at Blairgowrie are described in Volume 1 of this biography. His partner in this 'wonderful find' was the journalist Maurice Fleming, whose dedicated support is evident from his earliest letters. On 17 October 1954 he writes:

> Dear Hamish – The tapes – I'm glad to hear you like them – especially 'The Twa Brothers'. Unfortunately the School hadn't told me I should ask for the sources of the songs – but I can ask for these

2 It is interesting that, whilst at the University of Edinburgh in the fifties, the Rev. Professor James Barr (theologian and Old Testament scholar) revived the 'idea' of storytelling as crucial to all theological interpretation – that the Old Testament was not 'mainly' history, but stories, revealing beliefs not historical facts.

3 HH, conversation with TN, 1995.

> sometime and send them along . . . at the moment the Stewarts are living in an old caravan whilst their bungalow is being built . . . Some tinkers are here for the tattie-howkin but Berrytime is the best time and next year I'll be ready for the onslaught . . . If I'm given a machine, I'll be ready to start as soon as the first tinkers arrive.

By Christmas their friendship was so close that, by a strange process of osmosis, Maurice's letters begin to carry strong echoes of Hamish's voice and writing style:

> I may be making the devil of a mistake, but I think I have to thank you for a book. I was sure it was Archie MacPherson's [a local schoolmaster] but I've just phoned him and he denies all knowledge of it – anyway it was a delightful surprise and a most welcome addition to the library of Scots poetry I'm trying to build up. I've long wanted to read your *Elegies* which I've heard so much about and now, I have it – and to keep . . . Reading it last night I was extremely interested to find that you have been influenced by Cavafy – his poetry appeals to me strongly . . . A woman married into tinker stock promises she'll teach me some cant – you probably know already how close a secret the 'language' is. I hope to record a verse or two of a song in cant . . . I'm sorry I was rash enough to send in an article to the Evening News on my folklore experiences to date. Mr Sanderson was most annoyed. But he should have made the position clear to me from the beginning. My journalistic nose gets me into trouble quite often I'm afraid. And then I need the money so badly. However, I won't be a naughty boy again . . . I wrote two irate letters to the BBC this week – I'm a great believer in the power of the radio in the spreading of an art form. Look what they've done to boost country dancing . . .

This letter shows the grip that Stewart Sanderson was exerting on all aspects of the School's research. It also confirms that Hamish's research into Traveller cant was underway in 1954 and that Maurice Fleming was the first 'assistant' to join him on his great 'Tinker Project': the most ambitious of all the anthropological/folklore enquiries Hamish was to mount. In 1955 the Canadian anthropologist Frank Vallee joined the team. On 1 June Maurice wrote to Hamish:

> Thank you for inviting me to Ella Ward's party, which I enjoyed very much – delicious curry and excellent wine! . . . I understand from Sanderson that you are coming with a machine and Frank Vallee's to be picking berries. Would you like me to try to get you a hut which the two of you could share? It might be possible to get one near the Stewarts' berry farm at Essendy – or perhaps you'd rather just land here and let Fate guide you where you will.

Hamish described the Tinker Project as 'designed to survey the whole traveller set-up in Scotland from an historical, anthropological and folk-cultural point of view'. In-depth studies of individuals would become the key methodology, and Davie Stewart – a seasoned east-coast entertainer who had married his amazing 'rough-house voice to a battered squeeze-box, held by an otter-skin band' – soon forced himself to the forefront. Hamish described Davie as 'one of the Brochan Stewarts, the extensive remnant of what seems to have been the great royal clan itself', and their first meeting was memorable:

> I found Davie entertaining a cinema queue. With Scotch-Roman nose and bunnet cockily, aggressively, tilted back on his head he conveyed a spirit of rodomontade – a swaggering devil-may-care attitude to the world at large – that, immediately, drew me to him. It was 'MacPherson's Rant' he was playing – 'Sae wantonly, sae rantingly' – his voice coming out of the darkness like the surging of the sea, the notes from the squeezebox rising and falling like the distant sound of keening women. Davie had a tendency to fill in partly remembered lines with meaningless syllables and this 'habit' gave his delivery an uncanny edge, a rhythmic energy that probably predates set-piece singing. When Davie sang – an ecstasy, something primeval took hold.[4]

Davie (whose by-name was 'the Galoot') made many recordings, the best being the Topic LP 12T293 released posthumously in 1978, with a splendid introduction by Hamish. The milieu within which Davie lived, however, was harsh, as these extracts from letters from Fleming (1957 and 1962) make clear:

> Dear Hamish, The Galoot is now back in Dundee – filled with enthusiasm. He seems to have had a wonderfully successful trip to London, apart from that unfortunate night in the cells – which wasn't his fault . . . What a tragedy it should have happened on one of those precious few nights when he had the chance to sleep like a lord in a luxury hotel . . . He met Ewan MacColl and Robin Hall and earned himself three guineas per club.
>
> Dear Hamish, I was along to see our old friend the Galoot – he has boils on his backside and was groaning a good deal. He looks older. He (and his wife) are wondering why you never come to see them . . .

Hardship, however, did little to blunt the joys captured and released by Hamish's researches. And, in Ottawa, Frank Vallee was using his Scottish experience to begin new work amongst Canada's Native Americans. The

4 HH, unpublished notebook, Henderson archive.

emotional intensity that the work engendered is given beautiful expression in this letter written by Vallee in December 1955:

> Dear Hamish, The tape arrived, and Oh! what it means to us! . . . The tape had not unrolled more than ten feet or so before Anita allowed herself the luxury of a good cry. My own eyes were not too dry. I can't say how much we appreciate what you've done . . . The selection of numbers was excellent and the inclusion of thoughts from friends very thoughtful . . . I take my new job 'in stride' – my boss, the director of citizenship, is a cultivated French Canadian, a thorough gentleman with no pretensions. My own staff is most helpful, pleasant and charming . . . Anita misses Scotland as much as I do . . . but the kids are really blooming out here – in the snow, tobogganing and sledging . . . Please remember me to the folk in the School, in Aberdeen and Blairgowrie.

In October 1955 Hamish had presented the fifteen-year-old Sheila Stewart as one of his 'new generation' of traditional singers – on the solitary BBC broadcast he had been allowed to make. Like the discovery of Jeannie Robertson, it proved a pivotal moment in the history of Scotland's Travelling People. Over the national airwaves praise was afforded to a group widely regarded as beyond the pale. Hamish also acknowledged the contribution Maurice Fleming was making to his research. On air he behaved as his normal courteous, Highland self – committed to changing and elevating public perceptions. In private, however, he remained brutally honest, noting, for example, how centuries of deprivation had introverted certain aspects of Traveller culture:

> Tinker singing: that perpetual wail which in certain songs can be effective and even attractive, but which lifts the lid from what wells, ye gods, of savaged human-kindness, what deeps within these most driven shufflers of self-pity.[5]

During 1956 Maurice moved out of his parents' home in Blairgowrie to settle in Dundee, closer to his work with the D.C. Thomson Press. With time to himself, he wrote a stream of plays – several influenced by Hamish's interests. Maurice was a folk enthusiast but, by profession, a journalist with literary ambitions. These worlds were, however, not separate and when he later became editor of the *Scots Magazine*, Maurice frequently gave Hamish the page.

Acting as Hamish's 'ambassador', Maurice persuaded Kenneth Ireland, innovative director of the new Pitlochry Theatre, to make 'Folk Song and Folk Music' part of his Summer Programme. Hamish noted, 'For the

5 HH, unpublished notes, Henderson archive.

first time since the reign of James VI, the Travelling People were being paid to appear on the national stage of Scotland.' In September 1956 Maurice encouraged Hamish to visit Davie Glen of Tealing: 'He sings mostly comic songs; he sings them well and I like his use of dialect. He is, as you may know, the champion diddler[6] of Scotland. He lives alone in a railway carriage at the back of Tealing village and has a large beard. He's always away at weekends, hill-climbing from Saturday morning till Sunday night.'

It was, however, 'the Stewarts of Blair' who dominated folksong in Angus and East Perthshire, and it was with them that Hamish worked most closely. At the centre of the clan were Belle and Alec Stewart, then living in Rattray. Alec was a handsome, commanding man but it was Belle (MacGregor) who – with queenly authority – carried the culture. For Hamish, she was a tradition bearer second only to Jeannie Robertson. There were six children, with Sheila Stewart the most gifted. She had a dark Scotch-Romany beauty, with a character to match. Fourteen when Hamish arrived on the scene, the tinker lass and the wandering scholar began a lifelong folk-love-affair. Maurice was equally enthralled; he writes to Hamish:

> Sheila is a singer who astonishes me afresh every time I hear her. She always sounds better than I remember! She's just great to my ear in all her songs and could make a great record all to herself. Think of these: 'Blackwaterside', 'Hatton Woods', 'The Galway Shawl', 'The High Gelty Mountains'. Superb! In fifteen or twenty years time, she could be a big figure, couldn't she?

Two decades later Sheila was singing before the Pope and half a million people in Bellahouston Park, Glasgow. Today, on the edge of old age, she is an MBE, author of several books, dozens of records, discs, DVDs, appears regularly on television and the international folk circuit. For many years she has represented the Travellers on councils and committees – and her remembrances of Hamish are warm as the day:

> Coming into the house to do a night's recording – he sets up, places a bottle of whisky on the table and says 'There you are.' But the Stewarts don't drink! And through the evening – as the songs, stories and riddles flowed – it's Hamish, alone, who drains the bottle! For him, drink went with the socialising, so we never thought he drank too much. He would drop off for five minutes and wake up sober as a judge. I've seen him slip slowly under the table, for about five minutes hard-sleeping, then up he comes and the tape-recorder's still

---

6 Diddler: maker of mouth-music.

going, as fresh as a daisy. Everything was a wonderment to him and he wanted to capture it.

Andra, my father's brother, was a great storyteller but it was Donald MacGregor, my mother's brother, who learned me most of my big ballads. He was a great teacher – he would know whether I was 'ready' or 'not ready' for certain songs. Looking back I can see that he was like a theatre director, a choreographer – using me, according to the stage I was at. And Hamish was like that, he took every man as he was. The old man, Brazil, he cudnae sing, but he could dance – tap-dance – and I remember Hamish turning to my mother and saying, 'That man's singin' wi' his feet!' Old Weeny Brazil, he carried his board wi' him wherever he went and Hamish would put the microphone up to his board and record the tap-dancing. Whenever he felt like it – he'd throw down the board and start dancing! It was one foot in diameter.

Hamish told us about the Homes he was in. He had a hard life but he said it wisnae hard like the Travellers had – living in tents wi' every hand against them. He had the grieving for his mother – but we had 'the Tinker's curse'. People think that it's the Tinkers put a curse on people but the reality is that for centuries the Travellers were driven from the habitations of men; it was them who were cursed, accursed by the settled people – with guns on their backs. People hated us, and they were terrified of us. It was Hamish who drew us back to the fire. You see, the *Sidhe* have never left Glenshee and they've never left Scotland – they're still here, in us and in our stories.

I've been thinking back to all my ancestors and – over the last year – one of them has been reaching out to me, through all the generations. He's my mother's great-great-grandfather, Elijah Stewart. He became a self-taught minister, and he ministered to the Travelling people and he died in Logierait Poorhouse. And Hamish told us *his* own mother died in a Poorhouse. We always felt so close to him and he felt close to us. When he heard a new ballad sung, or he found something he'd been looking for, for years, he'd be ecstatic. He would retreat into himself – into a reverie – and then come back to share his joy with us. There'll never be another Hamish Henderson, he was the *Beinn Coul*. We'd been persecuted, ridiculed all our lives – we trusted nobody – then Hamish comes in and, after just a few weeks, we completely and utterly trusted him. He had no fear of us. He fed us with a great sense of worth and made us citizens of Scotland. We were no longer the lowest of the low: we had been identified by – the *Beinn Coul* – a man of standing and education. He came and he shared with us all that he had – not money but knowledge, and the standards of the modern world. He put us on the map as human beings – rather than sub-humans or animals. We were trapped in the darkness and he took us by the hand and brought us out into the light.

People ask me what we mean by the *Beinn Coul* and I say – it's not easy. It means 'the learned gentleman' but, also, for us, it means the high-up one, the man of good spirit and feeling, the noble one, the man 'with us'. We use *Beinn Coul* as we use the term *the conyach*. When a singer's singing with spirit, soul, deep-feeling, a complete immersion in the song – they have *the conyach*. A man with *the conyach* in his life and behaviour was the *Beinn Coul*.[7]

That marvellous oral portrait captures Hamish as seen by the Travellers, and by 1960 he was a legendary figure across the whole Traveller community. In the spring of 2007 I asked the great storyteller Duncan Williamson what the Travellers thought of Hamish when he first came among them:

To the old Travellers, Hamish was a God. I remember the first time I saw him coming down through the berry fields pushing his bike – with this big tape-recorder strapped to the carrier. Everyone stopped picking as he came down the dreel. You see, the women loved Hamish. And there was no jealousy amongst the men, with Hamish. And the children loved Hamish. Of course some of these collectors coming in were after the women, but not Hamish: everybody trusted Hamish more than their own fathers.[8]

Maurice Fleming also recognised an 'otherness' in Hamish: in June 1962 he writes

Dear Hamish, I am reading a book called 'The Man who Saved London' – it is about a highly successful French resistance man who passed on many secrets to us during the war. His method was to have a whole chain of agents working for him in a great many districts, passing on all they could find out. On a very much smaller scale it seems to me it would be the best arrangement for a song collector. And an ideal plan for the School . . . I wonder if, by making it a more deliberate policy, it might bring you in a greater flow of stuff. Your man in Dundee, Perth, Blairgowrie, Stirling, Aberdeen – you might need three there. To link them all together, a small magazine . . .

7 Sheila Stewart, conversation with TN, 2004.
8 Duncan Williamson, conversation with TN, 2007.

In reality Maurice was codifying a work practice that Hamish had been using all his life. He had no money or staff so it was totally impossible for him to do alone all he believed needed done. But, by using charm, drink, infectious enthusiasm and 'the sweet promiscuity of song', Hamish drew an extraordinary, ever-changing band of 'agents' towards him. A few were professionals, most were amateurs and as early as 1957 Hamish made notes on Traveller behaviour by means of which he would prepare *his* researchers for folk work amongst Travellers:

a) T. personal qualities. Teasing and humorous exaggeration – taking the piss – by-names – the marriage of first cousins – the necessity of hospitality – slanging matches – jam – blacking – competitive cultural activity. (Who can tell the longest story? Two went on, every night, for six months!) Mock wrestling matches – fights at weddings and funerals – obscenity amongst the women – the gravitas of the elderly – the grandeur and heroics of the men: Caliban and Prospero.

b) T. social attitudes. The concrete awareness of the dualities of existence – the different families of the husband and the wife – the sense of their being two clans, and two tribes – the acceptance of the normalcy of alternate generations marrying – cooperation and conflict built into these relationships as a stable and dependable factor – the fear of the technologically superior settled population (the aversion to the carrying or use of guns). Scotch doctors are known as stiffy-lifters; (a Townsley putting up his tent in an Aberdeen slum speaks of being 'Afeart o' passin' Kings College – efter six o'clock in the evenin'). The sacrificial table of the traditional mid-wife . . . These ideas are the ideas of primitive peoples everywhere – but also echo the history of modern Europe?

The Scots' competitive edge is equally apparent in Traveller society, and the nature of Hamish's work led to a number of jealous squabbles that lingered for decades. He could not record or reward everyone, or assume all Travellers equally talented singers and musicians. In Blairgowrie, Charlotte Higgins felt neglected; in Aberdeenshire, James Stewart of Alford still struggles to get taken seriously as a folk artist. Andra Stewart (Sheila Stewart's uncle) remains undervalued, partly because he and his family emigrated to Canada in 1956. Andra was a storyteller, piper and 'magnificent pub diddler'. Diddling (mouth-music) is a highly developed and ancient musical form – used by the Travellers to teach piping, for dancing (when no instruments are available) and for spontaneous revelry. Hamish's recordings of Andra singing song/diddles like 'I'm aye drunk, I'm seldom sober!' and 'I'm drunk since ever I saw your face' display an amazingly Palaeolithic, bacchanalian energy. Not surprisingly these recordings had a powerful influence on both the Folk Revival and commercial developments. They are Rock and Roll – well ahead of the clock. And it seems highly likely that Ewan MacColl's great love song (for Peggy Seeger), 'The First Time Ever I Saw Your Face', is based on Andra Stewart's 'I'm drunk since ever I saw your face'.

Andra Stewart's repertoire of 'druidic type riddles' was exceptional. One of the stories–riddles recorded from Andra in 1955 was used by Hamish, thirty years later, to open his last poem – 'Under the Earth I Go'. Hamish always recognised his debt to Andra and was proud to have gone down to the Broomielaw in Glasgow – to wave farewell as he and his young family emigrated on their £10 package deal to Canada, in 1956. He told me, 'It was a journey undertaken by hundreds of thousands of Scots before them; history unfolded before my eyes. Andra played the pipes; Lizzie and the five children were waving from the deck. It brought the tears to my eyes.' It seems likely that Hamish's song 'The Freedom Come a' Ye' began forming in his mind at that moment (though it was not composed until 1959/60).

> Nae mair will the bonnie callants
> Mairch tae war when oor braggarts crousely craw,
> Nor wee weans frae pit-heid and clachan
> Mourn the ships sailing doon the Broomielaw.[9]

Hardship can nurture art but Hamish fought long and hard to alleviate the hardships of the Scots Travellers. On 9 March 1956 he got the Scottish Diary of the *Daily Worker* to speak up for the Caithness MacPhees:

> Six formerly nomadic families of the Clan MacPhee – otherwise tinkers – have endured a bitter winter in a water-logged quarry up in Wick. Their huts are falling to pieces. Drinking water has to be carried in buckets from a well three quarters of a mile away. Four of the families are ex-servicemen's families. One, 44 year old Hugh MacPhee, was awarded the MM for bravery in Malaya and has six children . . . One person who killed stone dead prejudice against tinkers in her area – except amongst the most bigoted and flint-hearted – is authoress Naomi Mitchison. In her Kintyre fishing village of Carradale the MacPhees recently got their homes and are proud of them . . . Definitely a victory for humanity . . . Nearly all the tinkers in Scotland are MacPhees. Why I don't know. An old Gaelic legend declares they came from the Nile valley, led by Scota – a beautiful daughter of one of the Pharaohs. They brought

---

9 'The Freedom Come a' Ye', first published in 1961 in a leaflet of 'Anti-polaris songs', later published in *Hamish Henderson: Collected Poems and Songs* (Curly Snake 2000). [Hereafter abbreviated to *Collected Poems*.]

with them the Stone of Destiny – Jacob's Pillow – migrating along the North African coast, over to the Iberian Peninsula, thence to Ireland and eventually to Scotland. A lovely tale . . . and we owe the music-making nomadic MacPhees a great deal. They helped the art of piping from dying out after the Jacobite risings.

Today, educated people treat the very idea of a communist newspaper with contempt. Yet the *Daily Worker* gave Hamish a freedom that the BBC never gave him. Hamish's commitment to the Travellers and the best of Traveller culture was many-faceted but it had a good deal to do with 'the love that passeth understanding' and in 1954 he was delighted to get involved in a real-life runaway-love story that unfolds like a *nouvelle vague* film. The two lovers came to him from France. She was Danielle Fieguette, he was Claude Paul Charrayne. Their story unfolds across Europe as Hamish led their parents – and Interpol – a merry dance.

Claude Paul was the son of a Valence fruit merchant. Hamish notes that his father 'weighs 100 kilos!' Danielle was the youngest daughter of a sixty-year-old haut bourgeois industrialist (*constable dans usine électro-céramique)* who objected to his daughter 'marrying a boy from the market place'. From a bus Claude 'glimpsed Danielle and fell in love'. He was nineteen and studying law; Danielle was seventeen and still at school. On a skiing trip they became lovers. Learning of the relationship, Danielle's father denounced it and forbade marriage. In May 1954 the lovers holidayed, secretly, in Scotland and somehow met Hamish. He put them up in his flat (at Royal Terrace) and encouraged them (if necessary) to return to Scotland and marry at Gretna Green. From France, Danielle kept in touch by letter:

> Dear Hamish, Since we left you our troubles have continued but the friendship you offered us during a difficult time will never be effaced. You became an integral part of our lives at a very important turning point – the deep feelings you showed us amounted to something magnificent and which we think about with great emotion . . . At the moment we are installed in a flat and Claude is on-call to do his Military Service (many young men are being called up to go to Algeria). We have not seen my parents – who totally ignore us. We have, however, seen my grandmother . . . We send you a memory of old French songs. With our friendship, accept our deepest affection – kisses – Tony [her alias].

Eighteen months later, not wishing to wait until Danielle's majority, in the spring of 1956 they returned to Scotland. Hamish arranged for them to lodge secretly, first in Edinburgh, then in Kirkcaldy and finally in Dundee – with Maurice Fleming, whom Hamish had not consulted! When Maurice heard that two fugitives from international justice were on the way to his parents' house he wrote to Hamish in some trepidation: 'Dear Hamish, I'm sorry I sounded inhospitable but I was not able to say – "send them at once to Craigard"! For several reasons I simply can't do that, much as I would like to . . . ' In reality Maurice soon got himself organised and everyone enjoyed a fortnight in which life, theatre and journalistic possibilities combined in a symphonic joy. Maurice writes:

> Dear Hamish . . . Do you realise how odd it is that you should have asked my help? The play I wrote which, Allah being willing, is to be put on for a fortnight from 28th May, at Dundee Rep., is called *The Runaway Lovers* and is about just such a couple. Originally they were French but owing to technical difficulties, George Holst [the director] asked me to change their nationality to English. In the play the couple come from Edinburgh to a glen hotel, her father in pursuit. I'm glad to say he never catches them up! . . . So you see why I want to help them. And why George Holst wants to help them. Although it will be kept strictly secret for now, it would make a wonderful story in three months time! Please, therefore, for their sakes and mine (!), if you wish to move them at any time, do not hesitate to contact either of us.

By the time the wedding was due to take place, at the Registrar's Office in Kirkcaldy on 27 March, Hamish was so confident of success that he asked Maurice to publicise the story in the *Dundee Courier and Advertiser*. On 24 March the story was headlined:

> Runaways in Hiding for Wedding at Kirkcaldy – Two young French lovers who are to be married in Kirkcaldy on Tuesday have gone into hiding – they left Kirkcaldy last Tuesday afternoon after staying for a fortnight with Mrs Agnes Johnstone, 6 Templeton Avenue. Said Mrs Johnstone – 'They asked for lodgings for only a fortnight. When the time was up someone called for them in a big blue shooting brake, and they went away with all their luggage, three large packing cases.' When she asked if they would be back to see her, Claude smiled and said, '*Mais Oui*'. Then he added in halting English, 'We have been so happy in this house' . . . The only man who knows where the lovers are hiding is Mr John Stuart, headmaster of Templehall School, where Mrs Johnstone works as a cleaner. 'I can't say where they are,' he said. 'Their happiness is at stake.'

The article describes how the lovers had received dozens of wedding gifts from local folk and that the wedding would take place at 3.30 the following Tuesday. This was disinformation planted by Hamish, and the whole piece carries echoes of his voice. As ever, Hamish was putting a political frame around poetical events and it was with self-evident purpose that he drew schoolchildren, janitors, theatre directors and the working women of Kirkcaldy into this *ménage* of pan-European brotherhood and sexual joy! He sought to stir the Auld Alliance and remind people that true love says boo to the goose of paternal authority. Consequently, as events climaxed, Hamish openly attached his name to the couple's cause: he wanted the Scots people to know he was in on this cinematic epic. As the big day dawned the women of Kirkcaldy turned out in their hundreds to serenade the happy couple – five hours before the police turned up! Next day the *Glasgow Herald* announced:

> The Playwright, the Poet and the Lovers – A poet, a playwright and a schoolmaster last night celebrated the perfect end to the runaway romance of two young French lovers . . . When Claude and Danielle left Lyon and fled 1000 miles to Edinburgh three weeks ago, they feared Danielle's wealthy father would follow. Then they met the poet Hamish Henderson, in Edinburgh – and yesterday they came out of hiding for their wedding . . .

The *Scottish Daily Express* ran a headline: '100 women saw the runaway French girl wed "secretly"'. The *Daily Record* reported: 'A happy ending for "lost" couple':

> The runaway wedding that was organised like an army exercise ended happily yesterday – acting as interpreter at the ceremony was Mr Hamish Henderson, of Edinburgh University, on whose instructions the young lovers – able to speak only half a dozen words of English – scurried around Scotland in a game of hide-and-seek with the press. 'I used to be an Intelligence officer in the Army,' said kilted Mr Henderson yesterday. 'And I really enjoyed organising this affair'.

FIVE

The Summer Walkers

By Klibreck and Ben Loyal and the bonnie Kyle of Tongue
That road we often travelled in the days when I was young:
There's magic and there's beauty in those hills when passing through
There's many miles from Lairg to the Waters of Kylesku.

Brian Stewart[1]

Hamish liked to call the early years of the School of Scottish Studies the Golden Age of Scots folk collecting: 1952 was the year of the Horsemen, 1953 the year of Jeannie Robertson, 1954 the year of the Stewarts of Blair, 1955 the year of Ailidh Dall – Blind Alec Stewart of Lairg. He was the patriarch of the Stewarts of Remarstaig, Gaelic-speaking Travellers who, every summer, still roamed the wilds of Wester Ross, Sutherland and Caithness as their ancestors had done since time immemorial. Hamish's Gunn ancestors came from Sutherland and here, as in Perthshire, he felt instinctively at home. When stating 'my very early collecting was done on a G string', Hamish liked to add, 'but my time with Stewarts of Remarstaig was the top of my life'.

Folksong may have had a tarnished reputation at the BBC in Glasgow, but in London – by the mid fifties – it was on the verge of becoming the rage. With the English scene covered, younger programme makers began looking north of the border. Peter Kennedy, son of Douglas Kennedy (president of the English Folk Dance and Song Society (EFDSS) at Cecil Sharp House), an independent collector and record producer, was particularly interested in Scotland. In 1955 the BBC asked Kennedy to make a Scottish tour. Initially, Hamish was not involved but whilst employed as an adjudicator at the English Festival of Spoken Poetry, 'I asked Peter if I could tag along, as I had done with Lomax four years previously. Peter told me he was heading for Orkney, so I told him that I'd be happy to be his guide – as far north as the Pentland Firth! And that's what happened.'[2]

Hamish had already made three major tours that year, to Blairgowrie, Dundee and Aberdeen, but when Kennedy arrived in June with a car, a caravan, his wife – plus a young Devonian, a Northumbrian piper

1 Traditional song 'updated' by Brian Stewart of Culrain, Sutherland.
2 HH, conversation with TN, 1995.

called Bob Rundle – he knew something special lay ahead. Today, this Kennedy/Henderson Highland Tour is recognised as one of the great folk-recording trips of all time. In less than a month 142 songs and folktales were recorded – most in Scots but many in Gaelic. This trip is documented in the book *The Summer Walkers* but some of Hamish's statements are worth quoting here.

> The first place we stopped at was Perth. And there I went looking for an old Traveller I'd met in the berryfields, Henry MacGregor. I took pot luck and asked at a house where he lived and we stayed for three hours! It wasn't his house but the folk there had heard of me, via my work amongst the berry-pickers over at Blair and a Ceilidh broke out. We got a dozen good recordings, then went on to the real MacGregors! There the same thing happened. Half his friends and comrades came in to Ceilidh with us! Songs, music, liquor flowed all night . . . We had begun what Alan Lomax later described as 'the most productive recording tour ever undertaken'. He qualified it by saying, 'up till that time!' but I don't know who has got more, better, since. Euphoria! Peter Kennedy knew he'd entered a goldmine but, as the hours flashed by and the night grew wilder, both he and Tommy (Kennedy's Welsh wife) began to chaff at the bit. They had to get to Orkney, to start work! And so it was all the way up. We drove through the Highlands shrouded in the spray of Niagara!
>
> From Perth we detoured north east to Blairgowrie, where I introduced him to Alec and Belle Stewart . . . South of Newtonmore we found a huge Traveller encampment [here they heard talk of a round-up of Highland horses, at the start of the Second World War, with over six hundred horse mustered, Wild West style, and rail-shipped south]. At Kingussie we found Travellers – pearl-fishing the Spey – mostly Stewarts. Peter Kennedy was now getting the impression that every Traveller in Scotland was a singer named Stewart and, in a way, he wasn't far wrong! In Inverness we met more, and in Easter Ross we met Williamsons married into Stewarts. We might have stayed at Muir of Ord for a fortnight – but the Kennedys had to get to Orkney! On we went. My final throw was to persuade them to drive to Scrabster via Lairg and Tongue, rather than north east, via Golspie. That was an inspired ploy I've never regretted.
>
> Then Tommy Kennedy began to react very badly to what seemed like an endless expanse of peat-hag, barren deer forest and bleak distant mountain – she was almost hysterical, desperate to turn back – but when we stopped, I persuaded her that to go back would

> be worse than to keep pressing on! 'If we go back now we'll just see everything in reverse and still have the drive to Scrabster to do!' Gilding the lily, I said 'If we go on we'll quite soon leave these mountains and come down to the ocean and the white sands of the north.' Fortunately, she bought this. We went on, and that evening we camped in a small quarry high on a brae above the sands of the Kyle of Tongue. It was late, it was drizzling, but the clouds were lifting and the light was just strong enough, there on the waters below, for us to see 'the pale sands yonder'. And the tensions began to slip away. The shallow tidal waters of the Kyle can make the Caribbean look very much second best and next morning was perfect. I rose from my tent and walked over the brow of the hill to look south across one of the great landscapes of Scotland: Ben Hope and Ben Loyal silhouetted above the small illumined fields of the croft lands. Suddenly my heart went cold: there, just below me, was a half circle of tents with chimneys smoking – bow-tents – the domed, grey-green galleys of the Stewarts of Remarstaig. A small remnant of a people I would soon know as 'The Summer Walkers'. I might have been in Mongolia. I might have stood there any summer in the last eight thousand years and seen a similar sight. I know no more beautiful landscape in the world, no grander campsite under the stars. The Stewarts call Brae Tongue the King of Campsites. It remained Ailidh Dall's favourite camping place, long after he went blind, until he died. No wonder.[3]

Within an hour of meeting these Stewarts, Hamish and Kennedy were making recordings that would thrill folklorists around the world – and which would inspire Hugh MacDiarmid to write the poem 'King over Himself' (a tribute to Hamish and Ailidh Dall, quoted in Volume 1). Hamish had found his Gaelic equivalent to Jeannie Robertson: not the aesthetic equal, perhaps, but something ancient and unique in the world, an old blind man who told archetypal stories with inimitable gravitas, stories like 'The Bride of Ossian' and 'Am Maraiche Mairnéalach': stories that Campbell of Islay had heard fragments of – from a MacDonald tinker in Inveraray – but never managed to get whole.

Hamish returned to Edinburgh determined to make a proper study of this Travelling family whose roots seemed to be old as Scotland herself. His School of Scottish Studies report for 1955/56 gives a factual glimpse of this historic year:

> Storytelling among the Highland tinkers is still a living art . . . It is still possible to record stories as they were told in their heyday as popular entertainment – and not emaciated relics of a departed

3 Timothy Neat, *The Summer Walkers* (Birlinn 2002).

> culture. Mr Calum Maclean considers the style of the tinker story-tellers comparable with the best of the Hebrideans . . . Last year I investigated the Scots-English traveller cant – this year I began collecting examples of the 'Beurla-reagaird', the cover-tongue of the Gaelic-speaking tinkers described by David MacRitchie in Vol. 24 of the 'Transactions of the Gaelic Society of Inverness'; its relationship to the Irish traveller cant 'Shelta' is also of the highest interest . . . In the Reay Country information was gathered on Rob Donn and stories relating to Coinneach Odhar (the Brahan Seer) whose prophesies, like those of Nostradamus, were in rhyme and who met his end in a blazing tar-barrel at Fortrose in the Black Isle. From Henry Henderson, the Bard of Reay [a distant relative of Hamish's], I recorded reminiscences of the Land League and Crofter War. His voluminous diary of over 60 volumes he has consented to bequeath to the [School] . . . I spent three weeks in the berry-fields of Blair with Dr Vallee – and collected a fine version of an exceedingly rare ballad, 'The False Knight upon the Road'. The return of Dr Vallee to Canada has meant the dissolution of a partnership which in a short time achieved much. He has left behind a lucid and perceptive 'report of a pilot study'. The 'tinker project' should not be allowed to hang fire; entrée of the completest kind has been gained to a social group which exhibits characteristics of profound social and anthropological interest. In recent months Mr Herschel Gower and Dr Robert Botsford have been giving valuable assistance.

Hamish's relationship with Peter Kennedy was never close, and their correspondence always carries hints of differences of attitude and opinion. Having returned from Orkney, Kennedy writes, very formally, on handsome BBC letter-headed paper – London 22 August 1955:

> Dear Hamish, Many thanks for your letter and book. I'd be very glad if you would send any reels from which you have dubbed . . . I am sending you some photographs of yourself collecting – if you use them for any publication will you see that I get the usual copyright fees . . . Dough – I have twice told them to get on with paying you . . . as soon as you get it – will you let me have mine because we are rather 'in the straights' and I want to buy some stock for our next venture with Alan Lomax.

A few days later Kennedy wrote again: 'Tapes have arrived safely – yes, the results technically are not good – I have written a memo to say that we cannot get better recordings without better batteries . . . Had a telephone call last night from Belle Stewart and Sheila – they just wanted to hear our voices – my parents had a wonderful Ceilidh with them when they were on holiday up Glen Isla . . . Lastly Tommy and I would be glad if you could repay – we were anxious to help you, however, nothing will ever repay our initiation into Scotland by HH.' Napoleon might have described Kennedy as one of England's best 'shopkeepers', Hamish as a twentieth-century Ossian! As Kennedy aged and his hair fell out, he took to wearing a toupee; when Hamish's teeth fell out – he decided gums were all he had. However, their talents were genuinely complementary and the manner in which Hamish helped Kennedy is clear in this letter of 1959.

> Dear Hamish, as you suggested I put up the idea of a regular Light Programme Skiffle-Cum-Folk-Music-Programme – and have been amazed that the idea is more or less accepted. A resident band with guest fiddlers, pipers, and singers from all parts of Britain . . . I hope they will give us forty five minutes at a peak time . . . this is essentially an expression of young bloods . . . Could you jot down names . . . I shall get the best Skifflers and the best Ceilidh atmosphere.

As an independent collector, Kennedy had to make a living from his collecting and broadcasting, and important questions about ownership of copyright – of traditional material – soon arose. It was a general legal, financial and cultural issue but it also became an issue between the two men. Did the copyright reside with the singer, the community, the nation? What was the position, and rights, of the collector, the agent, the recording company, the broadcaster? What was the situation when professionals adapted or stole traditional material? Here was a serpent's nest of lawyers, innocents, go-getters and jealousies that Hamish, by instinct, wanted nothing to do with but – as a professional collector – it was an issue he had to address. And 'with bad grace' he did so, rather inefficiently, throughout his life. His personal position was that articulated by Burns in a magnificent letter to his publisher, George Thomson: 'As to my remuneration you may think my songs either above or below price: for they shall be absolutely one or the other – in the honest enthusiasm with which I embark on your undertaking to talk of money, fee, hire etc. would be downright Sodomy of Soul.' Hamish's problems with Peter Kennedy, in relation to copyright, are best mentioned very briefly. In 1959 Arthur Argo wrote to Hamish:

> Dear Hamish, One thing I want to bring to your notice. Peter Kennedy has done to Lucy (Stewart) what he did to John MacDonald, got her under contract – at two guineas for three songs. And again there is a ten year clause. Perhaps you could tell me what you think of this. I told Lucy I would consult you.

Lucy Stewart was the head of a family of remarkable Traveller singers from Fetterangus in Aberdeenshire, whom Hamish had introduced to Peter Kennedy, and the entanglements precipitated are indicated in this letter from Mervyn (Plunkett?) written on 20 November 1959:

> I don't know if you still make a habit of staying with Peter Kennedy when you're in London, but as the years go by I find him progressively more dishonest and two-faced and long since ceased to trust him. He's been an absolute bastard on the Festival Committee and has stopped doing any field work. He has lost interest in traditional performance and is at present cooking up another E.P. with phoney singers on it.

Meantime Hamish was planning new field work, with the Stewarts of Remarstaig as the centre of his focus. During 1956 Hamish, already committed to ongoing projects in the Central Belt, Perthshire and the Western Isles, was unable to revisit Sutherland but, in 1957, 'a properly resourced research trip to Sutherland became my overwhelming priority'. Early in the year he wrote to the Stewarts at their wintering place, by the railway line at the top of the Remarstaig Pass, and – once they were out on the road – Christine Stewart wrote back:

> Dear Hamish, we were very sorry when we did not see you last year. But we are equally glad you are coming this year. Well – you ask me to write to let you know where we will be, but I'm afraid it would be rather difficult. As you know we do not stay very long in each place. Just now we are in Assynt and will be for a fortnight. But after that I'm not sure myself. Maybe in Durness, or maybe around Tongue. You could enquire in the neighbouring villages . . . Grandpa [Ailidh Dall] is in quite good form and I am sure it will be a pleasure for him to make recordings for you.

Hamish noted himself 'A frogman amongst the battered hulks of Scottish folksong' but he planned this tour with military precision. In 1995 he described the process to me:

> I knew that what I had to do was of such importance that I decided to go straight to the top and request funds, not from the School of Scottish Studies, but from the University of Edinburgh itself. I went round to see Mr R.O. Curle, who was then the chief accountant, and I explained what I was going to do and how important it was; that things needed to be done, had to be done, 'here and now'. And he gave me three thousand pounds. It was the first and last time I got real funds for my work . . . I lived most of that summer on the road with the Stewarts – sleeping out in my tent for much of the time

> – and I came back to Edinburgh with what can only be described as priceless historical and cultural material. Curle sent me forth, and money made me free as a bird. The Stewarts were a tiny band, but their lifestyle and their culture were affirmation of a major strand in Scotland's history: what Scotland was, is, and will be. It was at the beginning of July the three of us set out, myself, Norman Maclean and Bobby Botsford.[4]

Botsford was a visiting American scholar who shared Hamish's flat in Edinburgh (and had a driving licence); Norman Maclean was a student from Glasgow. In 2004 Norman told me how he had met Hamish, by chance, at the top of Leith Walk the previous year:

> I was Pipe Major of the Glasgow University OTC [Officer Training Corp] Pipe Band. We were camped out at Milton Brig by Penicuik and we'd been playing up at the Castle. I was in my kilt, walking alone, when this man came up and started talking – he had an unusual, languorous gait, a moustache and fine wavy hair; he was tall, with flat feet: he had these badly dropped arches. It was Hamish Henderson! He asked me who I was and we immediately got on – like two policemen at the Policeman's Ball! We went for a drink. Lager. He spoke a sparkling dialogue. 'There is,' he said 'a laager within the University of Glasgow'. We went back to his flat in Royal Terrace: we read poetry, talked pipe music and sang till, suddenly, like Cinderella, I remembered I had to be back at camp by ten! I ran, got a taxi! Too slow! I got four hours in jankers! That was my introduction to the man who was, even then, changing the consciousness of Scotland. All that winter he was fighting the battle against the Benbecula Rocket range. This was on my Uist doorstep! But he was the one doing the fighting. He was like a bright bulb – in the candlelight of a Scotland governed by Sir Anthony Eden. Then, in the summer of 1957, Hamish invited me to join him on his tour of Sutherland and of course my heart leapt at the opportunity. He said he'd share his expenses with me! We travelled up by van. And there I met Ailidh Dall, and Essie his beautiful daughter, and Gordon Stewart, and Maggie the white mare: Hamish bestrode her like Genghis Khan! Those days may be thousands of years in the past now but I remember them like yesterday. That trip made me the Wandering Fool I became.

Hamish continues the story:

> Norman was a student, a native Gaelic speaker, a piper, singer, poet and future television comedian and it was as an apprentice he sat

4 HH, conversation with TN, 1995. See also Neat, *The Summer Walkers*.

> at the feet of old Ailidh Dall. Bobby and Norman soon returned to Edinburgh, so, there I was – stranded – with nothing but a Landrover, a tape-recorder and the Stewarts of Remarstaig! It was the cream of my life, the top of my life – those two months up there with the Stewarts – the first song I recorded from Ailidh Dall was 'The Sweet Sorrow' (*Am Bron Binn),* one of the oldest songs in Europe. It tells of Arthur 'King of Britain' and makes a direct link between the twin worlds of P Celtic and Q Celtic, the two great branches of Celtic language and history.
>
> To start at the beginning is always good! But to get started in 500AD was the stuff of dreams . . . I remember one milky white night camped on a little plateau, high on a cliff looking north across the Pentland Firth. The tents were set out along a gently sloping lawn of grass above what seemed an endless sea of heather: Ailidh Dall was playing the pipes. Couples began dancing. An eightsome reel got under way. All the family joined in and the lines of dancers gradually widened and the couples, swinging, spread out in great parabolas down the slope and away into the heather. It was a night that will stay imprinted in my mind as long as I live. So far north, in summertime the darkness is always incomplete; on a clear night one has to look hard to see the stars. I danced with Essie, she was sixteen then, with Mary her mother, with Black Anne, with her daughter Joanne. The tents were humped round in a semi-circle and at a short distance the horses watched us. With the heather in bloom, the perfume – coming off 'the flower of the mountain' – seemed to become substantial nectar as the dew came down. I went back to my small ridge-pole tent thinking, 'Life is good – life is very good like this'.[5]

On 11 July 1957 Hamish received a letter, poste restante, at Bettyhill Post Office – from Calum Maclean. 'Thanks very much for your card. Old Alec must be very grand indeed and you have done a very fine job. The stuff sounds great. Old Alec's style is much better than young Alec's.' Young Alec was Ailidh Dall's nephew, Brian Stewart of Culrain, a singer, piper, storyteller and tinsmith who had spent two years in Burma with the Chindits. Despite Calum's 'mild criticism', Brian Stewart would soon be recognised as a major Sutherland tradition bearer himself. He features prominently in the beautiful notebook/diary Hamish kept during this tour, and Hamish's interest nurtured affection across the whole band.

Hamish lodged a few nights with Archie C. Macpherson (from Blairgowrie) in Lairg. He noted that Hamish's mission 'was to take

5 HH, conversation with TN, 1995. See also Neat, *The Summer Walkers*.

down some wonderful tales of the Fians, in Gaelic. To my amazement he was completely fluent in Gaelic and conducted the whole matter in the language.'

The fact that Hamish was not a photographer curtailed one aspect of his work as folklore researcher but during the 1957 tour Bobby Botsford took two rolls of black and white 35mm film of great documentary interest, showing the reality of the Stewarts' life on the road (see the first plate section). In 1959 another American folklorist, the young Sandy Paton, accompanied Hamish on what proved to be the Stewarts' last summer tour and took additional excellent photographs. On 20 July 1960 he writes:

> Dear Hamish, my favourite photo is the one of Blind Sandy sitting by the wagon, looking without eyes into the late evening sun . . . And the real news, we have a fine new son – named James Robertson Paton (James for James Scott Henderson – to be called 'Hamish' later, if he chooses – and Robertson for Jeannie Robertson the world's greatest ballad-singer!).

The Williamsons of Ardgay continued to travel throughout the sixties but the Stewarts were too few and too old to continue trading. In June 1962 Essie Stewart wrote from Remarstaig: 'Dear Hamish, this will be a surprise to you. I am married since almost three years. My husband is a pearl fisher, so if you see a blue van, KST 389 on it, that's us! Mum and Dad don't go on their rounds any more . . . Haste ye Back – yours always Essie.' This pearl fisher was Eddie Davies, with whom Essie was soon to rear four children.

In 1975 Hamish re-established contact with the Davis family – so that we could make the documentary film *The Summer Walkers*. As pearl fishers they continued to live a nomadic life and can rightly be described as the last old-style Travellers in the north-west – where the old bonds between the settled population and the Travellers remained strong into the late twentieth century. In the summer of 1976 Mrs Mary Cowan, of the Strathy Inn, Sutherland, wrote to Hamish: 'I have a very fine collection of Eddie Davies' pearls which I should be very happy to show you . . . I love the pearl fishers and have been associated with them a very long time – my eldest daughter went to School with Eddie's youngest sister in Dornoch.' During the filming of *The Summer Walkers,* Hamish frequently reminisced about his tours in the fifties:

> We had been walking for miles, around the head of Loch Tongue, so I went in among the birches and lay down for a kip in the pleasant heat of the afternoon. Suddenly, aware of something beside me, I awoke from my doze to see a fawn looking at me from a few inches away. It bounded away, almost immediately, but my memory is of

> one enchanting stock-still moment . . . All my life I had dreamed of meeting a family like the Remarstaig Stewarts and here they were – living their lives as custodians of Homeric, Ossianic Scotland – silent as that fawn on the moss, and now gone. 1957 was the last full year the Stewarts spent on the road; so there I was – at the well at the end of the world. To hear Ailidh Dall begin one of his stories was to have your faith in mankind renewed: 'There was a king, long ago. There was a king and a queen – as many anes been – few have we seen, and few may we see . . . ' I felt like Gauguin when he stood to begin painting, in the Marquesas, that great painting: 'Who are we, where do we come from, where are we going?' Monumental simplicity, Ben Hope and Ben Loyal.[6]

Hamish's work with the Sutherland Travellers stimulated numerous other research workers. For example, John MacInnes began a still unfinished study of the *Beurla-reagaird* (the ancient cant language of the Gaelic-speaking Travellers) and in 1984 Linda Gowans[7] published a study of Ailidh Dall's sung-poem *'Am Bron Binn'*. Hamish was thrilled and described it 'as an important and original piece of research'. And Hamish's own work with the Remarstaig Stewarts might be described as coming full circle when, in 1994, STV commissioned me to make a half-hour documentary, *Rathad nan Ceard* (*The Traveller Roads*), in which Hamish and Norman Maclean retraced their journey of 1957 (see Chapter 24). Their meetings with Essie Stewart proved 'compulsive television' and Essie gave up pearl fishing to begin a mini-career as a Gaelic broadcaster and storyteller. This documentary encouraged me to transform the 1976 film *The Summer Walkers* into a book of the same title. It was published by Canongate (Edinburgh) in 1996 and became the first of a quintet of books on Highland life in the twentieth century.

Hamish saw these projects as realising important aspects of the researches he had begun half a century earlier and, in one conversation, he spoke of how the poets in Wales had maintained the cultural traditions

---

6 HH, conversation with TN, 1976.

7 The Henderson–Gowans relationship began in the spring of 1968 when she wrote, out of the blue: 'I am twenty years of age – though I have always lived in the South of England, I have visited my father's family in Scotland many times. My interests are in the field of folksong, folklore, and history, particularly that of Scotland. I have the General Certificate of Education in 8 subjects, shorthand and typing skills and hope to combine my secretarial capabilities with some aspect of Scottish folklore.' By June she was writing to thank Hamish for 'the interview' and asking, 'Is there any chance that you might be able to employ your own secretary when the autumn term starts?' Unfortunately, Hamish had no money to employ her – and the SSS would not countenance it. Thus, at a distance of five hundred miles, Hamish became Miss Gowans' mentor, private tutor and research-assistant.

of the Welsh Court, after its dissolution in medieval times, by going on 'perambulations'. 'Here, in Scotland, the Travellers did something similar but – we were more practical, we also wormed dogs, tamed horses and made pots and pans! After the First World War, the Scoots – in Argyll – took the whole idea literally, and got themselves perambulators!'[8] And he roared with laughter.

8 HH, conversation with TN, 1995.

SIX

Folklore and the Sexual Revolution

Mr Legman is the person, more than any other, who made research into erotic folklore and erotic verbal behaviour academically respectable . . . He's utterly famous in the world of erotica for making his materials accessible – providing them freely to anyone who asked – and for finding stuff that nobody else knew about. He also introduced the art of Japanese paper-folding to Europe in the fifties, coined the phrase – 'make love not war' and published a stream of major books, including The Limerick, The Horn Book, Rationale of the Dirty Joke *and* Oragenitalism.[1]

Media commentators and modern historians tend to refer to Britain's sexual revolution as beginning in 1963 – the year of the Beatles, Philip Larkin's public celebration of penetrative sexual intercourse and the introduction of the contraceptive pill, but this is an Anglo-centric and partial view. The Folk Revival preceded all of them, and long before Philip Larkin, Kenneth Tynan or Tony Harrison were making public use of the word 'fuck' Hamish and Gershon Legman were broadcasting it far and wide. The bawdy was part of the folk tradition they celebrated.

The name Gershon Legman is not well known. He was an American, a sexual revolutionary who became a driving force behind the cultural liberalism of Western civilisation in the second half of the twentieth century. Hamish was a close friend and one of his prime informants. Like Hamish, Legman was anti-war and anti-imperialist but it was the cause of sexual freedom, particularly in literature and on the stage, that makes their relationship important. Legman was an autodidact, a folklorist, an obsessive archival researcher and a hugely productive author. The two men first made contact in 1952/53 when Legman was working on his book *The Limerick – 1700 Examples, with Notes, Variants and Index* (Paris 1953). Hamish sent off a selection of his favourites, including this surreal creation:

---

1 Obituary of Gershon Legman 1999, by Bruce Jackson, Professor of American Culture at the State University of New York, Buffalo (the university to which HH sent his *Elegies* manuscript in 1949); obituary published in *New York Times*.

There was a young man of the Niger
Who had an affair with a tiger.
The result of the fuck
Was a bald-headed duck
Two snakes and a circumcised spider.[2]

Born in the United States in 1918, Legman was one year older than Hamish. His parents hoped he would become a rabbi but in his late teens he dropped out of college to start gainful employment – including a little lecturing on the birth control circuit! It was revolutionary work in the America of the 1930s and he claimed to have invented the sexual vibrator in his spare time. Like his academic contemporaries, Wilhelm Reich (1897–1957) and Alfred C. Kinsey (1894–1956), he wanted to confront the puritanical mores of America because he believed hypocritical propriety had transformed human sexuality into something obscene. This in turn had turned sex into a commercial commodity and a reason for inter-racial killing. By 1942 Legman was in New York leading a campaign against 'the prostitution of natural sexuality' and delving the vaults of the city libraries determined to make himself a world authority on sexuality in Western literature. The deeper he dug, the more he found that it was the world's folk traditions that addressed the subject most honestly and naturally. Hamish had come to similar conclusions.

Legman was part of a literary circle that included the young Allen Ginsberg and Marshall McLuhan. As editor of the Freudian quarterly *Neurotica*, he published a series of essays attacking the violence endemic in American comic books. In one of these essays he asked, 'Why are children exposed to destructive violence and totally sheltered from the image and idea of people making love?' When his first book, *Love and Death: A Study in Censorship*, was published, all postal services to Legman were suspended indefinitely. During the McCarthyite era, sexuality and communism were frequently attacked as a single evil gnawing at the heart of America. Facing regular police harassment, in 1953 Legman decamped to Paris with his young wife Beverley Keith. Photographs show Legman to have been a Clark Gable look-alike; a heavy-headed man with a leonine mass of hair (as in many Sheela-na-gig carvings). Legman had long admired Hamish's *Ballads of World War II* and as he learned the extent of Hamish's knowledge of 'Scotland's unequalled bawdy heritage' he nurtured a relationship that would last three decades.

Legman was a workaholic with magpie propensities. Hamish was ridiculously generous with 'his' material, but the relationship, self-evidently two-sided, would have surprising consequences on Western culture and social mores. Legman wrote regularly to Hamish from France:

---

2 HH, unpublished, Henderson archive.

> *7 November 1955*: Dear Hamish, Thank you for 'The Workman's Grave', and 'The Hieland Tinker', and the variant of 'The Hero Alexander' . . . If you should ever have the time and strength to sit down to 'The Ball of Kirriemuir'; that is of course the prize modern piece anywhere, in the English language area, and I could no more publish my proposed volume without a good and thorough extensive text for that, than I could omit 'The Bastard King of England'.
>
> *16 February 1956*: I have been teaching Japanese paper-folding folk art to 8000 children in Amsterdam . . . On the way back through Paris I had occasion to spend some time with Alan Lomax . . . he solemnly adjures me to keep in touch with you because of the unparalleled collecting you have been doing right where the stuff comes from . . .
>
> *1 June 1957*: The Harvard Library writes to me that they do have Peter Buchan's 'Songs of Silence' ms. that you mentioned. It is 196 pages – would you be able to give me some idea what is *in* them . . . Are they Buchan's own art poems, or folk materials, or what? . . . Do you know the book 'Forbidden Fruit' about which Mr S.G. Smith once wrote me – noting that the earliest known text of 'The Ball' is printed in it?
>
> *1 August 1957*: Here is your copy of 'Explorations' (under separate cover) – foolish of me ever to have thought that I could get paid for such mildly revolutionary stuff . . . The references to your own work are on page 142 . . . Alan Lomax, in London, has suggested that you are in a position to offer more than anyone else 'in these islands'.

In April 1960 Legman writes: 'I still think you ought to make a serious effort to get every goddam one of your texts (clean and dirty alike) out of your "private shorthand" – as you call it – and get them *written out* . . . In the end no one cares about the notes: Kittredge said it and it's true: *the text is the thing*.' Hamish, however, remained loath to put too much on paper but, now married, his need for cash was acute and he began to send more and more of the uncensored material Legman wanted: for example, important information about Scots Masonry. In October Legman writes:

> Dear Hamish, I thank you for your quick response to my SOS about the 'Masonic Song'. About ritual homo-sexuality in North British Secret Societies – have you seen the Records of the Beggar's Benison Society, Anstruther, Fife (ran from 1730 to 1890s) – the secrets being published in 1892 on the dissolution of the Society? . . . [I am reminded] of the way the Knights Templar carried on, over yon mountains on my left, some centuries back . . .

In February 1962 Hamish sent Legman a dozen copies of the world's first anti-nuclear songbook, *Ding Dong Dollar,* plus a manuscript copy of his song 'The Freedom Come a' Ye'. Legman wrote back: 'Thank you so much for the Valentine's Day gift of the "Ding Dong" songbooks, of which I consider the copy baptised in Guinness to be beyond price. The ms. song, hot from the singer-composer's "wallet" is of course the prize piece, to any collector, but I feel ashamed having the firstling of it. (I have sent the sum of 10,000 francs to your friend M Charrayne by Postal Order).' In November Hamish sent out a new batch of bawdy, plus a cheque. Legman replied:

> Dear Hamish, Your staggering letter, and stupefying enclosures (!) arrived while I was out of the country on a folklore expedition . . . Allow me to congratulate you on the victory for determination, character, strength, perversity (I mean perseverance) and everything else in the book! This is one check we never thought to see! We thank you, we love you, we admire you! . . . Your *Chansons de Salle de Garde* interest me – let me know what you find . . . Congratulations on the coming bairn. If you have twins, please send us one: there is some trick to having babies we have somehow never learned.

Unfortunately, Beverley Legman had now been diagnosed with cancer. Hamish and his wife Katzel were invited to France: 'You two are special, and Beverley loves you even more than I do, and so – if you can put up with no electricity and no toilet – make sure, sure, sure to come and stay with us, as the spirit moves you. Please come. I also have a priceless collection of "folklore" recordings – Sir Harry Lauder, 1900s pressing! To inflict upon the School's files.' Katzel, however, was now heavily pregnant and no visit proved possible.

Hamish described the best of the great Scots ballads 'as plays that begin in the fifth act': and 'The Ballad of the Legman Marriage' was no exception. In February 1964 Legman informed Hamish that he was divorced, this being 'the 20th wedding anniversary present' that Beverley had demanded. 'I have swung a year's appointment to teach folklore and French literature at the University of California – of which my new wife, Christine, is an MA . . . I can and do love an awful lot of people all at once. That is my downfall or glory – take your pick!' This was also the year in which Legman's magnum opus *The Horn Book: Studies in Erotic Folklore and Bibliography* (New York: University Books 1964) was published, and his slogan 'Make Love, Not War' began circulating across American university campuses. *The Horn Book* proved a seminal publication. Hamish was the source of many of the published items, and important passages bear his very strong imprint.

When Hamish received his copy, he wrote to commend Legman, who was delighted: 'Dear Hamish, Your compliments on the style of the Horn

Book have meant a lot to me, because lots of the folklore people have been quite *éblouis* by it – and don't understand this combination of intense research and Carlylean fulmination. Whereas you are yourself a writer and stylist and, when you understand, then I know that I am being understood.' Shortly after this, Legman returned to France. His second marriage had collapsed and he was looking after Beverley – now near death; he asked Hamish 'to write her a funny letter to cheer her up', which Hamish did.

After Beverley's death, Legman married Judith, a Californian librarian he had met while she was touring Europe. Legman wrote to Hamish:

> Dear Hamish, Judith is terribly happy here on the farm: she is that sort of girl and only waiting to start having babies! I am working hard getting the first issue of *Kryptadia: the Journal of Erotic Folklore* in shape for Spring 1967. Please consider that we can't publish without some type of contribution from your pen . . . My new book, *The Guilt of the Templars*, is out.

In September 1968 Legman published another huge tome, *The Rationale of the Dirty Joke*. Hamish had had a small part in its genesis but Legman kept him in touch with developments, writing in October to announce, 'censorship of sex has collapsed in the US'. The two men agreed that it was no coincidence that the Scots and the Jews have produced so many of the world's best comedians, and jokes. Both peoples share highly literate oral traditions; both use humour as a tool with which the confusions provoked – by migration, alienation, poverty, great wealth and murder – are addressed and come to terms with. Legman's book opens with the rubric, 'the secret source of humour is not joy but sorrow; there is no humour in heaven'.[3] Tragedy is part of all human experience but notably part of Scottish and Judaic culture. Jokes are psychological safety valves that function as surreal, redemptive forms of identification and understanding. In his introduction to *The Rationale of the Dirty Joke* Legman writes:

> It may be axiomatic that: a person's favourite joke is the key to that person's character [but] the aggressiveness of most jokes, and the purposeful unpleasantness of many 'dirty' dirty jokes – marks them almost always as a bid for sympathy or a cry for help. Your favourite joke is your psychological signature. The 'only' joke you know how to tell, is you . . . Tell me what you laugh at, and I will tell you what you are . . .[4]

---

3 Mark Twain, *Pudd'nhead Wilson's New Calendar*.

4 Gershon Legman, *The Rationale of the Dirty Joke* (New York: Basic Books/ Grove Press) 1968).

Hamish's own brand of humour was established early and it colours many of the recitations he copied out in his mother's recipe book of 1928/29; they echo and prefigure the Legman thesis:

> Two teachers on a tram one day. Says one to the other, 'How many children have you got now, Mary?' 'I've got sixteen. How many have you got?' 'I've got sixty-four and I'm expecting another twelve next month.' Flanagan leaned forward and said, 'Excuse me, milady, but what part of Ireland does your husband come from?'

Legman saw his life's work as essentially led by moral imperatives and by love of his fellow man. He was in many ways as self-dramatising and authoritarian as the worst of the Old Testament prophets but human affection remained his guiding star: in 1972 he writes:

> Dear Hamish, I am planning a new book on Concertos and Chamber music of the C18th – from Bach to Beethoven and Schubert, it should take about three lifetimes . . . The extra love you send, from far away, helps very, very much too. I am living only for music and the love of a good woman – Judith is radiant nursing the baby.

In 1988 Legman's last letter to Hamish sums up with grand aplomb what had been a thrilling collaborative relationship:

> Your translation of the Gramsci Prison Letters is wonderfully done, alternatively powerful and touching. Judith has stolen it. I get quite a bang out of your appreciation of Joe Gould, who was my first guru and one of the most brilliant talkers I have ever met: he sounded to me the way people say Lenin sounded. Insiders try to credit Gould with inventing 'oral history' because of his collection of graffiti, which has disappeared since his death. But in fact (not mentioning the Apostles of the New Testament) oral history as a conscious science was begun in France in the late 1770s on the eve of the Revolution by Restif de la Bretonne, who called himself 'Le Spectateur Nocturne' and stalked Paris at midnight searching for Significant Detail with an owl perched on his shoulder.

Academically, Legman's work has never been highly regarded, but his legacy is everywhere apparent: in the explosion of 'uninhibited humour' on radio, television, stage and cinema; in the stand-up comics who now dominate the Edinburgh Festival Fringe and 'the whole world besides'. In America, Lenny Bruce, the Limeliters, Alex Hassilev, Glenn Yarbrough, Mike Nichols and Elaine May, Allan Sherman and Tom Lehrer were influenced by the work of Legman/Henderson. In Britain, Billy Connolly is just one of many 'stars' who used folk bawdy as their lift-off point (it was Hamish who told Connolly 'to ditch the ukulele and be the Fool you are!'). That Rabelaisian humour dominates contemporary world humour owes much to Gershon Legman, and to Hamish.

SEVEN

Marriage, a Family and New Horizons

The Hero Cycle: Beowulf leaves . . . Ivan leaves . . . Jack leaves . . . the young aboriginal on Walkabout leaves . . . even the antique Don Quixote leaves. And these Wanderjahre, *and combats with the Beast, are the story-teller's version of the incest taboo; whereby a man must first prove 'fitness' and 'marry far'.*

Bruce Chatwin[1]

Hamish had limited domestic experience but the idea of marriage and the stability of family life appealed to him – emotionally, intellectually and as a social mechanism. Most people assumed him 'a bachelor type' but, once his financial situation stabilised in the mid fifties when he was given a permanent post at the School of Scottish Studies, Hamish seems to have consciously started looking for a wife. In June 1956 he met Felicity (Katzel) Schmidt.[2] She and her sister were on a working holiday in Scotland and were chatting, in German, at the top of Leith Walk, in Edinburgh. He overheard them and called out to them. She was nineteen, he was thirty-six. After a three-year courtship that mixed passionate closeness with long periods of separation they were married in May 1959. During those years, however, at least two other women had vivid relationships with Hamish.

The first was Isabel Sutherland, a folksinger from Edinburgh whose father was an antiques dealer. In 1955 she accompanied Hamish to the Blairgowrie berryfields, where they both made recordings and possibly became lovers. The relationship did not last and Isabel soon moved to London where she became a resident singer at Folksong Unlimited (a leading London folk club) and made a number of excellent records, including 'Pinch of Salt', 'Rocket Along' and 'Banks of Red Roses'. Hamish, however, soon became disturbed by the manner in which Isabel 'used' tradition and in the late 1980s wrote her a series of letters in an attempt to recover, for the School, 'copies of the many valuable tape-recordings made – as the direct result of my introductions in the berryfields and elsewhere'.

---

1 Bruce Chatwin, *The Songlines* (Picador 1988).

2 It was Hamish who first used the pet-name Katzel ('little cat') by which, in time, she became known.

The second relationship blossomed just weeks after Hamish's meeting with Katzel. Working in Armagh with the Irish folklorist Sean O'Boyle, Hamish was introduced to Fionnuala Ni' Naghallaig, a final-year student at Queens University. A colourful literary romance flared up:

> Dear Hamish, I haven't seen Sean since I came here, but I'm sure we'll be out visiting soon – your extended pun was delicious . . . I'm afraid my present existence admits of no cultural interludes. But yet, yesterday afternoon Father Collette and myself repaired to Lenny's kitchen – for a companiable three bottles – and really stimulating conversation – embracing Nancy Mitford's U and Non U – and naturally thence to Richard III . . . Olivier's *Richard III* film is still running in Dublin and my eye I'd give to see it! I don't think I've confessed to you but I'm a Shakespeare addict . . . *Le gias gach heannacht* – Fionnuala . . . *Sheamais a chroi* – How's your epic poem by the way? . . . I graduate on 9 July and the next day proceed to Donegal. So that will be my farewell to Queens – they were the happiest and most discontented days of my life . . . Life in Armagh is very ordinary – pedestrian in fact . . . When will you be visiting Ireland again. I'd just love to go across to you – but times is hard – you understand how I'm fixed. P'haps at the Summer's end?'

At Christmas 1956, Fionnuala wrote a rather depressed letter that seems to accept the unlikelihood of their relationship becoming permanent. Perhaps she pushed her literary ambitions – for Hamish – too hard:

> *Sheamais a stoir* . . . Yesterday in Belfast for the first time in months I was seized with black melancholy – entirely inexplicable – I just felt drained of any slow-motion *joie-de-vivre* I ever had . . . I don't know which state of mind is preferable – the alternative Titanic glooms and explosions of happiness (a favourite expression of your own which never fails to recall me to the dusky, musky stout-drinking sessions here in the kitchen) or no ups and downs! I've become complacent! . . . I saw 'The Quare Fellow' last week in Belfast – I enjoyed it very much – but it's not a great play – altho' it could be! . . . They had a record of your friend Brendan Behan singing '*Se Fath mo Bhuartha*' – and only played it for a split second – I was furious. I haven't been at a sing-song for ages.

Hamish remained attractive to many women throughout his life – his evangelical interest in people and hunger for companionship meant that his net was cast unusually wide. He responded to the moment, to the person, to the situation – and his meeting with Katzel Schmidt was classic 'Henderson'. Katzel remembers:

My sister Eli and I were walking at the top of Leith Walk when we saw a tall man in front of us stop – turn round – and say, in excellent German, 'Do I hear German spoken?' He was dressed in corduroy trousers and a short jerkin. He came up to us and started talking. At first we thought he was Austrian! He was very charming and invited us back to his flat – at 20 Royal Terrace. When we told him a lorry driver was expecting to take us back to Perth at eight o'clock – he said we could stay the night with him! Eli and I were full of trepidation about what this lorry driver wanted in exchange for the lift! So we were very pleased to be taken up by this German-speaking, older man – whom, we assumed, had other ideas entirely! We agreed to go back with him and we all climbed the stairs to this handsome, high-ceilinged Edinburgh flat, and Hamish was soon singing German folksongs and we were singing and we had a wonderful, magical evening.

Hamish was nice to Eli but he fell in love with me. I remember sitting in his big armchair and he was on the arm and we were all singing and when – in the song – we came to the section where all the girls stand up, I stood up and he slid into my place! So, when I sat down, I had to sit on his lap! We were so happy that night that it was ten o'clock before we realised our lift was gone! So we'd have to stay with this man! He'd told us he was a poet, and it was as though we had known him all our lives. I'm surprised, now, how bold we were. The flat was large but Hamish shared it with two friends, Jeffrey Jones and Bobby Botsford, so there wasn't much room. Eli had a corner to herself but I had to share the bed with Hamish! He said he'd be good. But, of course, all night long we fought like cat and dog! Me – to save my virginity; he, carefree with passion and laughter. All night long it was giggle and offer, struggle and refusal. All night long it was pleasure and laughter – but I survived. Much to my surprise – then and now! However, in the morning, Hamish decided we should stay with him – permanently – and that Eli should go back to Scone and collect our belongings, whilst I would spend the day with him in Edinburgh. Eli's visa had run out, so, it seemed to us that it was a great idea to stay with him, in this beautiful Edinburgh flat. He said he would look after us till we went back to Germany! That night Hamish and I became lovers. He was always very careful about contraception.

But the flat didn't stay quiet for long! Very soon Farnham Rehfisch, the folklorist, was banging on the door, wanting to start work on Hamish's 'Traveller Project'. So the next thing we knew, we were all upping sticks and decamping to the berryfields of Blair! There Hamish made sure Eli had a small tent to herself. And he and I shared a slightly larger one. Farnham Rehfisch got himself a hut. And so began what, looking back, was the happiest two weeks of my life. We picked berries with the Travellers, cooked out in the open, joined in the sing-songs around camp-fires. Hamish was making recordings, visiting the pubs and being entertained like a king. We met all the Stewarts, and Bella Higgins. We didn't have much money – but Hamish said it was best that he look after it! And, when a £50 cheque came in from Africa (from my brother in Namibia), he took charge of that as well.

Then he had to go out to the Hebrides with Sean O'Boyle and we had to go home. Hamish bought us rail tickets and put us on the train to London. And he gave us a couple of pounds pocket-money! But fortune stayed with us; in London, a German Jewess heard us speaking German – and took us in for the night! Next day, when we arrived at Aachen on the German border, a lorry from Coburg was parked in front of the station and it took us to the very doorstep of our house! Of course, we told our parents not a word about our adventures – especially mine! We said we'd stayed with an old professor and his wife – who'd looked after us very well! I was nineteen, Eli was twenty-two and Hamish was thirty-six.[3]

Felicitas Schmidt was born in eastern Germany on 3 March 1937 – with a twin brother – one of five children. Her parents, Felicitas and Friedrich Wilhelm Schmidt, were landed gentry with an ancestry that included Count Max von Schwerin, Count Heinrich von Schwerin, Heinrich von Muhler, a distinguished Minister of Education for Prussia, and, pre-eminently, Friedrich Daniel Schleiermacher (1768–1834), a friend of Goethe's and one of the great Protestant philosophers of the German Enlightenment. In 1945 the family estates were confiscated by the Soviets as the Third Reich collapsed. The family then escaped to the American Sector and settled near Coburg. Years of hardship were soon replaced by relative prosperity, and Katzel grew up in a conventional, well-to-do, Lutheran environment. At the age of eighteen she decided to visit Britain to improve her English. Her older sister Elizabeta (Eli) had recently completed a two-year course in Catering Management, so she accompanied her as a chaperone and workmate. They had always been close, and the trip sealed a lifelong, sisterly love–friendship. In January 1956 they hitch-hiked from Dover to Berwick-upon-Tweed where they worked as domestic helps at the Lebanon Mission Bible College, run by a Mr and Mrs Lambert.

All the students had felt the Call by Christ. The bedrooms were named Long Suffering, Hope, Courage, and on the bathroom door was a notice: 'This is the Lord's House: don't bang the door!' The Lamberts believed that 'the Lord will provide', so food was often

3 Katzel Henderson, conversations with TN, 2003/4.

> in short supply. Everything came from well-wishers! All our pocket money was spent in the Berwick Woolworths – on biscuits and cheese![4]

At Easter Katzel and Eli decided 'to do a runner'. After a short stay in Saltburn on the Yorkshire coast with an elderly German relative, they headed for Scotland and got themselves jobs at the Windsor restaurant in Perth. They rented a cottage on the banks of the Tay, at Scone. After an idyllic six weeks, 'the police came looking for us at the restaurant because Eli's visa had expired. "We could lock you up!" they said – but if we stopped work and agreed to leave Britain by 1 July they would let us go. They were very civilised. It was after that that we started hitching round Scotland and met Hamish.'

Hamish's diaries contain little about his adventures with the Schmidt girls but a number of jottings seem to allude to his relationship with Katzel: 'All the brutal facts of life need to be announced at once – we are all born, we copulate, we die. Consequently we are all entitled to an exaggerated plethora of sexual joy. So the immediate response is to treat the softer member as rough.' He also wrote a quatrain that addresses defloration with a directness straight out of the Horseman's Word:

> I took her through a field o' neeps,
> I hadnae time to louse the beasts
> I took the knife and slit the threads
> And gied her serendipity![5]

It was a rough wooing, but a splendid series of photographs of Hamish with the Schmidt girls in the berryfields documents sheer happiness. The girls hitch-hiked home and Katzel wrote a letter poste restante to Blairgowrie PO, but Hamish was in Ireland and the letter came back 'return to sender'. Katzel finally made contact via the School of Scottish Studies and on 13 September 1956 Hamish rekindled their friendship:

> Darling Katzel, This time I'm going to write in English . . . First of all, here are the photos – most of them come out quite well, I think (although there are only one or two which really do you justice!). But isn't it marvellous to have them, and recapture the happiness

4 Katzel Henderson, conversation with TN, 2003/4.

5 HH, unpublished notebook jottings, Henderson archive. This verse owes something to a fragment Hamish had collected from a Kintyre tinker, Jim McCallum of Ardrishaig: 'Ah laid her doon amang the whins / She pulled me hair and kicked me shins / But that's the night I got her wi' twins / Upon the banks o Tinmathaw – Jarra-ma-jow, Jarra-ma-jow . . . '

of our time together in the berryfields. I only wish it could have been ten times as long. Even the weather did us proud – we had the only ten rain-free days in the whole of this disastrous summer . . . The photo I like best is the one which shows us feeding each other berries. I bet anyone looking at this photo, and not knowing where it was taken, would think that we were in some tea-plantation in Assam – or maybe even among the vineyards of Calabria or Sicily! . . . The two taken in Lisa's bivvy are very good of you – the one in which you are looking straight at the camera makes you look even more like a gypsy (*eine Zigeunerin*) than usual! Those dark flashing eyes – *Mein Schwarz-braunes Schatzelein!* . . . You'll be delighted to hear that Daiches succeeded, at the court in Perth, in getting all the charges against the campers thrown out – the Sherriff agreed that the by-laws were just so much 'meaningless verbiage'. This means that all the ordinary tinkers camping at the top of the field got off Scot-free. However, Belle and her son Andy have had fresh charges made against them – and a new summons has been sent to both of them. I saw Daiches yesterday, and he seemed pretty certain that he would be able to get these charges thrown out too . . . The Irish folksong collector and I had a great time in the islands. We enjoyed ourselves a great deal, and collected quite a lot of interesting material. But I was always thinking of you, and wondering how you were getting on without me. How lovely it would have been if we had been able to go over to the islands together, just as we were together in Edinburgh and the berryfields! Think of it – together on the boat slipping past the green islands of Oban Bay in the early morning, and seeing the sun shining (it did occasionally) on Barra and Uist in the far Atlantic. Some time in the not so far distant future we must do a tour together. May it be soon.

The attempts by the Perth sanitary inspectors to terminate camping in the berryfields 'on the grounds of hygiene' enraged Hamish and he led a battle for the Travellers' 'historical rights'. He enrolled his old friend Lionel Daiches, one of the defence lawyers at the Conspiracy Trial in 1953, as the Stewarts' defence councillor, and summoned the press to Blairgowrie. The *Daily Express* headline ran: '2000 Berry-pickers say: We're Staying'.

Two thousand tinkers, camped in East Perthshire for the berry-picking season, have been told to quit. But if they do, they will have no place to go, and the berries – worth thousands of pounds – will be lost. They are being put out because, says a sanitary official, 'there is no proper water-supply and no proper drains'. But the tinkers are going to fight . . . Backing them is 36-year-old Hamish Henderson,

> a researcher at the School of Scottish Studies, and an American, Farnham Rehfisch.[6]

The report then quotes Hamish: 'Andra Stewart says, "We're going to stay until the last berry". And he's right! Margaret McPhee says, "This is our life. They can't just take it away from us – like that!" And she's right. I intend to stay put. And I say this – we will fight – where we stand: by the Standing Stones!' Hamish presents the problem as a clash of civilisations and a potentially revolutionary situation because two thousand tinkers, led by an experienced guerrilla leader, would be no push over! Sensibly, the police held back and, when the case came to court, the Travellers won a famous victory. Belle Stewart celebrated by writing a ballad in honour of Daiches and Hamish. Next day the Suez crisis erupted. On his thirty-seventh birthday, Hamish writes:

> *Katzel, mein Liebling*, Many, many thanks for the wonderful birthday present – a big hug to you, and a thousand, thousand loving kisses. It was lovely to get your letter too. And please thank Lisa for the card she sent . . . The Suez business looks a good deal quieter now, so I don't think there's any chance of HM's government trying to obtain my services. To tell you the truth I saw enough of Egypt last time! I've no wish in the world to ever see Cairo again . . . What you said in your last letter about wanting to come over straightaway and see me almost made me wish the crisis *had* got worse, so that I could have told you to come at once. But why not come across in the holidays for a week or two? You could hitch-hike again without much bother – and as soon as you got here you wouldn't have to worry about money.

In the summer of 1957 Hamish went to Germany to meet the Schmidt family. Not surprisingly, Katzel waited at Coburg station in a strangely heightened state of mind, and when he loomed up through the smoke – in a tattered much-stained kilt and looking every one of his thirty-seven years – she wondered for a moment whether this was the Man. 'Then, the whole platform turned its head – as we embraced!' Hamish had just completed his two months on the road with the Stewarts of Remarstaig. He was bronzed and fit – the sight of this huge, thin Highlander walking-out the young Coburger induced a mixture of envy and awe. Katzel was frequently self-conscious but also deeply happy, and Hamish was soon charming her parents.

When Hamish returned to Scotland things went quiet. In March 1958, losing patience with Hamish's long silence, Katzel applied for a teaching post in Iran. When she told Hamish, he exploded – writing to say that

6 '2000 Berry-pickers say: We're Staying', *Daily Express*.

he had hoped and expected her to become his wife! So what was all this nonsense about Iran! Katzel replied in some confusion that she was 'not sure about the future'. Hamish wrote back, 'How can you do this to me?' The Iran plan did not materialise. Katzel took temporary work in Switzerland and things again went quiet – until two separate events triggered the couple's formal engagement. Visiting Jeannie Robertson in Aberdeen, Hamish spoke about Katzel. After a short while she announced: 'Hamish, I can see you've lost yer hert to that lassie!' With those words Hamish's doubts and hesitations fell away and he decided he was destined to marry this woman. Meantime Katzel was in Coburg for celebrations marking the twenty-fifth wedding anniversary of her parents. On the evening of 6 November 1958 she got a surprise:

> I was alone, in the sitting room. I switched on the radio and heard a voice I recognised. It was Hamish. He was talking about the Travelling people and he was introducing Jeannie's great ballad, 'Son David'! It seemed as though the whole broadcast was directed at me. At the end, the announcer said, 'That was the distinguished Scots folklorist, Hamish Henderson, speaking from London about the song culture of Scotland.'[7]

Hamish's thirty-ninth birthday was just five days away so Katzel decided to send a parcel. 'It contained a sausage, a tie and a letter. I sent it to Hamish's flat at Royal Terrace. A fortnight later it was returned – marked, "Gone Away"! I took out the old sausage and readdressed the parcel with a new letter, to the School of Scottish Studies. After that I asked him to spend Christmas with me in Coburg. He agreed to come, and on Christmas Eve he asked me to marry him. Then, at the New Year, our formal engagement was announced.' Returning to Scotland, Hamish wrote:

> My darling Katzel, Here I am in London, after a '*Kleine Ewigkeit*' in trains and on the boat . . . Just after I got out of the train at Wurzburg, I noticed two girls I thought I had seen before – one a blonde, the other a brunette. So when I saw them again, waiting to board the same train as I was catching, and obviously looking at me with interest, I spoke to them. Do you know who they were? Two class-mates of your own from Coburg – Rosaline Kunze, and Eva Marie Wentzel . . . Needless to say, they too had seen the announcement of our engagement in the Coburg paper, and were obviously interested to talk to a real life Scotsman engaged to Felicitas! And – on the boat I met Pat Shuldham-Shaw, a folk-song enthusiast . . . I hadn't seen him for months, and there were

7 Katzel Henderson conversation with TN, 2003/4.

> a whole lot of things I wanted to talk about. We had a few Dutch gins together, and eventually started singing . . . Ever since I left Coburg I've been missing you more than I can say, my darling – it seems a long time till April . . . I enjoyed my Christmas and New Year with you tremendously – it was for every reason the most lovely 'festive season' of my life . . . I'm doubly fortunate – not only have I got the most marvellous little Katz in Germany, – but I've become a member of one of the nicest families. What have I done to deserve all this? I must give you all – and you above all – my love in return. *Wie ich Dich liebe*! With a thousand kissings and blessings – I love you! *Auf Wiedersehen!* Hamish.

When Hamish arrived back in Edinburgh, news of his engagement was greeted with a mixture of confusion and pleasure. Most of his friends were delighted but some of the most politically and culturally ambitious began to wonder whether the revolutionary was going soft. MacDiarmid, Morris Blythman, Simon Ward and Tom Scott all dropped hints that suggested that Hamish was yet another 'lost leader'. Hamish, however, embraced marriage as a new adventure and initially he certainly saw Katzel as a 'field partner'; he writes:

> Katzel, my own heart's darling, you'll be delighted to hear that among the many letters of congratulation I've received since my return to Scotland, was one from Alec and Belle Stewart, our good friends of the berry fields . . . Well, there you are darling – it's nice to know that the tinkers too are fond of us, and wish us well! Jeannie Robertson – who is now in London recording more songs for another extended play record – was very positive that she had 'seen it all from the stert, and could have told it to both of us, in our fortunes'. And the more I think of these incredible 'Zufalle' which attend our steps all the time, the more I tend to feel that she's probably quite right! . . . My darling I've already begun to make a few plans for Italy [Hamish's planned honeymoon destination], but I wont tell you about them yet – I'll leave them to your imagination. A hundred thousand kisses, my sweetest darling. I love you.

In March he sent her a card of the great Beech Hedge at Meikleour, Perthshire. 'How I wish you were with me my darling – the Scots landscape would sparkle like a diamond if you were beside me! But soon you will be, and we'll have hundreds of marvellous wanderings through the beauty spots of the country. Roll on the day!' He also set about buying a top-floor flat at 20 Melville Terrace, just across the Meadows from the School of Scottish Studies in George Square, Edinburgh. The Halifax Building Society agreed to advance him £1,250 – to be repaid over 20 years at £8 12s 4d per month. To fund the down-payment, Maurice and

Marian Sugden in Cambridge loaned him £200. A letter, to an unknown Dublin friend, shows how he advanced financial pleading and poetry – together:

> 'Come gather roond – roond the City Hall'. I've just been looking again at the Cuala Press edition of the 'Last Poems' (of W.B.Y's). They bring back memories of the Anzio Beach Head, where the book landed and helped me face the Huns; and of Easter Sunday years ago when I marched as a Glaswegian behind the Finton Lodge Pipe Band – down Baggot Street in the spring of 1939 . . . As for myself I'm getting spliced on May 16th among the people of the Black Forest in Germany. But I have one problem. An interview with my bank manager has at last convinced me that this commitment has vastly outstripped my slender savings. (As you can imagine I have spent as much on folksong and folksingers in the last decade as a Sultan might have spent on ten extra-luscious Lolitas.) In fact I need urgently to raise a loan and I have only 400 quid. Could you lend me anything – please let me know soon, as time (never a friend of mine) has begun to take me by the tentacles.

Before leaving for Germany, Hamish enjoyed a splendid mixed-sex stag night in Edinburgh. A young Canadian art student had constructed a papier-mâché head of Hamish and, 'ceremonially pulled from a bottle o' malt', it opened proceedings. Folksingers Ella Ward and Dolina MacLennan were in charge and they ensured that a Gunn-tartaned, all-singing, all-dancing Hamish set off for Germany 'in the good auld style'. On arrival, he found that the Schmidt sisters, having clubbed together to buy him a brand-new suit, demanded the removal of his much-tattered kilt. The suit, bought off the peg from High and Mighty, was huge! 'It shimmered silver-grey like a Rolls Royce', said Hamish. He didn't like it much but wore it 'for best' for the next twenty years. 'My dowry,' he said, 'was a huge marriage bed, seven feet by seven feet! It came with a huge feather duvet – the first ever seen in Edinburgh. We set the fashion for a generation – Katzel and me!' He wired Katzel: *'Alles erfolgreich heimgebracht ich liebe dich uber alles in der welt Auf wiedersehen Dienstag dein Hamish'*.[8]

The wedding was formal, and Hamish was glad of the telegrams from across the North Sea. From the 'Blythmen' of Glasgow:[9] *'Cha Duine Duine'n agnar guid luck'*; from Dominic Behan,[10] *'Gach beanact*

---

8 'I've brought everything home successfully [gifts of furniture from Katzel's parents]. Love you more than anything in the world. See you Tuesday.'

9 Hamish's friends Morris and Marian Blythman (see Volume 1 of this biography).

10 Brendan Behan's brother. The Behans (from Ireland) were great friends of Hamish's since the 1950s (see Volume 1 of this biography).

Croide on Dominic is a Clann ar do Poiste'; from Dry Drayton,[11] 'Our Renegade brought to heel me Boys / Smitten cold by a Kitten Bold / To Awake to what Rapturous Joy's Love'. He himself set down these lines:

So glory be to him that planted the golden jars;
Undo your kirtle, J, and let's pull down the stars.[12]

Italy was the natural place for Hamish and Katzel to honeymoon: 'it would provide us with bed and vino – for ever – for free!' Unfortunately, Hamish had forgotten 'the exclusion order' placed on him in 1950. At the Brenner Pass, armed Italian guards took the newly weds off the train, rigorously interrogated them and sent them packing – back into Austria. After ten days in Innsbruck, with his funds running out, Hamish decided that Hans Heini Meier, an old folklore friend in Switzerland, would put them up for a few days. Then the couple moved on to France – to visit Gershon Legman. Unfortunately Legman was in the British Museum hunting out bawdy songs and dirty jokes; Hamish told me 'Legman would have got a lot more – if only he'd stayed at home, with us!' Beverley Legman looked after them well but before long the bridal couple were heading homeward. On the ferryboat to England, Hamish announced, 'When we get home, we'll buy a car – I'll take the test and upgrade my Provisional Licence. We'll be able to go out into the country.' Unfortunately, lack of funds and Hamish's drinking ensured that when his fifth Provisional Licence expired, on 19 December 1960, this idea took more and more of a back seat – and the Hendersons would never own a car. Arriving in Edinburgh – so young and so much a stranger amongst Hamish's bohemian but highly intellectual friends – Katzel found herself an object of some curiosity. There were still pockets of strong anti-German feeling, but Hamish himself was, initially, a romantic, considerate and playful husband. For example Katzel found herself being introduced to Basil Megaw, the director of the School of Scottish Studies, after crashing into him outside the door of the University Staff Club: 'Hamish was chasing me – like a schoolboy – and I ran straight into the arms of the headmaster!'

The top-floor flat at 20 Melville Terrace had splendid views in three directions but almost no furniture. It was cold and draughty and, as Katzel reports, 'within days, there on the doorstep was Hamish's friend, Calum Black – with his wife and children, all needing a bed. They had come down to Edinburgh for a holiday, from Lismore, where Calum was the Minister. And none of them were easy to get on with!' Also, Hamish had almost Victorian ideas about 'meals-on-the-table', and Katzel soon found

11 Dry Drayton: the home of the Armstrong family, who became Hamish's second family from his Cambridge days onwards (see Volume 1 of this biography).

12 HH, unpublished notes, Henderson archive.

herself being tested by what might be described as a series of 'labours'. Did she really love him, would she scrub for him? In 2003 Katzel told the sculptor Tony Morrow that, within a few hours of their arrival home from honeymoon, Hamish gave her a heap of old and very dirty handkerchiefs to wash. Some had been brought back from France but others seemed to have been lying about since the spring! 'I threw most of them away but didn't tell him.'

Did Hamish have no idea how to behave towards a young wife? Did he just assume she would serve him like a school-maid or an army batman? Did he seek to test her commitment to him? Did he want to rub her bourgeois nose in 'the sacred filth of the living'; show her that, to rephrase Shakespeare, 'vilest things become themselves in him'? Hamish would, on occasion, confront both friends and foes with wounding directness, and a number of aphorisms jotted down in this time echo this brutal directness. 'A standing cock knows no conscience; the moment of truth for the saint is when he realises that there is some fun in the world after all; the sacrificial table / the traditional midwife; A crew of Thistle Street lawyers.' Of John MacInnes, after a session in Sandy Bell's, Hamish notes 'spurious kindness, disingenuous goodwill, bitter benevolence': of Gauguin: 'not only did he indulge in the pleasures of the flesh but he enjoyed them greatly.'

In Edinburgh Hamish and Katzel regularly attended folk clubs, theatrical shows, public demonstrations and political meetings together. In September 1961 they visited Belfast, lodging with Davie Hammond, a young communist Hamish had known since 1948. Hammond was developing his career as a singer, teacher, broadcaster and film-maker – in a very Henderson mould – and when he died in 2008 it was Seamus Heaney who wrote his obituary, in the *Guardian*. Hamish and Katzel moved on to Armagh to stay with the Sean O'Boyle family. Here, Hamish introduced Katzel to Fionnuala Ni' Naghallaig, now married with two young children. In Dublin, Brendan Behan roared – with open arms – 'Hamish's wife!', then whispered 'is she a dove?' What he meant is anyone's guess. In McDaid's pub, Hamish was always greeted like a hero, and never allowed to buy a round himself – a great week unfolded.

From the start of the marriage, Hamish had been keen to start a family, Katzel less so. She was still very young, preoccupied with the task of adapting to married life, and learning the ropes in what for her was an exciting but very foreign country. However, when after eighteen months no pregnancy had occurred, Hamish suggested they visit a fertility specialist. When it was revealed that his sperm-count was low, he was given hormonal stimulants. On 26 February 1962 Maurice Fleming, whose wife Nanette had recently given birth, offered his advice:

> I suppose you have tried adopting the Rhythm Method of ensuring – or trying to ensure – that 'the breakin' o' delight' bears fruit? It

entails watching the dates etc. I expect you know all about it . . . if you want details, I'll gladly send them. Good Luck, M.F.

That might have done the trick but it was not until the university term ended and Hamish and Katzel were holidaying on the Yugoslavian coast that the Mediterranean began working its timeless magic. In March 1963 their first daughter, Christina (Tina), was born. Naturally, Hamish had consulted the 'stars' in *Woman's Own* magazine – and copied them down for the week ending 16 March:

> *Pisces* (Katzel and Tina): An opportunity week. A slow moving project begins to show life. Other people seem willing to lend a hand, and social connections could help this trend. A gift delights you.
>
> *Scorpio* (Hamish): Home and family interests show very pleasing aspects this week. If there has been conflict, now comes your chance to get things on to a happier footing. Later you enjoy the company of someone 'special'.

Alexander Keith of Balmedie sent immediate congratulations: 'Dear Hamish – delighted to hear the good news. "Fresh April and then a boy". She'll teach you "Songs before Sunrise" to begin with; later you must instruct her in the true barbaric strains!' Such messages pleased Hamish but, as ever, short of cash, he was soon using the new arrival as a reason to encourage those who owed him money to pay up. On 27 February 1963 he had written to the American folklorist Ken Goldstein: 'Dear Ken . . . If it's a boy his name will be Patrick, and if it's a girl she'll be Christine Felicity. I'll be delighted – whatever and whichever . . . With this bairn on the way, we could certainly use some overdue dollars: I have heard that a "pirated" edition of my "Ballads of WWII" has been on sale in the States. Have you heard anything to that effect? I've also written a dance-tune love song that Jean Redpath should have a go at.' On 28 March Goldstein wrote back:

> Dear H. and K., Congratulations on the birth of your daughter. We couldn't be more pleased . . . I am hoping to take up an appointment at the U. of Penn . . . Also received a formal offer of a position in the Folk Life Department of the University of Leeds – the thing was arranged through your old nemesis, Stewart Sanderson on the recommendation of Archie Taylor . . . My reprint of Greig's *Folk-songs of the North East* has just come off the press [Hamish subsequently writes out a definition of the word 'nemesis'].

Goldstein's efforts resulted in a cheque for $5! But on 30 March 1963 Hamish struck it rich: he got a cheque for £53 5s 5d from the University of Chicago Press as his share of the advance for a book of Scottish folk stories he was to collect and edit with John MacInnes. Much cheered, on 23 April he wrote Goldstein a letter that shimmers with satisfaction and fatherly pride:

> Christine Felicity is now over a month old and by and large treating us very decent. The sight of Katzel with her baby daughter must go right ahead to the finals for the loveliest sight in the world. We've had some wonderful letters of congratulation, including one from Pete Seeger welcoming Christine into this 'crazy, rough and beautiful world' . . . I had no strong feelings, either way, about the bairn being christened, but Katzel's parents are devout Lutherans, and would have been very sad if the job had not been done. So, today, we took her to St Columba's by the Castle and unlike Presby ministers, who only give a bairn a cat's lick, our Episcopal Kirk ministers are quite lavish with the water – one took a conch and gave her three generous libations over the head like the Jordan – Jatsus. I was expecting an ear-splitting yell at the very first douche but she remained as quiet as a wee mouse.

The Celtic scholar Dr Anne Ross turned up with an antique pram; it was not casy to propel up four flights of stairs but provided Tina with a fine high viewpoint when crossing the Meadows. It was Katzel who had to do most of the pram pushing. In fact she soon found herself practically housebound as Hamish re-immersed himself in a plethora of public and professional demands. In the summer of 1964 Katzel and Tina went alone to Germany whilst Hamish stayed to work on in Edinburgh. However, invited to a major international folk conference in Athens, he made a one-night stop-over in Coburg. Hamish greatly enjoyed his week in Greece, phoning Katzel to tell her: 'Going up to the Acropolis was like coming home'. He also went out to Marathon to pay homage to the 192 Athenian hoplites killed in the battle that saved Greek civilisation. It was the mound within which they are buried that particularly impressed him. Their sacrifice inspired the subject matter of the Parthenon Frieze, one of the great achievements of mankind. Hamish told me of how, standing there, he thought of Samuel Johnson's statement:

> 'That man is little to be envied whose patriotism would not gain force on the field of Marathon, or whose piety would not grow warmer among the ruins of Iona.' I also said a prayer for Grigoris Lambrakis.[13] Then I walked from the Mound towards the sea.

13 Grigoris Lambrakis (1912–1963), Greek politician and pacifist, murdered in 1963 (see Chapter 8).

> I turned to look back – and noticed a black dog following me. It stayed with me to the shore. It sat by me as I undressed. Then I went out into the waves – to swim round in a semi-circle. Standing up, I looked back for this dog: it was gone.[14]

Hamish made an impact at the conference and was invited to take up a sabbatical six-month research post at the University of Athens. He was keen to accept, not least because he wanted to finish the 'Heroic Song for Grigoris Lambrakis' that he had been attempting to write for the last two years (see Chapter 8). Unfortunately, the university authorities in Edinburgh proved uncooperative and, with Katzel soon pregnant again, this possibly life-changing opportunity slipped away.

When the birth of Janet was imminent in March 1966, Katzel asked Hamish to attend the birth. He refused. The labour proved long and difficult, and the baby had to be delivered with forceps. Hamish awaited news, drinking with friends in Sandy Bell's Bar. News of the birth was telephoned to him. At the Simpson Maternity Hospital, he was asked to wait till visiting time. By the time he entered the ward he was in a highly agitated state and deeply shocked to find Katzel completely exhausted and their new daughter bruised and bloody. Filled with guilt and indignation he returned to Sandy Bell's to make a series of angry phone calls to the family GP! When Katzel finally got home – to be cared for by her ever-loyal sister Eli – Hamish sought solace by sticking to his merciless public routine. Katzel found this behaviour callous and inexcusable.

There were external reasons for Hamish's lack of humanity. By the mid 1960s his professional life was lurching from crisis to crisis. The great period of folk-collecting had passed, he believed he was getting little support within the School, his muse had left him, Scottish politics was in the doldrums, the Vietnam War was raging, he was drinking heavily and short of money – both for his family and for himself. He loved Katzel and the two girls dearly. He knew marriage had brought him much needed domestic support and security, but these benefits were now clashing with what he regarded as his public responsibilities. When forced to choose, Hamish had always felt impelled to put his art and public commitments before personal wellbeing; and this was still true now – even if his family had to suffer. His sense of virtue was Roman. He felt guilt and savage remorse for the pain he was inflicting but – suffering an extended dark night of the soul – was unable to solve the problem. Katzel remembers eruptions of real temper. One night, two months before Janet's birth, Hamish came home early to watch a television programme about the Nazi holocaust and insisted that Katzel and Eli watch it with him. Katzel, conscious of her pregnant state, refused. Eli sat with him but, as the programme ended, Hamish turned on her to denounce not just the Nazis

---

14 HH, conversation with TN, 1999.

but 'the complicity of the ordinary Germans – like the Schmidts'! A point of no return in their relationship was passed.

Hamish could still, of course, be extremely charming. He would sing to his children and delight in them. Christmas Eve was always a very special night. He would buy a large Christmas tree at the street corner in Sciennes and the whole family would gather to decorate it and then open their presents, in the German style. But when, in 1970, Katzel received a family bequest she decided the best thing to do was to buy a small flat – on the other side of Melville Terrace – as an insurance against what seemed likely to be a complete breakdown of the marriage. This breakdown did not happen until the autumn of 1975 but – when it came – the break was hard on all concerned. Hamish felt betrayed, whilst Katzel and the two young girls suffered real anguish and hardship. Regular personal contact, however, was maintained – across the street. Two parallel lifestyles emerged, and Katzel's decision proved to be to the long-term good of everyone. New lifestyles were constructed. Katzel knew she was a brake on Hamish's bardic compulsions and, looking back in 2004, spoke with exemplary understanding of the situation:

> Hamish was a poet. His marriage was to poetry, to ideas, to Scotland above all. The break was like putting an injured animal back to the wild. It was risky but his windows looked on our windows. We were just across the road. The girls still saw a great deal of him. It was not easy for them, or for me – but he would come over for Sunday lunch – and, after twenty years of estrangement, we would come back together.[15]

15 Katzel Henderson, conversation with TN, 2004.

EIGHT

Missile Crises and Peace Campaigning

I ask you – the youth of Scotland
(Our hope in the nation's future)
To help us in this struggle –
Which is only beginning.
HH, 1957[1]

In an interview with Patricia Wall of the Imperial War Museum, Hamish was asked, in 1978: 'Do you feel cut off from contemporary English poetry? I'm thinking of people like Ted Hughes, Thom Gunn, Edward Lucie-Smith, Peter Porter, etc.?' He answered, 'Oh – I *am* cut off. I like their stuff but I think I'm doing something different. I don't make any boundary between poetry and song. I write about the most pressing problems of all – namely those of our continuing existence, the Bomb.' Since the thirties Hamish had been a public campaigner for peace with a wilfulness rare amongst poets. In the immediate post-war period his prime concerns were the dangers posed by the Cold War. His activism was always political, cultural and practical. For example, in 1948 as secretary of the Scottish USSR Friendship Society, he initiated plans to get Samuel Marshak, the Russian poet and Burns scholar, to tour Scotland. In January 1956 Marshak arrived. Emrys Hughes, Labour MP for South Ayrshire, was in charge of events but Hamish was delighted to meet one of the world's great cultural ambassadors and it was with pride that he noted the key elements of Marshak's 'Homage to Burns', delivered in Edinburgh on 24 January:

> My fellow countrymen have learned to love and appreciate the rich, virile, abundant poetry of your rantin', rovin' Robin. Burns has become part of our daily life . . . Our best composers – Shostakovitch, Kabelevsky, Krennikov – have set his lyrics to music. My translations are to be found in the houses of intellectuals, in the cottages of collective farms, in the apartments of workers, on the tables of students . . . He is loved especially by our young people – his poetry is simple but deep. What attracted me to Burns in the first place was his lust for life – his honesty, open-mindedness, his magnanimity,

1 HH, unpublished notes, Henderson archive.

> his vitality . . . He is the best proof that only a national poet, true to his own country, can become a great international poet . . . Peace and freedom and the brotherhood of man – the doors of the parliamentary buildings of all nations should be emblazoned with his common-sense words: 'The deities that I adore / Are social Peace and Plenty. / I'm better pleased to make one more – / Than be the death of twenty.' If anyone can put it better, let him.[2]

During the mid fifties Hamish also made his presence felt in China where his friend Nan Green was working as Peace and Publications Representative of the Communist Party of Great Britain (CPGB). In October 1955, he received this letter from Green, then in Beijing. It came to him via their mutual friend Queenie Moncrieff, in London:

> Can you go to Collets [bookshop] and buy a copy of Chinese Literature No.3 1955 (a quarterly). I want you to send this as soon as possible to *Hamish*, and ask him – with my sincerest urgency, to write to the Foreign Languages Press, 26 Kuo Hui Chieh, Peking – his opinion on this. (Without saying the request came from me, or mentioning my name – and finally, for him to send me a copy of the letter he writes.) He should say frankly what he thinks. Hard criticism is appreciated here. And it is fifty times more closely listened to if it comes from abroad. If on top of that it comes from a poet who knows something about folk-poetry (which is folksong in this instance because the minority peoples of China are, some of them, in the stage where they sing all their poetry) it will be additionally valuable . . . It is a very difficult job to translate any poetry unless you are a poet. This job was done for CL by an excellent but heartless prose-writer . . . It makes me weep. I think Hamish will recognise both the aspects I have mentioned and it would be very helpful if he would write and *say so* . . .

At a time when isolation of China was order of the day, Hamish was delighted to do all he could, and on 19 February 1956 Moncrieff wrote to Hamish: 'Thank you for sending the Chinese literature letter. I received a letter from Nan the same day in which she said, "I am so glad Hamish wrote – the custom is to have a yearly summing up of the work in every branch [of cultural activity], and coming just now his words will have just the right effect.' Hamish's willingness to be open-handed with China is affirmed by two anecdotes. In the 1960s when Chairman Mao's 'Little Red Book' appeared, Hamish was presented with his copy in the Blythmans' house in Glasgow. Marian Blythman told me in 2004: 'He opened the book and read the first lines that caught his eye: "A song for

2 HH, unpublished notes, Henderson archive.

every mountain".' In 2008, on a singing tour of China, Sheena Wellington (the singer who sang at the opening ceremony of the Scottish Parliament in 1999) was thrilled to find herself approached by Chinese folklore professors asking: 'Do you know Hamish Henderson? Is he still alive? He is an honoured figure here in China.'

In the spring of 1956 Hamish circulated 'a round-robin' – calling for the release of Paul Robeson from the US asylum in which he had been incarcerated for extended bouts of electro-convulsive therapy – and sent it to the American Ambassador in London. This however, was the year in which Hamish focused his political energies on the island of South Uist. The Government had decided that Britain should build a military rocket range on Benbecula – at the very heart of Gaidhealtachd. Hamish opposed it in principle because of the devastating cultural impact such an establishment could have on Hebridean life. The plan was for a permanent RAF base, including a military town, stretching from Sollas in North Uist to Bornish in South Uist. From the base, missiles would be test-fired over St Kilda and the eastern Atlantic. Canon John Morrison of Ardkenneth led local resistance. The sculptor Hew Lorimer was commissioned to build a 25-foot stone-carved statue of the Madonna and Child overlooking the range (*Moire ro Naomh nan Eilean: Ban-Tighearna nan Eilean*, unveiled on 17 August 1958) as a public reminder to visitors that the island was a different world. On the mainland, Hamish – with Calum Maclean – became one of the 'the resistance leaders'. The Government claimed the base a necessary 'Cold War Emergency' and advanced its plans as rapidly as possible. The following notes – setting out the reasons why Hamish believed the base should not be built – formed the basis of a speech to students, in the Edinburgh University Students Union, in 1957:

1) A Public Enquiry was promised but never held.
2) The government claims no objections were lodged – this is untrue.
3) 80 crofters are to be dispersed.
4) £12,000,000 is to be spent. The money should be spent on Disarmament!
5) An alien population of 'builders' is set to swamp the local population (3,000).
6) Gaelic civilisation – amongst the most ancient in Europe – is under threat.
   The Hebrides are a place of pilgrimage for scholars and artists from all over the world. In WW I the slogan was 'Defending our way of life'!
7) No limits have been laid down re developments in the future.
8) The Western Isles have been historically neglected by successive governments and the suggestion that Rockets will remedy this neglect is Absolutely Baloney!

9) The Crofters feel the time for compromise is over. It is necessary to stop the scheme. Passive resistance is contemplated. An ultimatum must be sent to the present government.

The siting of the Rocket Range is not a problem for S. Uist or the Hebrides alone – thousands of people from one end of Britain to the other regard this action as the wanton desecration of a unique regional culture. Thus while a single crofter is prepared to resist the taking over of his land, on the isle of Uist, every man and woman of goodwill in Scotland should be prepared to render active assistance. We call upon all the churches, the cultural organisations, the trades unions, political parties – and especially those building contractors and site workers who may be called upon to build this Rocket Range – to stand with us.[3]

Hamish made a separate note. 'A prophecy from a decapitated head: "Quite a sizable piece of land for a language to get its teeth into"!' Hamish saw resistance to the rocket range as part of an ongoing moral battle for values. In April he visited Benbecula and subsequently was at least twice in London, lobbying MPs at the House of Commons. In May, Sean O'Boyle[4] wrote to him: 'Dear Hamish, I was delighted to see your enthusiasm for all things Gaelic has suffered no diminution from your contact with the Sassenachs in the House of Commons. I feared for your ideals whilst you were in their midst.' Exactly what O'Boyle feared is unclear but a number of rocket range protesters had been 'roughed up' and on the night of 30/31 July 1957 Hamish became the victim of a street incident. It seems he was found unconscious and taken to St Mary's Hospital, Paddington. Next morning, he picked up the doctor's notes from the end of the bed and put them in his pocket (they are now in the Henderson archive): 'This man fell on 31/07/57 and sustained an injury to his head. A wound on the occiput was dressed and he was given ATS 1 – X Ray of skull – no fracture.' On the back of this note, Hamish wrote out a series of questions and answers – associated with the rituals of the Horseman's Word. Presumably he wanted to check whether he had been 'properly brained' or just injured.

Q: Far did ye leave yer plou, laddie?
A: Abeen the steen
Aneen the meen
At the side o' a dang guid fearin . . .

---

3 HH, unpublished speech notes, Henderson archive.

4 Sean O'Boyle was an expert on Irish folksong and poetry.

Satisfied that his memory was in good order, he added a question of his own:

Q: Why is a horse put in blinds?
A: It doesn't need to tak aff his blin bridle
Until he sees the shite.

Was Hamish the victim of a drunken fall or was he attacked by muggers as an intimidatory warning? A letter from Calum Maclean to Hamish in June 1957 suggests how high passions were at this time.

> All is well in Uist and the enemy is being held at bay, I hope. I am much perturbed by the way they messed up the big protest meeting. Wendy Wood and Wilkie [well-known Nationalists] ought not to have been allowed. Poor Donald Archie [MacDonald] has come in for a lot of abuse for his attack upon Macmillan. I am afraid the Uist people regard Friar John as a fool and publicity hunter. It is all pretty bad but I'm really afraid the old Highland spirit is as dead as could be. The young girls will love being courted by airmen, the bitches. The School of Scottish Studies should shut up about Uist. They ought to pay Donald John [Macdonald, the Uist crofter-poet captured at St Valery in 1940] more and Sanderson less and be done with it. *Beannachd Dhu leat* – Calum.

The mention of Stewart Sanderson (Secretary–Archivist at the School of Scottish Studies) is interesting because in January 1957 he is documented as attending meetings in London and a press conference in Edinburgh on the rocket range issue – and taking a very balanced stance. Donald Archie MacDonald (who would later join the staff of the School), on the other hand, was a friend of Hamish's and his attack on Harold Macmillan (the new Prime Minister) may well have encouraged Hamish to write a new ballad entitled 'Scabby Tash'. It starts as a ferocious attack on Macmillan and ends as an attack on nuclear weaponry – seen as the Death Wish of power-debauched governments. Each verse of the ballad begins as a tirade against imperialistic brutalism before ending with this gentle and affirmative line: 'If you sit close tae me I winna weary'. Hamish made this an alternative title to the song: it suggests that there is a peaceful Burnsian alternative to war and that Scotland can rest assured that he (Hamish) will not weary in his efforts on her behalf.

I saw Macmillan doon the toon
Wha's that my dearie?
Hey, Jimmy Tyrie
Blundermac, Scabbytash
That's a', my dearie.
If you sit close tae me, I winna weary.

I saw a Tory doon the toon
Wha's that my dearie?
That's a bonehead
Hey, Jimmy Tyrie
Boneheid, Blundermac, Scabbytash
That's a', my dearie.
If you sit close tae me, I winna weary . . .[5]

By verse six, the repeated fifth line is seven words long; by verse ten, fourteen words long, and the object of attack has changed from Harold Macmillan to police informers and the murderous madness of national nuclear policies:

I saw a nark abuin the brae
Wha's that my dearie?
That's a hornygolloch
Hey, Jimmy Tyrie
Hornygolloch, Croakerjack, Bullyboy, Poodlefaker, Boneheid,
    Blundermac, Scabbytash
That's a', my dearie.
If you sit close tae me, I winna weary . . .

I saw the Hunley on the loch
Whit's that my dearie?
That's a Daith Wish
Hey, Jimmy Tyrie
Daith wish (nae mine!), Coonter-doon, Button-pusher, Bamstick,
    Hornygolloch, Croakerjack, Bullyboy, Poodlefaker, Boneheid,
    Blundermac, Scabbytash
That's a', my dearie.
If you sit close tae me, I winna weary.

This is not one of Hamish's best ballads but it has claims to be amongst the earliest and most complex of all anti-nuclear songs. It certainly preceded the foundation of the Campaign for Nuclear Disarmament (CND) in February 1958 and the subsequent Peace March from Aldermaston to Trafalgar Square in London.

Whilst Hamish saw the rocket range as a political issue, two of his friends – Ian Hamilton (of Stone of Destiny fame) and Sir Compton Mackenzie – used it as a literary opportunity. Frustrated by the manner in which the BBC played down the rocket range controversy, Hamilton decided in 1956 that Scotland needed an independent radio station. Such stations were illegal, so he wrote a play: *The Tinkers of the World*. It

5 HH, 'Scabby Tash', in circulation in oral tradition since 1958.

opened at the Gateway Theatre, Edinburgh, in February 1957. Hamish greeted it with enthusiasm, and Douglas Henderson[6] wrote a review that Hamish tucked away in his archive.

> *The Tinkers of the World* is a healthy and much-needed purgative to the modern Scottish theatre. Superficially the play deals with the immediate topic of a Rocket Range on a Hebridean Island . . . but the fundamental conflict is much deeper. *In ultimo* it amounts to what Bernard Shaw in a brutal flash of insight labelled 'the incompatibility of the Scot with British "civilisation"'– After a good deal of extravagant protest the old chief sells out, the young Highland Civil Servant sells out, the local MP sells out – and only two people (and two types) continue the struggle. They are the Chief's English educated and idealistic daughter and an aging hard-line socialist, ex-bus conductor from Glasgow – who is quite prepared to pursue armed rebellion in defence of his homeland . . . to the last, even when the boats are waiting to evacuate the islanders, he believes that only armed sabotage and irreconcilable defiance can save the island.[7]

The play can be interpreted as a celebration of Hamish's vision for Scotland and a thinly veiled attack on Hamish as yet another 'lost leader'. Hamilton was now a successful Edinburgh lawyer and increasingly frustrated by Hamish's espousal of the rude folk tradition and pub life that went with it. Hamilton saw this as a blind alley. The two men, however, continued to admire each other's native compulsions.

In 1957 Compton Mackenzie published his novel *Rockets Galore*. It never gained the success of the earlier *Whisky Galore* but in 1958 it was turned into a film and at Hogmanay 1959 Mackenzie invited Hamish to spend the New Year with him at 12 Marchmont Road, Edinburgh. Perhaps it was a thank you to Hamish for 'his part' in the story and it certainly wasn't long before Hamish came up with a new scenario for Mackenzie. 'I told him that just as *Rockets Galore* had followed *Whisky Galore*, his next novel should be *Congregations No More*! I told him about Calum Black's predicament on the Isle of Lismore – where the island's whole population had gone on strike, in protest, at their Minister's Christian radicalism! Calum was an ex Highland Div. Communist! It was perfect material for a Hebridean Trilogy!'[8] (see Chapter 16).

---

6 Douglas Henderson (1935–2006) had chaired the 'Welcome Home' dinner for the Scottish Republican Army conspirators in July 1954; see Volume 1. He later became an MP for the Scottish National Party.

7 Unidentified/dated review, Henderson archive.

8 HH, conversation with TN, 1995.

In November 1960 Hamish found a new focus for his peace-mongering. The British Government announced that it had offered Holy Loch to the United States of America for permanent use as its Polaris submarine base for the North Atlantic. The following spring the nuclear submarine USS *Proteus* sailed up the Clyde. Hamish, Morris Blythman and many of Scotland's folksingers were there – with CND – to meet it. A great protest campaign erupted and, over the next forty years, folksong, and Hamish, were to play a leading role in a campaign that continued until the base was finally closed.

The anti-Polaris demonstrators created a battery of new songs that were soon published as a booklet *Ding Dong Dollar*. Within a few months Folkways, a leading New York record company, agreed to make an LP entitled *Ding Dong Dollar* (FD5444, 1962). The lead singers were Josh MacRae, Bobby Campbell, Nigel Denver, Gordeanna McCulloch, Ray Fisher, Hamish Imlach, and Jackie O'Connor (who sings Hamish's song 'The Freedom Come a' Ye'). This ground-breaking record was to have a seminal influence on the International Peace Movement and the music of protest movements throughout the sixties. The sleeve notes for this LP are unsigned – but were written by Hamish and they remain a *tour-de-force*. All the *Ding Dong Dollar* songs were initially published as if they were anonymous folksongs but all were composed by contemporary songwriters. Most were the work of Morris Blythman; Hamish himself contributed only two: 'The Freedom Come a' Ye' and 'Anti-Polaris'. Hamish knew they were very different songs and deliberately published them together as an experiment. The first is a finely wrought 'art song': the second was, deliberately, loosely composed and sent forth unfledged – in the hope that it would be 'work-shopped into a new and better form by others'. 'The Freedom Come a' Ye' was quickly recognised as a classic, but to Hamish's disappointment 'Anti-Polaris' never took off. The most popular song amongst the demonstrators was the title song, 'Ding Dong Dollar', written by Morris Blythman, and it spread round the world.

> O ye canny spend a dollar when ye're deid
> No ye canny spend a dollar when ye're deid
> Singin Ding-Dong-Dollar; Everybody holler
> Ye canny spend a dollar when ye're deid.

Folkway Records was run by Moses Asch, and Hamish was greatly impressed by the courage with which the project was advanced. He writes, 'Dear Moses, the more we read of the present political and cultural set up in the USA, the more admiration we feel for your willingness to publish a Ding Dong Dollar disc. At any rate, it can hardly fail to make its mark in American disc history . . . ' On 16 February 1962 he wrote again: 'Dear Moses, I enclose textural transcriptions of the Scots anti-monarchist and anti-Tory songs . . . I hardly need to remind you that there is no need to mention the SSS on the disc or its cover (or the booklet)!' Many of these songs were his own and Hamish was beginning to hope that the *Ding Dong Dollar* record would open up a whole new world – to him, and the Scots and Celtic Folk Revivals. Unfortunately, Hamish's hopes ran ahead of actualities. The record did not sell well. After some argument, Asch sent Hamish a cheque for $50, and Blythman sent him twenty-five copies of the *Ding Dong Dollar* record 'at cost'. Hamish writes:

> Dear Morris, thanks a million for the 25 DDDs just received. I enclose a cheque for £1-10-00. Thanks also for 'The Holy War' – though I won't sing that in Eireann. A plague on both your bonces. Frankly I see little difference (except for the taste of the songs) in the bleeding billies and the bloody dans – let us keep our particular aberrations out of the scrimmage!'

Blythman's willingness to sing sectarian songs was just one of several disagreements that distanced Hamish from Blythman at this time but a remarkable new song-writing friendship was already underway – with Pete Seeger, the leading American protest singer. Seeger had known of Hamish's *Ballads of World War II* since 1947 but it was not until 5 January 1960 that they made direct contact – by letter – Seeger writing:

> Dear Hamish Henderson, I write you on the spur of the moment, because I have fallen in love with two songs you wrote the words for: Farewell to Sicily and D-Day Dodgers. Until this time I had only heard your name as a professor and collector of Scottish folk music . . . Re 'Sing Out' [Seeger's magazine] would you have time to write for it . . . might we print these two songs, and also at the same time print one of your favourites of the old Scottish songs . . . it reaches thousands of young people who are exploring the problems of how to reconstitute valid folk traditions . . . PS how I wish American audiences could sing with the deep-throated full tone that I heard in Glasgow.

In April Seeger informed Hamish, 'your songs will go in "Sing Out" in the next edition, and I'll send you a copy immediately . . . I am in England first three weeks of November.' Appearing at the Usher Hall in Edinburgh, Seeger spoke publicly of his great admiration for Hamish, and in his notebook Hamish was equally complimentary about Seeger: 'I have achieved a personal ambition in meeting this man.' In October 1961 Hamish wrote:

> Dear Pete, I've just come back from a late holiday in Ireland and found a leaning tower of letters – including your own, and one from a lad who listened to your rendering of 'The Freedom Come-All-Ye' at Carnegie Hall on 16 September. I'm most pleased to hear you like the song, and that you're already singing it . . . Of the songs in Ding Dong Dollar, only two – 'The Freedom Come-All-Ye' and the sequence called 'Anti-Polaris' are by me. These you are at liberty to print in 'Sing Out'. For the others you should contact Morris Blythman – who is the inspirer and begetter of the whole collection, and author (or part-author) of most of them – Here is a glossary for my own song.

Hamish enclosed a £4 cheque for the Committee defending Seeger against charges by the Un-American Activities Committee. In December Seeger wrote to thank Hamish and Katzel for the hospitality they had offered him: 'Toshi [Seeger's wife] and I are still full of warm memories of the people we met in Scotland and England. And what we learnt and what we saw we only hope we can repay some way during our life . . . how I wish some of you could visit our cold country, because all the records and song books are not as good as meeting face to face.' In June 1962 Seeger sent less welcome news:

> The 'Ding Dong Dollar' record has not received the explosions we had hoped for. I think frankly the people who oppose it are scared to publicise it. Unfortunately, however, even people who support it are not giving it enough publicity . . . My favourite song on the record is still the 'Freedom Come A' Ye'. However, I must say I sing mostly, everywhere I go, the theme song 'Ding Dong Dollar' and also 'Ye'll no sit here'. The chorus of 'Ding Dong Dollar' appears to me more fundamental and greater every time I hear it. 'Ye cannae spend a dollar when you're dead': – this is a theme song for the world these days . . .

Finally, in 1962, the criminal charges against Seeger were flung out by the US Court of Appeals – acting with the authority of President Kennedy's new broom. That Christmas, Hamish sent Seeger his 'Song of the Gillie More', and the warmth of his feelings for the man whom he described as his 'closest American friend' are clear in this diary note made in the seventies:

> Pete Seeger – 'If I had a song to sing / I'd sing out a love between / My brothers and my sisters / All over the world' – those words sum up the man – 'America's Tuning Fork'. Seeger's variation of the traditional spiritual 'We Shall Overcome' was to become, as the Black Civil Rights movement gathered momentum, the anthem of the crusade for equality in America . . .

It was Seeger's manager (Harold Leventhal) who, in April 1963, organised Bob Dylan's first major public concert, at the Town Hall in New York. This followed the Cuban Missile Crisis and it is important to remember that Scotland's Anti-Polaris Campaign – and the songs it engendered – preceded this great 'Dylan moment' by two years. Throughout 1962 Hamish was active in CND's attempts to forestall the crisis looming – frequently in league with Dorrie Dickie, Bertrand Russell's Committee of 100[9] representative in Scotland. On 24 March 1962 Hamish published an article in *The Economist*. In April 1962 he gave the keynote address at an Edinburgh symposium, 'Scottish poets and the Bomb': he began by quoting the Brahan Seer:[10] 'When the black rain falls, Scotland will rise . . .'

In the autumn, as the crisis became intense, he (with a group of CND activists) wrote to the Soviet leader: 'Dear Mr Kruschev – we ask you to understand that if, as you say, the USSR really wants disarmament and a peaceful world, it should stop trying to turn revolutionary nations like Cuba into military satellites.' He wrote to the *Glasgow Herald* (using the pseudonym Mr L. Sand): 'Dear Sir, The USA can no longer encircle the world with military bases and insist that there can be no Communist base on the American continent.' Speaking at an Edinburgh anti-war rally, he was even bolder:

> It is incumbent on all of us to disassociate ourselves from this madness and, once this crisis is surmounted – for I do not think Khrushchev will allow the world to destroy itself – we must labour with redoubled energy to try and secure unilateral nuclear disarmament on the part of Britain . . . Karl Marx wrote that previous philosophers had tried to explain the world – but the point is 'to change it'. We can now revise that: 'the point is to save it!' . . . Kennedy, as a philosopher, is the 'last of the Whigs'. What is there in the conventicles of the West that puts conscience before life – even the life of the world? Kennedy – the millionaire – is a man who by the very nature of his background has very little in common with 99% of toiling humanity . . . Khrushchev is a professional politician who, in spite of deformation, is a member of a movement which has its roots in a millennial wish to benefit humanity, and bring human beings to fulfilment, and not to destroy it. As for Castro allowing Russian bases in Cuba, let those who hold up their hands in horror remember that every reactionary government in the world that had land to donate to the USA was delighted to do it! . . . Castro and his revolution: every generous longing in the youth of Latin America must respond to him . . . And Scotland

9 A radical British anti-war group set up in 1960; Russell stood down from his presidency of CND to form this group.

10 The Brahan Seer was a seventeenth-century Scottish visionary.

> – Scotland must be in the United Nations. But who will speak? Lord Home, Harold Macmillan? No! We need a Scottish Voice. We need Home Rule!

On 24 October 1962 (United Nations Day) – the day that President Kennedy announced his Blockade of Cuba – Hamish sent this letter to Harold Macmillan: 'We the undersigned members of Edinburgh University staff, aware that we are in danger of world nuclear war, urge you to disassociate Great Britain publicly from both the recent Russian acts in regard of Cuba and the precipitous and illegal American response to it . . . We ask that you press for immediate action through the United Nations alone, to prevent any hostility.' As the Crisis dissipated itself Hamish jotted down a few more aphorisms: 'No taxation without representation / No annihilation without consultation!', 'The strain of hysteria in US life / The rich nation which makes next / To no provision for the poor and the old . . . '.

The Missile Crisis engendered a worldwide demand for peace – not least in Greece where, in April 1963, Grigoris Lambrakis, a charismatic socialist member of Parliament, helped organise a huge anti-nuclear peace march. The plan was to march from the Mound of Marathon to Athens. When the march was banned, Lambrakis (asserting his rights as an MP) marched alone. It was a heroic, symbolic act and he became a hero of the International Peace Movement. A month later, after giving a speech in Thessaloniki, Lambrakis was killed by rightwing extremists in a well-planned 'road-accident'. Hamish felt it his duty to honour him in song. He gathered all the news reports he could lay hands on: 'Women dressed in black threw red carnations on the coffin of Grigoris Lambrakis, the left-wing Greek MP who was killed by a motorcycle in Salonika after a "peace rally", when he was borne to burial in Athens today . . . When the coffin was carried out of the Cathedral to be put on the hearse 20,000 Athenians blocked the square shouting "Peace", "Pace", "no more blood", and "democracy". A huge procession formed and 50,000 people lined the route to the cemetery – where more than two hundred wreaths scented the air and made red the earth around the waiting grave.'[11] On 31 May Hamish wrote to the Greek Ambassador in London:

> Dear Sir – I am engaged in writing a poem, Heroic Song for Grigoris Lambrakis – in honour of the latest in the renowned roll of Greek heroes. The poem extols his noble act in managing the Marathon-Athens march alone, and tries to do justice to his intrepid courage. As the facts about his atrocious murder are rather hard to ascertain from the short accounts in the British press, I should be most grateful if you could give me the full picture and the real facts as known by the

11 Uncaptioned newspaper cutting, Henderson archive.

Embassy. I am particularly interested in the identity of his murderer – or murderers – and what their background is.

Not surprisingly, Hamish got no satisfactory answers from the Greek Ambassador and few politicians, anywhere, addressed the murder with the seriousness it deserved. Even the Manchester *Guardian* ran a supercilious headline: 'Political Jamboree at Deputy's Funeral'. Stan Awbery, MP, responded with anger:

> The death, your correspondent said was the best opportunity that the anti-government forces had had for years of showing their strength in the streets of Athens. No word about the respect that was shown to the great man. Even the peacefulness of the crowd was given a slant to sting the Opposition. They wanted, he said, to create a contrast to show that the government could only keep the peace by the use of thugs . . . To call the funeral gathering a jamboree (a jolly gathering) was nauseating . . . The article did not express the intimate and intense emotion of the 200,000 people who came to mourn the man they loved, and one the world can ill-afford to lose. Whatever we think about Nuclear Arms we must recognise that Grigoris Lambrakis has been made a martyr for world peace and friendship. His death and the circumstances around it will have great repercussions in Greece and in many nations . . . Lambrakis was an assistant professor at Athens University, an outstanding gynaecologist and also a great sportsman . . . The incidences are reminiscent of the rise of Fascism in Germany which was permitted to pass unheeded at the time and ultimately led to world war. The nations cannot afford to ignore this fact.

On 1 June Hamish wrote to the *Guardian*: 'Sir . . . It is quite amazing to me that a paper with the traditions of the Guardian should ever have published a piece like "Political Jamboree at Deputy's Burial". At the moment I am writing an "Heroic Song for Grigoris Lambrakis" which tries to pay tribute to his noble act in marching alone from Marathon to Athens to take part in the Bertrand Russell March . . . In the poem I shall try to put some of my feelings about his death into words. My thanks, again, to Stan Awbery for the timeliest and most eloquent letter I have read for a long time.' There is, however, something lame about this letter and – hard as Hamish tried – he was never able to finish his song. A new baby, drink, lack of funds, lack of intellectual support all conspired to exhaust his capacity for creative and intellectual work.[12]

---

12 In 1969 Vassilis Vassilikos published 'Z', a novel centred on the Lambrakis affair. It became an international bestseller and seethes with exactly the passion that Hamish had hoped to articulate in song. (Hamish's poetical jottings are in the Henderson archive.)

During the mid sixties Hamish campaigned against American involvement in the war in Vietnam but this was one campaign in which his role was not a leading one. An elected member of the Edinburgh Council for Peace in Vietnam, on 9 August 1965 he signed a letter to the *Scotsman* welcoming the public to a meeting: 'at which Mrs Verdun Perl and Lawrence Daly will speak for Peace, free elections, withdrawal of foreign troops'. He wrote this haiku:

> Viet Cong: peak of valour,
> This name becomes them,
> – Now, what name becomes us?[13]

A friend of Hamish's who saw service in Vietnam was Mary Brooksbank of Dundee, a self-educated mill-worker who gave her life to peace campaigning and the communist cause. In the early sixties Hamish helped Maurice Fleming organise publication of a book of her poems and songs. In 1970, at the age of seventy-three, she went out to Hanoi to tend the wounded and help rebuild a city being bombed 'round the clock' by B52 bombers. In the 1930s Mary Brooksbank had spoken out against the brutalities of Stalinism; now she kept Hamish informed of an equal brutality. On St Andrew's Day 1970 she posted him a card with an image of the North Vietnam leader Ho Chi Minh:

> Dear Hamish – To celebrate our national Saint's Day – I send you a thought – I think I am the only Scot in Vietnam, certainly in Hanoi! But what about you? I saw a rumour just before I left that the hound of the law had been after you. I cannot believe this is true! How safe I feel here. Ah Hamish how I wish we in Scotland were in this condition! When I say this to the Vietnamese they laugh – surely I must be joking. 'We are so poor', they say. If they could see us at home they would know what I mean. There is a quality of life here which seems to me, the more I know of it, like paradise – like the dreaming of all great revolutionaries. Send me a card – a view from Arthur's Seat.

The following year, Mary wrote to Hamish from London. She extols the virtues and power of song as a force for peace and human brotherhood and ends her letter with a quotation from James Connolly, the Irish socialist republican – whom her father had known in Edinburgh – executed in Dublin in 1916:

> No revolutionary movement is complete without its poetical expression. If such a movement has caught hold of the imagination of the masses they will seek a vent in song for their aspirations, their fears

13 HH, unpublished haiku, Henderson archive.

> and hopes, loves and hatreds engendered by the struggle. Until this movement is marked by the joyous, defiant singing of revolutionary songs, it lacks one of the most distinctive marks of a proper revolutionary movement. It is a dogma of the few and not the faith of the multitude.

At about this time, Hamish wrote down this quatrain:

> The crowd hailed Jesus
> That soon howled for his blood –
> How glad they must have been
> To get back to normal.[14]

14 HH, unpublished quatrain, Henderson archive.

NINE

The Politics of Action

Scottish Nationalism is not a temporary phenomenon. It will remain a political issue until Scotland enjoys political autonomy . . .

HH, 1967[1]

The adventurism that marked Hamish's political activities in the immediate post-war period reached a climax with the Conspiracy Trial of November 1953 (see Volume 1), but neither his work at the School of Scottish Studies nor the gradual return of economic prosperity to Scotland reduced his revolutionary ardour. At the time of the trial he noted, 'Motto: damn the turning back.' On Saturday 19 February 1955 he notes, 'Pay Calum for 4 conspirators.' This payment involved a car with number plate FOU 4531. If the Calum referred to was Calum Campbell, the nationalist publisher, Campbell's subsequent imprisonment for 'embezzlement' may be explained. At about this time Oscar Brand, an American folksinger, wrote offering Hamish his support in relation to 'the four convicted . . . My hand will always be on your shoulder when you need someone to stand by.' Throughout the fifties Hamish remained in close contact with the Behans and Irish Republicans in Dublin. In January 1957, Dominic Behan[2] wrote to him from London.

> Hamish *a Cara dil* – The Burns Nicht. Down here we have two technicians (real ones) and the most modern equipment ready for transportation to Glasgow on 25th January [Burns Night] – Hamish MacAndreass – Spike Milligan (Immortal Memory), a piper, Jimmy Callan choir . . . We await, by return, your assurance the blessing of *an Taeseach* [the war-chief] Henderson will descend on the Night . . . Ah Hamish, the liberties I take with that Highland generosity of yours, is sometimes beyond me. And yet look at all the important things I can do for you, I can for instance, introduce you, anytime, to the governor of Mountjoy, of Brixton, Portlaishe, of Wandsworth – wherever you wish. You don't wish – oh well, just thought I'd offer.

1 Unpublished notes, Henderson archive.

2 According to Marian Blythman, Behan claimed to be a captain in the IRA.

1956 had been a year of international political turmoil. Soviet communism was in crisis. Israel, Britain and France were planning an autumn invasion of Egypt, and the Hungarian Uprising would follow it. As was often the case, Hamish seems to have been ahead of the game. In March 1956 he informed his communist friend Phil Stein that he was writing a history of the failure of the Communist Party in Scotland.

> Dear Phil, I am at present writing a short account – purely historical and for the archives – 'Scottish Left-wing politics and the national Question 1945–55'. In this I am recording the reasons for the stultification of the most promising national revival of Scottish Home Rule agitation for many years – the high point of which was the Covenant with its two million signatures. The general thesis is that the leadership was not forthcoming in the quarters that might well have provided it, and I am examining the reasons for this in the light of recent developments in the Soviet Union [the exposure of Stalinism by Khrushchev].

Stein did not reply. On 19 June 1956 Hamish wrote again:

> Much of my study is complete – however, in spite of offers from several Communist Party sources, including yourself, so far not one line has materialised . . . Instead of being able to quote documents verbatim I shall be forced to paraphrase them as accurately as my memory allows. I do not think the general authenticity of these passages will be questioned by future historians . . . This is the last letter I shall send to trouble you in this connection.
>
> I was glad to see a letter in the 'Worker' a week or two back about the persecution of the Jewish cultural minority in the USSR. It was signed P.S., so I presumed it was you. In any case I applaud it 'whether or not'. It was also heartening yesterday to read the resumé of Togliatti's article in 'L'Unita'. This confirms my respect for Togliatti himself, worthy heir to the great tradition of Gramsci. Let's hope that in the not too distant future Scotland too will throw up someone of like calibre prepared to fight boldly and intelligently for working class emancipation within the context of his own national tradition. No future seller-out, or subordinator, of his country to England, no burker of his nation's most pressing needs and aspirations, no abdicator or acceptor of a 'line' from outwith Scotland's borders. Do you think it possible? Who knows? Maybe Stalingrad at some future date might acclaim him as enthusiastically as it has Tito.

Hamish was pursuing intellectual ends but also advertising his availability – as the leader of a new, humanist Communist Party in Scotland. Neither

Stein nor the Scottish leadership responded. In November (the month of the suppression in Hungary) Hamish stopped thumping his head against a wall of Party obduracy. He wrote to Stein: 'Dear Phil – Interested, as you can imagine, in the simple problem: who is a crook and who is not, in your set-up – I look forward to your next Friday's "Scottish Diary" – either people mean what they say, or they do not. I am not prepared to tolerate "Rakoci tactics" any further . . . ' He then jotted the stirrings of a poem:

> There is the crowning in thorns
> Our heids under
> Our whole lives long
> Or the faces of bronze
> Who gave to the workers
> A ragged pottage of red banners – chairborne
> tartuffes.[3]

In England, Hamish's old friend E.P. Thompson[4] was endeavouring to effect a similar 'velvet revolution'. Having abandoned the CPGB, Thompson was working to found a new Communist Party with a 'human face'. He launched a magazine, *The New Reasoner*. Over the years it published various articles by Hamish (and some of his Gramsci letters) but its influence, beyond narrow intellectual circles, was small. The tide of history had turned and there was nothing for men and women of their persuasion to do but batten down the hatches. In 1967 Hamish wrote to Stein, 'Perhaps I told the truth about the CP too soon?' Stein's reply was a mixture of anger and wisdom-after-the-event:

> Dear Hamish, You are a great lad for seeing sinister bogies where none exist – what put me off in maintaining the warm and sympathetic personal relationship we had built-up, was the violence of your attack on my probity some years back. It came right out of the blue one day in the International Club and left me completely hurt, flabbergasted and disorientated . . . You undoubtedly saw the truth about the CP and the USSR a lot sooner than me. You might be described as 'a premature anti-Stalinist'.

Far from appeased, Hamish wrote back on 3 March 1967:

> As for your 'probity', you know as well as I do that Stalinism played havoc with the probity of a whole lot of people. If you feel that you are the exception proving the rule, I will freely leave that to your

3 HH, unpublished notes, Henderson archive.

4 E.P. Thompson (1924–1993), Marxist historian who helped found CND.

> own conscience . . . I think that an impartial study of your own development as a writer and journalist would show that you owed me not a little when I was seeing a lot of you and discussing politics and literature with you . . . You even took over some characteristic phrases that I used, and indeed I was pleased at this . . . I was also the more annoyed therefore, when I discovered that you were perfectly capable of drawing a line of silence under all this . . . I first invited you to the School over 14 years ago. This was one of the great periods of modern folk collecting – I renew the invitation but if you come we shall not talk about these past failures, but about the political and artistic possibilities of Scotland, which I am more than ever convinced are fruitful and promising.

* * *

When friends or relatives died, Hamish always quickly moved on: so it was with politics. By 1960 he was close to two independently minded Scots intellectuals, Tom Nairn and a communist school teacher, Jack Mitchell. Mitchell found work in East Germany and played a seminal role in nurturing Scots folksong behind the Iron Curtain. Hamish helped him translate a number of MacDiarmid's poems into German and with research for a book about Willie Gallacher (a former leader of the CPGB and father-in-law to Phil Stein) and the history of communism in Britain. When Mitchell translated 'The Freedom Come a' Ye' into German, Hamish gave him the manuscript of his first draft of the last verse. In a series of articles exploring Hamish's work as a poet, songwriter and political thinker, Mitchell presents Hamish as a representative of a Scots–European tradition going back to Duns Scotus, George Buchanan and Hume.

As the CPGB floundered into obscurity, Hamish was delighted to be invited to become a founder member of Fife Socialist League led by Lawrence Daly, a miner at Glencraig colliery near Kirkcaldy. Daly was a Scots Home Ruler, a singer, a self-educated intellectual, and Hamish soon had a very high opinion of him. The south Fife Coalfield was one of the poorest areas in Britain and it remained a hotbed of leftwing activism. The Socialist League called for 'Peace, Prosperity and Scottish Self-Government'. In 1958 Daly was elected Fife County Councillor for the Ballingry Ward. In 1959 Hamish joined the campaign to get Daly to Westminster as an MP, the year of Harold Macmillan's 'never had it so good' General Election. E.P. Thompson and John Saville[5] came up from England 'to help found a Party with intellectual depth and organisational rigour' and, on platforms, Hamish would introduce Daly as 'a man with the makings of a Scottish Statesman'. Daly did not

5 John Saville, socialist economic and social historian, co-editor of the *Dictionary of Labour Biography*.

win his seat, and the Tories won the election handsomely. Daly's regard for Hamish is clear in this letter of 26 January 1960:

> Dear Hamish, Thank you sincerely for the 'Elegies' – it is a gift which I will greatly treasure . . . The ceilidh was so popular that there is a great demand for another. I enclose a draft policy statement. It was written by Alex Duncan of Glenrothes, a solicitor. The style suffers in consequence. You'll also note he's a bit over cautious on self-government, even not using the word 'Parliament' – is there any way you can come over to our next meeting to steer a firm course between the contending parties?

In April 1963 Hamish portrays Daly with equal generosity in a letter to the American folklorist Ken Goldstein (to whom Hamish had introduced Daly in 1959):

> [Daly and I] had a most interesting talk about Peking polemics, and Yevtushenko's in the soup again, and Silent Spring, and Warfare States, and mask-makers, and hidden persuaders, and professional folk-singers, and indeed about most everything. It's a great pity Lawrence is not at Westminster, for he is a born Statesman with the soul of a poet. Maybe the trouble is he's too honest to be a politician. Anyway he's doing a lot of people a lot of good in the Fife Coalfield.[6]

Hamish liked to think of the Fife Socialist League as having taken up the banner advanced by John Maclean fifty years previously and he used the League as an instrument to revive interest in Maclean. Plans to found a John Maclean Society were set in motion but progress was slow – perhaps because MI5 appears to have sought to destabilise the Society even before it was formed. On 10 November 1967, having been invited by a 'Mr Smith' to support 'a proposed John MacLean Society', Hamish replied with a letter of testy wariness:

> Before I give you permission [to use the John MacLean March], I'd like to know what you propose to put on this leaflet, apart from the text of the song . . . Re the projected 'John MacLean Society'. May I ask who the 'prominent Scots' are who have called for its formation with such forceful unity? So far no Scots, either prominent or obscure, have succeeded in bringing about such a simple thing as the publication of John Broom's biography [of Maclean]. Any society

6 Edinburgh was now Hamish's adopted home, and the city's architectural heritage meant much to him. In the fifties he fought hard against the university's plans to redevelop George Square. In the mid sixties he was active in the campaign to stop a planned Inner Ring Road for Edinburgh.

> using the name Maclean, and inaugurated in his honour, would have to be genuinely broad-based, with no sectarian overtones, such as the thoughts of Chairman Hoxha etc. If it started as – or degenerated into – a mere 'front' organisation, it would assuredly come to grief, and be less than useless.

If this 'Mr Smith' is the same Mr Smith who was within a few years to become a leading figure in British Intelligence in Scotland, Hamish's 'antennae' must be adjudged highly sensitive. He was, however, equally demanding of genuine Maclean enthusiasts. For example, when approached by Matthew Lygate, a youthful member of the Workers Party of Scotland (WPS), he writes:

> There are few Scots in our whole history who so fully deserve the honour and love of those who come after as John Maclean, and few who have had less recognition . . . I hope that a word of warning will not seem out of place. Any 'cult of John Maclean' which in any way resembles the Burns cult in Scotland would saddle him and be worse than useless. We must aim to guard against any type of sectarianism that could be used as a death-mask for John Maclean, or used to cover his noble features and ideas. If the society keeps these twin dangers in mind and acts with sure-footedness and skill I believe you cannot fail to do great work for Scotland and the Scottish people in the days that lie ahead.

Hamish recognised Lygate's strengths and weaknesses. In 1966 Lygate had helped Tom Murray (a Communist International Brigader) to set up the WPS (along Marxist–Maoist lines) and enticed distinguished figures such as Naomi Mitchison, Douglas Young and Hugh MacDiarmid to contribute articles to the Party magazine, *Scottish Vanguard*. During 1968 Lygate played an honourable role in establishing the John Maclean Society but – both disturbed and provoked – he subsequently joined a subgroup of the WPS that robbed banks and slid into pure criminality. It is a pity he did not heed the warnings implicit in Hamish's letter.

Meantime Hamish's recurrent skirmishes with Wilfred Taylor at the *Scotsman* continued. The 1966 Edinburgh Festival featured a new play about Garcia Lorca, by Bettina Jonic. Hamish saw it as 'wilfully revisionist and a plain-wrong interpretation of the Lorca story'. When the play ended he publicly decried the production: 'Lorca was a Republican, Lorca was committed to the revolutionary cause, Lorca's death was no accident! Lorca was murdered by Falangist fascists! This play is an assault upon the facts of history.'[7] He suggested that there were clear parallels between Spain in the thirties and the new civil war unfolding in South Africa. 'The

7 HH, conversation with TN, c. 1987.

armed struggle in South Africa is a direct result of the murderous suppression of the black population by the Apartheid government – orchestrated by that infamous ex-Nazi, Dr Verwoerd! Fascism continues its dirty work here and now! This production is a disgrace to Edinburgh!' Such public interventions tend to be frowned on in Edinburgh, and Wilfred Taylor used his 'A Scotsman's Log' in an attempt to turn the tables on Hamish:

> . . . So many of us, far from events, and without a true appreciation of the complexities involved are inclined to impose a quick emotional solution which makes us feel good without having to suffer any consequences. It's just as important to understand the Verwoerd mentality as to abhor it . . . Verwoerd is an intellectual . . . Dr Verwoerd's political philosophy led to apartheid which presumably stemmed from his reasoned conviction that in a society like South Africa if you can't or won't integrate two distinct populations all you can do is segregate them and allow them to develop independently.[8]

This public rebuke stimulated Hamish to make private notes about the history of 'the criminality' associated with the name 'Log', its being the *nom de plume* of a friend of William Hare (of Burke and Hare): 'Hare inherited both the lodgings house and the widow of a man named Log – when he died in Tanner's Close, Edinburgh . . . Mrs Log put out a board advertising "Beds to Let" and Mr Hare moved in.' Historical synchronicities delighted Hamish and it was with interest that on 12 January 1968 he notes 'Log' announcing: 'it is exactly 28 years since we started writing a newspaper column'. Their paths crossed again in the autumn when another 'extraordinary killing' hit the headlines – 'The Garvie Affair'. Maxwell Garvie, a wealthy farmer from Aberdeenshire and Scottish National Party (SNP) activist, had been brutally murdered. After months of delay, Garvie's wife and her mysterious young lover were charged and convicted of murder. During the trial Garvie's personal and political reputation was 'dragged through the mud' and salaciously taken up by the tabloid press – and by Wilfred Taylor. On 12 December 1968 Hamish wrote an indignant letter to the *Scotsman* criticising Taylor's involvement in a gratuitous and unnecessary assault upon 'the victim' of a murder. 'What is one to say of the oleaginous religiosity which accepts and appears to confirm the defamation of a dead man, put into circulation by his murderers, just because it can be used as a peg on which to hang a swatch of dubious "moral" pleading. I find this quite disgraceful.' Helen Cruickshank wrote a ballad about the murder. Hamish made a final note: 'Wilfred Taylor is the sort of journalist who loves awards. He loves them as Ramsay MacDonald loved a duchess.'

---

8 'A Scotsman's Log', *Scotsman*, August 1966.

In 1967 Winnie Ewing had won the Hamilton by-election for the SNP. Hamish had long predicted that the National Question would return to the high table of Scottish politics. He was delighted, and briefly tempted to join the Party. His excitement at the SNP's burgeoning growth is clear in this addendum he added to a questionnaire he returned to Sandy Hobbs, a member of the Labour Party in Glasgow, that year.

> Scottish Nationalism is not a temporary phenomenon. It will remain a political issue until Scotland enjoys political autonomy . . . At this moment Scottish Nationalism is in many ways an aspect of world-wide 'protest'. It is no accident that the authors of the most vigorous anti-Polaris songs are also the authors of the most effective nationalist songs (Morris Blythman, Jim MacLean etc.) By contrast Wilsonite Labourism seems a buttress of the establishment: it supports Johnson in Vietnam, recognises the Colonels in Greece, kow-tows to the bonces of international finance . . . On balance, we should give our support to the SNP in the present political circumstances.
>
> Nationalism, which in the C19th meant Garibaldi and Mazzini, has in this century acquired a bad name, being associated in the popular mind with Hitler and Mussolini. This semantic obfuscation need not worry us. Scottish fascism (demanded by Hugh MacDiarmid in the early 20's) has never been more than a lunatic fringe of the Scottish Home Rule movement. Anglo-phobia – a racist anti-Englishness – is self confessed political infantilism. The SNP, to its credit, has shown that it does not want racists and anti-democrats as members. Scottish Socialists have everything to gain – and darn little to lose – by reinforcing the leftward looking ranks of the SNP, before the next Tory landslide in England.

The nationalist revival revived Hamish's own political ambitions. On 28 November 1967 Marian Sugden wrote to him: 'Winnie Ewing's Hamilton by-election must have delighted you – and I really do hope you are considering nursing a constituency yourself. As an extra carrot to dangle for you towards that, we've got a tiny flat in Westminster which is largely unused in the week.' No Party made him an offer and he was soon embroiled in another colourful sideshow. With the rise of the SNP came a revival of romantic nationalism and in 1967 the 1320 Club was formed. It took its name from the year in which the Declaration of Arbroath had been signed; Club president was Glasgow nationalist Oliver Brown; vice president, Ian Taylor; secretary, Max Bancroft; treasurer, Edwin D. White; and the coordinator, J. Russell Thomson. Lord Boyd Orr of Brechin was chief patron and Major F.A.C. Boothby (an English in-comer) asked that he be known as 'the organiser'. Its aims were fourfold:

1 The Club has as its object the re-establishment of a Sovereign Independent Scotland.
2 It seeks to assist this aim by publication of controversial literature, and by the holding of debates, conferences and rallies.
3 It seeks to ensure that Scotland, on regaining its freedom, shall not fall victim to English-style Party Politics.
4 It seeks to ensure that the ancient Scottish tradition of the Sovereign people shall be maintained and that politicians shall ever be servants, not masters, of the Scottish State.

Hugh MacDiarmid became an enthusiastic adherent. Hamish was invited to join but refused when he learned that membership lists would be secret and 'unavailable to the public, or to members who are not on the Club Executive, which is solely responsible for choosing members'. Indeed, he quickly realised that the 1320 Club was an establishment grouping to which he was utterly opposed and, constitutionally, likely to derail the nationalist cause. Winnie Ewing agreed, and on 21 February 1968 Hamish wrote a letter to the *Scotsman* articulating the dangers of allowing the nationalist movement to be high-jacked by 'the 1320 dead-enders':

> Groups of 'self-elected elect' have always been the bane of Scottish Home Rule politics. Gathered in disputatious huddles on the periphery of whatever rational and coherent activity they can find to disrupt, the self-elected Elect have done much to make Scottish self-government a subject of mockery not only South of the border but amongst broad masses of the Scottish people as well. As often as not, their farcical, self-important professions of secrecy arouse a healthy public mistrust as regards the intention, capability and motives of the national movement as a whole . . . I for one, am absolutely convinced that about the only thing that can now seriously hinder Scotland's development into a self-respecting adult community in effective control of its own affairs is the big-headed presumption of the 'Self-elected Elect'. It is surely more than ever vital that the advance to Home Rule, so urgently needed, should not only be democratic but be seen to be democratic. Also there is no use blinking at the fact that the self-elected Elect are a pure godsend to the vast army of narks, agent provocateurs and political agents of all persuasions who are a disagreeable reality of mid-twentieth century politics . . . Mrs Ewing and her associates are surely to be congratulated for doing the necessary and no doubt harder thing, showing *them* where to get off.

This is an important letter, not least because it was written at the moment when sectarian antagonisms were about to precipitate two generations of 'civil war' in Northern Ireland. Not surprisingly, this letter aroused the wrath of the 1320 Club's 'organiser', Major F.A.C. Boothby. On 26 February 1968 he wrote to Hamish:

> I refer to your letter in today's Scotsman – I do not think any intelligent person could doubt that you are referring to an article by Hugh MacDiarmid entitled 'The Close Brethren of the SNP Junta' and that the object of your accusations and insinuations is the 1320 Club, of whose committee I am a member.
>
> It would appear to be necessary to draw your attention to the heading of the above mentioned article, which reads: 'any attempt to attribute the article to anyone else, or to any form of Association will result in proceedings being taken . . . ' Further the article is marked 'copyright'.
>
> The public knows that you have an apparently irresistible impulse to intervene with dubious comments in matters which only marginally concern you. Perhaps you will now say whether you are desirous that I should implement the warning contained at the head of the article quoted? I am enclosing a copy of a letter to William Wolfe, which may show you how uninformed interventions can prejudice delicate negotiations.
>
> You and I both fought for the same cause, in the same Army, in the same desert at the same time. I would like to think we are still fighting in the same army. Consequently it would greatly upset me to move against a man of your standing and reputation. I would suggest to you that some form of redress is indicated. Perhaps another letter to the Scotsman indicating that you wrote without full information?

The Major's letter was designed to intimidate so Hamish wrote back:

> You are wrong. I have not seen MacDiarmid's article . . . In the same post which brought me your bad-mannered screed I received half-a-dozen letters of support . . . I have used the term 'Close Brethren' for years in this context to describe the people in Scottish politics, literature and life, who adopt a bumptiously exclusive attitude to others. If MacDiarmid thinks he has copyrighted the phrase, he had better think again . . . Since you are not above personal rudeness – 'the public knows etc.' – I see no reason why I should not tell you that your letter is a load of nonsense, and if you were 'to move against me' (as you put it) on such ludicrous nugatory grounds, you would make yourself a laughing stock.

By return of post, Boothby sent this lame but vainglorious and patronising reply:

> I must apologise for having dinged you on the neb without, as it turns out, proper provocation. Never mind, you dinged back with spirit! It is tragic how people base their actions on gutter press and gutter snipes without checking the facts. More tragic still that Nationalists should attack Nationalists, and yet more tragic that the SNP should be bent on cutting its own throat on Saturday, despite non-stop efforts by the more intelligent and imaginative of its members to prevent this rather permanent process. Can you do anything? I would hope to meet you one day. Boothby.

There things might have rested but MacDiarmid, having taken Hamish's remarks about an 'army of narks, agent provocateurs and political agents' as a reference to himself, joined the fray with this letter to the *Scotsman* on 26 February 1968:

> Sir, It is natural that Mr Henderson should inveigh against intellectuals and dub them 'self-elected'. His concept of 'democracy' is what concurs with majority opinion . . . People do vary in intellectual status. Why defy this in favour of the undifferentiated mass, or accede to the demand of the latter that superior brains should acquiesce in the delineation of their political and other objectives to conciliate the mass who cannot see beyond their noses?

Hamish believed this letter showed MacDiarmid at his worst and replied with brutal directness, in a letter published in the *Scotsman* on 29 February. His aim was to alert the Scottish public to present dangers by making reference to MacDiarmid's fascist past (and by association, Boothby's):

> Hugh MacDiarmid's contempt for the 'undifferentiated mass', and his predilection for a kind of 'samurai sword' politics, with a high-tone elite holding sway over the common weill, are by now well and truly familiar to your readers. What they may not so widely realise is that Mr MacDiarmid has on occasion given these attitudes quite concrete political expression. For example in his article, 'Programme for a Scottish Fascism' (The Scottish Nation, Montrose 19 June 1923), he wrote: 'The entire Fascist programme can be readapted to Scottish national purposes and is (whether it be called fascism or pass under any other name), the only thing that will preserve our distinctive national culture' . . . He wrote those words after the march on Rome, and at a time when beatings-up and castor-oil dosings were

> causing as much concern throughout Europe as the revolting details of torture in Greek prisons currently being investigated by Amnesty International.
>
> I am quite aware, of course, that since then MacDiarmid has changed sides politically as often as a Chinese warlord during a civil war – but if there is any single thing which gives a kind of unity to his various tergiversations, it is precisely this authoritarian strain.

Hamish's critique was devastating and Tom Hyde of 'Earraid', Edinburgh, immediately took him to task, writing: 'Dear Sir, I am appalled that a Scot in your position should allow yourself to be used to create dissent and confusion in the ranks of those fighting to save their country from extinction . . . One can only suppose that you are working off some personal spleen, which may be understandable but hardly excuses you. (The man is over eighty you know). And "The Scotsman" will use anything to discredit us.' Hamish was not persuaded and wrote back:

> Thank you for your letter. Chris Grieve is not 'over eighty'. He is an exceedingly swack 75, and his polemical vigour remains unabated – as anyone who has read his recent articles and letters will know . . . I have a great admiration for Chris's poetry [but] this does not mean that one has to support his political cantrips. He lost his way politically many years ago, and is still in the wood. For years I have held my tongue on his bad influence on the Scottish Home Rule movement, but this 1320 nonsense is too much. I am surprised that anyone who considers himself intelligent should fall for it.

In March 1968 the 1320 Club met at Glasgow University. A number of inflammatory resolutions proposed by Hugh MacDiarmid were seconded by Nicholas Fairbairn (soon to become Tory MP for Perth and Kinross) and Major Boothby was elected convenor of the Club's Armed Forces Committee! When, at the General Election of June 1970, the SNP share of the vote plunged to 11 per cent, Boothby decided to 'up his game' and initiated a series of hair-brained acts of 'terrorism' across Scotland. Following an attempting to entrap Willie Wolfe (SNP President) into giving him 'the go-ahead' to blow up oil pipelines, Boothby was, finally, exposed as a charlatan. By April 1972 even MacDiarmid had his doubts, writing to the 1320 Club magazine, *Catalyst*: 'If Boothby is playing a double game, he must be exposed and got rid of . . . ' Boothby then disappeared into well-earned retirement – leaving eleven of his fellow 'Scots activists' in prison.

The discovery of North Sea oil had re-ignited 'dreams of Scottish statehood' on foundations of wealth not poverty, and Boothby was just one plank on a raft of measures floated against the very idea of such dreaming. In 1971 Douglas Hurd's novel *Scotch on the Rocks* was published. It was a dramatic story about nationalist ambitions and terrorism in Scotland. At that time Hurd was an MP and Private Secretary to Ted Heath, the Prime Minister; later he would become Home Secretary and Foreign Secretary in the Thatcher governments. The novel quickly became a bestseller. At much the same time the Queen's Private Secretary, Michael Shea (writing under the pseudonym Michael Sinclair), published a similar novel entitled *The Dollar Covenant,* but Hurd's book is of particular interest because the name of his – fictional – SNP leader is James Henderson. He, and everyone around him, are presented as being both dangerous and foolish. The authors of *Britain's Secret War* describe the stereotypical approach taken by Hurd:

> James Henderson, the canny SNP leader, is a composite of several well-known SNP figures, while the impassioned and cranky Mrs Merrilees is a mocking portrait of Wendy Wood, the leader of the 'Scottish Patriots'; then there is the token SNP socialist (and typically he also turns out to be the leader of the terrorists); a glamorous and promiscuous aristocratic blonde, Sukey Dunmayne; and a selection of rude Caledonians, mostly called Hamish, representing a mythical nationalist army, the 'Scottish Liberation Army'.[9]

This Scottish Liberation Army burns down St Andrews House, blows up the Forth Bridge tollbooths, assassinates (by mistake) the Secretary of State for Scotland and eventually 'occupies' Lochaber as a prelude to a new 'Jacobite Rebellion'! The rebellion is crushed but not before 'Moscow Gold', French communists, Breton extremists and Glasgow 'razor gangs' have reduced Scotland to a broken society ruled by terror. Hurd's introduction of 'razor gangs' as the Shock Troops of the Home Rule movement sounds bizarre, but Graeme Noble, a social worker in Glasgow at the time, reports being approached by MI5 officers who were worried that Glasgow's razor thugs might be recruited for just this purpose.

When *Scotch on the Rocks* was reprinted in 1972, Wendy Wood went on hunger strike in protest. Unabashed, the BBC decided to present the novel as a five-part television series. When it was broadcast the following year the SNP protested that the BBC was disseminating government propaganda. The Director-General of the BBC, Charles Curran, defended his programme makers: 'I can see no likelihood that this fictional series will establish any kind of pattern for the real future.' When the Principal of the University of Edinburgh, Sir Michael Swann, backed him up by describing

9 Andrew Murray Scott and Iain MacLeay, *Britain's Secret War: Tartan Terrorism and the Anglo-American State* (Mainstream 1990).

the series as 'relevant, high quality television drama' Hamish wrote to the *Scotsman* (21 May 1973) to dismiss *Scotch on the Rocks* as third-rate establishment agit-prop.

By this time the likelihood that Hamish would emerge as a national leader – like General de Gaulle – had passed, but, five years earlier, his political ambitions were still real and personal. For example, in January 1968 the *Scotsman* published a letter from Hamish, which was, in essence, an address to the French nation:

> Sir – As one of the custodian nations of Celtic language and tradition, Scotland should make it perfectly clear to France that there is not the remotest chance of a 'New Alliance' in any shape or form unless and until she starts introducing a little civilisation into her treatment of the persecuted Breton minority . . . It is not sufficiently widely known that France's record in this respect is much worse than that (say) of the old Austro-Hungarian Empire, known in its day as 'the prison house of nations' . . .

The following December, the *Scotsman* published a letter from Wendy Wood in which she envisions Scotland's future national leader as a man 'beyond party' – and very like Hamish.

> Sir – It is not a 'party' leader figure that is required, but a 'national' one for the whole movement and ultimately for the nation . . . A leader who will hold the faith of the people of Scotland for Scotland through the difficulties and entanglements ahead, outwith any political party ties whatsoever, is our urgent requirement.

That Wendy Wood is trailing a cloak is obvious, and the reasons why British Intelligence should seek to watch Hamish, sow distrust and undermine the cause of the nationalist parties in Scotland is clear. One of the most unsavoury by-products of this kind of intervention concerns a friend of Hamish's called Osmond Robb. Robb had helped organise the Edinburgh People's Festivals. He seems to have been a communist and fought to keep the Festivals going. On 8 November 1955 the *Daily Worker* published a letter from Robb praising MacDiarmid's poem 'In Memoriam James Joyce'. He describes the poem as containing 'the most seething attack I know on the hypo-critical cult of "Law and Order" in the "free world". MacDiarmid's line "The Law more lawless than any criminal" sums it up – and his emphasis on individuality is much needed in our movement.' Some time after this Robb was incarcerated in the Secure Unit of the Crichton Royal Infirmary in Dumfries. He had been declared insane. Perhaps he was, but when Marian Blythman, a distinguished educationist, who knew him in the fifties, was asked about him she replied: 'Osmond Robb – I haven't thought of Osmond Robb for forty years. He was a small man. He was said to be connected with the SRA. We heard that he got delusions of grandeur, was declared paranoid and put away in a mental institution.'

Whatever the facts of Osmond Robb's history or mental condition we know he was in the Crichton Royal for many years and that Hamish was one of the very few people who kept in touch with him. He sent him bundles of Scottish literary magazines, and Robb's letters to Hamish, although occasionally self-pitying, are not irrational. In February 1974 he asked Hamish to send him 'The New Edinburgh Review – with the translation of the Gramsci Letters . . . I am as happy here as you can be in a looney bin. I have to watch it though, if you are too obviously happy they conclude you are "elated" and put you on dampening down pills which are not at all nice. I've had some . . . All the best to your wife and family . . . ' Two weeks later he wrote again:

> Dear Hamish, I am reading the Gramsci letters and can see why you think so highly of them. They remind me in some ways of Lenin's letters. There's the same keen and observant interest in everything and everybody about him, the same dialectical transition from the particular to the general and back to the particular, the same passion for philosophy . . . and there is his humour, his 'ironical' approach. In other circumstances he might have been a fine creative writer. And like Lenin, these letters show Gramsci as having the same deep concern for the health and well-being of his correspondents . . .
>
> For six years after I came here, Pat [his wife] wouldn't let me see Jenny [his daughter] – I was as cut off as Gramsci from his family and as eager for photographs and news . . . Like him I felt I was missing my child's most fascinating years – from six to twelve. At last I got the doctors to intervene on my behalf: now I see Pat and Jenny once a year . . . I have been reading Solzhenitsyn's books and enjoyed them, although I do not think he is a great writer.

Did modern Britain – like many modern totalitarian states – incarcerate a selection of its more outlandish political opponents and thinkers? Only the signatures of two medical doctors are required for someone to be declared insane. One fragment of information – from Dr Ian Olson of Aberdeen, a clinician specialising in mental health – suggests that such practices might indeed have gone on. In September 2004, Dr Olson told me that an Assistant Prison Governor had told him that 'the leadership of the SRA had been put away in the fifties and never heard of again'. When I asked, 'Are you suggesting these men were assassinated, or put away in prison?' Dr Olson replied, 'not assassinated – put away'. Some months later I linked these statements to Osmond Robb's letters. Renewing contact with Dr Olson, I told him I now understood what the

Assistant Prison Governor had meant and that the SRA leadership had been 'put away' in secure psychiatric hospitals. Dr Olson replied, 'No, Tim, he didn't mean the psychiatric hospitals – they are all inspected and anything like that would be impossible. These men were in prison – out of communication with the world.'

TEN

From Folk Tradition to the Folk Revival

I've been to balls and masquerades
I've been to London and Balquidder!
But the bonniest lass that e'er I saw
She was herdin' her yowes amang the heather.
Trad.

Hamish always took his role as an academic folklorist with a pinch of salt: he liked to 'risken things up'. After visits to the Hawick Common Riding he would buy himself a box of snuff – and take it with style. After trips to Somerset he would drink cider for weeks; coming back from Ireland it would be Bushmills and Jameson's whiskey. He liked to entertain himself as well as others. In 1956 he notes: 'All folksong kids us on. And why not? Folksong after all is largely myth, so why expect its practitioners to stick to facts when they are dealing with one of the great unrealities of life?' Consequently it is not surprising that 'Folklore' remains a controversial 'academic study' in Britain – even in the twenty-first century. During the fifties the very idea that British universities employed people to research traditional folk culture – let alone popular culture – provoked recurrent anger in sections of the academic community. The idea that a university should teach folk tradition or get involved in the creating of new folk material was anathema. However, once the archive of the School of Scottish Studies (SSS) had been set up, that is exactly what Hamish wanted to do. He saw the School as a means by which the best, the most authentic, the most poetical was used as source material – and measure – for the future wellbeing of art in Scotland. A Folk Revival had slowly been gathering momentum since the War and he believed Scots folk tradition to be an unequalled and inspiring resource not just for Scotland but the contemporary world.

Hamish did not pretend that his folk interests were unprecedented – he proudly hoped to continue the work done by earlier folk collectors like John Lorne Campbell, Gavin Greig and Cecil Sharp; writers like Whitman, Wordsworth and Burns; Shakespeare, Rabelais; singers like Homer and Ossian. Many of the world's great composers had refreshed their genius at the font of their various folk and national traditions. Hamish believed that a twentieth-century Scots Folk Revival would propel modern Scottish culture onto the world stage like nothing else. Ridiculed he might be, but across sixty years he refused to be intimidated; and gradually the cultural community in Scotland has come to see itself – and the world – from his general point of view.

For Hamish the verse that sums up the quality, mystery and reach of Scots folksong is the opening quotation of this chapter. '"I've been to London and Balquidder!" – it says the universal thing in its own way – our way!' In a world driven by materialism, institutional structures and commercial exploitation Hamish believed folksong – tested by the ages – affirmed the deeps of human nature and communal understanding. He liked to quote Vernon Watkins' poem 'The Childhood of Hölderlin':

> Because his song was pure false tongues are silent.
> Through him the dead speak, and the quick are changed.

Hamish's initial appointment at the School of Scottish Studies was as a collector, transcriber, conserver and researcher but as time passed his wish to see the tradition maintained and developed became, to him, even more important, and he was soon spending as much time cultivating new musicians and singers as recording tradition bearers. By the late fifties the Folk Revival was a worldwide phenomenon. Looking back in the early 1970s, Hamish noted the following reasons for this:

> 1) The H Bomb 2) Auschwitz 3) Anti-semitism 4) Racism 5) Colonialism and the end of empire 6) The Cold War 7) Authoritarian Government:
>
> Folksong is part of the Eternal Human Underground that stands against authoritarian government and culture. It stands against war and for protest. It embraces the bawdy and stands for 'human truth against the mummy-wrappings of sexual convention'. This Underground stands against 'leafless, commercial, pop-folk skulduggery and with the help of the TSMA [Traditional Song and Music Association] and a few just men from Blair and Kinross 'we'll tell the truth and shame the Deil' . . . Communities that have folksong have a sort of sap which rises in them continually – by comparison communities which have lost folksong make a very dry and sticklike impression . . . [1]

1953 witnessed the publication of two important Scottish songbooks: *Scotland Sings – A collection of Folksongs and Ballads* compiled by Ewan MacColl, and *The Rebels Ceilidh Songbook* compiled by the Bo'ness Literary Society. Hamish had a great deal to do with both, though the manner in which he was excluded from MacColl's book is interestingly

1 HH, unpublished notes, Henderson archive.

documented in this letter from Janey Buchan, the wife of Labour MP Norman Buchan (27 October 1952):

> Dear Hamish, When the Scottish Workers Music Association was formed one of the first ideas we ever had was to have a Scottish Song Book . . . We took the opportunity of asking you if you would be interested. However, unknown to me a lad of Scottish background living in London had given £150 as a donation to the Workers Music Association – for a Scottish Song Book – and Ewan [MacColl] was asked to do the main work . . . When I heard about it – it was agreed that if possible you and Ewan would jointly edit it. Now here's the rub. I presumed that since Ewan was in Edinburgh he would see you about this . . . What can I say to you – I know that you will feel insulted but nevertheless I think you should give your support . . . with publication of this book we can make the most tremendous contribution ever towards the interesting of thousands of young people in Scottish folk song . . . bearing all this in mind, I'm sure you will cooperate. I know that it seems a colossal bloody cheek on our part and everything else, and if the blame for the mess lies with me, then I abjectly apologise for it.

Janey added a motherly footnote in the hope that solidarity would be maintained despite MacColl's egotism. 'I personally consider that *your* most important task is to write more songs for us. Consider how everyone really loves the John MacLean March and how readily they join in, don't you think the new songs you can give us are ten times more important than any amount of recording?' Janey, her husband Norman and brother, Enoch Kent (singer and songwriter), all played long-term roles in the Revival. Norman got himself a folk column on the *Weekend Scotsman*. Later he edited *101 Scottish Songs* (Collins 1962) and *The Scottish Folksinger* (with Peter Hall, Collins 1973). By that time Norman was not just an MP but Deputy Secretary of State for Scotland and – bending protocol – saluted the ageing Jeannie Robertson by swanning her through the streets of Aberdeen in his chauffeur-driven ministerial limousine.

Hamish's 1956 annual report for the SSS documents him twice visiting Allan Glen's School in Glasgow, 'where the poet Morris Blythman has succeeded in transforming the current folk revival from a bobby-soxer vogue into a flourishing and many-sided artistic movement'. Glasgow School of Art was another centre of folk activity, producing Jimmie Macgregor and Robin Hall and other excellent musicians. The city of Glasgow also played a vital part when Lonnie Donegan, Nancy Whiskey and Bob Kelly emerged as three of the leaders of the Skiffle movement. Between 1956 and 1960 Donegan was a regular chart topper and influenced the young John Lennon, Paul McCartney and George Harrison. Donegan's admiration for Hamish is clear in a letter from his London manager, Peter Buchanan, in May 1958:

> Dear Hamish, I am immensely pleased to have finally contacted you – and the other gentleman [Blythman]– who arranged the 'caley' during our Glasgow visit . . . Would you accept Lonnie's invitation to become President of our Edinburgh Club? . . . Our two main objects in forming these clubs have been to foster the interest in skiffle and folk music in general in as many towns as possible . . . I hope you will afford us a favourable reply as Lonnie and myself will be deeply indebted to you.

The previous year, the BBC had invited Ewan MacColl and Peter Kennedy to present a documentary radio series, *A Ballad Hunter Looks at Britain*. Hamish worked as a consultant on the two Scottish programmes: he gave pride of place to the Stewarts of Blair. Charles Parker and Alan Lomax were also involved, and a series of benchmark programmes was made: *Singing the Fishing, The Big Hewer, The Travelling People* and *The Song Carriers*. 1957 also saw the launch of the first major British folk magazine, *Sing*. It was produced in Cambridge by Eric Winter, and Ursula and John Hasted. Hamish's 'Song of the Gillie More' was featured in the first issue and he remained 'an adviser to the board' for many years. By this time Robin Hall and Jimmie Macgregor were in London having established successful television (and recording) careers. They openly acknowledged that they were folk apprentices, that Hamish was the master. In January 1958 Robin Hall wrote:

> Dear Hamish – Thank you for your letter and information, I have now got a copy of 'Last Leaves of Traditional Ballads' from the library – so all I have to do is learn some of them . . . I have also met Dominic Behan about the Folksong Club and it really sounds great. Dominic came down to the 'Troubadour' (I sing there once a week) and introduced himself . . . I have received a letter offering me a guinea fee for accompanying Rena Swankey [Swankie] on 'The Programme' for which I want to thank you . . . If I can make enough money to keep myself for the duration (down here) – would it be possible to go with you on one of your trips? I reckon I could learn more that way than any other and it would be a marvellous experience and opportunity. P.S. I have met an American girl, Peggy Whelan . . . .

The poet Edwin Morgan was one of a number of people disappointed by the manner in which Robin Hall and Jimmie Macgregor popularised Scots traditional music, but Hamish was thrilled at the thought that young singers were making the old songs 'their songs'. However, when Robin Hall became an 'overnight' national success, following an appearance on the BBC's *Tonight* programme, the issue of copyright raised its ugly head and, much to his chagrin, Hamish found himself drawn into the arguments. On a philosophical level, Hamish felt that the copyrighting of traditional material was a nonsense but money, reputation and the law are facts of modern life and he was willy-nilly bound to be involved. He felt himself to be responsible for 'his discoveries' and the song culture of Scotland and was determined that lawyers and purely commercial organisations would not take all the cream – if there was any cream. That poisons were already circulating within the song-body of Scotland is clear in this letter from Robin Hall dated 10 November 1958.

> Dear Hamish, I have just read your note, which to say the least, prompts a very quick and annoyed reply . . . Do you really think I have become some crummy 'Tin Pan alley' bastard who goes about stealing songs from friends I USED TO HAVE . . . If I may jog your memory, on several occasions in the past you have expressed the desire for me to sing *The Banks o' Sicily*, which I learned about a year ago and have been singing since . . . Always on any record or concert or broadcast (where possible) I refer to you as my greatest source of material and knowledge . . . Now Decca (and Beltona and Collector) know the song is yours and will act accordingly . . . I am not a coward or a crook, and, most important of all, I still have the greatest admiration for you as a poet, as a folklorist and a person – this is not Bullshit! Yours sincerely, Rob. P.S. I still wish to remain your friend.

Soon to be married, Hamish needed all the money his own songs might engender but his distaste for 'the cash nexus' remained almost pathological. The idea that his art and 'the art of the people' were there to be bought, sold and copyrighted by 'the brightest and best of the sons of the morning' revolted him. His wider vision is, however, well expressed in an article for the magazine *Scotland*, published in November 1958. It celebrates what he saw as the happy and creative marriage of folk tradition and the new 'pop culture'. Entitled 'Rock and Reel', the article begins with a quotation: 'I'll sell my rock, I'll sell my reel / I'll sell my grannie's spinning wheel', then moves forward to suggest that Scotland's youth could and should lead a revolt against the proprietorial, metropolitan culture that had dominated Britain since the First World War. Hamish argues for provincial and Scottish revivals, suggesting that the genius of Europe's periphery has remained too quiet for too long:

> Folksong is on the way back, these days, both north and south of the Border. Bothy Ballads have been featured on TV and teenage

> skiffle groups in Glasgow have started to sing the breezy vivacious street songs of their native city . . . Will this wave of interest in folksong subside? And can those of us who are interested in safe-guarding the Scottish cultural heritage do anything to direct the enthusiasm of younger folk into channels which will lead to the reinforcing and strengthening of a genuinely native tradition? . . . And what about the influence of radio and TV? Well, here again, I think the tendency has tended to be too pessimistic by half. The coming of print and the broadsheet did not kill folksong; it merely meant that another and less assimilable strain entered it, leaving gobbets of material which might take decades even centuries to dissolve. The radio and TV are by comparison much more fluent media – they are (or can be) in fact, a powerful ally of culture, and offer immense possibilities for the diffusion of the best and most virile in our national culture . . . Needless to say, people wishing to use them for this purpose will have to fight a lot of vested interests and old fogeyisms. But that they will win through in the end I have no doubt whatsoever.

Hamish's focus was on Scotland and a new generation nourished by contact with genuine tradition bearers. In 1958 he set up the Edinburgh University Folk Club – in close liaison with a young medical student, Stuart MacGregor. The two men were already friends but their relationship now became close and richly creative. Almost immediately they conjointly discovered a wonderful 'new folk voice' – the Gaelic singer Dolina MacLennan. A native speaker from Lochs on the Isle of Lewis, Dolina had come to Edinburgh in 1956 to study occupational therapy. She was young, innocent, beautiful, intelligent and hungry for the burgeoning freedoms of post-war Edinburgh. It was meeting Hamish and Stuart MacGregor in 1958 that launched Dolina on her fifty-year, Edith Piaf-like career as one of the most characterful singer-personalities of the Gaidhealtachd:

> I had been invited to a dance at Moffat in the Borders. Dressed to the nines – in a white waisted dress decorated with small flowers, and wearing high-heels – I found everyone else in boots and clod-hopping clothes, ready for a barn dance! Mortified, I did a runner! I came back to Edinburgh and with my friend Christine Fletcher we got ourselves invited to a party by Robin Scott Moffat – a New Town grandee – very wealthy and gay! We two girls were in the kitchen when Scott Moffat called for a song. I sang and, as they say, the rest is history! . . . [Stuart MacGregor] came up to me and embraced me – bending over me like a hawk over its prey – and he whispered: 'Nobody tell Hamish Henderson about this!' He didn't mean it, of course, and, after my next song – there he was. And he

came towards me with these great arms high above his head and he encloaked me – and a feeling of pure benevolence came on me. It was like a blessing that has stayed with me till this day. And there was Stuart, announcing that the Edinburgh University Folk Club had made its first great discovery!'[2]

Hamish and Dolina became lifelong friends and he often spoke about meeting her:

> Dolina was just twenty. She came like a shepherdess, trailing these songs of gold from ancient times. Looking back across half a century – on that one wonderful night, Dolly established herself a pivotal figure in the history of Folk Revival. In those days she was a singer and beautiful, now she's an actress, script-writer, theatre director, hotelier, you name it![3]

Within days of meeting her, Hamish had recorded the bulk of Dolina's youthful repertoire and within weeks she became a semi-professional singer, 'She fell in love with a handsome young man named Robin Grey and the two of them started earning their livings "pub-singing around Edinburgh".'[4]

By the late 1950s folk enthusiasts were visiting Scotland just to see Hamish. He was *the* authority on traditional Scots music, he had ideas, he was launching new singers and musical groups by the month. Hamish began receiving letters, loosely addressed, from total strangers: 'Hamish Henderson, Bard Extraordinary, Folk Collector par Excellence, Singer Fantastic, School of Scottish Studies Edinburgh.' Conscious of the dangers of becoming a folk guru, he was determined to keep his feet, and those of his followers, firmly on the ground. He was part of a process: as he made clear in an interview with David Ward:

> Collectors have always tended to think of themselves as the end of the chain. They think in terms of their own mortality and consider the folk arts are like the last raindrops coursing down a window pane after the rain has stopped. The idea of folklore as a continuum is a relatively new idea promoted by the Americans. Here is an example of how the tradition continues to create itself. At a sing-song in a pub, after a Miner's Rally in Edinburgh, I heard 'King Fareweel', a previously unrecorded Jacobite song. Jeannie Robertson then heard it and liked it and, not to be outdone, sought and learned another

2 Dolina MacLennan, conversation with TN, 2008.

3 HH, conversation with TN, 1995.

4 HH, conversation with TN, 1995.

> 'stronger' version in Aberdeen. One day she sang it to a group of Glasgow school children amongst whom was Andy Hunter . . . In time he created his own version of 'King Fareweel'. He was waiting there – as a tree to deliver the fruit – and he created what, I believe, is the finest Jacobite song of all. It was written not in 1745 but in 1964! That story shows you the working of the folk-process, like nothing else.[5]

It was Morris Blythman, at Allan Glen's School in Glasgow, who set Andy Hunter on 'the folk road'. When Hunter went to university – to study French – he chose Aberdeen so that he would be close to Jeannie Robertson. When, in 1964, Hamish completed 'The Flytin' o' Life and Daith', Andy Hunter wanted to sing it. He was teaching in Brittany and sent a tape of the song to Hamish. In 1965 Hamish wrote back:

> Dear Andy, You make a fine job of 'The Flyting', and the tune really comes into its own when you sing it. If I have a criticism it is that the argument is a little too 'noble' . . . I don't visualise the song as a stair-heid rammy, exactly, but it is meant to be a real conflict, with blood on both sides: – this said – your version is by far the best I have heard: when you get back to Scotland I would like to use it on an L.P. of my own songs . . .

This is the Henderson method in action: Hamish encourages, guides, affirms a 'gold standard', and his criticism provides foundations to build on.[6] On 12 February 1968 Hunter writes: 'Dear Hamish, I have just received an offer from Edinburgh Film Productions re the German programme on the Origin and Influence of Scottish Folklore . . . It was you who put my name forward – this is just another example of the magnificent help you have been to me throughout the years.' When the SNP began to use Scots song as one of its campaign tools in the late sixties, both Hamish and Hunter challenged their selection and taste. Hunter writes to Hamish:

> Look at some of the songs you and I have written – is it not true

---

5 HH, interview with Dave Ward, text in Henderson archive.

6 The following letter from Lorn Macintyre (19 April 1967) is another example of the Henderson method: 'Dear Hamish, Now that I have arrived back at my father's silent villa by the sea to brood on Calvinism and the Highland Renaissance, may I say that I spent a memorable day with you in Edinburgh. Your kindness towards me is much appreciated . . . I am hoping to borrow MacLennan's book on Sorley MacLean in translation; and when I've read his poems I shall write to you.' Macintyre was twenty-four and, within a few years, he was writing articles, poetry and novels and would later work in Gaelic broadcasting at BBC Scotland.

> that we have had to face right up to ourselves and express what was there whether we like it or not – no easy task. Hamish, you have shown the way – art is tied up with values, love, affection and respect for our people – and I am right behind you there. It is for this reason that I wholeheartedly endorse your attack on an insidious and destructive genre [nationalist kitsch].

A very different product of the Glasgow folk clubs was Matt McGinn. From an impoverished working-class Scots–Irish background McGinn emerged in the late fifties as a pioneer of the kind of anarchic folk-comedy that would, a decade later, set Billy Connolly on the road to fortune. As a member of the Communist Party, McGinn campaigned against compulsory National Service and, in 1960, became one of the leaders of the anti-Polaris campaign. On Hamish's advice, Pete Seeger invited him to sing on the American circuit, where he made a notable contribution to the Newport Folk Festival, alongside Norman Kennedy and Jean Redpath.

In 1969, at a party in folksinger Robin Laing's flat in Teviot Row, Edinburgh, McGinn and Hamish 'workshopped' a song about Paddy Meehan – a loose-cannon MI5 agent and self-confessed criminal then imprisoned at Peterhead.

> Free Paddy Meehan from Peterheid prison
> Free Paddy Meehan from down in the hole . . .
> He is no saintly fellow, he has no golden halo
> He has blasted some safes in his days here and there
> But of one thing we're certain he had nae part in
> That murder committed six years back in Ayr . . .[7]

Hamish had hit the nail on the head: in 1976 Meehan was given a Royal Pardon when his case was recognised as 'police entrapment'. Unfortunately, by this time McGinn was himself the victim of destructive circumstances – marginalisation, poverty and drink – and in January 1977 he killed himself.

Hamish's third great ally in the Glasgow Folk Revival was Adam McNaughtan. Blessed with a remarkable bass voice, Adam began his career as a primary school teacher and, from the start, championed the Glasgow vernacular. He was an exceptional teacher who could, at the drop of a hat, become 'a classroom street singer'. When his reputation as songwriter, humorist and club-performer took off, McNaughtan left teaching to become an antiquarian bookseller and song collector. Today he is a folk scholar at the School of Scottish Studies, cataloguing and transcribing Hamish's personal tape-recordings. McNaughtan was

7 Unpublished song, Henderson archive.

always interested in the connections between folksong and the Music Hall and linked performers like Charlie Chaplin and Stan Laurel, Harry Lauder and Chic Murray to street theatre, balladry and pub entertainment. One of McNaughtan's own 'star turns' is his song 'Oor Hamlet', an extremely truncated Glaswegian version of Shakespeare's original. It has spawned worldwide imitations and stands as a classic example of the folk process in action.

During the 1960s two million people joined folk clubs in Britain alone. For some it was a passing 'student phase' but for many people the Folk Revival set the moral compass of their lives. Hamish jots in a notebook: 'I love you love – my only true love'. He was a teacher and, very consciously, worked to link young singers to mentors, and singers to songs. He made lists entitled 'Songs for Ploughing Back': for example, 'Picket's Hoose at E'een, Rock of the Dee, Jimmy Young, Twa wemen Talking, Busk, Busk – Catherine Grant, The Little Drummer.' He also tried to link his singers and musicians with appreciative or deserving audiences. Since boyhood, he had had a special concern for the blind. He spoke to me on several occasions about a war-blinded match-seller he met on Saturday mornings outside the Clapham orphanage. And as soon as he was employed at the School of Scottish Studies he began organising ceilidhs for the Scottish National Institute for War Blinded. On Armistice Day 1958 he organised a day-long Folk Music Festival for the War Blinded at Linburn House in Edinburgh. The programme reads like a 'Who's Who' of the Scots folk scene c.1960:

> *Pipers*, John Burgess, H. Forbes, Norman Johnson, Alistair McCallum; *Fiddlers*, Tom Anderson, John Arthur; *Scots singers*, Jimmy MacBeath, Jeannie Robertson, Tom Scott, Ella Ward; *Gaelic singers*, Iain Campbell, Joan MacKenzie, Helen T MacMillan, May Margaret MacMillan; *Dancers*, John MacLeod, Farquhar MacNeill, Jean Reynolds; *pianist* Willie Hunter; *Accordionist*, George MacPherson; *Groups* – Auld Reekie's Moonrakers, and MacGregor's Night Hawks.

In north-east Scotland one of the first traditional singers to embrace the Folk Revival was Zetta Sinclair – mother of the singer and television celebrity Isla St Clair. Zetta's brother, Alexander, was Commando No.3 in the British Army. He was killed during the D Day Landings of 1944, and his death greatly affected Zetta. After attending the unveiling of the Commando Memorial at Spean Bridge, in 1947, she wrote a song, 'The Commando's Lament'. This song released Zetta from three years of grieving and drew her into contact with Hamish. Her family were fisher folk from the Morayshire coast. Hamish encouraged her, both as a tradition bearer and creative song-writer. Zetta, however, was a strong-minded woman well able to keep Hamish himself up to the mark.

> Dear Hamish – Give all the credit due to the Travelling People because they have a wealth of song and story – but I've felt often that from the fishing way of life has come just as rich a heritage of traditional song, story, custom, superstition and love of all kinds . . . they made little separation between the auld folksongs, popular songs and hymns – and this has swayed the judgement of the folklore purists.

In May 1966 she wrote to explain the origin of one of the songs Hamish had admired: 'Dear Hamish . . . "The Blind Maid o' Moray": it starts "As I wandered the Laigh o' Moray a bonnie lass passed by me". It was prompted by a sympathy for the blind with whom I worked at one time, and a love of the Laigh o' Moray . . . The singer's job is not to say "look what a beautiful voice I've got" but to get the story through – intact.'

Zetta's daughter, Isla St Clair (b. 1952), was a child prodigy – making her stage debut at the age of three, in the Salvation Army Hall at Findochty, Banffshire. Hamish was soon taking a fatherly interest in her and recorded her, aged thirteen, singing 'The Dowie Dens o' Yarrow' to an audience of 1,500 students at Pollock Halls in Edinburgh. At the age of eighteen she released her first LP and in 1971 the *New Musical Express* declared her Female Folk Singer of the Year. Celebrity followed. Isla was petite, dark, innocent and charming; the purity of her voice demanded attention and – after successful tours of the USA and the USSR – she became co-presenter of *The Generation Game* with Larry Grayson (the first openly gay TV personality). In 1979 Isla was voted Best Female Television Personality in Britain. Once she had children of her own, however, she lowered her profile and returned to her folk roots. Having sought advice from Hamish, she made a series of programmes for BBC Children's Television entitled *The Song and The Story* (winning the European Television Prix Jeunesse in 1981).

The tradition of individual singers singing unaccompanied songs lies at the core of Scots folksong but – as the Revival got going – Hamish became increasingly keen to encourage the young to form bands and use instrumentation as an integral part of a new folk pop. In the west of Scotland, the Tannahill Weavers from Paisley took the lead. In the early sixties they began making music that combined Highland and Lowland tradition with their own very contemporary musical interests. Hamish knew the group's leading musicians, Roy Gullane and Phil Smillie, before they set up the band and encouraged them to give their Burnsian pastoral heritage the energy of rock and roll. It was the Tannahill Weavers who brought the Highland bagpipes on to the rock stage, and Hamish praised their seminal work.

In Edinburgh it was the Corries – Roy Williamson and Ronnie Browne – who pioneered popular developments. They had begun singing at Edinburgh College of Art in 1955 but it was after teaming up with the Irish singer Paddy Bell in 1962 that they formed a group and made a public impact. In 1964 they topped the bill at the Usher Hall (with the Dubliners) and were soon fronting the BBC's *Hoot'nanny Show*. Hamish helped them find good source material, and the Corries claim they made history when – in their search for authenticity – they got themselves filmed singing 'The Braes o' Killiecrankie' at the Pass of Killiecrankie. It was Hamish's version they sang; today it is claimed as the first 'music video'! When the Corries became financially successful, Hamish tried to gather a portion of the rewards. On 13 March 1967 he wrote to the MCPS:[8]

> The Corries sing my traditional version of the 'Haughs o' Cromdale' on a new LP and have agreed to give me the copyright royalties (credited to me in Norman Buchan's collection 'One Hundred Scottish Songs') . . . I may have told you already that a new song of mine, 'Ballad of the Speaking Heart' is beginning to get sung around the Clubs.

In April 1968 he wrote again: 'The Corries, who sing my "Paddy's Hogmanay" on a Fontana Record (TL5465) inform me they have used its alternative title "The Shamrock and the Thistle". They credit me as copyright holder.' When Roy Williamson wrote 'Flower of Scotland' in 1974, Hamish's initial response was lukewarm, partly because it owed much to him, partly because he thought it verged on Scotch kitsch. But once the folk process and the rugby terraces had turned the song into a sporting national anthem, he was happy to accept 'the wisdom of the folk' and applaud it. When Roy Williamson died in August 1990, Hamish wrote a moving obituary for the *Scotsman*.

Stewart and Williamson are the commonest Traveller names in Scotland, and Hamish was not surprised that the names Stewart and Williamson keep reappearing in the pantheon of Scots popular song. Robin Williamson of 'The Incredible String Band' was close to Hamish over many years. In the early seventies he wrote: 'The I.S.B. was a fusion of folk at its best, often built around religious themes – Celtic, European, Indian. The group's music was like an esoteric rite that, once passed through, bound for ever its initiates.'[9] In 1973 *Melody Maker* musical magazine reported that 'such diverse persons as John Lennon and Bob Dylan have confessed to an admiration for the Incredible, and in particular the song-writing talents of Robin Williamson'.

The Clutha formed itself around Gordeanna McCulloch in 1964. She

---

8 MCPS: Mechanical Copyright Protection Society, now the Performing Rights Society for Music.

9 HH, unpublished notes, Henderson archive.

was a pupil of Norman Buchan's Rutherglen Academy and studied with Ewan MacColl in London but always remained close to Hamish – singing his songs, and those songs he collected, with inimitable passion. The first Clutha LP, in 1965, was entitled *Gordeanna McCulloch: New Voices from Scotland*. It featured Norman Kennedy and the Exiles, another group that Hamish and Katzel knew well.

The group's second LP, *The Clutha: Scotia!*, produced in 1971 by Arthur Argo, is even more 'a Henderson record'. It opens with 'The John MacLean March' and closes with the great ballad 'Harlaw'. In October 1972 Hamish wrote to the Scottish Arts Council in support of the Clutha (who were planning a trip to Sweden): 'Of all the folk groups who have emerged from the present revival, the Clutha are without doubt the most serious and imaginative artists. They have taken great trouble to go to the authentic source material for their songs and instrumental pieces, and in dealing with them have achieved great artistic success . . . it is exceedingly encouraging that a group like the Clutha should have the opportunity of presenting the genuine article to young and interested foreigners.'

Since the 1940s Hamish had championed the waulking songs of the Hebrides as ancient and dramatic music of worldwide interest. They are communal work songs, sung by women beating the tweed, dipped in urine, to strengthen the fabric and raise the nap. The beat is hypnotic, the songs frequently erotic: tensions often broken by humour and insult! Gradually, these very ancient songs have exerted a profound influence on contemporary Scottish music – both popular and classical. Since the 1980s Runrig and Capercaillie are just two of many bands that have used them as starting points to create thrilling modern music of their own.

Hamish now also became interested in the possibilities of 'electronic folk', in particular the group Steeleye Span, formed in 1969.[10] Steeleye Span was an English/Celtic group, formed after a break-up within Fairport Convention. Its eclectic electrification of traditional music quickly proved highly commercial. It was their experiments with 'blues-rock' that encouraged Hamish, a year or two later, to join Serge Hovey in his equally dramatic work, updating the songs of Robert Burns. Hamish's enthusiasm for this kind of experimentation, however, opened up his old quarrels with Ewan MacColl in London. Whilst Hamish championed Scottish groups and organic, mongrel, international developments, MacColl was becoming increasingly egotistical: a purist, resistant to change and innovation. In the mid seventies Hamish wrote this letter to an unknown recipient:

---

10 Hamish wrote to the MCPS in 1969 to inform them that the group was using his song 'Young Neil my Darling'.

> The counter-agent of all the phonus balonus of MacColl's censorious puritanism – was the knowledge, patience and artistic skill of young apprentice singers who weren't out for a quick buck, but knew there was no replacement for acquaintance with the tradition, and were prepared to devote time and energy to acquiring it: Sheila Graham, Ray and Archie Fisher, Andy Hunter, Tom Speirs, Isla St Clair, Alison McMorland, Dick Gaughan, Jean Redpath – to name only a few – well and truly leavened the lump; I can't describe to you the joy and felicity when I realised that each and every one of them existed . . .
>
> Incidentally I'd been pleased enough to know that Ewan MacColl existed, during the People's Festivals of the early fifties . . . It wasn't till he took Jeannie [Robertson] for a ride that things got difficult. After that he gradually turned into the prophet Ezekiel, giving his acolytes received truth about folksong, *'de haut en bas'* and generally, in my opinion, doing the revival a lot of harm. However he, and Peggy Seeger, remain a quite extraordinary phenomenon.

Other groups Hamish championed were Campsie Folk, Drinker's Drouth and the Boys of the Lough, who in the mid seventies became one of the earliest Celtic folk bands to tour the world as a professional group. The stresses and strains of this meant that (like the Battlefield Band) the Boys of the Lough might be described as a slowly evolving 'workshop' of master musicians. Many of them graduated via sessions in Sandy Bell's bar. The great Aly Bain was one. Tutored by the Shetland fiddler Tom Anderson, Aly Bain was immediately recognised by Hamish as a musical genius.[11] The Edinburgh singer Dick Gaughan was another of the Boys of the Lough who went solo and gained worldwide renown. He is a stylist whose very personal interpretation of songs has thrown new light on the Scots tradition and several of the best of Hamish's songs. Cathal McConnell (from Fermanagh), the group's tin whistle player, became one of Hamish's close companions in Sandy Bell's, and in 1976 the Boys of the Lough gave Hamish permission for their superb rendition of 'Lochaber No More' to be used in the pearl-fisher sequence of the film *The Summer Walkers* (for no fee). Later, the group's leader, Robin Morton, set up Temple Records as one of the leading recording studios in Scotland.

Billy Connolly is not a name usually associated with Hamish but the superstar's status owes more than a little to furrows ploughed by his one-time chum, Hamish. For example, in 1967 Arthur Argo featured Connolly on the front cover of the magazine *Chapbook*. Connolly was

---

11 Aly Bain later teamed up with accordion player Phil Cunningham. As Silly Wizard, solo artists and TV presenters they have developed their reputations over thirty years.

then in a band called the Humblebums and unknown. *Chapbook* lauded Connolly's potential as a performer and documented his marriage to Iris Pressagh. An argument had broken out at the wedding reception about the honeymoon destination, Connolly shouting, 'We can't decide – between Bermuda, or Saltcoats – depends on the weather!' Brought up in a slum, bullied at home and at school, Connolly found his feet as an apprentice in the Clydeside shipyards, got interested in leftwing politics, motor-bikes, sex and the folk scene, and met Hamish. A friend of Matt McGinn and Hamish Imlach, Connolly flirted with groups called the Skillet-Lickers and the Acme Brush Company, before forming the Humblebums with Tam Harvey and Gerry Rafferty. When Hamish met Connolly, he recognised him as a comedian, not a banjo player or singer, and, quite consciously, pushed him in a new direction. Connolly spent time in Sandy Bell's and several evenings in Hamish's flat. Things took off at the Royal Command Performance of 1971. Prince Philip and the Queen were greatly amused and Deeside loomed up like a vision before the bearded ruffian! After that Connolly wrote *The Great Northern Welly Boot Show* with Hamish's friend Tom Buchan, and Danny Kyle of Radio Clyde was soon describing Connolly as 'the world's first verbal cartoonist'. Hamish was delighted. He had found his 'Caliban'.

Hamish's work brought him into contact with an ever-changing circle of cultural activists. One fractious but productive relationship was with the young Richard Demarco. By nature an apolitical radical, Demarco was an art enthusiast who, during the mid 1950s, helped transform 'the rump' of the Edinburgh People's Festival into what quickly became the Edinburgh Fringe. In 1961 when Jim Haynes and Demarco set up the Traverse Theatre[12] its programme had a strong 'folk aspect' and Hamish was frequently involved in events. For example, he wrote to Midlothian County Council to support Demarco in an application for funds for a show presenting 'authentic traditional singers and the best versions of Scottish folksong. By doing so he is undoubtedly doing a service to the public and especially to young people.' Once Demarco had the money, however, things went haywire. Hamish's singers found themselves left high and dry and he wrote a letter of complaint that included a verse telling things as they were:

---

12 Jim Haynes was an American from Louisiana. He was one of the Beat Generation and in 1959 established the first paperback bookstore in Edinburgh. By 1960 he knew Hamish well. From 1961 he was centrally concerned with the Traverse Theatre. Later he helped run the 'Arts Lab' and Canongate Press. In the 1980s he moved to Paris where his house in Montparnasse became a 'Salon for cultural enthusiasts', a twentieth-century nuit Parisienne – drinks, conversation and dinner.

De Marco, ye hae made it plain
Why a' your ploys will be in vain.
Justice ye've earned, and, by the Book,
Your just deserts ye winnae jouk.
Ye'd fairly mak a body boak.
If this is how ye're treatin folk
That micht be willin tae befriend ye,
I rede ye richt – your slicht will end ye.

Demarco apologised but Hamish was unappeased: 'Dear Richard – thank you for your letter. I accept your apology, but I have to say I remain pretty sore about the whole episode . . . I do find it a strain to excuse that sort of conduct. The show last Tuesday was a success and I see no reason why I should have lost money on it . . . I realize you have difficulties, and I make allowances for that, but failing to keep an appointment with a person who has given up time to help you is just bloody impertinence. Also, it is exceedingly unintelligent.'

Hamish's overriding interest was in Scottish developments but the London folk scene had a strong Scottish component and his close ally Bruce Dunnet kept him in touch with the metropolis. When Dunnet's 'The Singers' Club' proved both successful and resilient, London City Council helped him set up the Folk Music Record Club in Shoreditch and establish a Folk Song Agency. In 1961, with Paul Carter and Douglas Moncrieff, Dunnet set up Folksong Unlimited. He informed Hamish that its aim was 'to present good public performances of folksong, make records of traditional performances – and, most important, to look after the artist'; his letter ends, 'We should like you to accept this card making you the first member.'

Dunnet later became Jeannie Robertson's London agent. Hamish, ever hopeful, assumed her fortune was made – but, in April 1963, he was brought down to earth by this letter from Dunnet: 'Hamish . . . for the love of Jesus there is no gold on the trees . . . I lost £107 on the Jeannie Concert. I still don't know what happened to the audience.'

One important visitor from London to Edinburgh at this time was folklorist and songwriter Sydney Carter, later composer of 'The Lord of the Dance'. He stayed several days with Hamish and Katzel and a letter he wrote to the *Observer* (17 February 1963) shows how similarly these two men viewed the folk and political worlds:

> The rebirth of British song may seem a small thing set against the liquidation of an Empire: but it's healthier to hail the one than bewail the other. The new folk singers are young men and women looking forward, not old men and women looking back. They may sing medieval ballads but they were also singing songs of political

> and social satire long before 'Beyond the Fringe' made the phrase fashionable.

Carter's viewpoint here is important because when Michael Frayn wrote *The Book of Fub* he snubs the contribution of men like Hamish and Carter. Writing of the Scots Folk Revival, Frayn opines: 'Roy Guest, a Welshman of multi-racial origin, did what Ewan MacColl, Joan Littlewood, Hamish Henderson *et al* the academicians failed to do – bring Scottish folksong into the market-place and the coffee houses.'[13]

Who is this unknown Guest whom Frayn praises so highly? Guest was an interesting character and he did set up a coffee house, 'The Howff', opposite St Giles' Cathedral in August 1960. He was a good singer, and Hamish helped this new arrival in Edinburgh to turn 'The Howff' into 'a bohemian-seven-day-a-week-folk-club'. Historically, Guest had a role in nurturing the folk scene in Edinburgh but, compared with Hamish and many local Scots, his role was minimal. However, it may be no coincidence that his role was well marketed from the start, notably by W. Gordon Smith and Charles MacPhail, two senior figures at the Scottish BBC. In a series of contemporary media articles Gordon Smith praised Guest generously. At the same time Charles MacPhail extolled his colleague – stating that it was W. Gordon Smith who had created the Scots Folksong Revival by 'introducing Robin Hall, Jimmie Macgregor, the McEwan bothers, Burl Ives and Cy Grant, Lonnie Donegan, the Corries, and Ray and Archie Fisher to BBC Television . . . '[14] W. Gordon Smith did some important work for the Scots Folk Revival, but all the singers mentioned owed far more to Hamish than to him – yet he gets no mention. This did not go unnoticed and in November 1964 Hamish wrote to the *Weekly Scotsman*:

> Sir, I am interested to learn from W. Gordon Smith's letter of 23 November that 'it took Roy Guest to bring folk-singing into the marketplace – or coffee den.' If Mr Gordon Smith is referring to folk-singing in Edinburgh, he should know that it has been going on in howffs, dens, open spaces, and even private houses for several hundred years. The modern folksong revival, as far as Auld Reekie is concerned, began not with Roy Guest but with Ewan MacColl and Joan Littlewood of Theatre Workshop, in 1947, the year of the first Edinburgh Festival. We even served coffee with it! . . . Roy Guest arrived in Scotland at the invitation of the 'Sporranslitters', in August 1960. The Howff (their name not his) was already in existence. While it lasted, it provided a congenial central meeting place for all interested in folk music, and Roy Guest was undoubtedly

---

13 Michael Frayn, *The Book of Fub* (Collins 1963).

14 Letter to the *Scotsman*, 23 November 1964.

> a major attraction. Unfortunately, as it turned out, neither the 'Sporranslitters' – a most promising and enterprising Scottish cultural society – nor their experimental Howff survived Roy's picturesque tap-and-run raid on the Scottish folk scene.

Hamish's letter hints that there was more to Guest than meets the eye. Certainly the mid sixties was a hard time for Hamish. On 10 February 1967 he wrote to Jimmie Macgregor:

> As I told you in the Traverse, the royalties still outstanding are performing rights royalties for 'live' performances at concerts etc . . . As you know I have taken an exceedingly liberal attitude towards performances of my own songs by the folk singers of the revival, especially those ones who are just about making a living jigging around the clubs. However, you and Robin [Hall] are now in a totally different position. I don't think you could altogether deny, furthermore, that it is partly at least due to my own work (not to mention, in the case of one of you, a fair amount of practical assistance) that you are in a totally different position.

But having made his grumble, Hamish moves sideways to keep Macgregor informed about his public commitment to his ongoing grand plan:

> As for the songs I collected and put into circulation, I did this in the context of a definite cultural strategy, and as in war one must always allow for losses of one sort or another. (I am not now referring to financial losses.) My hope – and it has been realised in quite a large number of cases – has been to encourage young folk to approach their cultural heritage with creative elan.

Hamish expected difficulties and opposition to his more radical ideas but he was surprised by attacks from unexpected quarters, particularly from Scotland's literati, some of whom seemed determined to join the media in its attempts to either silence him or to corral him 'within shabby confines of the folk arena'. The jotted beginnings of a series of unresolved poems show his pain:

> There is one sin,
> To call a green leaf, grey,
> Whereat the sun in heaven, shuddereth.
>
> There is one blasphemy,
> For death to pray,
> For God alone knoweth the praise of death.

There is one creed:
    Neath world terror
Apples forget to grow on apple trees.

There is one thing needful –
    Everything
The rest is vanities of vanity.[15]

He writes of 'having tried to steer the Scottish folksong revival between the shoals of dusty archivism on the one hand and commercial prostitution on the other', and notes that modern Scotland's attitude towards the poet:

> is one of amused contempt, mixed sometimes with hostility – particularly in Edinburgh – the only town I know where the bourgeois mental attitude – the attitude related by Robert Fergusson in his 'Guid Braid Claith' – has soaked down through to the entire working class. A few Scots have a grain of civilisation and courtesy, but the vast majority are 18 carat blunts . . . It is only the diminutives among the art poets who openly attack and despise oral folk culture, usually for vulgar reasons of exclusiveness and precocity – but the top-notchers sense the stimulus that the ballads and vernacular austerity can give . . . Both Yeats and Auden experimented successfully with the folk idiom; writers like W.S. Graham, Charles Causley and Arish Loyne have carried the experiments a stage further. And, rather differently, one gets the songs of Bob Dylan in whose, now hugely popular, work one can perceive veins of genuine poetry. The same is true, of course, of Ewan MacColl.[16]

His poetical jottings expand on these philosophical musings:

Folksong belongs to the body
    As if in some mystic way
        Folksong had been implanted
            Like the soul in every body.

Folksong runs unofficial and anti-cultural
    It is the bawdy in the bothy
        The *thried o' blue*
            The Horseman's Word.

15 HH, unpublished jottings, Henderson archive.
16 HH, unpublished notes, Henderson archive.

The rebel song, and army songs.
Folksong belongs to everybody –
A mystic Rousseauesque idea
And true.[17]

1966 was the year in which the Traditional Music and Song Association of Scotland (TMSA) was founded. Various enthusiasts did the hard work – Pete Shepheard, Mairi MacArthur, Sheila Douglas, Peter Hall – but Hamish was the moving light. Mairi MacArthur and Pete Shepheard were both members of the St Andrews University Folk Club. Mairi, a Gaelic speaker, later did important research in Argyll and re-established the Iona Press, in Inverness. Pete Shepheard had come north from the Cotswolds but – having fallen for a Scots lass – fell in love with Scots song and dedicated his life to the advancement of traditional music. In the early 1970s Hamish wrote Shepheard this 'job reference':

> Pete has had an impressive career as paladin and standard-bearer of the Contemporary Scottish Folksong Revival – no single figure has done more to infuse it with enthusiasm and intellectual curiosity, and so get it off the ground . . . The achievements in Ireland under the aegis of *Comhaltas Ceoltoiri Eireann* made an enormous impression on him and in 1966 he organised the first Festival of Traditional Music and Song at Blairgowrie. He wanted to create and succeeded in creating the atmosphere of an Irish *Fleadh Cheoil.* This led to the foundation of the TMSA.

Hamish gave the TMSA a 'Foundation Lecture', which was typically wide-ranging:

> Scotland has no Shakespeare but it has its balladry – and existing across the English-speaking world balladry has become, and remains, an equally powerful force . . . From America, via Ezra Pound and T.S. Eliot, modern English poetry has been revived by the appropriation of demotic English speech. Anglo-American Pop Art (in the post war period) was forestalled by an Anglo-American literary revival fuelled by popular music and song. Alistair Cooke created a real bridge across the Atlantic with his radio series 'I hear America Singing' but it was a bridge already carried – across the generations – from Walt Whitman back to the early colonists, from Buchan to Appalachia . . . And, today, we have to recognise that the American pop-folk scene, with its escalating onslaught on the sensibilities – for better or for worse – is going to be part of our scene too . . .

17 HH, unpublished jottings, Henderson archive.

Hamish, School of Scottish Studies, George Square, Edinburgh, 1954 (KH).

Hamish with James Robertson Justice (actor), Inverness-shire, 1957 (KH).

The settled Blairgowrie Traveller Bella Higgins mothers Hamish with song, 1955 (KH).

Belle and Alec Finlay, Strathdon tradition bearers, 1955 (KH).

Hamish with young folksingers, St Andrews House, Ayr, 1965 (Photo: K.M. Andrew; KH).

ıternational House, Edinburgh: Hamish in conversation with the poets Alan Riddell and
\dam Drinan (broadcaster Joseph Macleod), in kilt, c.1953 (MF).

:hool of Scottish Studies folklorist Calum Maclean with Angus McNeill, Moidart, 1959
'hoto: Ian Whitaker/School of Scottish Studies [SSS] Archive; KH)

Jeannie Robertson, the Aberdeenshire Traveller widely regarded as the finest European traditional singer of the twentieth century, c.1954 (KH).

Lucy Stewart of Fetterangus, another Traveller tradition bearer, c.1955 (KH).

Alec MacPhee, Argyllshire Traveller, brother to Hamish's long-time friend Willie MacPhee, tradition bearer, singer and storyteller (WM/TN).

Hamish with an Irish lady friend, c.1956 (KH).

The Clydesdale horse was the totemic animal at the centre of the cult of the Horseman's Word 'discovered' by Hamish in 1951 (Photo: Clydesdale Society).

A group of bothy workers in North-east Scotland, of the kind amongst whom Hamish found and recorded a great, still living Scots ballad tradition, c.1935 (DA/KH).

Kintyre tinkers on the road, c.1900 (WM/TN).

A tinker funeral: the burial of Donald Reid at Dunkeld, c.1910 (WM/TN).

Curly Kate Williamson, Sutherland Traveller, c.1935 (AJW/TN).

Duncan and Shaunas MacPhee, Sutherland, c.1950 (AJW/TN).

Hamish astride 'Maggie', Sutherland, 1957 (Photo: Bobby Botsford/SSS Archive; TN).

Chrissie Davies Stewart with bairn, Sutherland, 1957 (Photo: Bobby Botsford/SSS Archive; TN).

Hamish with Joanne Stewart, Sutherland, 1957 (Photo: Bobby Botsford/SSS Archive; TN).

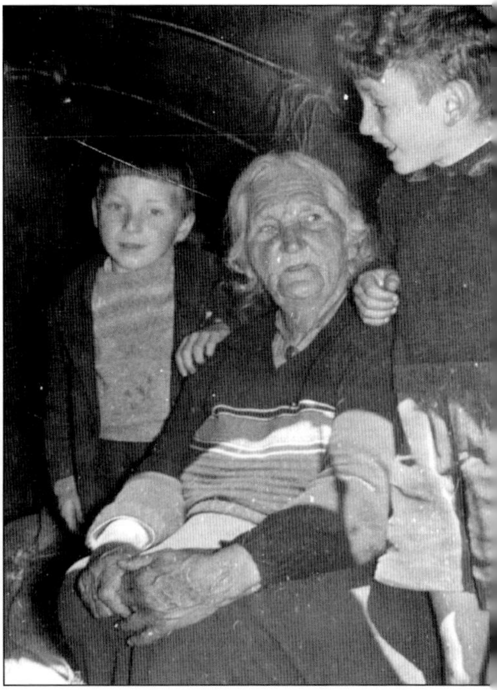

Black Anne Stewart with grandsons, Sutherland, 1957 (Photo: Bobby Botsford/SSS Archive; TN).

Hamish spent two months with the travelling Stewarts of Remarstaig in the summer of 1957, recording Gaelic oral tradition and documenting their ancient lifestyle (Photo: Bobby Botsford; TN).

The Stewart clan patriarch Ailidh Dall tells a story at the roadside, Wester Ross, 1957 (Photo: Bobby Botsford; TN).

Hamish recording Ailidh Dall in the heather, Sutherland, 1957 (Photo: Sandy Paton/SSS Archive; KH).

The Stewarts of Mintlaw, Aberdeenshire. The singer Jane Stewart (Cameron/Turriff) is the dark-haired girl in the centre, c.1940 (TN).

Aly Bain, Shetland fiddler, one of the great musicians of the Scots Folk Revival, c. 1957 (KH).

Hamish with the Stewarts of Blair, one of the outstanding tradition-bearing families of Scotland, Rattray, c. 1956 (KH).

Hamish feeding raspberries to his girlfriend, Felicity 'Katzel' Schmidt, in 'the Berryfields o' Blair', 1956. Katzel and her sister Elizabeth had come to Scotland on a working holiday and been embraced by Hamish into his recording project (KH).

Hamish in the tent of the Schmidt sisters, Blairgowrie, 1956 (KH).

After their marriage in May 1959, Hamish and Katzel planned to honeymoon in Italy; turned back as 'political undesirables' at the border, they found sanctuary in Switzerland, where this photo was taken (KH).

The newly weds in clover, Germany 1961 (KH).

John Elliot 'cries the Fair', Langholm, c.1960. Hamish established a friendship with Elliot and recorded the drama of the Common Ridings across the border counties (AE/TN).

By the late 1950s the Scottish Folk Revival was a dynamic phenomenon. Here, Hamish celebrates with tradition bearers and revival singers in the Clifton rooms, Edinburgh, August 1959 – from the left Jimmy MacBeath, Isaac Higgins, Robin Gray, Ella Ward, Hamish, Ray Fisher, Jean Redpath, Stuart MacGregor, Jeannie Robertson and (seated) Dolina MacLennan (Photo: Edinburgh Evening Despatch; KH).

In November 1959 Hamish organised a historic School of Scottish Studies Ceilidh for the Scottish National Institute for the War Blinded, at Linburn, Edinburgh (Photo: Norward Inglis; KH).

Hamish supported the American folksinger Pete Seeger in his battles with the Un-American Activities Committee. Here they sing on stage in Aberdeen 1961 (KH).

25 May 1967, Hamish – in his element – in 'the Woolpack', Edinburgh: Jeremy Isaacs and Edwin Morgan enjoying themselves, Lawrence Daly (the Scottish Miners leader, in front of Hamish) less so (KH).

Modern singers of the 'revival' range far and wide in search of material but they are increasingly finding their way back to the native product – the wine of the country . . . This is surely a natural development. Given a chance, folksong always finds its own level. Roving out and returning with their spoils, these young singers are doing no more and no less than countless singer-ancestors have done before them. However, at some stage or another, the folksinger of today is bound to feel the pull of his own ethnic tradition and he then embarks on the most thrilling journey of all: the voyage of re-discovery, the journey home! If he can resist the Siren's song, there's every chance that, like Ulysses, he will reach his own native isle, and recover his own native inheritance . . . In order to do this he – and she – must steep themselves in the best traditional song and the best traditional singers . . .

Scots songs are evidently full of heart and reality. They are not written for the stage. They were the slow growth of intense passion, simple tastes, and a heroic state of society. Love, mirth, patriotism were not the ornament but the inspiration of these songs. They are full of personal narrative, steaming hopes and fears, bounding joy in music, absolute disregard of pettiness.[18]

The TMSA festival at Blairgowrie precipitated an avalanche of small-town folk festivals across Scotland – from Newcastleton to Castlebay, from Auchtermuchty to Orkney, from Shetland to Berwick-upon-Tweed. When asked why Blairgowrie had provided such lift-off, Hamish answered proudly: 'Why Blairgowrie? Because the truth is – this town has been enjoying an *unofficial* Festival of Music and Song for centuries!'

Meantime the Director of the School of Scottish Studies, Basil Megaw, had taken early retirement. In 1969 Dr John MacQueen, a medievalist and Scottish Literature scholar at the University of Edinburgh, took up the Directorship and began changing the School from a research department into a normal university teaching department. Margaret Mackay had come from Canada to begin work as the School's first postgraduate student, in 1967. Hamish slowly assumed a number of supervisory roles but became increasingly involved in the production of records that made use of the School's sound archive: notably a double volume LP, *The Muckle Sangs*, released by Tangent Records of London. It featured many of the best singers recorded by the school over the previous twenty-five years. At Berkeley Professor Bertrand (Bud) Bronson, the world's leading ballad scholar, was hugely impressed:

18 HH, unpublished lecture notes, Henderson archive.

> Dear Hamish, 'The Muckle Sangs' reached me a fortnight ago. What a splendid album! And what an enduring treasure! My cup runneth over. I rejoice to possess it, and have read every word of your signed jacket summary and the handsome booklet. You have put it all in proper perspective . . . it is wonderfully satisfying that living tradition continues to unlock its secret repositories to the deserving seekers. And it was your divining-rod, Hamish, that beyond all others in these latter days, found the springs of native song and brought them again to the surface for the refreshment of our generation and generations to come. It must be enormously gratifying, and exhilarating, to you to realize how fructifying your discoveries and your influence has been. You touched the rock and living waters gushed forth. Posterity's debt to you is incalculable and will not be forgotten . . . Yours Aye Bud Bronson.

In 1969, the School hosted the 20th International Folk Music Council Conference, in Edinburgh. Hamish gave a keynote address. He entitled it 'The Coming of Age of the Scots Folk Revival' and he started by reminding his audience how William Blake liked to ask Mrs Linnell (wife of the painter John Linnell) to sing Scots songs for him: 'My Nancy's hair is yellow as goud / And her een as the lift is blue . . .' He then spoke of how 'Blake was deeply moved by such songs. Just as poets in our generation are moved by Bob Dylan. Just as the technology of "Electric Folk" and innovative bands like "Steeleye Span" are exciting a new generation today.' Many in his scholarly audience found their hair standing on end as, to make his points substantial, a medley of young Scottish singers – Bob Bertram, Matt McGinn and Billy Connolly – stepped up beside him to perform. He also presented a selection of fine tradition bearers: Mary Brooksbank, Jeannie Robertson, Calum Ruadh Nicolson and Willie Scott. His conclusion was equally dramatic:

> I'm very much in sympathy with what Stockhausen is trying to do – stimulate a new aural tradition – the tradition of learning by ear and composing orally. Stockhausen is trying to do this on the level of far-out avant-garde music – but it is my conviction that the same general principles hold good for poetry and music making for a wide range of the population – and this, in alliance with the latest technologies and electronic advances, is an important *popular* art of the future . . . There is near unanimity on one point – the quite distinctive and peculiar place Scotland has in the worldwide folk music movement, and the success of the 'join' we have made between the old and new. We have an unbroken great tradition and the children of our cities, Edinburgh, Glasgow,

Aberdeen and Dundee are, even now, carrying it forward into the electronic era.[19]

The extent to which Hamish had now won his battle to bring Scots folk tradition back to its honourable place in Scots culture and history is acknowledged in a seminal article by Alastair Clark, Britain's first daily newspaper folk correspondent, published in the *Scotsman* on 29 October 1970.

> . . . Davey Graham was the first great fusion man on the British folk scene – a tagsin from Syria here, a blues holler from Louisiana there – all tied together so you could not hear the join. – He took Beatles songs into the folk clubs when the Beatles were regarded as White Trash. And his daddy came from the Isle of Skye . . . Robin Williamson of the Incredible String Band had a good grounding in traditional ballads in Edinburgh before joining Mike Heron on a magical mystery tour of time and space and East and West. Hamish Henderson called them 'the wild rovers of the folk revival', two others were Bert Jansch of the Pentangle, and Hamish Imlach . . . Today even purists accept the folk-and-pop mixture purveyed by Billy Connolly and Gerry Rafferty of the Humblebums – and Dave MacNiven and Rab Noakes, one of the most prolific and gifted song-writers, graft the sounds of Presley and the Everly Brothers onto stalks of purist folk . . .

19 HH, unpublished lecture notes, Henderson archive.

ELEVEN

Three Flytings Atween Twa Bonnie Fechters

Death or the bed of contention – MacDiarmid or me
HH, 1958

For the ten years between 1947 and 1957 Hamish and Hugh MacDiarmid enjoyed a stimulating, though sometimes testy, creative friendship. In the late fifties their relationship became acrimonious and a series of angry debates flared into 'flytings' aired, particularly, on the letter page of the *Scotsman*. Flyting is the old Scots word for an intellectual dispute conducted in public: it is a form of 'literary theatre' in which insults are traded with brutal directness. *Chambers Dictionary* defines 'flyte': 'to scold, to brawl', and 'a flyting' as 'a scolding or poetical exhibition'. MacDiarmid's poem 'Skald's Death' shows how he believed such habits to be part of his poetic persona:

> I have known all the storms that roll.
> I have been a singer after the fashion
> Of my people – a poet of passion.[1]

That these two poets should seek to revive this probably druidic 'performance art form' in twentieth-century Scotland was in their natures but also part of a deliberate policy to stir the flaccid pudding that passed as intellectual debate in a Scotland content, in MacDiarmid's words, 'to be each of us no better than a carted stag'.[2] An article by Hamish for the *Saltire Review* in 1955 suggests something was brewing:

> The history of Scottish folksong has been chiefly a determined attempt to take all the guts and spunk, all the ardour, verve and raucle randiness out of the song of the people, and reduce it to the level of a Kirk social . . . [But, as Burns wrote] 'let our National Music preserve its native features. They are, I own, frequently wild and unreducible to the

---

1 Hugh MacDiarmid, 'Skald's Death', *Complete Poems* (Martin Brian and O'Keeffe 1978).

2 Huge MacDiarmid, 'Talking with Five Thousand People in Edinburgh', *Complete Poems* (Martin Brian and O'Keeffe 1978).

more modern rules; but on their very eccentricity, perhaps, depends a great part of their effect' . . . Was not Burns himself a recreator and reshaper, as well as a collector? Where does one draw the line between 'folksong' and the productions of the individual bard?

> The arts of the people display an amazing resilience – one thinks of the commons of Scotland who rallied to Wallace when the Scots nobility were treacherously deserting him . . . Young singers in Glasgow are learning old songs from our [SSS] tapes, and making new ones on the old tunes. Play the traditional music in schools, as I have done, and the effect is electric. The national consciousness is stirring; if we act promptly and boldly, we can make the folksong revival a powerful component part of the Scottish Renaissance.

MacDiarmid was jealous of *his* 'Scottish Renaissance', and on reading this article he probably sensed that he – as well as Scotland's intelligentsia – was being called to account. Other seeds of conflict were sown when MacDiarmid published his huge poem 'In Memoriam James Joyce' during the same year. It makes use of numerous 'ideas' brought to MacDiarmid by Hamish, and a good deal of material borrowed from other sources (as discussed in Chapter 13). Hamish had sympathy for MacDiarmid's omnivorous use of 'a collage of material' but saw that such actions, unacknowledged, might do him and the burgeoning Folk Revival real harm. Hamish believed the great strength of Scots literature was its collective dynamic and its permanent interaction with folk tradition: if this historical phenomenon developed into a plagiaristic free-for-all, the whole fabric of the culture could be damaged. He felt bound to act: even if it meant losing MacDiarmid's friendship and gaining a raft of new enemies. His notebooks document his thinking:

> MacDiarmid fears his sons will kill him.
> Wants to write prefaces to give birth to them.
>
> MacDiarmid: the Old Testament, vengeful God.
> Jonathan and David syndrome –
> The Greek myths tell the story:
> The political 'King' emerges as the dominant autocrat
> Out of the mythological line.
>
> Huge MacDrinkmind – as Sydney Goodgodsir Standing Stiff used to call him!

Their personal relationship, initially, remained good. In early January 1958 Hamish wrote to MacDiarmid to tell him how well his poems had been received at a Workers' Educational Association (WEA) lecture he had given; and he invited MacDiarmid to give 'The Immortal Memory' at a Burns Supper being organised by the Scottish Miners' Union. The whole event was to be recorded by Topic Records – with Dominic Behan one of the guest singers:

> Dear Chris, It will be the first Burns Supper LP. We're pulling a fast one on the official Burns cult with a vengeance! . . . Incidentally, Topic has another excellent idea – namely the issuing of records of Scots poetry. I suggested to them that the first of these should be your 'Hymns to Lenin' – or rather, the first two 'Hymns to Lenin' – plus a number of other poems which I would select myself. As readers I suggest yourself (for the First Hymn), Norman MacCaig, Alex McCrindle and Tom Scott.

This event proved a big success but, the following year, it was the bicentenary of the birth of Burns that triggered the first flyting. The Scottish Committee of the British Arts Council commissioned publication of an anthology of contemporary Scottish poetry, entitled *Honour'd Shade*. Published by Chambers, its editor was Norman MacCaig. Nothing by Hamish or 'the folk poets' appeared in the anthology. On 19 November 1959 an anonymous review of *Honour'd Shade* appeared in the *Scotsman* (if Hamish did not write it, he certainly had a word in the ear of the writer). It suggested that Burnsian values were notable by their absence in MacCaig's selection. It acknowledged the quality of the anthology but suggested that the editor's 'range' was self-consciously restrictive: Hamish Henderson, Alan Riddell, T.S. Law, David McEwan and *all* Scotland's female poets had been excluded. The article concluded by suggesting that the book might have been better entitled, 'like one of the poems it contains, "The Muse in Rose Street"'.

The jest struck home and next day MacDiarmid took up the cudgels on MacCaig's behalf. He wrote to the *Scotsman*: 'The Rose Street group of contributors are certainly head and shoulders above all the contemporary Scottish versifiers . . . I am satisfied that no contemporary Scottish poetry deserving inclusion has been excluded.' It was a headmasterial rebuke and Hamish's friends felt bound to respond – 'The *Honour'd Shade* Flyting' began. Over the next two months the letter pages of the *Scotsman* rippled with a mixture of anger, wit, insight and delight.[3] Douglas Young spoke up for the women poets; 'the reviewer' himself rebuffed MacDiarmid's reference to literary 'inferiors'; William Little asked 'what are we to make of an oracle [MacDiarmid] who speaks with two voices'. Goodsir Smith, Stewart Conn, Tom Scott all joined in the debate. On 28 November Hamish wrote a letter addressing the reasons for *his* exclusion:

---

3 Documented in *The Armstrong Nose: Selected Letters of Hamish Henderson* (Polygon 1996).

> . . . I do not believe my patronage of bars outwith the magic Rose Street circle had anything to do with my exclusion from the present volume. Mr MacCaig did, in fact, do me the courtesy of asking me for a contribution, and it was nobody's fault but my own that I did not submit one till it was too late. However, even if I had submitted a sheaf by return of post, and Mr MacCaig had rejected them holus bolus, it would not have upset me unduly. It is my opinion that few of the shorter poems I have written of late measure up to the standard that I should have felt obliged to impose if I had myself been in Mr MacCaig's position . . . I have come to set greater store by my songs 'in the idiom of the people' than by other kinds of poetry I have tried to write. By working in the Folksong Revival, therefore, I am paying what is probably a congenial tribute to the honour'd shade of the most famous Crochallan Fencible [Burns].

MacCaig – by excluding song, the bawdy, the sporty, the popular and any female contributor – had, inadvertently, raised important questions about what Scots poetry is, what the Scottish tradition is, what Scots culture is and what the Arts Council was doing! The emperor had been caught with his pants down, and Hamish encouraged Scotland's younger poets and singers – from the Old Town, from Sandy Bell's and the wilds of Glasgow – to take the debate on to the streets, to write poetry and to sing! In February 1960 'a sound-tape of new poetry' was released entitled *Dishonour'd Shade: Seven Non-Abbotsford Poets.* It featured Ian Hamilton Finlay, W. Price Turner, Tom Wright, Stewart Conn, Shaun Fitzsimon, Anne Turner and Tom Buchan. Other poets who enrolled on the Henderson side included Thurso Berwick, Stuart MacGregor, Edwin Morgan and Norman Buchan. This flyting solved nothing, but literature and song became, briefly, part of 'a national conversation', and the Folk Revival began to be seen as a cultural force as well as music for pleasure.

Hackles, however, remained raised and Ian Hamilton Finlay soon found himself the object of a sustained attack by MacDiarmid; anyone daring to side with 'the folkies' knew they risked opprobrium – administered either by the literati or the academic establishment. A remark by the poet Albert Mackie sums up the tensions. In May 1960 he stopped Hamish, at the top of Middle Meadow Walk, Edinburgh, and said to him: 'Hamish, you are the bravest man in Scotland!' Hamish would not allow the 'the stone of the Folk Revival to gather moss' or be defeated, and MacDiarmid features large in his notebooks:

> Although MacDiarmid has long wedded himself to the Scottish National movement – he is now a widower . . . Perverse as he is, he likes to play the wicked nurse who lets the baby out with the

> bath water. He is the lone wolf . . . If Scotland, led by some miracle, worked up enough smeddum and direction to achieve independence – or even moderate Home Rule – MacDiarmid would desert at once to the English side and start intriguing against the new Republic . . . MacDiarmid is the apostle of a kind of spiritual apartheid and there is an acrid anti-humanism in his writing: 'As I have said in one of my poems, I on the other hand would sacrifice a million people for one immortal lyric. I am a scientific socialist. I have no use whatsoever for emotional humanism'[4] [but] MacDiarmid's ecstatic marathon walk through the snows and hailstones of a disorientated and spiritually divided Scotland must be one of the most extraordinary feats of endurance in literary history.
>
> MacDiarmid interpreted my wish to elevate Jeannie and the song tradition as an attempt to bring *him* down! I thought of Ferrey's description of Voltaire, 'What a pity that such a great genius should have a heart so mean.' By the late Fifties MacDiarmid, obtusely, began to regard the Folksong Revival as the new Kailyard and a threat to his Renaissance. I think it probable he intervened to stop the BBC using traditional singers at this time. George Bruce was his ally . . . Back pocket: re MacDiarmid 'I let the great captive albatross quiver for a minute in my hand.'[5]

In 1962 the Edinburgh Festival hosted a major International Writers' Conference. Two thousand guests attended. Special delegates included Dame Rebecca West, Angus Wilson, Muriel Spark, Stephen Spender and Norman Mailer. 21 August was Scottish Day. Unfortunately, the Cuban missile crisis was brewing, many of Scotland's writers were at daggers drawn: a mild hysteria – not unlike that which had produced Dadaism at the end of the First World War – pervaded the air, with the Glaswegian beatnik Alexander Trocchi hungry to play the role of a Tristan Tzara. Having serenaded London, Paris, New York with cane, black cape and a wide-brimmed hat, he descended on Edinburgh determined to lift lids and spill garbage. The novelist Walter Keir set the tone of Scottish Day by declaring: 'There is hardly any Scottish literature worth speaking about. We are a nation of schizophrenics. We are attending the wake of Scottish literature.' David Daiches chaired the keynote debate on 'Contemporary Scottish Literature'. MacDiarmid and Trocchi were the lead speakers. Trocchi began by denouncing the cultural climate within which artists had to work in Scotland: 'The whole atmosphere here seems to me petty, provincial, stale porridge – Bible-class nonsense! It makes me ashamed to sit here with writers from other parts of the world.'

---

4 Letter from Hugh MacDiarmid to Leslie Mitchell (Lewis Grassic Gibbon).

5 HH, unpublished notebook, Henderson archive.

MacDiarmid accepted much of what Trocchi said but then savagely attacked his competence and 'canvas' as a writer: 'Trocchi seems to think that what matters in the world are lesbianism, homosexuality and matters of that kind!' It was all red rags and bulls. Looking back, Hamish told me:

> Trocchi lost his temper and glorified in it. MacDiarmid kept a firm grip on his. Trocchi shouted his defiance of MacDiarmid. MacDiarmid maintained a ferocious argument! For some time sixteen hundred people sat in stony silence but gradually, perhaps half of them began to erupt in vociferous applause in support of this or that assertion. Daiches tried, unsuccessfully, to keep order. With things getting out of hand, he asked Josh MacRae to conclude the session with a series of songs – anti-Polaris songs! MacRae invited others to join him, including Morris Blythman, and me!

As these singers took the stage it became clear that some were drunk and the McEwan Hall – a splendid amphitheatre – witnessed a series of scenes from the Theatre of the Absurd. Hamish found himself part of a spectacle that he realised – too late – would be likely to do both him, and Scotland, considerable harm. Next day a *Scotsman* letter, from C.M. Gibson of Carlyle Hall, Edinburgh, paints the scene:

> It was indeed a wake . . . Celtic in spirit, bickering in tone, aided by shots of the cratur . . . That Mr Trocchi should put on a beat act was perhaps to be expected but what hardly anyone had bargained for was that what had set out to be a serious discussion of Scottish writing would end up with a ballad singer (with guitar) rendering an incomprehensible number about Lady Chatterley and a plug for someone's pamphlet. It is to be hoped that the conference will ignore this debacle and yet go on to retrieve itself.

Magnus Magnusson, then a young reporter on the *Scotsman,* recorded the day's events with commendable lightness of touch, but Hamish sensed that he had been both used and humiliated. Still ambitious as a political leader, he penned a letter of apology:

> 22 September 1962 – Your correspondent Magnus Magnusson has considerately drawn a veil over the fantastic episode which brought Tuesday's session of the Writers' Conference to an end. I refer to the tasteless cabaret turn which caused an immediate and understandable exodus from the hall. As a Scottish writer involved (suddenly and without any warning whatsoever) in this fiasco, I undoubtedly owe an apology to the audience in general, and to

> foreign visitors in particular. The invitation to come forward to the platform to join the singers took me completely by surprise and had I not known them – and worked together with them in the Scots folksong revival – for many years, nothing on earth would have induced me to accept it.

When Hamish, later, asked Daiches why he decided to wind the session up with 'a drunken chorus' he replied: 'The BBC people asked me to – they thought it would make a good ending.' This poses the question: were Scotland's anti-nuclear folkies set up – to be gunned down? Whatever, Hamish found himself on an abyss of public ridicule and he determined to watch his step more closely. Indignities were part of his bardic lot, but intellectual shame something else.

Hamish jotted down the beginnings of his 'The Flyting o' Life and Daith' during the war, inspired by some medieval German verses and his visit to Pompey's Pillar in Alexandria, but it was his battle with MacDiarmid and MacCaig – and the 1962 Festival Conference – that impelled him to complete what is now regarded as one of his most profound songs:

Quo life, the warld is mine.
The floo'ers and trees, they're a' my ain.
I am the day, and the sunshine
Quo life, the warld is mine.

Quo daith, the warld is mine.
Your lugs are deef, your een are blin
Your floo'ers must dwine in my bitter win
Quo daith, the warld is mine.

Quo life, the warld is mine.
I hae saft win's, and healin' rain,
Aipples I hae, and breid an' wine
Quo life, the warld is mine.

Quo daith, the warld is mine.
Whit sterts in dreid, gangs doon in pain
Bairns wintin breid are makin mane
Quo daith, the warld is mine . . .

. . . Quo daith the warld is mine.
I hae dug a grave, I have dug it deep,
For war an' the pest will gar ye sleep.
Quo daith, the warld is mine.

Quo life, the warld is mine.
An open grave is a furrow syne.
Ye'll no keep my seed frae fa'in in.
Quo life the warld is mine.[6]

In 1964 the BBC Third Programme commissioned David Daiches to chair a series of broadcasts about contemporary Scottish culture. In the third of these broadcasts, MacDiarmid and Norman MacCaig renewed their attack on the Scottish folk tradition. They spoke with patrician disdain, and a second major flyting – the folksong flyting – was ignited. On 4 March Hamish's friend the Marxist literary critic Dr David Craig responded to the BBC broadcast with this letter to the *Scotsman*:

> . . . Norman MacCaig [said] that folksong might be good enough for berry-pickers and steel mill workers, but not for him – he had read Homer. The two poems we now call Homer's are believed by modern scholars to have been pieced together out of short lays chanted by minstrels at the Aegean courts . . . Scotland's lays are the ballads, and it is no exaggeration but the sober truth to say that in Jeannie Robertson Scotland has her own Homeric-type singer, whose work is equal in quality, in beauty and truth if not in scale, to the great European epics. If she is allowed to pass her time without being heard to the full over 'our' national radio service, it will be an irretrievable crime done to our culture.

A selection of the most relevant letters in this flyting is presented in *The Armstrong Nose* (Polygon 1996) but it was a public 'Talk Out' at the Traverse Theatre in Edinburgh that provided this second folksong flyting with high drama. Talk Outs were the fashion in the United States, and Jim Haynes (of the Paperback Bookshop and Traverse Theatre) decided that Scotland should have one. Haynes wrote: 'Hamish – would you be interested in participating in an experiment to be called a "Talk Out"? Monday night 13 April 1964? Would you be prepared to make a 15 minute statement vis-à-vis your position to Scottish Poetry and Folksong; with Chris Grieve also making a statement regarding his position? You both might have another "second" of your choice. I think that I have Lord Kilbrandon to chair what I hope will be the first of a long series – the BBC are very interested in putting it out as a sound broadcast – please write or phone me straight away.'

MacDiarmid got MacCaig to act as his second. Hamish invited Dr David Craig to be his. Craig was then working for the WEA in Yorkshire.[7]

---

6 'The Flyting o' Life and Daith', published in the *Collected Poems* (Curly Snake 2000).

7 Later first professor of Creative Writing at the University of Lancaster.

Craig studied English at Aberdeen University in the early fifties: after an Orwellian spell as a lecturer in Ceylon (Sri Lanka) he returned to Britain to pursue a doctorate in 'Scottish Literature and the Scottish people' at Cambridge. Like Hamish, his life had an uncommon drama; he told me:

> From Aberdeen, I travelled 'old style', by boat, from Aberdeen to Leith, and Leith to Lowestoft. My approach to literature was Marxist; my exemplars Leavis and Speirs. I did research in Edinburgh – where I found David Daiches so nervous and conventional that he never said anything of much use to me. I used to go running instead out into hills. I did work under the wing of David Murison – Hamish's friend – in George Square: he was so shrewd, sardonic and exact that you would feel ashamed to say something that you couldn't back up with evidence . . . I enjoyed some very provocative evening classes with Hugh MacDiarmid but after ten years of studying art poetry I began to latch on to song. Song was in the air, and the influence of Hamish everywhere apparent. When I heard his 'Freedom Come a' Ye' I recognised immediately that it stood up absolutely as literature, without the music.
>
> When Bob Dylan's 'Blowin' in the Wind' was published, in *Sing Out*, I wrote to Stephen Sedley (now a judge!) to say, 'There is a new Shelley.' Times they were a changing! And it was Hamish who crystallised all that for me. Hamish had written a letter to the *Scotsman* [November 1959] to say that he'd come to set more store on his own work in the idiom of the people than on his Elegies. This struck home to the centre of my brain; this was a fundamental truth: 'the idiom of the people' must be the living core of living literature. It was like a veil torn away. Never again could I be patient with elitists ploughing their narrow furrow. Thus, I was very proud to be asked to be Hamish's second in the Traverse debate. His cold-shouldering by the BBC was a horrible cultural crime: I hoped our debate might lessen, for a moment, the anger of Lenin! . . . Once the debate was scheduled, Hamish invited me to join him. However, with a full-time job, a wife and family, and very little money – I could not get up to Edinburgh to coordinate our position. In those days, I was a scholar-critic rather than a writer – so I saw this debate as a crucial literary, cultural and political event and I prepared my case, very seriously. When the day came I set off at lunchtime in my van – a Commer Cob – no trim inside, no heating. Six hours on the road from York: ice crystals on the metal above my head. I arrived after dark. I met Hamish at the door of the Traverse and we walked straight into the cockpit that the Traverse was in those days.
>
> MacDiarmid was a good debater, and MacCaig had any amount of *savoir-faire* – tall, handsome, speaking slowly with great poise

and clarity of expression. They thought on their feet. Hamish did well enough but, even with Jeannie Robertson there, to sing for our side, we landed no *coup de grâce*. As soon as the debate was over, a newspaper man came up to me and said, 'You boys had the best ideas, but they had the best speakers.' As far as speaking went, they won – on points – and I did feel crestfallen afterwards. I was coming back to Scotland after three years away. I'm proud that it was me that decided Jeannie should sing 'The Butcher of Crieff'.

> There was a bonnie lassie
> An' she was gaen tae Crieff
> She met in wi' a butcher laddie
> And he was sellin' beef . . .

The glorious libidinous symbolism, and the great draught of sound Jeannie gave it transfixed the audience. She sang so slow, so that those two jog-trot verses became a love lyric of great nobility. 'And he was sellin' beef': that line reveals itself like a Rubens, or a Titian, or a Goya. But the unfolding amplitude – the epic quality of the Bronze Age – was all her own. She had developed those lungs and diaphragm long before Hamish met her – but he slowed her up and encouraged her to bring the powers of opera to Scots folksong – her tempo, volume, cadence, inspire awe in me yet.

Darkness, rows of faces, we all stood up in turn and did our piece. Hamish spoke as usual without notes. I always began a public statement with the word 'Friends' and, as I did so, Valda Grieve, who was sitting in the front row of the audience, shouted out – 'and Comrades!' I could see her extraordinary strawberry blond hair glowing in the darkness. She practised disorientation tactics. A big jeer went round the house – even though I was an active member of the Communist Party at that time! The whole debate was being recorded by George Bruce and the BBC. And Hamish – suspicious that we were being set up – seemed, on occasion, to lose confidence. He was good but not 'the success' that our case merited. Time, however, has proved us right: 'the idiom of the people' will remain the core of living literature.

Once the Talk Out was over, George Bruce took charge of editing a two-hour event into a half-hour broadcast. Hamish, doubting Bruce's intents and purposes, asked to be allowed to hear the edited version of the debate before it was broadcast. The BBC (perhaps rightly) refused and shelved the programme. Bruce and MacDiarmid, however, then circulated rumours that Hamish had vetoed the broadcast 'because he lost the argument and had made a fool of himself'. This infuriated Hamish and he asked Bruce to acknowledge that this was not the case, in writing. Arguments rumbled on for months. On 6 June 1965 Hamish wrote to Bruce:

> I remember that I phoned you, and asked you to acquaint him [MacDiarmid] with the true facts; this you promised to do . . . Chris Grieve should withdraw a statement that has been shown to be incorrect – and which was quite gratuitous . . . I have learned to my cost that one can be too easy-going in these matters . . . I have put the facts on record in my own private 'archive' to Scotch (or kill) the untrue statement whenever I encounter it.

On 14 June, Bruce replied: 'It is very doubtful if he [MacDiarmid] would remember exactly what I said, though it was to the effect that you did not put an unqualified embargo on the broadcast to the discussion.' On 19 June the correspondence ends with Hamish informing Bruce that 'your present letter makes it clear that you *did* do the necessary correcting, so (together with the relevant entries in my own diary) this puts the truth on record . . . One has got to be careful these days.'[8] Who 'won' the debate was, however, less important than the fact that it took place. The Talk Out showed that Scotland remained a place open to what the philosopher George Elder Davie described as 'the democratic intellect'. And Hamish had powerful supporters: Douglas Young wrote to the *Scotsman* to say, 'I am in general on the side of Mr Henderson and Dr Craig in the issues they argue' and in 1967 MacCaig sent Hamish this ultra-friendly letter, plus an unpublished poem in manuscript.

> Honestly you seem to persist in misunderstanding my estimation of folk-songs. If you were to plot a graph, my dot would be a lot nearer to yours than to Chris's. There is surely evidence for this – think of the hours and hours and hours I've spent listening to them and howling their choruses. Would I do that if they bored me? And that doesn't take account of the time I've spent soberly reading them, and about them . . . There are bad ones and good ones, just as you've written bad ones and good ones. That's no insult. Shakespeare wrote bad plays and good plays. Whether you can write a 'folk-song' which is also a poem is proved – one needn't go further – by your 'Flyting of Life and Daith' – never mind the 'Banks o' Sicily' . . . I would like to see a much greater cross-pollination between 'folk-poems' and

---

8 In May 2003 Dr Ian Olson, whose father was an engineer with the Scottish BBC, wrote to TN: 'The conflict between Hamish and MacDiarmid (the latter supported by MacCaig) came to a head in a famous debate on the matter of folk song and Scottish culture at the Traverse Theatre in 1956 [1964], chaired by Magnus Magnusson, when MacDiarmid and MacCaig "ran rings around Hamish" (Bruce). It was recorded for the BBC – but Hamish refused to let it be broadcast.'

'art poems'. (I think in terms of music, what Bartok and Kodaly did). This would fertilise both and perhaps bridge the surely artificial gap that seems these days to separate them. I suppose this is a job (amongst others) that you, perhaps more than anyone in Scotland (Britain?) are fitted to do.

MacCaig and Hamish, however, remained ever prone to rub each other up the wrong way. Hamish notes in a diary, 'Norman MaCoy: behind the facade of gloom, their lurked an interior of complete and utter despair. Grovelling down in the primeval slime.'

During 1968 a third flyting, concerning the 1320 Club – already discussed in Chapter 9 – took place. In 1969 the fourth and last flyting began: it rumbled on for several years and involved numerous people and various publications. It is best described as 'The Plagiarism Flyting'. The causes date back at least to the mid fifties but things began to move, in the early sixties, when the source of MacDiarmid's beautiful short poem 'The Little White Rose of Scotland' (written in the thirties) came under increasing scrutiny. Hamish, like many others, believed that the poem owed a great deal to Sir Compton Mackenzie. On 13 February 1965 Edwin Morgan wrote to Hamish:

I was interested in what you said about 'The Rose of All the World'. When I first read this poem I was sure it was something I had read before, but I have never managed to track it down. I'm pretty certain, however, that it isn't MacDiarmid's own work. If ever you do find out the original I'd like very much to know! I suspect a great deal of his poetry is unacknowledged quotation – especially in the long poems. I had an article in 'Notes and Queries' about a long passage in 'In Memoriam James Joyce' which was taken with no acknowledgement from Sherrington's book *Man on his Nature*. Some day this will all have to be sorted out. What a bibliographical hunting ground for someone![9]

Hamish had no interest in an academic witch-hunt; he sympathised with MacDiarmid's 'artistic kleptomania' but felt unable to let things pass:

It is probably easier for the folklorist than it is for the literary critic to come right out and say boldly that plagiarism is often an intrinsic part of the creative process . . . Most Scottish plagiarists of any eminence use pseudonyms – thereby tacitly admitting the presence of an alter-ego. Indeed one of the most curious things about 'MacAlias' [Hamish's general term for the multitude of Scots who have used aliases – including himself] is not only that he calls himself something else, but that he not

9 Amongst the many scholars who joined Hamish in his plagiarism enquiry it was his Irish friend Douglas Sealey who made the most brilliant contribution (by letter).

> infrequently turns out to be someone else into the bargain . . . Plagiarists of genius are the justified sinners of literature and we know them well in Scotland . . . Hugh MacDiarmid's poem 'Perfect' is a classic case of what his roots know and what his branches say.[10] May I say I'm full of admiration for MacDiarmid's plagiarism: 'The skull on the Machair' is the most uncompromisingly 'found' of all 'found poems' – which MacDiarmid lifted from an excellent article into poetry.

Things remained under wraps until 1967, the year in which Duncan Glen prepared a special issue of his literary magazine *Akros* – to celebrate MacDiarmid's seventy-fifth birthday. Glen invited articles and tributes, and Hamish gave him the poem 'To Hugh MacDiarmid, on reading *Lucky Poet*' (written in 1945, revised in 1947 and, probably, polished in 1967). MacDiarmid and Valda Grieve were not pleased and sent new shafts in Hamish's direction. The poem is a surgical evaluation of a ferociously brilliant poet:

> . . . If there were just two choices . . .
> Mine would be yours, MacDiarmid!
>
> . . . But what about 'Scotchiness',
> This awful dingy bleary blotchiness?
> You list 'Anglophobia' as your recreation,
> But it's Scotland that's driven you to ruination.
> Why not admit it? The meanness, the rancour,
> The philistine baseness, the divisive canker,
> The sly Susanna elder-ism, McGrundyish muck-racking
> Are maladies of Scottish, not English making.
> If we think all our ills come from 'ower the border'
> We'll never, but never, march ahead in 'guid order' . . .
>
> And you've said it all before. So we're back where we started.
> Yes, you said it all before. And are broken hearted?
>
> Did an unlucky break befall the Lucky Poet?
> Just what *do* you stand for, MacDiarmid? I'm still not certain.
> I don' wanna step behin' dat tartan curtain . . .[11]

---

10 The previous year rather similar charges of plagiarism had been raised against Lewis Grassic Gibbon and his North East trilogy *Sunset Song*. Unfazed, Hamish explained his position to Maurice Fleming: 'I try to take the discussion "beyond plagiarism". The important thing seems to me not whether Gibbon knew [Gustav] Frensson's book or not, but how and why he made use of its "scaffolding". In Crocean terms, Frenssen supplied the "structure" to "Sunset Song", and Gibbon the "poetry".'

11 Published in the *Collected Poems*.

On 5 May 1969 Hamish informed Arthur Clark at the *Times Literary Supplement*, in London (which had already published material about MacDiarmid's plagiarism): 'I have assembled quite a lot of information about MacDiarmid's work as a "collage artist" . . .'. On 5 July 1969 Hamish wrote to MacDiarmid:

> Dear Chris, I've been working on an essay – or rather a series of essays – which attempts to survey your later poetry through the eyes (so to speak) of the people who contributed to it, e.g. Gramsci, Karl Kraus etc. I have often wondered if you know (or have guessed?) who wrote the unsigned article in the TLS ('Satirist in the Modern World', 8 May 1953) which you turned into a poem in 'In Memoriam James Joyce'?

Erich Heller was author of the article referred to, and on the day Hamish wrote to MacDiarmid he also wrote a long letter to Heller, at Northwestern University, Evanston, USA. It ends: 'May I add that I am full of admiration for MacD's inspired plagiarism, and I am sure you will not mind finding yourself part of the English poetry of the mid-century.' Heller, however, was not fully placated, writing back: ' . . . half a dozen pages of unacknowledged quotation is a bit much!' Hamish now became interested in plagiarism as a psychological phenomenon. Why, for instance, did so many Scottish writers use pseudonyms? He notes it being

– a by-product of Calvinist inhibition
– a product of close communities (literary and other)
– a device used by 'the right' to make ex cathedra statements
– a consequence of the social disposition of Scotland's middle-class to 'behave yourselve afore folk!'
– a democratic wish to disown a superior status (as judge, critic or artist), i.e. it wasnae me (Chris Grieve), it was that licensed fool Hugh MacDiarmid
– a necessity for certain political journalists and women writers[12]

As the controversy petered out, Ian Hamilton, a London literary critic and poet, struck up a correspondence with Hamish about pseudonyms and aliases – suggesting that the hectic use of aliases in Scotland indicated a native difference of character between the Scots and the English. He encouraged Hamish to start a serious study of the subject. Nothing happened but the flyting stimulated Hamish to write a fine poem of his own. Based on MacDiarmid's 'The Little White Rose of Scotland', it is an example of 'the folk process' in action. It seems to have been written in collaboration with another person, as yet unknown:

12 HH, unpublished notebook, Henderson archive.

Against the cold blue-black of the evening sky
Among the bitter grey fronds of the sleeping trees
That blackie sang so sweet, so long
I thought the dawn would break.[13]

13 One of a sequence of unpublished poems (by HH?) in the Henderson archive.

TWELVE

America: Goldstein, Redpath, Farina, Dylan

Folk songs were the way I explored the universe, they were pictures and the pictures were worth more than anything I could say.

Bob Dylan, *Chronicles*, 2004

Historically, the twentieth-century Folk Revival started in the USA but American folk music had strong Celtic roots and Hamish was determined that contact across the Atlantic should be not just maintained but developed. In retrospect he can be seen to have implemented a four-point plan. First, he worked with folklorists like Alan Lomax, Gershon Legman, Farnham Rehfisch, Herschel Gower, Bertrand (Bud) Bronson, etc. Second, he cultivated the interest of record producers and broadcasters like Ken Goldstein, Moses Asch and Studs Terkel (Alan Lomax above all). Third, he developed direct contact with creative American artists like Paul Robeson, Paul Strand, Tom McGrath, Jean Ritchie and Pete Seeger. Fourth, he became an unpaid musical entrepreneur 'exporting' Scottish singers and musicians to America and generally encouraging 'folk exchanges'. One amateur enthusiast who exemplifies the dynamic consequences of cross-fertilisation is Howard Glasser, a New York artist and designer. In the summer of 1960 he visited Scotland to collect songs, met Hamish and began a forty-year collaborative friendship. Returning to the States, Glasser used his recordings to spread Scots song through the folk clubs and college campuses along the east coast. In February 1962 he wrote:

> Dear Hamish, since the time of my Scottish holiday, a great deal has happened to change my life . . . I shall never forget those wonderful three months collecting in Scotland – I brought back forty hours of tapes – and a lifetime of memories – nor will I forget your kindness . . . We need more people in this world with the Scottish temperament to help make it a decent place to live.

Hamish's closest academic relationship was with Ken Goldstein. The two men first made contact in 1954 when Goldstein was working on Jeannie Robertson's first LP, *Songs of a Scots Tinker Lady* (for Bill Grauer Productions/Riverside Records, New York, 1956). When a financial dispute broke out, Hamish represented Jeannie, and Goldstein represented Grauer Productions. The problem was never satisfactorily resolved but Goldstein developed a love for Scots balladry, and the two men became friends. By 1957 Goldstein had plans to make a record with Hamish, present Scots traditional music on the Riverside Records label, and become himself an academic folklorist. The following year he applied for a Fulbright Scholarship, to spend a year working with Hamish on the 'Scots Tinker Project'. His application met opposition. In March 1959, Basil Megaw, the Director of the School of Scottish Studies, asked Hamish to write to Goldstein, 'qualifying the School's willingness to sponsor him'. Megaw saw Goldstein as an American go-getter likely to use his time in Scotland purely to advance his own career. Hamish, however, was glad to get any assistance at all and realised that Goldstein had managerial skills, media connections and academic virtues of the kind he lacked. Consequently, in October 1959, Hamish greeted Goldstein in gleeful excitement, not least because he was smuggling back to Scotland a copy of Peter Buchan's *Secret Songs of Silence* (the unpublished manuscript had been sold to an American buyer in the late nineteenth century). After just one night in Edinburgh, Hamish drove Goldstein north with Katzel in the back seat. 'He was on his fifth, and last, provisional licence. He drove leaning forward, peering out of the window – leaning this way and that as though he was still on a bicycle!'[1] En route they detoured via Kirkcaldy so that Goldstein could meet Lawrence Daly and the members of the Fife Socialist League, then fighting the 1959 General Election. Hamish wanted Goldstein to experience the reality of modern Scotland and know that folksong here was a living political reality as well as an ancient art form. On 29 October Goldstein wrote to Hamish from Strichen.

> Moe Asch of Folkway Records definitely wants the Willie Matheson recording for the album . . . I'm looking forward to receiving a list from you of leads to informants in Buchan . . . I can't thank you enough for the wonderful way you and Katzel took care of me – a man can show no greater love than to wake up at 6.00am for a friend.

Back in Edinburgh Hamish arranged for Goldstein to present a documentary radio programme entitled *The American Stranger*. The BBC was willing to give the young American time that it would not give Hamish, but it was Hamish's voice that kicked the programme off:

> What makes a man travel thousands of miles in search of song? Why should an American come to Scotland when a more obvious opportunity for such work seems to be there in his own country? Ken Goldstein, a Fulbright Scholar, has the answer.

1 Katzel Henderson, conversation with TN, 2004.

> *Goldstein:* The well-spring of all balladry, in the final analysis, in the English language, comes from Scotland, and at one point or another in a scholar's career, he finds he must turn to Scotland for his researches. Scotland was the great treasure-house for balladry . . . Over one third of texts[2] come from the single county of Aberdeenshire . . .

Goldstein settled down with his family in Strichen, at the heart of Scotland's ballad country, and was soon out 'in the field' recording.

In January 1960 tragedy struck the Goldsteins when their eldest son died after a short illness. Hamish travelled north to visit them. On the train journey from Strichen back to Aberdeen, he completed the last verse of 'The Freedom Come a' Ye'.

> So come all ye at hame wi' Freedom
> Never heed whit the hoodies croak for doom.
> In your hoose a' the bairns o' Adam
> Can find breid, barley-bree and painted room . . .[3]

In May 1960 Goldstein informed Hamish: 'I have finished laying out the Burgess Bagpipe album, and I think it's great. Sounds absolutely wonderful, and if we can get some decent publicity we should make it sell.' Hamish was delighted that the career of John Burgess was being resurrected.

Home in Hatboro, Pennsylvania, Goldstein began work on the vast body of material he had assembled. His priority was to get a major new album of Jeannie Robertson ballads out for the Christmas market (1960). He asked Hamish to 'write a good introductory note about Jeannie and her being called "the greatest folksinger in the world" . . . Lomax was in for a visit the other day – I look forward to talking to him about my Scottish work. He's a very perceptive and brilliant ideas man and may give me some ideas on further analysis and reporting of the material.' Things went well and in 1960/61 three major discs were released. When

---

2 *The English and Scottish Popular Ballads,* edited by James Francis Child.

3 Published in the *Collected Poems*. In March 1984, knowing how deeply the Goldsteins' tragedy is part of this song, Hamish sent his 'train fragment' to Rhoda (the Goldsteins' eldest daughter) to mark the Goldsteins' thirtieth wedding anniversary. 'Dear Rhoda, I enclose the ms of part of the third verse of my song "The Freedom Come-All-Ye". This was written on the train between Strichen and Aberdeen after one of my visits to your family. I gave it to Ken as a keepsake when he returned to the US in 1960, but he was kind enough to return it to me in 1966 when Arthur Argo wanted to use it on the front cover of a number of *Chapbook* mainly devoted to my songs. This is therefore the third time this scrap of paper will be crossing the Atlantic – this time to its rightful owner.'

the first of these, *The World's Greatest Folksinger* (Prestige 1961), was ready, Goldstein wrote to Hamish: 'Jeannie's record should be ready this coming week. The cover is absolutely beautiful – Jeannie's singing is so glorious that no one will be able to complain about the recording quality . . . I am very grateful to you for your wonderful cooperation.'

The next project was with the Stewarts of Blair. On 15 May Goldstein writes: 'Hamish – would you be willing to put together the album of Blairgowrie material? We'll pay an advance of $200 for it.' He also enquired about an album of waulking songs and – working with Ewan MacColl on an LP of Burns's 'Merry Muses' – asked again for Hamish's cooperation: 'I need a top-notch name in Burns Scholarship to write the introduction – as a deterrent against government action against the issuance of the record . . . PS. Start thinking about Jeannie doing another album.'

1961 was the year in which Scottish song – both traditional and revival – really began to take off in the States. Goldstein's friend Paul Endicott organised a highly successful tour by Ewan MacColl, accompanied by his young wife Peggy Seeger, and invited Hamish to lead a tour of 'his singers' the following year. Hamish was delighted but showed no inclination to apply for a visa for himself. In March 1961 Goldstein suggested he must come:

> Dear Hamish – your good country folk will simply be lost and tired in the US – Endicott needs you to herd them as well as to introduce them and place their performances in meaningful context . . . You are the only man who can do it properly. I also informed him that you sing as well . . . I also took it upon myself to suggest that Jimmy MacBeath be *not* included on the tour. Don't get mad at this, but I was thinking of you . . . Jimmy is in poor health, and being such a bad drinker, he could well drink himself into one of those coughing and bad-breathing fits – his death could well be on yours and Endicott's hands . . .

Hamish wrote back to terminate the plan, and his letter raises some unexpected reasons. First he refers to the continuing shock he feels 'at Dylan Thomas's totally unnecessary death', then states how much he prefers 'the intimate atmosphere of the Ceilidh as opposed to the concert or lecture hall' and concludes with these half-humorous political points:

> I am more than doubtful whether the US government would admit me – the Embassy in Grosvenor Square has a dossier on me as long and loud as Niagara Falls – Paul Robeson's passport, Peace Committees, anti-Polaris, anti-Colin and Shine, the Pete Seeger Committee and much more. In the other direction the Russian Embassy has, I should imagine, a longish dossier on me as well

– anti-Pasternak persecutions, anti-Nazi executions, anti-Hyaica shambles etc.

At a deep level, perhaps, Hamish had no wish to experience, or be tempted, by the American world, and Donald Higgins (Jeannie's husband), following Hamish's example, soon announced that he 'would not allow Jeannie to go America'!

Goldstein, however, kept up his astounding productivity, informing Hamish: 'I will be reprinting "Scots Musical Museum"; in September, Dick's "Songs of Robert Burns"; in November, Taylor's "The Proverb", in January 1963, Greig's "Folksongs of the North East" and "Folksong in Buchan" (Arthur Argo and I will write the introduction).' And in May 1962 (after a series of hitches) he wrote to inform Hamish that all was well with the Stewarts of Blair project: 'I am putting in a bill for $350 for the Berryfield album. This cheque will be made out to you, and I will leave it to you to pay the individual performers – about $250–260 and you keep the rest for your work as collector, editor etc.' This letter marks the high point of the Hamish/Goldstein collaboration. Shortly after this, problems with copyright, contracts for singers, and the PhD Goldstein was writing began to cause serious strains in their relationship.

Fortunately, Hamish's revival singers were now making their mark on the American music scene. First amongst them was Jean Redpath. Fifty years later, she is still there, enjoying a career as one of America's best loved folksingers. Following Hamish's death in 2002, Jean sent me this email:

> Hamish first hove into view on my teenage horizon when he presented an illustrated talk on ballads to the Literary Society at Edinburgh University in 1959. There I heard Jeannie Robertson for the first time – introduced with the kind of wildly articulate passion that I associated always with Hamish on his pulpit of the moment. He opened doors, windows, prospects for me that I had no reason to suspect till then – access to songs and information, folk of like interests, all-night ceilidhs at an age when I could still survive them and always challenge, stimulus and encouragement. Every major move in my life seems to have had Hamish somewhere in the wings: – the recording connections in the early 60s with Ken Goldstein, my long association with Serge Hovey and the Burns project and all the questions over the years to which the easiest answer always was – ask Hamish. He was a brilliant, creative man, not always easy to deal with and his influence on all of us is impossible to gauge . . . Bon voyage, old Friend.

For Hamish, Jean Redpath was to the Scots Revival what Jeannie Robertson had been to Scots Tradition itself and with a touch of

Svengali cunning he consciously prepared her for greatness. She went to Aberdeen to sing with Jeannie and then it was off to America. He sent her – as though she were a scout – as a native tradition bearer, intelligent, beautiful, ready to learn, eager to send back reports. After some months in California, Jean moved to New York where, on 15 November 1961, she featured in a major review by Robert Shelton of the *New York Times*:

> The Scottish visitor is Jean Redpath, a big raw-boned, apple-cheeked, radiantly healthy girl. She is appearing at Gerde's Folk City . . . Miss Redpath would charm an audience with her repertoire alone – some 250 songs, enough to keep a ceilidh (jam session) going for days. These include luminously poetic folk ballads from plowman's shacks, mouth-music with which Scots supply their own accompaniment for dancing reels and strathspeys, songs of Robert Burns, and a round of drinking, bawdy, lyric-love and children's songs . . . Her voice is a clear, rich, beautiful mezzo-soprano, sure-pitched enough to sustain unaccompanied numbers such as a seal-charmer's song . . . Although Miss Redpath has no connection with the Scottish Tourist Board she is a resolute boaster of her land, its history, customs – and music.

With evangelical zeal Jean reported back to Hamish:

> I won't launch into a rigmarole about the things that have started popping up since I hit New York two months ago – a live week-booking in the village, all sorts of offers as a result . . . First big scheme is an album for Electra – a definitive album on the ballad . . . I'd like you to suggest material . . . I'm still haunted by an odd note here and there of the Breton melody of the 'Twa Corbies' you sang to me one day. If you've a tune and an opportunity could you tape this for me? I'd appreciate your help here, Hamish – this is a chance – and a responsibility – I don't want to mess up . . . I'll educate these foreigners yet! . . . P.S. Arthur [Argo] arrived safely – I hauled him on stage to do a couple of songs and they loved him!'

After his ten year 'Apprenticeship' with Hamish, Arthur Argo was a singer/journalist well versed in Scots folk culture and keen to be part of the American project. Jean, thrilled by what was happening, writes: 'Dear Hamish, Bless yer white cotton socks! The material sounds terrific – I'll have to talk someone into doing a few more records! I did a radio show with Studs Terkel.'

In New York, Jean was soon close to Bob Dylan and Joan Baez, whose mother was Scottish, and was 'in-there' as the music of the sixties began to happen. Celtic folk music was at least as important as Black music as a catalyst of change. The foundations of American Pop-Protest had been laid by Woody Guthrie, Pete Seeger and the Lomaxes but they all had strong Scottish connections. The age of the LP, jet planes and 'the public concert' arrived simultaneously and stimulated a revival of European influences on American music. Radio and television beaming new music into millions of homes changed millions of lives. One musician who briefly and brilliantly embodied the changing scene was Richard Farina, born in Brooklyn in 1936. He was of Cuban-Irish ancestry. At Cornell University he found fame as a writer (working closely with the future novelist Thomas Pynchon) and got himself suspended for organising student demonstrations. He then went travelling to Cuba and Ireland in search of revolution. Back in Greenwich Village, after an eighteen-day romance, he married the folksinger Carolyn Hester. In September 1961 whilst playing harmonica for Hester's third record, he met Bob Dylan at Columbia Records. Dylan was there because he'd had a chance meeting with Paddy Clancy of the Clancy Brothers (whom Hamish had met in Ireland and encouraged to take their music to America). Some years later Paddy Clancy described his part in the 'discovery' of Dylan in a letter to Hamish: 'I met him in New York and suggested he should back Carolyn Hester, a fellow CBS artist of ours . . . He jumped at the chance, and during the session the A and R man heard him humming away to himself and asked him if he sang?'

In 1962 Richard Farina and Carolyn Hester came to Scotland to make an EP with Rory and Alex McEwan, two folk-revival singers, who knew Hamish well. It was Edinburgh Festival time and Sandy Bell's was their watering hole. The EP was entitled *Four for Fun,* and Hamish was very much in the wings during rehearsals. The group made a live television appearance, and Hamish and Farina found they had a great deal in common. Farina's marriage to Hester was already collapsing. In October she returned to New York whilst Farina stayed in Scotland. Up till this time, Farina had played second fiddle to his wife; now – encouraged by Hamish – he suddenly blossomed as a song-writer and solo-singer. Leaving Edinburgh he headed for London to meet up with Bob Dylan, Eric Von Schmidt (a folk blues singer) and Mimi Baez, a younger sister of Joan Baez. Here they played gigs at the 'Troubadour', a folk club dominated by singers close to Hamish: Dominic Behan, Martin Carthy, Bob Davenport, Louis Killen. Within days Mimi Baez and Farina became lovers; within weeks they had eloped to Paris to sing for their supper in troubadour style. Farina later described how Mimi danced to a hat whilst he became 'a blind-singer who miraculously regained his sight each night!' They were a highly poetical couple and having settled in a log cabin outside Carmel in California dedicated their lives to the peace movement. In 1965 they released an LP, *Celebrations for a Grey Day*. All the songs were written by Farina and sung by Mimi; one of the instrumental pieces is called 'Hamish'. On the sleeve notes it is described as 'A smiling nod to olde Hamish Henderson, humming poems and songs aloud in all the prouder pubs of Scotland. The blend of "Banks o' Sicily" and Schroeder's Beethoven is half the devil's and our own.' Hamish was delighted but, four years after Farina's death, wrote to the MCPS (Mechanical-Copyright Protection Society): 'Dick Farina's "Hamish", which is based on my "Banks of Sicily" is my copyright. The Dick Farina L.P. on which this number appeared was a best-selling folk record . . . '

Many of Hamish's more radical friends died young; Farina died on 1 May 1966. A party was held to celebrate publication of his novel *Been Down So Long It Looks Like Up to Me*; it was Mimi's twenty-first birthday. During the evening a stranger at the party offered Farina a ride on the back of his motorcycle. A mile up the road, travelling at 90 miles an hour into a 90-degree bend, the bike crashed – throwing Farina, riding pillion, to his death. The biker, in the best Wild West tradition, seems to have disappeared never to be heard of again. For Mimi, for music, for the world peace movement, Farina's death was a terrible loss. In 2007 the Italian folk scholar Pino Mereu sent me an email describing Hamish's influence on Farina and Dylan.

> Richard Farina learned all Hamish's songs. Hamish's influence on Farina was huge: through Scots tradition bearers like Jeannie Robertson, Ella Ward, Jimmy MacBeath, Davie Stewart and Scots/Americans like Jean Ritchie (who taught Farina to play the dulcimer). Farina knew the Clancy Brothers very well. Their lead man Tommy Makem wrote: 'We must not forget the importance of Hamish in the anti nuclear movement of the Sixties. He was one of the first to fight against nuclear armament. And I think that songs such as "A Hard Rain's Gonna Fall" from Bob Dylan [were] inspired from the anti-nuclear marches in Scotland and directly from recordings such as Ding Dong Dollar – and Scottish Republican songs . . . Hamish with Norman Buchan, Matt McGinn and many others always choose as melodies for their words Scots/Irish tunes.'
>
> Dylan often sang 'Banks of Sicily'. It was available in the USA from 1947 onwards. He also knew Pete Seeger's song 'Where Have all the Flowers Gone' (recorded by Folkways in 1956). Jean Redpath sang various songs that Hamish had collected to Dylan in 1961. Hamish's 'The Freedom Come a' Ye' completed in January 1960 was regularly sung by Pete Seeger and it appears on the Ding Dong Dollar album released by Folkways in New York in 1961. The opening lines of Hamish's song are a brilliant evocation of the Nuclear Threat:

Roch the wind in the clear day's dawin
Blaws the cloods heelster-gowdie ow'r the bay
But there's mair nor a roch wind blawin
Through the great glen o' the world the day.

And there is no doubt that Hamish influenced Dylan's songs, 'Blowin' in the Wind', and 'A Hard Rain's Gonna Fall' – both of which deal, amongst other things, with the nuclear threat.

By 1963 Dr David Craig had encouraged Hamish to take a particular interest in Dylan as an artistic phenomenon on the world folk scene, and notes and letters suggest that Hamish believed he'd had something to do with Dylan's emergence as a great singer. In 1965, for example, he received this letter from Joe Morgan, 5727 South Kensington, La Grange, Illinois, 60525. 'Dear Hamish, . . . I heard that song you had written that Dylan sang before he was DYLAN (I can't remember the name of it just now). I heard it the night I played at the Grand and I really liked the song – could you send me a copy of the words, or any kind of recording of the song?' In 1966 Hamish made notes about Dylan's place in the Folk Revival ('Idea for an Article'):

> The best analysis of Dylan's work is the paperback "Freedom in the Air" by Josh Duncan, which looks at the new American song writers and relates them, correctly, to the British song-writing revival of the Fifties which gave them their inspiration . . . Bob Dylan is the tip of the iceberg. He personifies a historical phenomenon and we must recognise that the folk process is not only deep but slow-moving. There are many who are silent, who don't open their mouths – but two or three years later they become folk artists. The question of time – of slow (necessarily slow) maturing must be recognised; as must the dangers of the tin-pan-alley cash nexus, and the destructive power of scorn and scoffing. Endless patience and self-restraint are needed and the moment makes up for a good deal . . . The moment experienced by the creator of 'folk art' should be comparable with the moment created by the individual artist, poet or composer. And lucky are those societies in which 'folk' and 'art' cultures experience such moments intermingling.[4]

Since Hamish's death, new research by the Scots traditional singer Rab Noakes, and others, has confirmed numerous connections between Hamish's work and Dylan. In particular, Noakes has asserted that it was the tune of 'Banks o' Sicily' (Pipe Major Robertson's 'Farewell to the Creeks') that directly inspired Dylan's 'The Times They Are A-Changin'.

---

4 HH, unpublished notes, Henderson archive.

Perhaps more importantly, the words and imagery of this song owe more than a little to 'The Freedom Come a' Ye'. When, in 2004, the world's media took up this story, Dylan is quoted as saying: 'You use what's been handed down. "The Times They Are A-Changin" is probably from an old Scottish folksong.'[5]

5 Quoted in Senay Boztas 'Dylan song a-changed a Scots tune', *The Sunday Times*, 11 April 2004.

THIRTEEN

Literary Friendships and an Incompatible Rival

> *The non-genuine person cannot believe that the genuine (das Echte) exists.*
>
> HH, 1984

Hamish's relationships with his academic and literary peers were rarely as relaxed as his communion with 'the folk'. His life amongst the Travellers earned him respect but also a distanced antipathy. However, his natural generosity and warmth led him to form many close friendships with other writers and poets. During the early years of Hamish's marriage, three long friendships – with Tom Scott, Ian Hamilton Finlay and Stuart MacGregor – blossomed into creative relationships that have had a continuing influence on Scottish culture.

Hamish and Tom Scott[1] first met in London in 1946. In 1950 Scott worked with Hamish and Lomax whilst they made their Edinburgh recordings. In the sixties, when both men had young wives, their relationship was at its closest. Both men were singers and liked to drink. Scott often disagreed with Hamish but had permanent faith in his vision for Scotland and 'worried' about him. For instance the announcement, at New Year 1959, that Hamish was to marry spurred Scott to address the 'Hamish problem' – what was he, where was he going? And on 22 January he published an important article in the Edinburgh University magazine *The Student*. His subject was Robert Burns and the responsibilities and qualities any 'national poet' must have but – between the lines – Scott seems to address Hamish, at this make-or-break moment in his career as a poet.

> The national poet, when he comes, if he comes, will have to have epic and/or dramatic power, a universal mind as well as poetic genius (almost a term of abuse these scientific days), the ability to integrate Scots and English, a knowledge of Gaelic and awareness of the Celtic world, a feeling for the Admirable Crichton as well as Burns, and for Knox, James Simpson, and the great engineers. He

---

1 Tom Scott (1918–1995), poet and author of *A Historical Review of Scottish Literature*.

> would have to have the stature of a Walter Scott as well as poetic genius. I see no sign of such a man anywhere around us today, but until he comes it is folly to speak of Burns as a 'national' poet. It creates darkness.
>
> When I stand in St Giles on Sunday in honour of Scottish poetry, for which Burns gave all he had, I shall think also of John Knox, and wish that Burns could have had some of his guts and spiritual power, and that Knox's savage inhumanity could have been mellowed by the sweetness and geniality of Burns . . . I shall let them meet within myself and make at least that contribution towards the healing of that so-called Caledonian Antisyzygy, a polite name for a form of schizophrenia. It is ironical to reflect, too, that were Burns alive today he would be considered, like the late Edwin Muir, unqualified to teach Scottish bairns their A.B.C . . .

Hamish was exactly this kind of 'unqualified teacher'. By introducing the idea of a Caledonian Antisyzygy, Scott raises, and puts aside, MacDiarmid's claim to be Scotland's national poet, but 'the capacities' he suggests that Scotland's future national poet will need seem very much the capacities Hamish possessed in abundance. Or had possessed? In the article, Scott seems to be making a public plea to Hamish – 'to rise now or forever hold your peace'. It was the same plea that MacDiarmid had made to Hamish in the mid fifties – in poems like 'King Over Himself' (see Volume 1 of this biography). Scott, like many others, believed it a tragedy that Hamish had produced no significant poetry since his return from Italy in 1950.

Perhaps Scott sensed that the battle was already lost. In the mid twentieth century no university in Scotland had the wit to host a national poet. The Scottish Arts Council did not exist in 1959 and when it was established its brief was broad and short-term. And he knew no wife (without big money behind her) could set the stage on which a struggling 'national poet' might find himself. Thus, Tom Scott metaphorically 'cries out' in this article for his staggering hero to break mould – before time and drink take him down. And Scott was not alone: on 3 April 1959 – just weeks before Hamish set off for Germany to be married – the poet and playwright Joe Corrie wrote to Hamish from Glenrothes in Fife. His letter stresses how important it is that the BBC integrate 'good, relevant, modern Scottish songs' into Scotland's national life and states that he hopes Hamish will get back to song-writing:

> There are limitless subjects at the moment to sing about as we are living in an entirely new age, but who is to start the ball rolling? . . . a number of the lyrics of such poets as C.M. Grieve just don't have the lyric quality. A lyric should half-sing itself, have a beginning, a

> middle, and an end, and the poet must have the dramatic instinct to keep his best thought for the last. That was where Burns scored every time . . .

Corrie's words spoke straight to Hamish's heart and over the following four years Hamish wrote at least four great songs, 'The Freedom Come a' Ye', 'The Flyting o' Life and Daith', 'Rivonia' and 'Floret Silva Undique'. Scott and Corrie did their bit, and the happiness Katzel brought Hamish certainly played its part. And it is unlikely to be coincidence that the first of these songs, 'The Freedom Come a' Ye' (written September 1959 / January 1960) embraces exactly the kind of national/international issues Scott and Corrie had suggested should be pursued. Katzel recalls Hamish composing it, 'in a white heat of commitment! He pounded up and down the corridors of the flat, binding the words to the tune. I was terrified of disturbing him.'[2] From the beginning, Hamish knew this song was an anthem of real artistic and national consequence. Whether Hamish was conscious of the stimulus that Katzel, Corrie and Scott had given him is unknowable, but lifelong – within his limitations – he remained loyal to all three.

In 1967, when Hamish learned that Corrie had fallen on hard times and was living in frustrating isolation in Glenrothes, Hamish asked Arthur Argo to feature Corrie as 'a literary giant' in his magazine *Chapbook*. In the thirties, T.S. Eliot had described Corrie as 'Scotland's greatest poet since Burns', and *Chapbook* stimulated a critical re-estimation of a dramatist sidelined for years as a socialist has-been. Corrie suddenly found himself mildly lauded. He moved to Edinburgh, and Alex Reid, of the *New Yorker*, profiled him in the *Edinburgh Evening News*. His article concluded, 'Joe Corrie is certainly a most welcome addition to the literary world of the city.' The same year *Chapbook* brought out a special edition featuring Hamish, and it provoked this letter from Tom Scott:

> Dear Hamish, Chapbook certainly does you proud . . . You have deserved well of your country and its folksong, and if your country, as is its wont, repays you with impalement on the thistle, its highest award for its benefactors, at least the folksong elements are in no doubt at all about your importance, and rightly hail you, as the father of the folk-song revival in Scotland.
>
> I remember you once complaining to me about my lack of sympathy for your aims, at some long forgotten meeting with Tambimuttu[3] [1946/47] but you have more than justified your position, and I

2 Katzel Henderson, conversation with TN, 2007.

3 Meary James Thurairajah Tambimuttu (1915–1983) poet and editor.

> too, whatever my romantic attitudes of the time, have lived to be glad to strike roots of my own as deep into the folk as I can, in my way . . . You are a great romantic, and I envy your faith in that vision. For me the faith has long been overlaid by a profound scepticism, so that it has become more a wish than a faith now. But, still, my heart is with the vision of man restored to his wholeness, and whatever my sceptical mind may say, my work – and voluntary work is the only abiding good I have discovered – carries on the mental fight to build Jerusalem in every green and pleasant land.

> Needless to say I don't agree with Grieve [MacDiarmid], though I have sympathy with some of the motives that underlie his position. But I see no reason to create false antitheses all over the place, as if there weren't enough real problems without that. But he is divisive – there is an undeclared motive of hate for any face not his own in the glass. There is no reason to ask whether a child has a father or a mother – it's an unreal problem. And the mother of art poetry is the folk, out of whom the rocket soars – even Grieve – and back to whom it sinks. 'But the earth abideth'. To most people there is war enough without making one of poetry – in the Muse's house also are many mansions. That there are dangers attendant on your work you know yourself – but danger is the common lot.

* * *

Today, Ian Hamilton Finlay has a major reputation as an international artist but he always saw himself as a poet. It was as a young ex-serviceman – dedicated to poetry and working as a Perthshire shepherd – that Finlay first made contact with Hamish in the late 1940s. In 1959, having established the Wild Hawthorn Press, he renewed contact. Finlay got enormous intellectual and artistic pleasure from the manipulation of word and image and it was after he had founded his Art Press that his long march – as one of the most original artists of the late twentieth century – began.

The cultural visions of Hamish and Finlay were at once similar and very different. Both were classicists with an ear for the Scots vernacular but whereas Finlay was highly Apollonian, Hamish was romantic and bacchanalian. Both worked intensively with other artists but whereas Finlay pulled everything together, Hamish watched his bread drift away on the waters. They were good for each other and helped each other across fifty years. In 1959 Hamish encouraged Finlay in his plans for a revolutionary new magazine entitled *Poor Old Tired Horse*, better known as *POTH*. Today this 'little magazine' is recognised as a major Scottish contribution to the 'Concrete Poetry Movement'. On 24 February 1960 Finlay wrote to Hamish from 24 Fettes Row, Edinburgh:

> Dear Hamish, . . . I was very interested to see in today's Scotsman a wee report of your talk on two poet Macs [McGonagall and MacDiarmid]. Do you have any interest (it seems to me that it would be nice if people did have) in the *possibilities* of Folk? . . . i.e. you talk about the long folk line, of the concertina sort, with rhyme endings, and it's true, the earlier Mac is very inventive with this. Do you know my poem, Angles of Stamps, in *The Dancers Inherit the Party*? – I tried to use the long folk line there, with a kind of *ironical sophistication*, and it seems to me this *use* of folk – i.e., a deliberate use of it, putting it to use, has a lot of possibilities. As has the use of actual Scots, Glasgow Scots and so on.
>
> Do you know of any Russian poets of the time of the painters Larionov, Goncharova etc.? They used street – folk – speech (such as I horrified local folk by doing in *Glasgow Beasts*), and the painters, too, were crazy on folk art, and USED it in their work. We are trying to get together a special number of POTH to honour the Russian avant-garde of that time, inc. Malevich, Tatlin, etc. as well, and if you could do any translations of the folk-jazzy poetry they did, I would be awfully glad, i.e. I'm sick of folk as a DEAD thing, and they never treated it as such. Do you know Zoshchenko's angry words about the people who resented his using gutter-folk-idioms to make stories from? Of course, the thing is, to use – not to duplicate from outside, but to make from, by understanding. We are surely very narrow if we understand only one culture (they talk of two cultures, but it seems to me there are twenty two. And all of value).

Finlay's 'folk thinking' – along determinedly international lines – further stimulated Hamish's own and, together, they resisted MacDiarmid's mean-minded Scotch bullying. Hamish played a leading part in the *Honour'd Shade* Flyting, Finlay took Scots Concrete Poetry onto the stage of international Modernism. *POTH* did not actually appear until 1962, but it lived up to expectations. For example, *POTH* No. 6 presented *'poesia concreta'* by the Brazilian artists Marcelo Moura, Pedro Xisto and Augusto de Campo; *POTH* No. 18 presented stunning imagery by Bridget Riley with 'writings and script by Ad Reinhardt'. When MacDiarmid attacked the new magazine, Hamish jumped to Finlay's defence with public statements of support. MacDiarmid's tirades against Finlay, in a pamphlet entitled *Ugly Birds Without Wings*, so appalled Hamish that he jotted down these private counter thoughts:

Ugly birds:
It is nae sin to call a green leaf grey.

The mortal sin of antinomian Calvinism
Is the monstrous conspiracy of the old against the young.[4]

Finlay was soon writing to the Austrian poet Ernst Jandl: 'An extraordinary thing has happened – that Hugh MacDiarmid, who I told you of – our leading poet – has announced that unless I am *excluded* from the [Oxford] University press anthology of contemporary Scottish poetry, he will not permit his own poems to appear in it . . . Really Ernst, can you imagine such a thing!' In April 1966 Finlay commiserated with Hamish who had recently been similarly treated by Faber:

> I got the new addition of the Faber Scottish anthology, and find you aren't in it. Is there any reason? I mean, you didn't refuse to be in it, or anything, did you? I couldn't believe there was nothing of yours. It seems strange. Actually, it seems impossible . . . There's to be an Arts Council show of 'concrete poetry' during the Festival. They have asked Edwin Morgan to arrange it; I feel very strongly that it should have been jointly edited by Morgan and me, since – so far as the world is concerned – the Wild Hawthorn Press IS Scottish concrete poetry.

By 15 May, Finlay's problems were domestic as well as artistic. He was lodging in a cottage in grounds close to the Ross-shire home of Eric Linklater, the novelist. An obscene squabble broke out between various lairds and tenants. Finlay writes:

> Dear Hamish, Since I last wrote our lives have been turned upside-down – first, stupid gossip from the Linklaters to our landlord's wife, about us being unmarried (as if THAT was any business of theirs) – next, demand that I work as labourer for my landlord – to expiate my sins as it were . . . That is, so that they can feel I am not 'getting away with anything' by being a poet and building a nice garden and having a nice wee baby. Of course as we pay RENT and have a lease, I declined to work as a labourer – is my own work not work? . . . Finally, letters to third parties saying I am 'mad' . . . A quite impossible situation, based on nothing but greed – greed, licensed by idle gossip from the wife and daughter of a rotten Scotch novelist whose work I would not have in my house . . . I had actually to get my doctor to go and tell them I am 'sane' and to pay a lawyer to threaten them with an action for

4 HH, unpublished notes, Henderson archive.

> defamation . . . and on top of it all, Mavor of the Arts Council dares to come with the Linklater woman and ask to bring her in (here) 'for a literary chat'! . . . So we have lost our home – we have to be out in six weeks . . . and I immediately told the Arts Council I wanted nothing more to do with them (since they seem to prefer gossiping bitches and landlords to poets) we have also no doubt lost our wee POTH grant . . . Ironically, I had a nasty letter from Edwin Morgan telling me I've had my 'last chance'. Ah, fellow-poets are a great boon in this life . . . Well, to hell with them all. Such is life . . .

On 6 June 1966 Finlay wrote from Ardgay: 'Dear Hamish, please forgive my delay in thanking you for your kind letter, and your *very large* POTH sub. Thank you so much.' The following year Finlay, with his family, moved to Stoneypath, in the Pentland Hills. There they began creating 'Little Sparta', one of the great modern gardens of the world. Its centrepiece is an old byre transformed into a neo-classical garden temple, inscribed 'To Apollo / His Music / His missiles / His Muses'. Thus, at Little Sparta, the Scots folk vernacular runs in tandem with Greece and Rome, and the English landscaped garden. The effect is sublime, the scale small, but landscape, architecture, sculpture, poetry, history are orchestrated to brilliant, hard-head Aeolian effect.

This marvellous intellectual friendship flared again in the 1980s when Little Sparta found itself the victim of a destructive attack by the Planning and Taxation Departments of Strathclyde Regional Council. This matter will be returned to in Chapter 25.

* * *

Dr Stuart MacGregor was Hamish's closest personal friend during the period 1956–65. MacGregor was a medical student, a singer and writer in whom Hamish recognised many of the strengths and weaknesses of Scotland down the ages. The Edinburgh University Medical School abutted Forrest Road and Sandy Bell's Bar, and MacGregor took to the folk scene like a native. He was a Scots nationalist with a wild and rebellious streak. In 1958 MacGregor was the driving force behind the formation of the Edinburgh University Folk Club. After qualifying in medicine he served as doctor with the British Army of the Rhine but remained a big character on the Edinburgh folk and literary scenes – writing songs, poems and novels. Later, MacGregor got a job at the University of the West Indies in Kingston, Jamaica, where he died in 1973 aged thirty-seven. Today, his reputation as a writer and one of Scotland's most creative 'angry young men' is on the rise.

MacGregor's most important novels are *The Myrtle and Ivy*

(MacDonald 1967) and *The Sinner* (Calder and Boyars 1973). Both books have a strongly autobiographical basis and are set in the Old Town of Edinburgh. Both feature major characters based on Hamish. In *The Myrtle and Ivy*, Hamish appears as a radical university lecturer and folk-entrepreneur named Hector Gunn. In *The Sinner*, Hamish appears as Nichol Ross – a folk-poet-prophet who will be betrayed by his 'follower' Denis Sellers, a character based, largely, on MacGregor himself. The first book is centred on the folk scene of the mid fifties and dedicated to 'the Brotherhood of Sandy Bell's [and] the two great seats of Edinburgh learning – Sandy Bell's and the University'. The novel explores an 'underground Edinburgh' where sexuality, drink, medical criminality, republicanism and police surveillance provide the framework for a dramatic love story involving a medical student and two passionate women. Whenever Hector Gunn appears, the idea of 'the nobility of man' and 'Highland courtesy' come with him. *The Myrtle and Ivy* is at once imaginative fiction, social realism and a personal testament to a man of vision – Hector Gunn. During a Hogmanay police raid, for example, one of the drunks describes him as 'the saviour of Scotland'.

The Sinner deals with the Edinburgh of the sixties. Formally a more philosophical, modernist and experimental work, it ends with Nichol Ross (HH) dying mysteriously, by his own hand, in the Pentland Hills. MacGregor, however, makes it clear that it is the city of Edinburgh and the destructive forces of Calvinism endemic in Scotland (encoded in the character of Denis Sellers) that forced this sorry pass. 'We both crucified him, and rightly so.' Nichol Ross is already dead at the start of the novel: he is introduced as an enigma and remains one.

> The rumours, particularly in Connor's [Sandy Bell's]: a ruined aristocrat, the bottle. A fisherman's son, left home because of a woman, said Joe the Rat. Really an Englishman, said Starkey Shearer, there are Oxford undertones in thet eccent. An unfrocked priest, from Ollie the Bull, the Harlem schizophrenic. Deals in black magic, queer noises from his house at night. Best novelist we had fifteen years ago, hasn't written much since.
>
> We talk about you, Nichol, how could we help it? . . . Were you a fragment of God? But it's too late now. The Powers of Darkness, the two mad Johns, still rule this City . . . Together we raised a new rebel standard, then like all the others we went the way of history, turned on each other and . . .[5]

5 Stuart MacGregor, *The Sinner* (Calder and Boyars 1973).

The two mad Johns are John Calvin and John Knox. And against them MacGregor presents Nichol Ross – as a visionary, a saintly poet, a metaphysical philosopher and a modern Montrose. In one scene, Ross takes two lovers to the spot where Montrose was executed, in the High Street of Edinburgh. There, Nichol – raising his arms like a druid – oversees them being given Gaelic oaths of allegiance, to each other and to Scotland; then he blesses them in marriage.

The place of Montrose's execution is marked with a brass H amongst the cobbles. Hamish identified strongly with Montrose and with this spot. Montrose's heroism on the scaffold before his execution was something that Hamish honoured deeply. Hamish was not a suicidal type but, in the late sixties and early seventies, his creativity was in abeyance, his domestic situation fraught, his plans all over the place. The poet William Neill, like MacGregor, recognised this fact and gives it remarkable expression in a poem entitled 'Edinburgh Don, 1971'. Neill, a member of the radical literary group known as the Heretics (of which MacGregor was a member), wrote it after an afternoon in Hamish's attic study, in 27 George Square.

In this high centre
of all that's known and ever can be known
I gaze across the cities of the plain
to clearer skies beyond.

Soon they will come,
secure in their new prophecies,
sure their causes have the best effects.

Soon they will come, eager disciples;
seeking yearned truths, at last they will come to wisdom,
seeing the years bring no knowledge,
syllogisms no surety.

For my disciples I resurrect no gods,
only the whispering phantoms of old words,
the gibbering ghosts of long dead certainties.

I am the living link of the old chain,
my cell a little warmer than Lindisfarne,
a little less remote than Icolmkill.

Our faltering guidance still remains unhonoured,
the well-born lackey of the worldly-wise.

I pull my gown around me, close my window
lest in the traitor moment I should hurl
my body concretewards from this high temple.[6]

Neill, like Tom Scott and Joe Corrie, recognised in Hamish visionary genius and great flaws but it was Stuart MacGregor who most deeply understood his character. In *The Sinner* he writes: 'Dear Man of Men so strange thy words and strong / Below the spires that John had screamed among / Yet under madness in my heart a song.' When MacGregor left Scotland in 1972 to take up a medical post at the University of the West Indies, Hamish wrote a ballad in his honour, 'To Stuart – on his Leaving for Jamaica'. Here is the last verse:

Stuart, atween us braid maun roll
'A waste o' seas' – a vale o' water.
(What signifies a waste o' seas?
A waste o' beer's anither matter.)
But in their cups, in auld Bell's bar
The Legion o' the Damned will mind ye;
And howp that, noo and then, ye'll toast
The gallus crew ye've left behind ye.[7]

On 25 January 1973, Burns Night, MacGregor was killed in a road accident – after a visit to his friend Ian Sangster. A tyre blew out and the car crashed into a tree.

* * *

Another of Hamish's long friendships was with the poet W.S. Graham. They met regularly in the forties, but when Graham settled in Cornwall contact became occasional. On 24 January 1966 Graham wrote from Madron: 'How nice to hear from you Hamish, my seldom seen old fuck-recording friend of the North . . . Many thanks for the Chapbook and your wee mention of BALDY BANE. In a poem of mine, The Dark Dialogues, there's a section to do with a kitchen in the high tenement top of my childhood in Greenock which, I think, comes from realer folk springs than that. Anyway it was good to come across the BALDY BANE bit in your article suddenly. I was reading it before I realised it was me.'

Graham died in January 1986 but the previous summer his wife Nessa brought him to Edinburgh for the Festival. He was seriously ill and knew this would be his last visit to Scotland. On the evening of their

6 Published in *Aquarius* No. 6 (Scottish Issue), 1973 (with a related poem, 'A Celtic History').

7 Published in the *Collected Poems*.

departure, Hamish accompanied them to Waverley Station to see them off on the sleeper. When Nessa had settled Graham into his bunk, he asked Hamish to sing 'The Banks o' Sicily'. After that Hamish sang 'The Freedom Come a' Ye'. Back in Cornwall, Nessa wrote to thank Hamish and say how much that farewell had meant to Sydney, leaving his native land for ever.

Robert Garioch (Sutherland) was another poet of the war generation. Following publication of Hamish's *Ballads of World War II*, Garioch sent a letter and a selection of unpublished works for Volume 2, and a lifelong friendship began. In 1959, Garioch backed Hamish in his flyting with MacDiarmid, and his poem 'Embro to the Ploy' makes reference to it:

> The Café Royal and Abbotsford
> Are filled wi orra folk
> Whas stock-in-trade's the scrievit word,
> Or twicet-scrievit joke . . . [8]

In October 1962 Hamish and Garioch attended the annual gathering at the grave of the eighteenth-century poet Robert Fergusson. It inspired Garioch to write what Hamish thought was one of his best poems.

> Strang, present drool
> Ruggs at my hairt. Lichtlie this gin ye daur:
> Here Robert Burns knelt and kissed the mool.[9]

In September 1965 Hamish noted in his diary 'Robert Garioch Sutherland needs a job' (Garioch had been making a living as a teacher in Croydon for years). Shortly after this Garioch started work at the *Dictionary of the Older Scottish Tongue*, in the School of Scottish Studies building in George Square. It was a job for which he was brilliantly qualified but also brought Edinburgh's poet back to Edinburgh. Garioch was a small, shy man. When MacDiarmid took a strong dislike to him, Hamish became, in a way, his protector, and Garioch (a prisoner-of-war in Italy) looked on Hamish with something approaching hero-worship.

Hamish's friendship with Helen Cruickshank continued till her death in March 1975 and he makes several appearances in Cruickshank's autobiography:[10]

---

8 'Embro to the Ploy', published in *Robert Garioch: Collected Poems* (Polygon 2004).

9 'At Robert Fergusson's Grave', in Garioch, *Complete Political Works* (Macdonald 1973).

10 Helen Cruickshank, *Octobiography* (Standard Press 1976).

> through [Hamish's] introductions I had a host of interesting visitors from the folksong and theatrical world – he is now married to a charming German girl and I am the proud godmother of his eldest daughter . . . I had a feast of folksong. The dishes were washed up to songs in Scots, Gaelic, English, German, French or Italian. Visitors included Jeannie Robertson and several singers of bothy ballads from 'twal mile roun'. I had Alan Lomax, the famous American folk collector for the Library of Congress, as a one night guest. Isla Cameron pulled at our heart-strings as she gentled thro' 'I know where I'm going'. I think Norman MacCaig played the fiddle, Hamish sang in five languages and a French girl who was helping me in the kitchen moaned, 'Do these people *never* go home!'

By the mid sixties Naomi Mitchison was spending much of each year in Africa and kept Hamish in touch with her doings. In 1964 she writes:

> I am as deeply involved in Africa as one can be, having become a full member of the Bakgatla, taking all responsibilities. One might well be in C18th Scotland, only with a chief and half a dozen others who know their history and what at least to avoid. Sometimes I wish I could love them less and could see the vices that undoubtedly they must have, more clearly. At any rate they have the most lovely songs . . . I am so much struck by the similarity between the 'great music' of Africa and the 'great music' of the Highlands that I want them to have some of the latter – I am wondering if the SSS have any records?

Hamish wrote back, promising a bundle of tapes and his new song, 'Rivonia'. Mitchison told him to be careful: 'it would be nice to get the Mandela song but if you do put that on – don't put it at the beginning of the tape. If you started with a nice bit of Shakespeare, it would be all right.'

George Mackay Brown made contact with Hamish before becoming a student at Newbattle Abbey College in the mid fifties. Subsequently Hamish kept a distant fatherly eye on the young writer's development and wellbeing. In the early sixties Tom Scott wrote to Hamish: 'George Mackay Brown – his grant ends this term. He has told me he would like to do some work on the ballads . . . Have you any ideas? How is the School placed these days? If he works on ballads, obviously you will be one of his supervisors. What about Mrs Ross's dept? George is of delicate health – teaching is right out. It would be a disgrace to let him starve, for he is a genuine poet and has a good deal to contribute.'

Of Glasgow's many writers, the one who probably owes the biggest personal debt to Hamish is Eddie Linden. Eddie was born in Ulster in 1936, christened Sean Glackin Quinn and sent to Scotland for adoption. He was brought up a Catholic in a working-class Protestant house; he was a rebellious teenager, briefly became a miner, joined the Young Communist League, then found himself a janitorial job at Glasgow School of Art. Interested in literature, he joined the London gay scene of the sixties. He met Hamish via Father Anthony Ross, a free-thinking Chaplain at the University of Edinburgh. In 1969 Eddie launched his own, highly idiosyncratic literary magazine *Aquarius*, which ran for thirty years. Eddie delegated much of the editing to professionals with greater skills than his. *Aquarius* became a collective achievement (outside the Fort Bastion of academia) – and all the more important for that. *Aquarius* No. 6 (edited by Tom Buchan, 1973) was particularly impressive, featuring some ground-breaking poems by Tom McGrath. In 1979 *Who Is Eddie Linden?* by Sebastian Barker (J. Landesman 1979) appeared, and in 1980 *City of Razors*, a collection of Linden's poetry. Buoyed by this success, Eddie's visits to Edinburgh became, for a time, a little too frequent. He normally lodged with Hamish and could prove exhausting and difficult company. In 2004 Eddie jotted down his own remembrances of Hamish:

> I remember my first meeting with Hamish. It was a beautiful summer's day, midday: Sandy Bell's was packed and the musicians were there in the corner. I saw this tall-legged man wearing a sport's jacket and a white open-necked shirt, as he always did – entertaining in a very generous way. He approached me as if he'd known me all his life. He handed me a glass of whisky, and I handed him a copy of Aquarius, issue number one – and I read him one of my poems, 'City of Razors'. That day was to last into the evening – ending in an Italian restaurant. We became friends. There were rumours Hamish was a homo-sexual but he never made a pass at me.
>
> We did poetry readings together in London and Edinburgh and sometimes there were the four of us – Gerry Mangan, the artist, and Father Anthony Ross. One night I shared Hamish's flat with an entertaining old shepherd from the Hogg Country – Willie Scott. It was the time of the terrible tragic war that was going on in Ireland and me, with my Irish background, I was wearing a big sash round my waist, hanging down. We polished off a bottle of Glenmorangie; then Hamish took me down to the bus station to catch the overnight coach to London. Having climbed aboard, I declared myself an Irish Republican! I was taken off the bus and put in a police cell and questioned about a bomb that had gone off near the castle. It was said to have been planted by a Glasgow Irishman with a strong Scottish accent and red hair. That was me! So I got them to phone

> up and ask Hamish where I'd been that night, and next morning he came down and paid the fine for my drunkenness . . . I'm not in this game for money or rewards: I'm in it for love, a love of literature, a love of people like Hamish – and Colin MacInnes, Harold Pinter, John Heath Stubbs. What we need now is a new class of working class leaders! Like Hamish![11]

One literary figure with whom Hamish never got on was Alan Bold. Bold was precocious and productive as a poet, writer and editor. Born in 1943, he emerged on the Edinburgh scene with his own magazine, *Rocket*, in 1964. He had supported MacDiarmid in the folksong flyting, and David Craig was not impressed, writing:

> Dear Hamish . . . Re *Rocket* – Alan Bold's outpourings seem negligible to me, as they were in *Gambit* last summer. Surely he is hopelessly wordy and bludgeoning, with next to no edge, penetration, expressive qualities? Clearly he is doing a good job of polemic – organising. But I think it would only encourage a rough-neck atmosphere in Scottish cultural affairs if he were to be taken seriously.

Hamish, initially, was much less censorious and when Bold requested literary assistance Hamish responded generously. For example, in February 1965 Bold wrote to thank Hamish for a copy of the magazine *Sing* and various enclosures. Excited by Hamish's new song 'Rivonia', Bold sent him his own latest song, 'Rachman's Riddle'. This, however, was followed by a series of approaches that Hamish felt were demeaning and self-centred. On 29 May he wrote to Maurice Fleming:

> *Lines* has the most interesting record of all 'little Magazines' except *POTH*. As for *Rocket*, I am one of its 30 – or is it 40 – subscribers, but I have strong reservations about it, not unconnected with the personality and general attitudes of Alan Bold himself – a conceited 'gowk' if ever I saw one. God, how I hate this bumptious-blate cocksureness and overweening conceit which lies thick on practically everything he writes. (I can't deny there's a personal bias, too – one or two of Bold's missives to me might have been sent from Mount Olympus to a helot dimly discerned among the olive groves below.) Bold seems to have taken over holus bolus all MacDiarmid's most outrageous 'Great I Am' and 'elect of the elect' pretensions – pretensions which in the old man's case have led to what at times seemed like a clinical solipsism. If Bold isn't gey careful, he'll go the same way.

---

11 Eddie Linden, letters emailed to TN, 2004.

Alan Bold took Hamish's generosity (natural intellectual profligacy) well beyond the pale. For example, when Bold was commissioned by Penguin Books to edit a collection of socialist poetry (which he sensibly decided should include songs), he wrote to Hamish in January 1969 asking Hamish to supply him with the best socialist songs written since 1848 – from any nation in any language – as long as good translations existed!

In April 1973 the two men met when the student radical Ray Burnett invited Hamish and Bold as lead speakers at a weekend conference on the Culture of Scotland at Marischal College, Aberdeen. In the major debate, Bold and Burnett were to speak for the motion, 'This House Condemns the SNP as a Pedlar of Myths'. It was opposed by Michael Grieve[12] and the artist Donald Bain. Unfortunately, things got off to a bad start. 'Bold arrived', says Burnett, 'demanding his fee up-front. I got him his £8, which he immediately spent on drink in the Union bar. His performance was an insult. Most of Scotland's leading intellectuals were there. It was a good conference but Bold ruined the debate. Hamish spoke from the floor: afterwards we drank together and, looking back, I can see that he changed my life that day.'[13] Hamish knew that Burnett was deeply involved in the crisis in Northern Ireland and it is evident that he went up to Aberdeen with intent in his mind. On 13 April 1973 Hamish wrote this letter to Tom Scott.

> The conference on 'What kind of Scotland' will be useful and fruitful – an attitude which postpones a discussion of these issues until after the achievement of independence is absolutely crass . . . If the Irish had spent more time in rational discussion about what sort of state they wanted to be, and less blethering about Cathleen ni Houlihan, they might not have landed with the ghastly split-minded and split-bodied pseudo independence which has now gone absolutely rancid on them . . . The time to change Scotland is now . . . I do not fancy an independent Scotland in which the ideas of that bloke McGuire McLure bear the gree, and Free Church ministers from the backwoods become actual legislators. And make no doubt about it – they'll do their damnedest to get in the saddle, just as the Irish hierarchy got firmly into it in 1923 . . . I shall do my utmost to make the conference a success.

Burnett was an Edinburgh Roman Catholic. His mother was Irish and whilst visiting relatives in Northern Ireland he had joined in protests organised by the Provisional IRA. In 1973, after five years of Troubles, Northern Ireland was very close to open civil war. Burnett was strongly

12 Michael Grieve, journalist, son of Christopher Grieve (Hugh MacDiarmid).

13 Ray Burnett, conversation with TN, 2009.

tempted to throw in his lot with the Provisionals. During the Aberdeen conference Burnett and Hamish discussed the situation at length and consequently Burnett, whilst not qualifying either his radical socialist passion or his Celtic nationalism, took up the cudgels of democracy. Within months the first issue of his magazine *Calgacus* appeared and he began his career as a journalist and teacher – on the island of Uist where Hamish had worked to complete his *Elegies,* and Calum Maclean had done so much valuable collecting.

In 1980 Bold wrote to inform Hamish that he was editing a book on erotic verse, and requested any erotic verses or bawdy songs he might have! Hamish probably had more bawdy in his head than any man who ever lived, and his study was stacked to the gunnels with hundreds of unpublished bawdy ballads and scripts. He seems not to have replied. Meantime Bold's friend Alexander Moffat had been making a series of paintings of Scotland's poets, funded by the Scottish Arts Council. Hamish was not one of them.

During the early 1980s Bold worked on commissions to write the biography, and edit the letters, of Hugh MacDiarmid. On 2 June 1982 he wrote to Hamish stating that he 'believed' Hamish might have MacDiarmid letters and asking if Hamish would provide the texts so that he could consider them for publication. Given the number of letters exchanged between Hamish and MacDiarmid as a public correspondence printed in newspapers, Hamish took Bold's letter as an insult, and no accommodation was reached. When *The Letters of Hugh MacDiarmid* (Hamish Hamilton 1984) was published the whole extraordinary correspondence between Hamish and MacDiarmid was omitted. This was the last straw. When Hamish heard that Joy Hendry, of *Chapman* magazine, was organising a party to celebrate the refurbishment of Milne's Bar in the New Town of Edinburgh, he decided to deliver Bold his come-uppance. The opening was planned as a grand event. Hamish arrived in kilt and tweed jacket. Joy Hendry takes up the story:

> All went well for some time. Then, I saw Hamish wander forward to where Alan Bold was draped over the bar. Hamish showed his teeth and a great forced smile spread over his face. The teeth were false, they had been made especially for the BBC documentary *The Dead, the Innocent*, and he hadn't worn them for years! He leaned forward, close-up to Alan and said: 'I put my teeth in Alan Bold!' Alan leaned back, havering and conciliatory. Hamish said again: 'I put my teeth in Alan Bold!' Then he drew himself up to his full height and said, 'I do not like you Alan Bold!' He set his jaw, closed his right fist and very slowly – in slow-motion – delivered an upper-cut that gently grazed Bold's chin. He repeated the gesture, announcing loudly – 'I do not like you Alan Bold!' It was a challenge to fight and

the barmen quickly moved in. Hamish was escorted out, without protest. It was a memorable moment.[14]

This seems to have been the last occasion on which Hamish stood ready to fight, and the fact that he had put on Highland dress was no accident: he was again Cuchulin – 'the half-naked savage' about whom MacCaig had written in 1949. Was this bullying? Possibly, but Bold had been 'bullying' Hamish for years and, just as Hamish had felt himself goaded to take his intellectual stand against MacDiarmid, he, finally, felt bound to act against Alan Bold.

Throughout his life Hamish was recurrently treated as a shambling fool. In the Abbotsford Bar in the early sixties, a young female companion of Norman MacCaig's quietly tied Hamish's shoe-laces together. When he moved to leave the bar he fell to the floor. It was school-boy funny but also a humiliating insult. His poem 'When the Teased Idiot Turns' gives expression to feelings that haunted him across a lifetime:

When the teased idiot turns
And in his little eye, before so patient,
The quickening anger burns
                I think with faith
Of all the uncouth, humped, hooped, malformed,
                Wry-fashioned

In the traitor's gate of death.
They to their cramped ledge cling
Death's hostages from among the living people
                And in the torments sing.
                They give me power
To hammer out verse, who am learner yet,
                Time's pupil
And spurn this unheeding hour.

                Unheeding, because the sky
Draws eyes into its dark, and spikes their sockets
And drowns the blindbuff cry
                In silence. Yet
The blind man twists his poppies, clasps his lockets
And splits the enfolding net.[15]

---

14 Joy Hendry, conversation with TN, 2008.

15 Probably written during the Second World War, published in the *Collected Poems*.

FOURTEEN

Songs of the Sixties and the Anti-apartheid Campaign

The runners who would challenge
The rough bounds of the desert
And strip for the test
On this barbarous arena
Must have sinews like hounds
And be cunning as jerboas.
HH[1]

The best critique yet published of Hamish's anthem 'The Freedom Come a' Ye' was written by Duncan Glen for the magazine *Inter Arts*, in October 1988. It also uses, for the first time, the excellent phrase 'Poetry becomes People' to describe Hamish's literary vision:

> Hamish Henderson's greatest song, and most widely sung, 'Freedom Come all Ye' is firmly rooted in Scotland and Scots vocabulary and the native song tradition but in its final two great lines Henderson looks to the Third World to truly usher in the new, socialist, freedom.
>
> And a black boy frae yont Nyanga
> Dings the fell gallows o' the burghers doon.
>
> 'Freedom Come All Ye' was originally part of the CND movement and the anti-Polaris campaign but it belongs to all time and all people. It is unique in Scottish literature – a masterpiece without qualification . . . Behind the song is the Burns tradition and all before him in the Scots song tradition, but Thomas Crawford also links it to Shelley and William Morris as well as to that modern 'peace-song' 'Blowin' in the Wind' [written three years later] . . . The 'simple-seeming' words are richly heavy with the cumulated weight of references that lies behind all true art language . . . There are many great opening lines in Scots poetry but that of the 'Freedom Come All Ye' is fit to be put beside any of them.

---

1 'Heroic Song for the Runners of Cyrene', *Elegies for the Dead in Cyrenaica* (Polygon 2008).

Roch the wind in the clear day's dawin
Blaws the cloods heelster-gowdie ow'r the bay,
But there's mair nor a roch wind blawin
Through the great glen o' the warld the day.
It's a thocht that will gar oor rottans
– A' they rogues that gang gallus, fresh and gay –
Tak the road, and seek ither loanins
For their ill ploys, tae sport and play.

Nae mair will the bonnie callants
Mairch tae war when oor braggarts crousely craw,
Nor wee weans frae pitheid and clachan
Mourn the ships sailin' doon the Broomielaw.
Broken families in lands we've herriet,
Will curse Scotland the Brave nae mair nae mair;
Black and white, ane til ither mairriet,
Mak the vile barracks o' their maisters bare.

So come all ye at hame wi Freedom,
Never heed whit the hoodies croak for doom.
In your hoose a' the bairns o' Adam
Can find breid, barley-bree and painted room.
When MacLean meets wi's freens in Springburn
A' the roses and geans will turn tae bloom,
And a black boy frae yont Nyanga
Dings the fell gallows o' the burghers doon.

The opening line was probably conceived in the berryfields of Blairgowrie. Hamish was watching a young tinker boy – about to have his hair cut *al fresco* by a bigger, tougher, elder brother – when he pleaded: 'Ye'll nae be roch!' The lines 'But there's mair not a roch wind blawin / Through the great glen of o' the warld the day' refer directly to the threat of nuclear war, and the whole song challenges the self-justifying rhetoric of the militant democracies. Out of a past riddled with imperial injustices Hamish conjures a future of brotherhood, wellbeing and ecological harmony.

The reference in the penultimate line to 'Nyanga' is to one of the two black townships outside Cape Town, which were then becoming centres of Black resistance to the Apartheid regime. For Hamish, the name evoked the sounds, the sights, the smells, the gathering rage of Africa. And the line 'Black and white, ane til ither mairriet' affirms the reality of the post-racial world emerging in the twenty-first century. One month after Hamish completed this song, Harold Macmillan delivered his historic 'Winds of Change' speech to the South African Parliament (3 February 1960). Two months later the Sharpeville massacre brought the brutality of Apartheid to the consciousness of the world.

In June 1963 a letter sent to the *Guardian* – by an eighteen-year-old student named Elaine Goldberg – attracted Hamish's attention. It was high-spirited and heroic and promised resistance, as South Africa moved towards 'totalitarianism'. Hamish put the letter in his archive, and the seeds of his song 'Rivonia' began to germinate. In August he helped organise a round-robin on behalf of the Scottish Anti-Apartheid Committee, to be sent to Dr Hilgard Muller at the South African High Commission in London. It read:

> We the undersigned deplore the decision by the South African government to refuse permission to A. Luthuli, winner of the Nobel Peace Prize, to journey to Glasgow for his rectorial installation. And we earnestly request the S.A. government to reconsider its decision.

One month before this, on 11 July 1963, Nelson Mandela and nineteen members of the African National Congress (mostly communists involved in 'armed-struggle' against the Apartheid regime) had been arrested and charged with treason, at Rivonia near Johannesburg (exactly ten years since Hamish's SRA friends had been arrested on the charge of conspiracy in Edinburgh). The trial of the arrested men began on 26 November 1963 (exactly ten years after the Conspiracy Trial in Edinburgh). Hamish recognised several other peculiar coincidences and, quite quickly, his Mandela ballad was born. Some years later, lecture notes outline the history of the song's genesis.

> 'Rivonia' is the name of the farm in South Africa where the South African National Congress leaders had taken refuge and where they were captured. Their trial was often referred to as the Rivonia trial. I made the song just after Nelson Mandela made that magnificent speech from the dock in November 1963. I was in London at the time and singing various Spanish Civil War songs, including '*Viva la Quince Brigada*' which has this refrain '*Rumbala, rumbala, rumba-la . . .*' and it struck me that that was rather like the sound of African drums and almost immediately I extemporised 'They have sentenced the men of Rivonia.' It was one of my songs that came together very quickly. The names Carmela and Manuela were more or less interchangeable when the '*Quince Brigada*' was sung – and the 'Manuela chorus' suggested 'Mandela'. My song was first sung at the flat of Dougie and Queenie Moncrieff in South London. Shortly after that I remember a great night in the Waverley Bar with Dolina MacLennan. Later on it was sung by the Black South African group Atté, and it was their singer Mphima Yengwa who began adapting it.[2]

Hamish felt a kinship with Mandela and saw many parallels between

2 HH, unpublished lecture notes, Henderson archive.

his struggle in Scotland and Mandela's in South Africa; a subtle Scottish subtext exists in the song. 'Rivonia' was the first Mandela song and it remains one of the best – though not now widely sung. It was created at a time when the African struggle was a matter of life and death and addresses brutality and the need for resistance head on. The Communist Party in South Africa was at the centre of the Anti-apartheid regime; 'Rivonia' does not shy from that fact:

They have sentenced the Men of Rivonia
Rumbala rumbala rumba la
The comrades of Nelson Mandela
Rumbala rumbala rumba la
He is buried alive on an island
Free Mandela Free Mandela
He is buried alive on an island
Free Mandela Free Mandela.

Verwoerd feared the mind of Mandela
Rumbala rumbala rumba la
He was stifling the voice of Mandela
Rumbala rumbala rumba la
Free Mbeki Goldberg Sisuli
Free Mandela Free Mandela
Free Mbeki Goldberg Sisuli
Free Mandela Free Mandela.

The crime of the men of Rivonia
Rumbala rumbala rumba la
Was to organise farmer and miner
Rumbala rumbala rumba la
Against baaskap and sjambok and keerie
Free Mandela Free Mandela
Against baaskap and sjambok and keerie
Free Mandela Free Mandela.

Set free the men of Rivonia
Rumbala rumbala rumba la
Break down the walls of their prison
Rumbala rumbala rumba la
Freedom and justice Uhuru
Free Mandela Free Mandela
Freedom and justice Uhuru
Free Mandela Free Mandela.

Power to the heirs of Luthuli
Rumbala rumbala rumba la
The comrades of Nelson Mandela
Rumbala rumbala rumba la
Spear of the nation unbroken
Free Mandela Free Mandela
Amandla Umkhonto we Siswe
Free Mandela Free Mandela.[3]

That Hamish's song 'recognises' not just Mandela but four of the future leaders of South African was prophetic. That a song designed to be a popular rallying point should contain so many difficult and foreign words shows how deeply Hamish understood the oral process. Pure sound linked to melody and rhythm advances understanding faster than the written word – there to be read. Hamish, deliberately, did not get 'Rivonia' printed immediately. He sang it round the pubs and clubs, and tested it. During the spring of 1964 he made one or two changes. By the summer it had taken off and, by September 1964, Pete Seeger was singing it to big audiences in America. Seeger congratulated Hamish and told him it was becoming an 'anti-Goldwater song' in the 1964 Presidential campaign. Hamish then sent the song to the African National Congress Headquarters in London. On 13 October Raymond Kunene replied, from 3 Collingham Gardens:

> Dear Friend, we thank you most heartily for the song you have arranged. It is spirit of this character that will indeed carry us through the immense task of liberation. Your contribution is greatly appreciated, indeed there are great similarities between the Spanish struggle against fascism and ours. Anti-Apartheid has generally evoked the same idealism as the Spanish Civil War. We hope that ours will see the end of tyranny soon.

On 20 October Hamish wrote to Paul Nelson at *Sing Out* magazine in New York. 'Dear Mr Nelson – The song about Nelson Mandela which I sent you is going to be performed at a big anti-apartheid rally in the Usher Hall, Edinburgh, on the 29th of this month. Copies of it have been sent to Africa by the A.N.C. office in London. It is also going to be published in the 5th number of "Il Nuovo Canzoniere Italiano".' The British folksong magazine *Sing* published the song in January 1965 and Hamish noted, 'Mick Graves of "The Spinners" 'is singing it round the clubs'. On 22 January Hamish got a second more enthusiastic letter from the ANC:

3 HH, 'Rivonia', published in the *Collected Poems*.

> Dear Friend, Rivonia: when I forwarded the copy of your song to our main office in Dar es Salaam there were ecstatic comments from all the friends there . . . We heartily express our congratulations for this inspiring song. We hope to make a record of freedom songs and we shall be pleased to include this one . . . The song has, after all, been from time immemorial the most potent form of expressing protest. Yours fraternally Raymond Kunene.

This recording was soon top of the Tanzania 'Hit Parade' and stayed there for five months. On 30 March 1965 Hamish wrote to Marian Sugden: 'My song "Rivonia", for Nelson Mandela, is having quite a success in Africa . . . Some time in the future, I hope to collect some variants between Angola and the Cape! My hope is that it may be carried as far as Robben Island, and show Mandela and the others they're not forgotten . . . a hellish business altogether.' From Tanzania the song spread into South Africa and became part of the emotional fabric of 'ANC underground resistance'. Hamish was deeply moved when he heard that black fishermen hauling nets off Robben Island now sang 'Rivonia' in the hope that the wind would carry it to the prisoners breaking stones beyond the prison wall. For the next thirty years he was a regular speaker at ANC rallies in Scotland.

Because White South Africa was one of the world's leading sports nations, the ANC soon made sport an important plank in its Boycott Campaign against all things South African. In 1969 the Anti-Apartheid Campaign in Britain centred its activities on efforts to get the Springboks Rugby Union tour cancelled: the International against Scotland was scheduled for 6 December – and the demonstration turned into quite a battle. The aim was to disrupt the game so the rugby authorities marshalled a small army of 'rugger vigilantes' backed up by heavy police involvement. Katzel Henderson recalls how Hamish got his group to prepare themselves:

> Everyone was asked to wear white – with a black slash of solidarity. We practised singing 'Rivonia'. Hamish said the plan was demonstrate outside Murrayfield [Stadium] – then it was back to the Staff Club for celebrations! As it was, Hamish and some of his friends got involved in a fracas and I didn't see him for days.[4]

Hamish was forty-nine at the time of the battle of Murrayfield and probably marginally less fit than most heavy drinkers; however, he was determined to do his bit and never regretted his involvement in an event that had significant international impact. At lunchtime on 6 December he spent a couple of hours in Sandy Bell's gathering support and arguing the

4 Katzel Henderson, conversation with TN, 2004.

cause. Then, having sent his younger companions off, he ordered a taxi to Murrayfield and set off with three companions.

> We set off late. And with the crowds we got delayed! So, I arrived at the gates of Murrayfield at one minute to three. Everybody else was in the ground – so the stewards, seeing this tall, rugby-looking gent shambling towards them, waved me on straight through the gate and I just kept going. Suddenly there I was – with the whole arena before me – and the first bars of 'God Save the Queen' were sounding. That was our signal for the pitch invasion! Barricades of sleepers had been erected all round the pitch, with sandbag platforms on the inside – so that the defending police could hammer-down anyone attempting to leap or climb over. My God, forget the Queen, I thought, I'm at the barricades, and on I went! Being tall, I gave the police an advantage – they only had to aim a loose kick and get me in the head! So first in first out, I was pole-axed and slumped at the base of the barricade. This was just as all the other protesters surged forward. Naturally they climbed over us early casualties and soon enough there I was at the bottom of the pile. With the weight of the bodies I felt I was losing consciousness and this single thought came into my head: 'This is it! I'm going to die – for this great human cause!' A feeling of exhilaration swept through me. I hoped to shout 'Victory to the ANC!' before I died, but I was content – I felt my life had not been lived in vain.
>
> Well, the police quite quickly got the upper hand and the stewards began ripping these great piles of bodies apart. Suddenly there I was – stood-up and being marched out through the gate I had so recently come in through. All this was just what I needed – but some of the younger ones were getting a real beating. Well, there I was, outside the ground, wondering what to do. Large numbers of protesters – thought to be trouble-makers – had been arrested and I rather hoped I would be too. But the police were busy and I was exhausted, so I thought I'd better save some strength for the second round! But no second round came and I began to feel I'd let the side down – especially when I heard reports of the brutal tactics employed by some of the police. So, at about nine o'clock, with Bruce Bain, I phoned the *Daily Express* to complain about 'Police brutality at Murrayfield'. Then, with Stewart McLennan, Robert Waugh and A.H. Caldwell I went up to Police headquarters in the High Street.[5]

---

5 HH, conversation with TN, 1990s

At this point in the story a handwritten letter to Hamish, from Caldwell in December 1969, is the best account of events in the High Street that evening:

> Stewart McLennan half-hissed at the policemen passing us –'Shame, Shame, Shame,' whereupon the senior officer turned back and yelled, 'You can do that at Murrayfield sonny, but you can't do it here!' Henderson, Waugh and McLennan were then ordered to move off. Waugh and McLennan linked arms and Henderson moved forward to protest that he was an Edinburgh citizen and tax-payer and entitled to some respect – indeed, that he paid the salaries of the men now jostling them! The senior officer then announced that if they didn't move off quickly they would be run in. At this point Hamish produced a pamphlet from the N.C.C.L. [National Centre for Civil Liberties] and started to read a germane passage to the officers – crowding them. I saw that they were about to be arrested so I ran forward to identify the officers effecting the arrests – and shouted the numbers to Hamish *et al* as they were bundled through the door.

After a night in the cells all three were released pending trial. In mid December Hamish received a letter informing him that 'he, along with Robert Duffy Waugh and Thomas Stewart McLennan, was charged that 1) "on 6th December 1969, in Parliament Square, Edinburgh, you did cause an obstruction by standing along with others on the footway there, and did refuse to move on after being required by the constable: contrary to the Edinburgh Corporation Order, 1967, Section 464 (a); or alternatively 2) time and place libelled, you did stand and loiter to the obstruction and annoyance of Inspector Thomas Beasley, Sergeant Walter Hallyburton, and Constable William Copland, all of Edin. City Police; contrary to the Edin Corp. Order 1967 Section 464 9b)."' As usual Lionel Daiches came forward to defend the accused men. And Bob Waugh (son of the janitor at Sciennes Primary School where Hamish's daughter Tina was a pupil) decided to go on hunger strike 'to draw attention to police brutality – the Anti-Apartheid Movement – and to raise money for the Defence'. The hunger strike took place at St John's Church in Princes Street. Katzel reports:

> Their trial was set for January. So the younger ones – not Hamish – decided to fast until Hogmanay. It was a symbolic fast, not a fast to the death. Bob Waugh was their leader. We went down to see them each day and at midnight on 31 December they ended the fast. Hamish had arranged that they should all then be conveyed by car up to 20 Melville Terrace – where I had prepared haggis, tatties and neeps. Hamish got out the whisky and we had the best Hogmanay

> we ever had. Fortunately none of the starving men died and we had a real carnival Hogmanay![6]

When the case was heard, on 29 January 1970, the *Edinburgh Evening News* gave the accused significant, sympathetic coverage:

> 'Vigil' lecturer and students fined . . . A university lecturer and two students were fined a total of £30 [each] at Edinburgh today when found guilty of causing an obstruction outside Edinburgh City Police Station after the Scotland South African rugby international on 06/12/69. H.S. Henderson, Robert Waugh and TAS McLennan both of Edinburgh College of Commerce pleaded not guilty. Inspector Thomas Beasley said that 'Henderson repeatedly kept pointing out that he was a ratepayer and paid my wages – he also said "I understand your charge – I also know what I have seen at Murrayfield, and the British public will know that too"'.

Hamish's complaint was that many police officers had not worn identifying insignia or identification numbers. His protest was one of many made and on 10 February 1970, Willie Ross (Secretary of State for Scotland) announced that Scotland's chief constables had now agreed to have identification numbers attached to all police raincoats, after complaints by demonstrators at the Springbok International. On 17 February, Helen Cruickshank wrote to Hamish:

> I read somewhere that you had been fined £30 recently for something connected with the anti-Springbok demonstration – I am a little concerned that Katzel's 'housekeeping' money may have had to be tapered down in consequence. I'm 'in the money', in a small way, so please accept the enclosed personal gift – and let it be spent on the family.

On 25 June 1970 Hamish wrote to the new Prime Minister: 'Dear Mr Heath – If your government decides to supply arms to South Africa – this means you will be supplying a fascist Broederbond, which was our active enemy in WWII – which will be, at the start of your premiership, a truly disgraceful and infamous act. It is crucial to think about the long term and that everything is done to weaken Dr Vervoerd and to lower his prestige.' Today such letters can easily be dismissed as childish but the many-faceted campaign that Hamish was part of undoubtedly had a powerful cumulative effect on the South African establishment and their allies around the world. Without such efforts, Nelson Mandela might

6 Katzel Henderson, conversation with TN, 2004

never have been released, Barack Obama might have remained another Chicago black lawyer, and 'immortal moments' – like the one when President Nelson Mandela gave the white South African rugby team captain the World Cup trophy in 1995 – might never have happened.

FIFTEEN

Liverpool and English Connections

Shame, shame on all boundaries for ever
HH[1]

That Liverpool played a major part in the evolution of British popular culture in the 1960s is widely recognised: that Hamish and the Scottish Folk Revival played a significant role in developments has long been forgotten, but Liverpool has always been a Celtic melting pot with strong Scottish connections. The first successful group of the Folk Revival in Liverpool was the Spinners; they emerged in the late fifties and specialised in sea-shanties, street ballads and Hamish Henderson songs. In 1960 John Lennon took 'The Silver Beatles' on what was their first tour, to the ballad country of Scotland – to Alloa, Inverness, Forres, Fraserburgh, Peterhead and Keith. They performed as a back-up band to Johnny Gentle – a rock-crooner who sang ballads. In 1961 the Spinners launched their own 'folk magazine' called *Spin*. Leslie Haworth, the grand-old-man of the Folk Revival on Merseyside – and a long-time folk ally of Hamish's – masterminded developments, and Hamish made regular contributions. From 1960 onwards, Scots folk singers made regular visits to Liverpool, and, long before the famous 'Cavern' opened, Jeannie Robertson, Isabel Sutherland, Jimmie Macgregor, Robin Hall, Enoch Kent, Alex Campbell, the Stewarts of Blair and Hamish had made appearances in Liverpool. Ewan MacColl, Peggy Seeger and Dominic Behan made regular visits from London. In addition, one of the best local finds was Jacqueline McDonald, a Liverpudlian with strong Scottish roots.

The folk magazine *Spin* was cheaply produced and cost just a shilling but by advancing traditional, popular and experimental music, by printing songs, tunes, news, record reviews and articles, it made a big impact on the wider Liverpool scene. Leslie Haworth, Huw Jones, Fritz Spiegl and Stan Hugill were regular contributors, and Hamish was 'the authority'. Hamish used *Spin* No. 4 (Feb. 1962), to advertise the School of Scottish Studies' latest LPs: they are described as containing 'some of

1 HH, unpublished notes, Henderson archive.

the best material in its archives – stories, songs and instrumental music'. Just as he wanted Scots revival singers to know the best of the 'deep tradition', he also wanted the English singers to know it. In the same issue he wrote an article about James MacPherson, the Highland 'rebel hero', as though he were a Liverpool hero. At the same time he took the two best singers of 'MacPherson's Rant' – Davie Stewart and Jimmy MacBeath – to Liverpool to sing this revolutionary song. Following a visit with Jeannie Robertson, Leslie Haworth wrote to thank Hamish (3 August 1962): 'I want to thank you, more than I can say, for the wonderful evening you gave us, and the chance to meet Jeannie; what a lovely person she is, I feel we could always be happy together . . . It will be the happy time when I see you all again.'

It was six weeks later, in September 1962, that the Beatles made their first single, 'Love Me Do'. The closeness of Hamish's relationship with the Liverpool folk scene is made clear by this letter to Tony Davis, editor of *Spin* (3 April 1963):

> Today I got a letter of congratulations from an old friend of mine, Violet Hawkes, who is the daughter of a Church of Ireland clergyman, Allan Armstrong. Allan is a marvellous old man, a militant pacifist, and fearless mental fighter; he is also a lineal descendant of one of the characters mentioned in the ballad 'Johnny Armstrong' (enclosed). And how, you may ask, did the Armstrongs get into Ireland? Well, after 1603, and the Union of the Crowns, most of the boldest of the borderers were removed to Ireland; some went in chains, some went as convicts. This is true. I have seen the border they created in Ireland, and then they arranged to export it to Liverpool, and that is why you enjoy all the benefits you do today. They were not so much planters as planted. King James rightly foresaw that they would give the Kerries something to skip about!

Hamish's interest in sectarian songs dated back to before the war, and for some years he had been encouraging his friend Jim Ritchie to collect, study and nurture Scottish football songs.[2] It was in great 'divided' cities like Glasgow and Liverpool that such singing could be found at its best and worst, and it is no coincidence that the best of all modern football songs was 'invented' by the Liverpool skiffle artist Gerry Marsden. In October 1963 Gerry and the Pacemakers recorded his Liverpudlian version of 'You'll Never Walk Alone': within four weeks it topped the

2 James Ritchie published two books, *The Singing Street* (Oliver and Boyd 1964) and *The Golden City* (Oliver and Boyd 1965), on street songs, rhymes and games, and in March 1966 the *Scots Magazine* published 'Troubadours of the Terraces' about folksong traditions, songs and chants.

UK Pop Charts; within four months it was the Liverpool FC anthem. A similar thing happened with the Liverpool street song 'Johnny Todd'. In the late fifties the Spinners made it a hit, then it was chosen as the theme tune for the mould-breaking BBC TV police series *Z Cars* and gained worldwide fame.[3]

The music boom triggered a poetry upsurge, and the Liverpool Poets became part of a single cultural phenomenon: the Mersey Sound – it was egalitarian, youthful, working class, popular and oral literature and music walking hand in hand. The three leading Liverpool Poets, Roger McGough, Brian Patten and Adrian Henri, all emerged from the Folk Revival. In the early 1960s these young Liverpool Poets were regarded as scruffy outsiders; today, in the twenty-first century, they have a cult status. Indeed Roger McGough is part of the literary establishment – presenting BBC Radio Four's flagship poetry programme *Poetry Please*. In 2008 I spoke with him. The Liverpool Poets wanted, he said, 'to differentiate themselves from the London and Cambridge poets – who dominated the literary life of the time. We were Scousers! We were "performance poets". Our approach was informal and multimedia.' As part of a poetry and music group called the Scaffold,[4] McGough visited Edinburgh regularly and met Hamish. 'He was always bringing in shepherds from the Highlands to sing ballads, at the Traverse. Hamish made the Scottish folk scene part of the New Scene.'[5] McGough mentioned the group's success at the Beat Poets 'Wholly Communion' gathering in the Royal Albert Hall in June 1965. 'It was after that that Allen Ginsberg declared Liverpool "the centre of consciousness of the human universe". McGough's remembrances of Hamish were warm but within a narrow folk framework; twenty years previously he had been more generous, telling Michael Law: 'Hamish is – where the heart is!'

The poet, novelist and playwright Adrian Mitchell, although not from Liverpool, is often associated with the Liverpool Poets. He was a Londoner of Scottish ancestry, and his educational background was similar to Hamish's. As a libertarian socialist and a performance poet, he became a regular at the Edinburgh Fringe and got to know Hamish well.[6] In 1965 Mitchell gained a measure of real fame at Ginsberg's 'Happening' at the Royal Albert Hall ('Wholly Communion') with an

---

3 One of the best of the many scriptwriters employed on *Z Cars* was John McGrath, a Liverpool socialist with Scottish connections. A long acquaintance of Hamish's, he established the 7:84 Theatre Company in 1971 and moved to Scotland.

4 With Mike McGear/McCartney (brother of Paul McCartney) and John Gorman.

5 Roger McGough, conversation with TN, 2008.

6 In 2008, shortly before his death, Mitchell wrote the introduction to the latest edition of Hamish's *Elegies for the Dead in Cyrenaica* (Polygon 2008).

impassioned recitation of verses about the Vietnam War that stole the show:

> You put your bombers in
> You put your conscience out
> You take the human being and twist it all about . . .
> Tell me lies about Vietnam.[7]

This was five years after the *Ding Dong Dollar* songbook had appeared in Scotland, and it is surprising that neither Morris Blythman nor Hamish attended the Albert Hall event. In 1966 Mitchell sent a letter plus a poem, 'to Hamish Henderson with love', that reads a little like an apology:

> Dear Hamish, Thanks for your letter. It was great seeing the thing about you in the Sunday Times . . . I'm seeing a cultural lady here to see if the Bluecoats Arts Forum would get you down to do a Reading . . . I must say in retrospect how much I enjoyed Edinburgh and how much you've done to make it all worthwhile – not least my last night in the West End Hotel which was great – I enclose a belated copy of 'Scotland 1966'.

> Scotland/Liverpool poet[8] indecently assaulted by girl folk-singer in Grass Market, court told
> Scotland/meeting someone I'd always wanted to meet at a party and not knowing how it felt
> Scotland/dream schoolgirl refusing curry in an all night café
> Scotland/Rangers supporters sailing down the Clyde in an orange submarine
> Scotland/postman singing songs for love and whisky in public houses
> Scotland/a bronze dog waiting patiently for its master outside a public house
> Scotland/John Knox behind the counter shouting 'Time Please' at Sandy Bell's.

The following Easter, Mitchell sent an even more personal poem, entitled 'For William Blake and Hamish Henderson'. It meant much to Hamish at a time when he felt generally pummelled and up against the ropes.

---

7 Adrian Mitchell, 'To Whom it May Concern', in *For Beauty Douglas: Collected Poems 1953–1979* (Allison and Busby 1982); later published in *Heart on the Left: Poems 1953–1984* (Bloodaxe 1998).

8 This may be a reference to Brian Patton. In a letter to Hamish he writes: 'edinburgh . . . my head is still full of steps and kilts, and lovely men and girls . . .'

. . . You out-spat your enemies,
You irradiated your friends.
Always naked, you shaven, shaking tyger-lamb,
Moon-man, moon-clown, moon-singer, moon-drinker
– you never killed anyone.
Blakehead, babyhead,
Accept this mug of crude red wine –
I love you.[9]

With love from Adrian, Easter 1967

Hamish also made regular visits to Leeds and Newcastle-upon-Tyne throughout the sixties. In Leeds, he usually lodged with Mary Ringsleben, an old communist friend and translator. He spoke and sang at the University Folksong Society and helped recover costs with an occasional lecture to Stewart Sanderson's folklore students.

Hamish liked Newcastle: he knew he could say, 'I like Geordies because Geordies are Scotsmen – with their brains bashed out!' without them taking offence: 'They understand the double entendre!' He made several visits to the Morden Tower, a small-scale cultural centre run by Connie and Tom Pickard, two poets of the Beat persuasion. They drew numerous avant-garde poets to Newcastle and liked Scotland to provide the music. In return Hamish invited some of the north-east poets to Edinburgh. One visitor was the Northumbrian piper Billy Pigg. He came to the School of Scottish Studies in October 1964, played a number of gigs, and a revival of the cauld wind pipes began in Scotland.

One English writer with whom Hamish had a telling relationship was John Prebble, the popular historian. Prebble was a Londoner with Canadian connections. In the late thirties he joined the Communist Party and did war service with the Royal Artillery. After that he became a journalist. In 1961 he published *Culloden*, a controversial historical account of the battle that was to devastate eighteenth-century Highland society and change the course of Scottish history. It was a great success. Two years later he published a follow-up volume entitled *The Highland Clearances*. In 1964, when the BBC, with commendable boldness, turned *Culloden* into a mould-breaking documentary film – directed by the young Peter Watkins – Prebble gathered much of the kudos. That same year the movie *Zulu*, starring Michael Caine and co-scripted by Prebble, became a block-buster success. Within two years Prebble had gained himself an international reputation and financial security. Such success did little to improve his scholarship, however, and when his third Highland history, *Glencoe,* was published, Hamish decided that Prebble was peddling a

---

9 Published as 'Lullaby for William Blake', in Adrian Mitchell, *Heart on the Left: Poems 1953–1984* (Bloodaxe 1998).

new romanticism that was deeply English and that he must oppose. The book also contained factual errors and he acted to counter 'this prepotent Pebble!'[10] Perhaps Hamish was hungry for a new 'flyting'; *Glencoe* gave him a new opportunity to address the Scottish public, and he quickly got himself commissioned to write an article for the *Scotsman* (25 June 1966). He began by commending Prebble's 'fresh' approach to Highland history but then challenged his partiality and lack of knowledge. The article ends: 'Artfully camouflaged pieces of romantic history just won't do any longer. The Scots will have to come to terms with their history if they are to survive as a nation, and secure the elementary civilised right of a nation to control over its own affairs.' The same day Prebble wrote back to the *Scotsman*:

> The attack was on two fronts – a feint upon the errors he found and a frontal assault upon my manner of writing . . . the rest of Mr Henderson's article is concerned with my style and with what he thinks is my attitude to Scots history. What answer can one give to cat-calls like 'glamour-whimsey', 'romantic literature', and 'pop-historian', except to wish that Mr Henderson, in his disapproval of my style, had a more felicitous pen himself – he flails at me with phrases like 'jerry built reconstructionism' and 'costume-play posturing', stunning himself with his own ugly vocabulary . . . I write this way because I wish my books to be read by the ordinary man and woman who have an avid thirst for knowledge about the past . . . apparently [this] cannot be done without defiling the sacred cow of History which Mr Henderson worships, and which bores the ordinary man into ignorance.

On 10 July the Glasgow poet Edwin Morgan wrote to back Hamish up: 'although I have not read Prebble's book yet I am sure you are right! . . . When he began his book on the Clearances, "Mr MacLeod of Geanies

---

10 Hamish's notebooks contain some genuine 'second-hand' facts about the Massacre of Glencoe. 'There are a lot of stories told about the massacre of Glencoe. Here's one I heard from the old people. They used to say that there was one family that escaped – and this is how it happened. The soldier who was staying with them . . . went to the door before they went to bed and when he came back the man of the house asked him, "What sort of night is it?" "It's a good night," said the soldier, "but many a change comes over a long winter's night." But he saw they didn't pay any great heed to what he'd said, so he looked around for another pretext. There was a big dog lying beside the fire. The soldier went over to him and kicked him, and said, "grey dog, if I was in your place I'd make sure my bed was in the heather tonight." That's how the people understood for a certainty that something was to happen, and they got out of the way before the massacre was made.'

was 'much fatigued this Sunday morning'" one knew what to expect – I quite agree with you that this is the bad old way of writing history – we've got beyond that stage.' Prebble, however – as befitted an ex-communist – was already enjoying the dialectic Hamish had initiated, and the two men began a private correspondence that lasted five years and benefited the work of both men. In November 1966 the *Scots Magazine* published an article on the Highland Clearances, by Hamish. It was stimulated by Prebble's book, and Hamish writes challengingly with broad cinematic strokes of his own:

> In the last year or two the work of Peter Watkins has marked a new advance in the development of the television documentary. Using the techniques pioneered by Grierson and Flaherty, Watkins has brought on to the small screen an extraordinarily compelling recreation of an historic event (Culloden) and an apocalyptic look at the stark realities of a nuclear holocaust (The War Game). Culloden was largely based on research done by John Prebble, who wrote the much praised book of the same name. I'd like to suggest that Prebble's second book on a Scottish historical theme – 'The Highland Clearances' – would make an admirable – and even more ambitious – film or TV documentary.

Hamish then moves sideways to ponder the reasons why the Highlanders, so frequently courageous in battles abroad, were so supine in their response to suppression at home: 'the general picture is one of almost masochistic apathy and defeatism'. One reason for this, Hamish suggests, is that the post-Culloden suppression of the Highlands actually continued a previous suppression (by tribal chieftains and feudal lords), and that historic subordination, 'the folkways of a millennium', continued. 'Passing an Act to abolish the heritable jurisdictions does not mean that you get rid, automatically, of the mental attitudes involved, either on the victim's side, or on the side of the judges. Reading the accounts of some of the Clearances, one gets an impression of the ritual of "pit and gallows" still in operation, and the luckless clansman waiting to be topped by the chief's *crochadair* (executioner).'

Hamish is here addressing a truth 'that dare not speak its name' and with rare insight he 'wonders' at the greater courage frequently shown 'by the Highland women as opposed to their menfolk'. He presents these Highland women as heirs to a genuinely ancient Celtic tradition – whilst their men, more in tune with modern mores, had accepted subordination to feudal chieftains, to Church, State and property. As 'vassals', they asked few questions and offered no serous opposition. Hamish terminated his article by returning to the important role that 'the new media' could and should play if Scotland was to change and live more democratically in the future. Finally, he placed himself centre stage by stating that, in 1951, he had tried to interest the BBC in making a 'folk musical' in the form of 'a radio ballad' – dealing with 'The Clearances'.

> When Alan Lomax arrived in Scotland in 1951 he asked me what I thought would make a good subject for a BBC 'folk musical'. I suggested the Clearances, and we roughed out a programme something along the following lines: – 'A Sutherland glen hears with joy of the heroic deeds of its young men under Wellington in the Peninsula. 1814 passes, and the Hundred Days, but the young Gaels get no home leave. When the hero, Neil, returns, it is not to the glen he knew but to a devastated shambles. Mairi, the girlfriend of his childhood, is homeless. There are rumours that the same thing is going to happen in the great Strath to the north. The fatal eloquence of the ministers holds the people in thrall. Neil resolves to down-face them, tries to organise resistance, but is betrayed by his erstwhile friend, Norman, now one of the unco guid. After the Year of the Burnings – emigration of Neil and his young bride to Canada. '*Cha till, cha till, cha till mi tuilleadh*' (I will return no more). Needless to say, the BBC wouldn't hear of it, and Alan Lomax, in disgust, did a corny folk musical on Bonnie Prince Charlie instead. Frankly I wanted no part of it.

This article looks back at submerged history but also stimulated new developments. Just six years later the 7:84 Theatre Group started work on *The Cheviot, the Stag and the Black, Black Oil*, a documentary folk musical of just the kind proposed by Hamish in 1951, possibly the most radical breakthrough in the history of theatre in twentieth-century Scotland. In addition, Hamish's information suggests that the history of the great radio-ballads created by Ewan MacColl and Charles Parker c.1957 might need to be rethought somewhat. Hamish sent a copy of the magazine to John Prebble, in Surrey. As usual he responded immediately:

> I have just received your piece on the Clearances in the Scots Magazine. I understand, and agree with, your feelings about a film on this subject . . . I have talked about it with interested parties . . . I want to give you my thoughts, for what they are worth, on the lack of real resistance shown by the Highland man to the evictions. I have a theory about this . . . there might be a clue to this lack of resistance in the half dozen or more serious mutinies in the Highland regiments – from the well-known one in the Black Watch, 1742, to those scarcely known in the Revolutionary and Napoleonic wars . . . It is pretty clear that the Highland soldiers considered that they had been betrayed, that promises made to them (by chiefs, lairds and tacksmen) on enlistment had subsequently been broken. They

> had been enrolled on quite different emotional and psychological terms to those of the drumming up of an ordinary Lowland or English line regiment. There were strong family or traditional ties between the enlisted men and their officers. His loyalty was first to his captain or colonel (usually a member of the chief's family) and secondly, if at all, to the government . . . However, when troubles flared up none of these officers took a stand with the mutineers – and it soon became clear to the Highland soldier that whatever his chief might have been in the past, in a redcoat he was very much like an English gentleman, and would hand over his clansmen – his children if the word is not too emotional – to the hangman, firing-squad, and drum-major's whip . . . that while his chief's son was not defending him against the blind-stupidities of military law, his chief was selling the land beneath the feet of his relatives back home.
>
> The emotional effect on the Highland soldier must have been totally destructive of spirit – though he continued to fight brilliantly. The whole structure of his society, his traditional memories, had conditioned him to expect guidance and protection from his chief. This was now being betrayed on two fronts . . . In the clearances the people refused to believe that the chief was in any way responsible. Except for a few bards (and these late) they blamed the factor, the sheep-farmer, the English, the Lowlanders, everybody but the chief – and the returning soldier, with his bitter first-hand knowledge of his officers' indifference to ancient obligations must have had a profound emotional effect on other men of the townships . . . They sank into despair and inaction . . . What is the value of resistance, we cannot win?
>
> Thus, in the conviction that the campaign could not be victorious, what *man* could persuade himself that it was worthwhile winning a battle. The *women*, however, less rational, more impulsive and instinctive – not having a man's experience of betrayal in the regiments – could act emotionally and impetuously, thinking of this day not next year . . . To make it less simple, less black and white, one might also argue that the cruel suppression of the mutinies had taught the Highland soldier to respect authority, to fear it, to obey it . . .

How much Prebble knew of Hamish's role as an officer in the 51st Highland Division in North Africa and Italy (or his later association with the Scottish Republican Army) is unclear but when, on 7 December 1966, Hamish replied a feeling of elation is evident. Hamish knew he had been 'recognised' at his own estimation:

Many thanks for your letter which I found exceedingly interesting. During the war I served for a while with the Highland Div., when it was in the Desert and in Italy – one of the poems I wrote then (5th Elegy) expresses much the same thoughts as you have had on the Highland Regiments and the multiple betrayals . . .

I am sure you are absolutely right to draw attention to the slavish mentality of the senior NCOs. I found during the war that the easiest Germans to interrogate were the Oberfeldwebel. No doubt the returned ex-soldiers helped to communicate a feeling of abject gloom to the rest of the community . . . You know the stories of the fantastic piety of the Sutherlanders . . . 'The Man's World' therefore was broken, but 'The Woman's World' was not. Several correspondents have drawn my attention to a similar pattern in parts of Africa, where the male warrior world of the tribes has been shattered, and the women have the edge on the men – because many have become 'unemployed' they have lost their self-respect vis-à-vis their wives.

Commenting on my remarks about the hidden 'matriarchy' in Scotland, the poet Tom Scott has drawn attention to the *Lex Adamnani* [Lex Innocentium, Adomnan's law for Women, Clerics and Youths] which confirmed a decree of St Columba's that the traditional practice of the Celtic tribes, making their women fight with them in battles, was to be forbidden. 'It is said that Adamnan's mother made him promise to restore the Columban prohibition when she saw one woman in battle drag another from a battlement with a battle-hook through her breast.' I have been wondering whether the battles royal one finds among the tinker women, Highland and Lowland, might not be anarchic hang-overs from these pre-Christian times.

Gordon Donaldson has written, 'the point that impresses and puzzles me most is the way in which the Highlander's desire to find leadership could apparently degenerate very easily into a readiness to accept tyranny. But I wonder how far their whole outlook was shaped by a kind of apathy which was the outcome of their constantly dis-spiriting struggle against adverse natural conditions.' . . . I think this apathy may have been partly due to the exceedingly harsh realities of justice in the old tribal system. Romantics like Tranter talk weepingly about the act of abolishing the hereditable jurisdiction. I wonder how they would have liked to have lived under a set-up in which they could be caught by a wanton arbitrary despot for even trivial misdemeanours. The Chief's children could be well-thrashit, you know! No doubt you have heard the story of the Perthshire clansman who naturally hung back when the Chief's *crochadair* came to fetch him. His wife

> grasped him firmly and brought him out of the house, saying 'come awa, Donald and dinnae keep the laird waiting!'

The Marxist anger that flares in that last paragraph suggests Hamish wished to keep 'Surrey' at some distance from Scottish internal affairs, but ideas raised in the Prebble correspondence echo down the years: for example in Hamish's important essay 'Women of the Glen – Some thoughts on Highland History'.[11] The two men met face to face only once, in April 1968; for Prebble the meeting was memorable (like the 'made horseman' he was, Hamish was sounding the seller).

> Dear Hamish, I enjoyed meeting you. That was a long session for me, lasting from noon to midnight. But – because of the company, the malt, and the various locations – I suffered little . . . As always when I go north in spring and autumn, the Highlands were kind and sunlit . . . I seem to remember the Lone Highlander story being told during the war, an Eighth Army version. The best stories are eternal, and national pride – which frequently seems to be military pride – has its tap-root deep in their outrageous fictions.

Four years later, when Prebble offered public support for Douglas Hurd's anti-nationalist novel and television drama *Scotch on the Rocks,* Hamish terminated their relationship. The folksinger Jean Ritchie sent a note that sums things up:

> Dear Hamish, Is this definition in the Devil's Dictionary? *Clearances*: noun. Popular subject for best sellers, written by Englanders, feeling sorry for Hielanders, blaming the Lowlanders!

Despite his wariness of the English hegemony in public life in Britain, Hamish's love of the landscape, the architecture, the literature of England was permanent. He took his daughters to holiday at Dry Drayton, sent them pony-trekking in the Northumbrian hills, took them to dance in Padstow and up to Chagford on Dartmoor, where his mother and James Scott appear to have holidayed together. During the sixties he became a regular at folk festivals in Sidmouth, Keele, Cambridge. Sometimes he was an adjudicator, sometimes a performer, sometimes a recordist. Across Britain he was recognised as 'the tuning fork' to whom singers, musicians, enthusiasts and academics would turn for advice – though many would be unaware they had done so.

---

11 Published in *The Celtic Consciousness,* ed. Robert O'Driscoll (Dolman Press/ Canongate 1982).

SIXTEEN

Unknown Friends, Prisoners and Murderers

You are a King. Live alone. Take a free road and follow where your free mind leads you, bring to perfection the fruits of well-loved thoughts, ask no reward for noble deeds accomplished. Rewards are within you. Your supreme judge is yourself. None will ever judge your works more sternly. Discriminating artist, does it please you?

Alexander Pushkin, quoted by TN in postcard to HH, 16 July1991

Hamish liked the phrase 'the sweet promiscuity of song'; it captures an enduring aspect of his character: his all-consuming interest in people, his hunger for friendship, his appetite for life's pleasures, his compulsive need to draw people out. Many of Hamish's friends have national or international reputations but Hamish also enjoyed profound relationships with many people unknown to historians and society columnists. One such friendship was with a Church of Scotland minister, Calum Black, a crofter's son from Iona.

Calum Black's parents were native Gaelic-speakers – originally from Mull. His mother was Flora MacDonald; his father, Donald Black, known as 'The Sergeant' because of long service in the Territorial Army and his reputation as a crack-shot at Bisley. Calum was the youngest of four sons, all dark, handsome and physically strong. During the Second World War, Dougal, the eldest, stayed on Iona to farm the croft at Clachnacorrain. The two middle boys served in the Merchant Marines; both were killed. Calum joined the army and saw action from Alamein to the Alps. After the war he trained as a minister, met Hamish and recognised the importance of his *Elegies for the Dead in Cyrenaica*. Living on the Isle of Lismore, in the Firth of Lorne, Calum invited Hamish to visit. Lismore was one of the very early centres of Christianity in Scotland and the place where 'The Book of the Dean of Lismore' (one of the great Gaelic compilations) was written in the late sixteenth century. The island was still alive with Ossianic legends. Hamish visited in 1959 and, at Easter 1960, he took Katzel 'out to Lismore' – to enjoy the honeymoon that the Italian government had denied them the previous year. Unfortunately the people of Lismore were also censorious. Hamish and Katzel arrived to find Calum, his boisterous wife Mary Boyle and their two children at 'war' with their congregation! Hamish told me:

> A boycott had been placed on the Black family and the manse was a dog house! Parish life was in turmoil. The Lismore elders had appointed Calum because he was an Argyllshire man, a war-hero, a native Gaelic speaker; when they discovered he was also a singer, a revolutionary, and a Scottish nationalist, they turned against him with all the rectitude propriety could muster! No islander would attend any services conducted by Calum and the family lived in quarantined silence.
>
> Katzel and I were up there for a week and had a great old time, we rang the Kirk bell! Katzel and I, with Mary, were Calum's whole congregation! Calum preached, we sang – and the gates of Heaven might have opened if we'd had trumpets! For a time, Calum had been enjoying his 'sinecure' but the Kirk authorities wanted the people back at Church and the parishioners wanted Calum somewhere else. The hunt was on to find him a new parish – but there was a problem! What Church of Scotland parish would take a Jacobite, republican rebel like Calum, who was also a good friend of mine?

For Hamish one of the great things about Lismore was the manner in which the island had fused its pagan and Christian heritage. Ossian and the heroes of the Fianna are closely associated with the island, and the famous dialogue between Ossian (last survivor of the Old Order) and St Patrick (leader of the new Christian Order) in The Book of the Dean of Lismore may well have actually taken place on Lismore. It was an idea that thrilled the two battle-hardened Christians, and they spent the week talking and singing and drinking, at one with the ancients. Indeed, Hamish used the experience later to create 'a new dialogue – between Patrick and Hamish' (see Appendix 1). Calum was a Highland romantic and enjoyed boasting, 'like Cuchulan, of his dogs, his horse-riding, his exploits as cattle dealer, the wounds he suffered'.[1] Hamish described him as 'a contemporary ancestor' and, when he got back to Edinburgh, he reported to Compton Mackenzie: 'here is a story, tailor made for you'. Compton Mackenzie, however, was writing up his memoirs – octave by octave – and nothing happened.

When Calum and his family were finally removed from Lismore they began a period of rather unhappy wandering, and as the Edinburgh Festival of 1963 drew to a close Hamish found himself on the receiving

---

1 HH, conversation with TN (who spent his honeymoon on Dugald Black's croft in 1967).

end of Calum's demanding nature. In the middle of the night Calum thundered on the door of 20 Melville Terrace, demanding a dram and a bed. Hamish slammed the door on him. Two days later (11 September), he wrote a letter that might have ended their friendship:

> Dear Calum, In case you didn't get what I was telling you on the phone yesterday, I'm going to repeat it loud and clear. First of all, your outrageous bloody impudence in writing such a letter to Katzel and me after all the help and hospitality you have received from us, now you can fuck-off as far as we are concerned. The outline above is enough to show that you have a selfish ego as big and ugly as the north face of the Eiger . . . The other stories and your odious and disingenuous line about the Army has done one thing, if nothing else, left us in no doubt that you are a ruthless and unscrupulous 'bullshitter' . . . It was totally unfair on Katzel and the bairn – and you must have realized that after three weeks of the Festival during which there were never less than two and sometimes as many as six people staying overnight + work galore at the School itself, we'd both been nearly round the bend with accumulated fatigue.

The Black family later headed out to Australia where Calum joined a new church and made a new life for himself; he and Hamish maintained an occasional correspondence for thirty years. In July 1993 Calum wrote to thank Hamish for sending him copies of *The Gramsci Letters* and *Alias MacAlias*:

> I'm sure the Soviet collapse was as much the result of American harassment as of internal errors . . . Theoretically I like your book much better than Gramsci's – I'm always wary of systematic doctrines. I like your short chapters and the whole book was redolent of memories . . . I don't suppose there's one particular socialist or nationalist solution to the world's problems but those who oppose both are keen to suggest that nationalism is opposed to internationalism, that nationalism equals fascism and socialism Stalinism . . . Again adios amigo.

Hamish's sympathy for anyone in difficulties meant that many, in times of difficulty, gravitated towards him. In 1968 Michael Randall, a young artist who lived in Radstock Road, Southampton, wrote:

> Dear Hamish – friend and patron. I cannot thank you enough for your visit and appreciations of my work. I shall be indebted to you for your help and Understanding for the remainder of my life. As I said before, it was as if you were sent by God. Never in my

life have I needed help so desperately as then. Both spiritually and materially . . . I have hope.

When in 1970 Hamish sent a letter, magazines and chocolates to an old comrade, John Rae, who was dying in hospital, Rae sent back this note:

> Dear Hamish – I have been six months in this hospital
> Pleurisy, Bronchitis and Diabetes
> What a parcel!
> The Christians say that God
> Persecutes those that he loves.
> He must have a helluva love for me –
> Thanks for the John MacLean March.
> Magnificent.

A prisoner, Mr F. Screene (HM Prison Aberdeen), was a persistent correspondent. In October 1974 he wrote:

> Dear Hamish, I write this short manuscriptal letter in hope you will exult in giving me a chance in the field of Poetry. I gave you hundreds of my works quite a few years ago but you were doing nothing with them so I took them back. I wrote under the name of Fran De Bere. Do you remember me now. I can't come to see you, as I am serving a Life Sentence . . . but it's neither here nor there – its only another phase of my life, to me the Poet, a laugh? Yes, a laugh . . . My Poetry comes first even before freedom. Anyway what the hell is out there anyway. Sweet-Fanny-Adams. Oh I miss a fair chick now and again, but there's always masturbation . . . So bingo I am a sort of long-haired Existentialist Ecosse. I have written to Lord Burleigh at the Scottish Arts Council but would rather send my work to the School of Scottish Studies – for I am a true blue Scot not an English oink. Here is another poem for you – it's called 'A Super Heart'.

Screene came from the Edinburgh slums. His poetry has an ugly surreal power. One poem deals with matricide:

> . . . her heart falls out through her clothing,
> I retrieve it and turn it round in my hands –
> It has the trademark of my rubber ball
> I lost in the wall . . .
>
> How the hell could she have lived
> To produce a man like me.

Here, Mother, put your heart back in: –
She did, and smiled.
Both of us bounced away together
Through time back through the reversed wall . . .

This chimes with a poem Hamish had written ten years previously, entitled 'Ballad of the Speaking Heart'; he describes it as 'after La Chanson de Marie-des-Anges by Jean Richepin (1849–1926)'. It is, however, an original creation. Hamish sang it well, as did the Perth folksinger Sheila Douglas:

A puir lad yince, and a lad sae trim
(Hey the haw, the gilliefloor, hey the thyme)
A puir lad yince, and a lad sae trim,
He loo'd a lass that loo'dna him.

Says she, gae fetch tae me, ye rogue
(Hey the haw &c)
Says she gae fetch tae me, ye rogue
Yer mither's hert tae feed my dog.

Tae his mothers hoose gaed that young man
Tae his mothers hoose gaed that young man;
He cut oot her hert and away he ran.

Noo as he ran, he trippit and fell
Noo as he ran, he trippit and fell,
And the hert rolled on the grun as well.

Noo the hert it stotted against a stane
Noo the hert it stotted against a stane,
And the laddie heard it makin its mane.

The hert was greetin and cryin fu sma'
The hert was greetin and cryin fu sma',
Are ye hurt, my bairn, are ye hurt at a'.[2]

The stories of Hamish's involvement in the hunt for Glasgow's Bible John and the Yorkshire Ripper are too convoluted for this biography, but his part in the long campaign to obtain a pardon for Iain Gordon, convicted of the infamous 'Cullen Murder' of 1952, continued for thirty years and deserves documentation. Patricia Curran, daughter of a distinguished Protestant

2 HH, 'Ballad of the Speaking Heart', published in *Chapman* 1995 (*Norman MacCaig – A Celebration*).

judge in Northern Ireland, was brutally murdered outside the family house on 23 December 1952. Iain Gordon, a young Glaswegian RAF National Serviceman, was arrested on circumstantial evidence. He was convicted of murder, adjudged deranged, and given a life sentence. Released after eight years and, apparently sane, he demanded a pardon. None was forthcoming. In 1965 Hamish joined the campaign. In October 1968, he followed-up an article by James Fox in the *Sunday Times* with a letter suggesting that 'folk knowledge might help reveal the truth about this baffling case':

> Desmond Curran, the murdered girl's brother – gave an account of the meeting he had with Iain Gordon, the accused airman on 23 December 1952, and stated, as they were going up in the lift in the Presbyterian hostel, Gordon said to him, 'Now, we go up to the Heavens'. This remark, which Sgt. Capstick found so damagingly suspicious, is a harmless stock-saying which the folklorist immediately recognises; it has been floating around in Presbyterian Scotland ever since lifts were introduced. A variant was used by the poet Robert Garioch in his 'Masque of Edinburgh', first published 1940 when Iain Gordon was a child of eight. There is another and no doubt related gobbet of ironic folk speech which goes back at least to the C16th; it was said of the people living in the towering 'lands' of Edinburgh's High Street that it was 'the nearest to Heaven they would ever get' . . . It takes one's breath away to read that this was part of the 'particularly damning evidence' which helped to send Mr Gordon to a mental home for 8 years.[3]

On 30 October Hamish forwarded a copy of his letter to Ludovic Kennedy (author and campaigning lawyer) with this note:

> I am sure you know James Hogg's *The Private Memoirs of a Justified Sinner*. I reread some of the closing passages of that extraordinary masterpiece after reading Fox's article, and it seemed to me that there could hardly be a better description of brain-washing – in this case the brain-washing produced by an over-heated Presbyterian upbringing – than the following: 'I have been buffeted as never living creature was. My vitals have been torn, and every faculty and feeling of my soul racked, and tormented into callous insensibility. I was even hung by the locks over a yawning chasm, to which I could conceive no bottom, and then – not till then, did I repeat the tremendous prayer! – I was instantly at liberty; and what I now am, the Almighty knows! Amen.' . . . The moment when an innocent is forced through pain and desperation to sign a confession when he knows himself to be innocent must surely be a moment similar

3 HH, letter to *The Sunday Times*, October 1968.

> to this. These are points that might not readily be apparent to a Scotland Yard Superintendent or to an Irish jury.

Kennedy replied: 'I was delighted to get your letter and find another who has been stirred by this infamous case . . . Hugh Pierce sent me the papers on the case a number of years ago and when you read them *in toto*, they make up a devastating case against Capstick and his merry men. What you say about the incident in the lift is very revealing – it had not occurred to me before and I am sure the right interpretation was never even put before the jury.' Hamish then began a correspondence with Captain William Long, Minister of Home Affairs at Stormont. Long wrote back saying that the folklore theory 'could carry some weight and it is certainly a fascinating approach . . . I am sure Iain and his mother would be delighted to see you.' So, Hamish wrote to Mrs Brenda Gordon (3 March 1969), requesting a meeting with her son: 'I hope you won't mind me writing to you out of the blue . . . all the information I have come across has completely convinced me of your son's innocence . . . ' Mrs Gordon wrote back: 'Dear Mr Henderson . . . it has been an odd feature of this case that each time Iain and I grow discouraged, somebody comes forward to give us the push we need. We have always had to go on and we are anticipating meeting you and listening to a fresh approach, as you can guess, most eagerly.' Twenty-five years later, in 1995, Iain Gordon was given a full Royal Pardon.

SEVENTEEN

A Mirror up to Scotland: Five Tradition Bearers

Give this to the one you love best of all only
Duncan Williamson, 1999

Hamish worked with so many Scots tradition bearers that to profile some and ignore others is invidious but necessary. I have selected five. The first is John MacDonald, the Singing Mole-catcher. He lacked formal education but was a singer, storyteller, puppeteer and amateur folklorist who – with luck – might have 'made it big' like Harry Lauder. On 21 February 1957 he writes: 'Hello Hamish, 'Hoo are ye, a' ye dein'?' I thought I'd drop you a note to let you know I'm 'Broadcasting" a talk about moles in Farm Forum on Thursday 28th February, at 7.00 pm. I'm also broadcasting about birds and animals for the Children's Hour on March 14th . . . Poor old granny Bochel is gone at last.' (Hamish had recorded her the previous year, at the age of 103.) In October 1959 Hamish wrote to inform MacDonald that he was doing a broadcast featuring singers from the North East; MacDonald replied with news of his own:

> Dear Hamish – I got a pleasant surprise this week when I opened the Radio Times – Man, they should have put in your whole photo – but, perhaps, the page wasn't long enough! I'll be listening to you. Are you using any of my recordings? Kindly let me know as I am planning a broadcast with Miss Adair and will hold back so as not to clash with yours.

The following year MacDonald reported his tour of England: 'Down in Manchester the old ballads just "brought the house down"! I made a record for overseas trade, "The Bonnie Woods o'Cawdor" (my own song) and "The Dying Plough Boy" – one of our best farm songs – but it has been altered so much and the air spoiled – those jean-clad singers on TV are making a fool of our songs – it's time they were stopped! Man, we could do with a good night again . . . I did a record for Peter Kennedy lately.' Perhaps a little put out by Kennedy's intervention, Hamish encouraged Collector Records to make an LP with 'The Singing Mole-catcher'. On 29 November 1960 MacDonald writes:

> Dear Hamish, about the Collector Records, I would be very pleased to record for them but I'm afraid that the "Roving Ploughboy" is out as Peter Kennedy put it on 'Cameleon Records' and asked me to sign a contract not to record it for anyone else for 10 years . . . but I have plenty more.

Indeed Peter Kennedy had now 'signed up' not just John MacDonald but a whole stable of Scottish singers. He was just one of many London-based collectors then 'invading' the Scots folk scene, including Ewan MacColl and Peggy Seeger. Hamish took up John MacDonald's case with Peter Kennedy. The case raised all kinds of financial, legal and academic issues and various disputes rumbled on for years. Hamish supported his singers and guarded his patch; in May 1961 MacDonald writes: 'Dear Hamish, 'Thank you so much for the cheque . . . Did you see my picture in last week's "Weekend" the London coloured paper? They came to one of my shows and now the "Daily Mail" is after me . . . any news of you coming north?'

In October 1962, excited by the enthusiasm of his huge Scottish audiences in Blackpool, MacDonald tried to lure Hamish back into politics:

> Dear Hamish, We had a grand time in Blackpool, on the third Saturday in September there were over 3,000 holiday makers from Glasgow. A concert in Blackpool, when the place is full of Scotch folk, would be a grand time to let them know we are still a nation, and to tell them what we think . . . The following week I listened at the Mound in Edinburgh to some of the Nationalist Party – it was grand but speeches there wont help – I would rather see them crossing the border and bringing it right home to the English. Blackpool would be the place for it, another William Wallace we need . . . It was very good of you to give STV my name, however, I only got notice on Friday afternoon and the rush was too much for me – I collapsed and had to be put to bed – whilst waiting for the taxi to take me to the station . . . My mother had died on Tuesday but I hadn't been well and I suppose the excitement proved too much – my singing has improved as my new melodian is not so high-pitched.

In November 1975 MacDonald proudly informed Hamish: 'The Topic Record is out and we are well pleased with it – you made a grand job of the notes, excellent in fact . . . Never hear from Peter Kennedy now – he wrote me some time ago asking me to send him a lot of songs but I wrote and told him, "No more songs for him. I was finished with him!" Ena dared me to give him more! Topic are different, very nice people . . . ' In January 1979 he prepared his own obituary.

Dear Hamish, I've been looking over all my achievements in life:
Collected hundreds of folk tales
Won English plaque as Champion Storyteller
Collected and composed hundreds of folksongs
(Many of which you still haven't heard)
Trapped 200,000 moles and won the British Championship
Won many prizes with my melodeon
Won Scottish Diddling Championship twice
Was Government Rat-Catcher during the War
And there isn't any claim but I can meet
First-class.

In fact the old mole-catcher lived one more year and, on 6 December 1980, his last letter congratulated Hamish on the excellence of the television documentary *The Dead, the Innocent* that he had made with the BBC (see Chapter 20).

* * *

Mary Brooksbank of Dundee was an equally exceptional character. In October 1964 Maurice Fleming informed Hamish of his latest 'folk find', in the Dundee Folk Club:

> Mary Brooksbank: her address is 145 Fintry Drive, Dundee – a flat on a large housing estate. She is a small motherly person aged 64. Strong-voice still. Born in Aberdeen – mother from Greenock, father from St Vigeans, Carmyllie District near Carnoustie. Lived at Ship Row, Aberdeen – and Blackscroft, Dundee. Father and husband both dockers. She has written many poems and knows 'folk' songs from the Dundee mills. She once won first prize in an essay competition in the People's Journal. Writing a character study of an old shepherd of great learning she met one day in Aberfeldy. In 1954 Mary sent a book of poems and songs to Ewan MacColl (whom she had met after a folksong evening at the Marryat Hall, Dundee). He neither acknowledged or returned the book.

Hamish made contact with Mary, and Maurice contacted MacColl, who duly returned the book. In November Mary received a cheque for three guineas for MacColl's use of her versions of 'To the Beggin' I will Go' and 'Come all ye Tramps and Hawkers'. Hamish and Maurice then moved to get a collection of Mary's songs and poems published – to local acclaim. Hamish's succinctly documents Brooksbank's qualities in this letter:

> Dear Maurice, It's a really remarkable exploit, this blend of the old Scots radical tradition (poems like 'Tom Paine' and 'Lewis Grassic

> Gibbon' and the indomitable gaiety of the urban folk idiom). You've done a remarkable job locating this old heroine. 'Journal of Democracy', her parody of Eliot's 'Journey of the Magi' is brilliant – as is her 'To the Reactionaries', the first verse of which goes:
>
> When Church and State amalgamate
> Tae preach us Law and Order,
> Ye wives and mothers sure as fate –
> Ye'll ken they're planning murder.

The closer Hamish got to Mary, the more he realised that MacColl owed her a good deal more than three guineas and, on 9 January 1969, he wrote to the MCPRS:[1]

> I notice that the 'Jute Mill Song' has the note 'Music by Ewan MacColl'. The music of this song is traditional, preserved by Mary Brooksbank, who wrote most of the words now sung. If you look up the notes to 'The Singing Island' (Mills Music Ltd, 1960) you will find that the note to this song states: 'Taken down from a manuscript submitted by Mary Brooksbank, jute-spinner of Dundee.' The ms concerned was a book of poems and songs, most of them original. Mary lent the book to Ewan MacColl, at his request, and she did not get it back for fully ten years, although she wrote several letters to Ewan (all ignored) . . . If you gave Ewan a guinea for his share in this song, I suggest you get it back from him, and send it to Mary who is an old age pensioner . . . She is also an amazing old lady, a heroine of the working class movement in Dundee, and a free-spoken, free-thinking old rebel who got thrown out of the CP for denouncing Stalin in the *early thirties*. When a plaque was put up in memory of James Connolly in the Cowgate, Edinburgh, where he was born, she travelled from Dundee to attend the ceremony – June 68 – and 'made' the occasion by singing her Connolly song at the end of the do.

Hamish was ever on the lookout for artistic talent, new informants and new historical sources and in May 1965, at a folksong course in Dundee, he made contact with a primary school teacher, Morag Muir, who encouraged him to contact her father, Donald MacMartin, 'because he has old songs'. MacMartin was a 60-year-old Berwickshire farmer but he had been brought up around Loch Tay and Hamish was soon describing him as 'the most valuable single informant on Scots folksong to come to light for several years'. A native Gaelic speaker, MacMartin was descended

1 The Mechanical Copyright Performing Rights Society, which became the Mechanical Copyright Protection Society (now rebranded as PRS for Music).

from the hereditary armourers to clan Cameron. In his annual report for the School of Scottish Studies Hamish noted:

> A 400 year old anvil lies in his back yard. He sings close on 50 songs, including Jamie Raeburn, Dowie Dens of Yarrow, The Plains o' Waterloo, Aberfeldy Feein' Fair, and The Auld Gardiner's Wife – not collected since Gavin Greig. He also has local stories, legends, lore and prophecies from the Lady of Lawers.

Donald MacMartin was proud to meet Hamish but one month after delivering his songs 'safe into the keeping of the School of Scottish Studies' he died. The death came as a tragedy to his family, as these letters from Morag make clear:

> *27 June 1965*: Dear Mr Henderson, We took my father home to Lawers yesterday to rest among his ancestors in the countryside he loved. His death was sudden and unexpected and a terrible shock to us all. My mother was with him when he passed away during a visiting hour – we had no warning that he might not be coming back to Silverwells . . . The day he spent with you was one of the highlights of his life and he spoke of it often when in hospital . . . It would be a great comfort to us to hear his voice, as it was during one of his happiest days. He was so proud to contribute something of value to your collection, and to have someone appreciate his knowledge.
>
> *17 October 1965*: Thank you so much for sending us the tapes for Dad's birthday. As the nights are longer we are more conscious of the empty chair – it's wonderful to hear his voice although we end in tears every time we play the tape. His voice is so true to life, whereas the rest of us might be anyone.

Another of Hamish's great friends from the Border counties was the ballad-singing shepherd Willie Scott. Willie was born in 1897, when many older people remembered people who had known the great generation of Burns, Hogg and Sir Walter Scott. Willie Scott had learned most of his folk repertoire before the First World War but was still attending Herd's suppers, Border kirns, Common Ridings, sheep fairs and cattle markets – from Berwickshire to Galloway – when Hamish first recorded him in 1958. Scott's biographer, Alison McMorland, recorded his reminiscences.

> I left School and started shepherding at 12 years old – and have stayed at it all my life. It was not till 1940 that I lived in a house with a road to the door. Till the road came, and the TV, people settled

> in the glens and made their own entertainment. I've enjoyed being among the hills and glens of Scotland among the black-faced sheep and the bonnie bloomin' heather . . . 'Ony fule can write a book, but it taks a man tae herd the Merrick!'[2]

It was Francis Collinson who first recorded Willie Scott (soon after the School of Scottish Sudies was founded) but, by the late fifties, it was Hamish who was championing his singing and encouraging him to join the Folk Revival. Scott's last years as a working shepherd were spent in the Cleish Hills above Kelty in Fife, not far from the folk clubs in Dumfermline, Kirkcaldy and Edinburgh, and Hamish was determined to get him involved as a performer and role-model for young singers. Willie was not a political man but Hamish soon had him singing at ceilidhs organised by the Fife Socialist League. It was, however, a ceilidh at the Howff Song Club of Dunfermline, in October 1961, that really launched Willie Scott's career as a modern singer. Hamish reports the occasion:

> It was not the young Turks of the Edinburgh Revival (Stuart MacGregor et al.) who stole the show – but the old Border shepherd himself! He gave a commanding rendition of his song 'There's Bound to be a Row' and the whole audience felt themselves – in the ancient capital of Scotland – in the presence of a tradition that had bonded the nation for centuries and still did . . . The world of John Leyden and James Hogg seemed to communicate directly with the new cosmopolitan folk audience of industrial Scotland through the lips and personality of this masterly veteran tradition bearer . . . He was a tall, slow-spoken, silver haired shepherd from the Borders, sixty-four years old at the time, and employed at Kingseat of Outh above Kelty.[3]

For the next twenty years Willie Scott was a regal figure on the British folk circuit. He also travelled across North America and gave a memorable performance in Sydney Opera House. At the Blairgowrie Folk Festival of 1968, Hamish introduced Willie Scott to Willie Mitchell – the singing butcher of Campbeltown. Scott later recalled their meeting with red-blooded glee:

> It was ae night in the Sun Lounge of the Angus Hotel. It was one of the best parties I've ever been at. I'd never met Willie Mitchell, I never kent there was such a man. He stole the show earlier at the Men's Singing. I asked him for songs I'd heard at the ram

2 Alison McMorland, *Herd Laddie o the Glen: Songs of a Border Shepherd* (revised edition, Selkirk 2006).

3 From McMorland, *Herd Laddie o the Glen.*

> sales . . . I ca'd him Mr Mitchell. He said, 'Dinna put handles on my name – nae misters. I'm just Willie Mitchell!' 'Weel' I said, 'I enjoyed you. Hearin' you in the hall. 'Nancy's Whisky' – made my festival.[4]

Hamish's notes about this felicitous coming together are even more enthusiastic:

> This impromptu ceilidh [in the Sun Lounge] will remain life-long in the memory of everyone who was there. Archie Fisher gave of his best and several other people sang, but Willie Scott demanded more songs from Willie Mitchell! And eventually he sang 'Callieburn' – Willie Scott was tremendously struck by the song – asked for it to be sung again and he got Willie Mitchell to write out the words. A few months later I recorded Willie Scott singing it. The words were as he had received them from Willie Mitchell, but the tune had been totally transformed. For me – the midnight ceilidh in the Sun lounge of the Angus Hotel marked a real moment of qualitative break-through – tradition and revival working together, had actually made it! As the late Arthur Argo once put it: if all our efforts in the Folk Revival were now to drain away into the sands, it would have been worth it for that midnight Ceilidh.[5]

The Mitchell family were Kintyre people, and Hamish had always had a soft spot for Argyll. Now, he began to develop a close friendship with the greatest Argyllshire tradition bearer of modern times, Duncan Williamson. Duncan was a Traveller: his mother had been born in the cave behind the shop in the village of Muasdale; he himself was born in a bow-tent at Furnace, on the shores of Loch Fyne. Duncan was the seventh son of a seventh son and, at the age of thirteen, left home to begin an impoverished, wandering Traveller life. He cut peats, worked horses, picked berries, made money as a sparring-partner to the Middle-Weight Champion of Scotland, had a family of seven children, and made himself master of thousands of songs and stories. One reason why Hamish felt such a strong personal attachment to Duncan is to be found in the long poem 'Journey to a Kingdom'. In one section the poet meets a young Traveller on the road between Lochgilphead and Inveraray (the road on which Duncan had spent so much of his boyhood): poet and Traveller find themselves in step, and a visionary experience unfolds. Hamish names his companion Peter, but the man he met might well have been Duncan Williamson, and he was extraordinary:

---

4 Letter from Willie Scott to HH, Henderson archive.

5 HH, unpublished notes, Henderson archive.

I had your company, Peter; though the road was hard
And your feet were sore,
There was light enough going for us – the
whole drum-thundering host
Of heaven was with us. Out of a Gaelic Bible
In your bundle came archangels and the
flaming angels
To go before us. O, on your noble head,
Grey-haloed like a Covenanting saint's
A hand (whose hand!) had rested –
which no fell, no fiend's fingers
Could claw away. In a corner of my brain
That knows the universe tiny and godless
I knew your vision Peter, and my own heart.[6]

On 23 January 2007, I visited Duncan at his small flat in Ladybank, Fife. He had been strong so long that I was surprised to find him looking frail: his death was just six months away. He insisted on giving my wife a small brass cow, and spoke at length of the weddings he'd recently been conducting 'in the old style, on the beach'. I asked him when he had first met Hamish. He replied:

> I heard about Hamish long before I met him. That first night in the berryfields, I went to the camp fire to watch him doing his recordings. And the thing about Hamish was this – he played his recordings back to the singers. Travellers, singing and playing the chanter, would hear themselves for the first time and it was like magic to them – hearing themselves come back out of this machine. Hamish was different. He was different to Ewan MacColl and the others. He would never correct a singer and say 'the words should be this'. To say, 'that's not the way it goes' was foreign to him. He never said, 'that was a mistake'. The travellers were not 'tinkers' to Hamish, they were his friends, and they knew he loved them. He was like someone you'd been brought up with all your life, the respect he gave was not put on. He liked the old grannies, he wanted to hear their side of the story. Hamish was a legend and he'll never be forgotten.
>
> At the School of Scottish Studies, when Hamish walked into the room one felt the air change. The atmosphere changed. I was with him once, up at Sandy Bell's, at the time the Brewers moved the juke

6 Extract from 'Journey to a Kingdom' (1935–40), published in *Aberdeen University Review* no. 178, autumn 1987 (Andrew R. Hunter, 'Hamish Henderson: Odyssey of a Wandering King').

> box in. 'Duncan' he said, 'you see that juke box – that Bloody Thing! It won't be here tomorrow.' And, before he'd finished speaking, a white van slammed on its brakes, in the street outside, and two men in black balaclavas banged-in through the door and went straight for the juke box! They pulled out the plugs – heaved the thing on its back and shouldered it out through the door – like a drunk! And away! And that was it! Of course, by now, the barmen were onto the police! So Hamish said, 'I saw the whole thing – I'll be a witness!' Sure enough the police came! But that was the end of the juke box at Sandy Bell's!
>
> And, as you know, it was Hamish paid for Jimmy MacBeath's funeral. He did that. Hamish always knew a good singer when he heard one – but he never divided the sheep from the goats: if somebody asked Hamish what he thought of a singer, he'd say 'he's one of us', or 'she's just one of us'. And that was it: we were one circle round the fire, one circle and one family – and the women trusted Hamish, and the men were never jealous. They trusted Hamish. They loved him, as he loved the children: and I never heard Hamish swear – but once! We were at David Campbell's flat in Edinburgh, David Campbell – the great story-teller – for two years he learned his trade from me! Well, there were about thirty visitors and I started by welcoming everybody: 'This is a Ceilidh – so – it's tell a story, sing a song, show yer bum – or oot ye gang! And we don't want to see any hairy bums here the night!' And, of course, Hamish had had a dram or two and he shouts out: 'Why shouldn't we see some bums!' That brought the house down! And that was the only time I ever heard Hamish swear![7]

It was not Hamish, however, who first recorded Duncan Williamson. It was Geordie McIntyre and Helen Fullerton who began recording the Williamson family, in 1958. Early on they worked with Duncan's mother and sisters – the men folk were suspicious. McIntyre was a teacher and folk enthusiast, Helen a folk researcher attached to Glasgow University. She was camping out with the workers building the hydro-electric dams in Argyll. Whilst documenting them she got to know the Travellers but it was not until 1967 that Geordie, having recorded Duncan, played the tapes to Hamish. He recognised immediately that 'a new planet' had arrived in the universe of Scots song; years later he told me: 'All the fey genius expected of a seventh son of seventh son, which Duncan was, was there for all to see and hear.' Naturally, Hamish encouraged Duncan to attend the 1968 Blairgowrie Folk Festival and he soon arranged for systematic recordings to be made at the School of Scottish Studies. Like John MacDonald,

7 Duncan Williamson, conversation with TN.

Duncan liked to say he knew 3,000 stories. His style was strangely gentle, his singing strangely gripping and suggestive of a very ancient ancestry; his voice entrancing and intriguing. Duncan's genius encouraged Hamish to re-activate his 'Great Tinker Project'.

It was not until 1973, however, that the project in Scotland got going with the arrival from America of Linda Headlee as a School of Scottish Studies postgraduate student. Almost immediately, Hamish described her to Professor John MacQueen (who succeeded Basil Megaw as Director in 1969) as 'a student of quite exceptional ability – who can revitalise the now languishing Tinker Project', and she soon proved herself one of the most innovative and productive 'freelance folklorists' in the English-speaking world. Linda worked with numerous Traveller families and it was with her help that Betsy Whyte of Montrose emerged, in the 1980s, as the author of two bestselling books, *The Yellow on the Broom* and *Red Rowans and Wild Honey*, books that raised the profile of the Travelling people, won critical praise, and stimulated all kinds of televisual and theatrical responses. Like many Americans, Linda Headlee was prepared to go the whole hog. She arrived in Scotland a newlywed but such was her determination to work in the field and give herself to her informants that, within a year, her marriage had foundered. Her commitment to the Travellers is clear in this unpublished letter to the *Scotsman* (November 1974).

> I have noticed since my first visit to the [Travelling] folk how excited and intent they become when they learn we are interested in their lives, their stories, songs and concerns. Our aim in collecting may be directed to the past, but the result belongs wholly to the present. We give our informants a feeling of self-respect, a deep sense of worth; and what else could ensure the strong survival of culture – in all its protean forms?

Eighteen months later Linda married Duncan Williamson. He was forty-nine. His first wife had died in 1971. The wedding took place at Cupar Registry Office in Fife, with Hamish in attendance. A few days later Duncan writes: 'Dear Hamish, We are all fine down here at Lochgilphead. Linda is happy and she is a good traveller and *ceard* and tries to do well. Hamish I must thank you again for your time and company. I think you would make a fine Traveller man and your cant is as good as your songs. I love the way you sing them . . . We'll have a night at Sandy Bell's and I'll bring my mouth organ.'

For the next four years Duncan and Linda lived the traditional Traveller life, camping for long spells in a large 'gelly' at a site run by the Council on the outskirts of Lochgilphead. Two children, Betsy and Tommy, were born but Linda continued work, recording hundreds of hours of songs, stories and Traveller lore from Duncan, his relatives and Traveller friends.

In 1977, camped in a wood in the Howe of Fife, Linda wrote to Hamish (her PhD supervisor):

> about your word *'rawkies'* (Jeannie's term for the Perthshire travellers), I think, and so does Duncan, that this must be *raw creish* – *creish* being cant for unrendered fat (usually pork). The Pitlochry Johnstones were nicknamed this (they were always begging for fat from the pigs the farmers killed in the Fall, or at Christmas or New Year.) It was Betsy Whyte and her sister Katie who told me this – and there is a parallel with the *buid and milk* nickname of the Aberdeenshire travellers.[8]

In the fifties Hamish had made a collection of Traveller by-names – *Wooden-sleeves – Love-in-a Close – the half-Hangit-Minister – the Big Mahungry.* Linda, with Duncan's help, now revisited this area of study. After Linda Williamson's PhD was completed she approached Stephanie Wolfe Murray at Canongate publishers, and Penguin Books in London, with plans to get Duncan's oral tales published in book form. When both responded positively the second stage of 'the Henderson/Williamson tinker project' took off. On 31 October 1985 Linda writes:

> Dear Hamish, I promised to have repaid your loan of £175 by now – I am just waiting on the Penguin advance . . . Enclosed is a narration of Duncan's *Cinderella,* the way he heard it first from his family . . . I think this is a perfect masterpiece of Traveller storytelling . . . The Penguin contract says 'app. 100,000 words by Sept. 1986' . . . Could you look through the card catalogue I gave you from Duncan's repertoire. It would be a great help to know which ones shouldn't be missed out for this World Folklore Library.

At Christmas she wrote again: 'The doors you opened for the travelling folk . . . Duncan with his book and opportunities now to express himself in his own words. . . We want you to know how our lives are given meaning by OOR HAMISH! God bless you aye!'

In 1987 Penguin published Duncan's *A Thorn in the King's Foot*, a 300-page paperback that was an immediate critical and commercial success. After this Duncan's career as a 'published author' took off. On 1 September 1992 Linda wrote to tell Hamish that Duncan's autobiography, *The Horsieman* (Canongate 1993) was finished, adding this comment: 'I

---

8 The Traveller lust for fat suggests the continuance of Palaeolithic, hunter-gatherer habits into modern times. The Inuit still eat vast quantities of fat, and Dr Julian Toms of Kintyre has documented how the teenage daughters of the Townsley clan – the Scoots – would regularly eat half-pound packs of butter – like ice-cream.

am reminded all the time of Bruce Chatwin's *Songlines* . . . Duncan's songs and poems, and ballads complete each chapter . . . Hamish would you be interested in reading some of the chapters?'

Linda's mention of Bruce Chatwin's last book, *The Songlines* (Picador 1987), is of interest because Hamish had met Chatwin, in Edinburgh, in the late sixties and had long believed he had some role in transforming Chatwin from a go-getting Sotheby's antiques buyer into a mould-breaking novelist of international importance. The history of the two men's contact goes back to 1966 when Chatwin, tired of the London business world, came north to the land of his Bruce ancestors to enrol as an archaeology undergraduate at the University of Edinburgh. Chatwin's interest in literature, gay politics, nomads, folklore and history coincided with Hamish's many interests, and the subjects and literary forms used by Chatwin in his first major books – *On the Black Hill* and *In Patagonia* – might be described as Hendersonian. When they were published Hamish read them with interest. When *The Songlines* appeared, he was thrilled but also disturbed because the Australian Outback that Chatwin was revealing was so like the Scotland of the Travellers he had 'discovered' in the 1950s:

> . . . the song and the land are one . . . song describes the nature of the land over which the song passes . . . 'Music', said Arkady, 'is a memory bank for finding one's way around the world . . . the world, if it has a future, has an ascetic future.'[9]

These words might have come from Hamish's lips at any time over the previous thirty years. When *The Songlines* was first published, Hamish and I discussed it at length, and a level of chagrin was obvious. Chatwin had turned aspects of *his* work in oral history into literary fiction (rather as George Ewart Evans and Ronald Blythe had, earlier, turned theirs into non-fiction) and Hamish, briefly, bristled defensively. But he was also proud to recognise Chatwin as part of the folk continuum:

> Chatwin has imagined an Australia very like the Scotland the Travellers inhabit. Our songlines go out, now, from Sutherland and Sandy Bell's – to Sotheby's and Alice Springs! It was Banjo Paterson who got Waltzing Matilda going, it's Eric Bogle who keeps things going today – and both of them came from the Scottish Border![10]

9 Bruce Chatwin, *The Songlines* (Picador 1987).
10 HH, conversation with TN, c. 1988.

EIGHTEEN

Ireland: A Continuing Love Affair

Hullo Pat Malone, sure I knew ye'd be here son:
The red and the green, lad, we'll wear side by side.
HH[1]

As a researcher at the School of Scottish Studies Hamish made regular professional visits to meet colleagues at the Irish Folklore Commission in Dublin. In January 1956 he made a broadcast with Ciarán MacMathúna of Radio Eireann and recorded twenty ballads from Kathleen Behan. Of her 'Lord Randall' he noted, 'like many versions of Child ballads collected in Ireland it is probably of Scottish origin'. Returning via the North Hamish got himself interviewed on BBC Radio Ulster, making the point, 'South-west Scotland and North-east Ireland may be said (from the point of view of folklore) to form a single cultural area.' Staying in Armagh, he began a long collaboration with teacher and folklorist Sean O'Boyle; their personal closeness is evident in this letter from O'Boyle:

> Seamus a Caraid . . . Never think for one moment because I've not written before now that I haven't been thinking constantly of yourself and the times we had around hogmanay and the times that we'll have with the help of God in the future . . . haven't you my own scallywag outlook on life, love, drink and all the more important aspects of our terrestrial sojourn? Wont we meet some day, anyway, in eternal light with Diarmid and Fionn and Oscar and the rest of the boys – to eat of oaten cake for ambrosia and drink the nectar of Glenlivet? And how many of those boys didn't answer a letter at all? Why, Oisin didn't even know the Fianna were dead . . . '

They were soon planning a summer collecting trip to the Hebrides. On 6 June O'Boyle writes in high spirits:

> Dear Hamish, I must remain at action stations until the end of the month then hey for the boot and the horse lad, and over the waves with me . . . I'll be seeing you in Edinburgh in the first week of

1 'The John MacLean March', published in the *Collected Poems*.

> August and, to begin our studious liaison, I'll bring with me the version of 'The Apprentice Boy' that I got in County Antrim in 1953 – yes, and sung to the Sarah Jane air too! Don't bother me with details about what we'll do in Barra – that will work itself out day by day and ceili by ceili . . . I'm certainly looking forward to meeting you again . . .

The Hebridean trip proved a great success. When Hamish, later, sent O'Boyle recordings of Gaelic psalm singing on the Isle of Lewis, he responded with delight. 'I don't know when I got a present I enjoyed so much as your Gaelic psalms: what a revelation about the widespread use of the good old Irish language. It's lovely, thank you . . .' The Psalms of David, sung by Free Presbyterian congregations on Lewis, are one of the glories of the School of Scottish Studies archives and provoked a story Hamish enjoyed retelling. Two female Jewish American scholars visited the School – to hear the best of Scots music. Hamish played them a selection of his favourite recordings. Nothing particular appealed to them until 'I played the unaccompanied Gaelic psalms! Their faces lit up. I didn't tell them what they were. They told me! They announced "these are the Psalms of David sung by the Iranian Jews!" They asked me where we'd got them? I told them the Isle of Lewis! When I saw their responses, I realised that a lifetime's research lay ahead – of them!'[2]

In July 1958 Hamish spent a week visiting the archives of the Irish Folklore Commission and enjoyed another radio appearance with Ciarán Mac Mathúna, entitled *Heritage in Sound*. He visited the great storyteller from the Blasket, Peg Sayers. 'Peg is lying blind and bedridden in a hospital above Dingle, but her mind is as alert as ever and she told me her version of 'Ri Na mBreag' (The King of the Liars), one of the stories I recorded from the Blairgowrie Stewarts.'[3]

During the summer of 1959 Hamish helped Francis Dillon of the Features Department of the London BBC arrange a recording session with Kathleen Behan in Dublin. She earned some cash and the BBC's interest helped change policy at the Irish Folklore Commission. Looking back in the seventies, Hamish made notes about state propriety in Ireland:

> The Behans were the embodiment of Irish, urban working class culture – but also part of the older Irish tradition that Peg Sayers represented: both these traditions were fundamentally challenged by the Catholic authoritarianism of the Irish Free State – with its censor, its anti-sex prudery and the all-pervading clerical preponderance. By the Fifties, Delargy [Head of the Irish Folklore Commission] had become a folk connoisseur. He wouldn't record the remarkable

---

2 HH, conversation with TN, 1980.

3 HH, unpublished notes, Henderson archive.

> Behan family – they were not recorded by the Folklore Commission and were banned from Radio Eireann. When I first met Delargy he knew absolutely nothing about the Behan tradition – the urban Dublin tradition – Irish nationalism had been pushed to the wall. Brendan Behan was almost totally unknown to the Irish public and what they knew they didn't like – but – by the time of his death he was the most popular character in Ireland.

Hamish's long collaboration with Dominic Behan continued as the Folk Revival gathered momentum. On Hamish's thirty-eighth birthday he sent this letter:

> Dear Hamish, The Lomaxes and MacColls are funny animals, they are not quite the same as us, they don't think like us, and, even more when they do, they don't act like us. In other words, they, and I'm damned if I don't believe this, have to be told what's good and what's bad . . . One of MacColl's ideas is to do a certain amount of work for the Bee Bee See, and it is here I want you to get down to some work in the Behan interest – it is absolutely imperative that I do a rapid amount of work on his programme.

During the spring of 1960 Dominic Behan made plans for a summer tour of East Germany – with Hamish and both their young wives.

> The idea is that you and I should go through for six weeks . . . We would visit the universities and an odd workers institution, singing and talking about the folk culture of these islands – it wont I imagine take long to deal with the English bit – we are transported both ways by plane at their expense, we will be paid and kept during our stay, and be allowed to record anything that takes our fancy . . . I think Hamish and I can have a right good time. They know all about the Nixon-McColl [Communist Party] plot against you, and were not impressed by either of these gentlemen.

For some reason this trip – like all the other major foreign trips planned by or for Hamish – did not materialise. Katzel was most disappointed, but Sean O'Boyle came to the rescue by inviting them to Armagh:

> *A Sheamus a charaid* – We'd all love to see you again – could you not manage some excuse to see me? – Here's one – I'm engaged on research into the Rhythm of Bardic Poetry – *Ranniocht Mhor, Ranniocht Bheag, Seadra, CasBhavidre*, the whole lot: I think I have established the interconnection of Irish music and the old Filiocht – in fact I'm sure of it. Now Irish music is Scottish Music: and the most consistent practitioners of the Bardic metre were the Scots.

This research is as important for the SSS as it is for Ireland – can't you get a short leave to discuss it with me?

Sean O'Boyle was working on a theory that 'Ogam was an early musical tablature'. He told Hamish, 'I wouldn't give up this research for all the money in the world.' Unfortunately, he was mortally ill and a year later Sean wrote this short, last letter:

> Dear Hamish, . . . say a prayer for me that I may bear it all usefully. I still feel fit before the frosts come. I do wish I could see Chris [Grieve] again, and all the boys and all the girls, and tread the streets of Edinburgh again. But it's not for me this time.

That summer at the Edinburgh Festival, Hamish met another Irishman who was to have a profound impact on his life, Brian Trevaskis. He came from Dublin but was of Cornish descent. He lacked formal education but, determined to become a writer, he was soon clinging to Hamish both as a father-figure and a literary mentor. Within a year Hamish had helped negotiate him a place at Trinity College, Dublin, and a meteoric career took off. In 1980 Hamish learned a good deal about the background to the Trevaskis story in this letter from Nell Bourke of New Hampshire.

> Dear Hamish, If you are who I think you are, there is no one in the world I would rather hear from . . . I first met Brian [Trevaskis] in a way that does him much credit. I had dragged Patrick [Paddy Kavanagh?] to a lecture at the Little Lecture Theatre in Kingston, Jamaica by, I think, Stephen Spender, a good twenty years ago. Sitting in front of us was a young man in faded, mended, very clean shirt and dungarees who asked a singularly intelligent question in a lilting Irish tone. He had had to leave school very young and was working as a donkey greaser on a cargo ship. Most sailors landing in the unsavoury part of Kingston head straight for the bars or brothels. The Little Theatre is a helluva way from the docks, and to make all that effort to hear a poet certainly substantiated his claim to be trying to self-educate. I was fairly, OK, financially, then . . . so was able to send him to a crammer's school in Scotland to get his G.C.E., O and A levels, which he did, which enabled him to get into Trinity College, Dublin.
>
> He was writing poems, novels, plays, and I had a lot of contacts in the literary world; through my now dead brother-in-law Robert Shaw, excellent connections in the theatre world meant that if he sent in a script – at least, it would be read – and he made a lot of useful connections, like you for example. But, he seems to be one

of those people with the seeds of disaster in them, blowing golden opportunity time after sad time – if he had an appointment with a publisher, the novel would get lost on a train – with a theatre producer we had practically blackmailed, he would mistake the day. And always in dire need of money . . . He did not mean to become one, did not want to become one, but became a severe financial drain once the children began to grow up, and as Kipling says, never-ending as 'once you begin paying the Danegeld, you never get rid of the Dane'.

Now to you. Are you the genius that wrote 'The Freedom Come a' Ye'?, 'The Farewell to Sicily'?, 'The D Day Dodgers'? (I heard them from Liam Clancy) – They are brilliant! . . . I have been in folksong for about 25 years, a great friend of the Jamaican Olive Lewin and the American Ed. McCurdy, but think your songs unsurpassed . . . My father's family were Malcolm of Gaylea, and my mother was a Semple, now spelt Sempil, of Craigivar in Aberdeenshire – please write – fondly Nell.

In September 1964 Trevaskis wrote to Hamish from Dublin:

Dear Hamish, You have returned from Hunland and the Aegean Isles . . . and I have been awarded a grant for Trinity College, Dublin – will you allow me to take you for a drink one evening, when I can repay you for the £s I owe you . . . It's just as Yeats said: 'only the wasteful earn the sun.' The Irish produce great writers because they're prodigals – they're willing to squander their lives on the gratuitous work that great art demands; whereas the Scotch, on the contrary, are only really good at economics and moral philosophy: I believed that till now . . .

Trevaskis was soon elected President of Trinity Philosophical Society and within a year had written two plays, *Killinarden* and *The Captain's Daughter*. He was also a controversial 'personality' on Gay Byrne's *The Late Late Show*, which over the years became a powerful force in the secularisation of life in Ireland. Trevaskis attacked the moral hypocrisy of the Irish Catholic Church, 'personified', he declared, 'by Archbishop John Charles McQuaid of Dublin!' In 1966 he wrote to describe how he had called 'the Bishop of Galway a moron, on television!'

Dear Hamish, I'm taking up where O'Casey left off . . . I'm having possibly the most glorious career at Trinity since Gogarty or Mahaffy . . . The success of *The O'Neill* [his latest play, presented at the University Drama Festival in Galway] was phenomenal and a necessary feather in my cap . . . Thank you for everything – delighted

> by Joan Littlewood's assessment of 'Killinarden'. Can you lend me some money? When the lights go up and the world looks at its programme for my next three plays it will read, 'By Brian Trevaskis with the assistance of Hamish Henderson'.

Trevaskis, like Sean O'Casey before him, felt bound to leave Ireland, and his next letter comes from Mousehole, in Cornwall, land of his fathers: 'I have left Trinity and Ireland. The real choice was getting out or into a state where a nervous breakdown would have been the consequence. I do not enjoy fame. I was running up a blind alley. I have chosen health and productivity, I am in Cornwall, and destitute. I have rent to pay next Thursday and God knows what will happen – can you wire me £20 for a couple of months?' Hamish sent money by return and took up the tutorial burden the lecturers at Trinity had put down.

> Dear Hamish, Another short-story enclosed. How about offering me some good down to earth criticism . . . I have taken you at your word and will not be repaying you for a few weeks yet . . . Some good news, *The O'Neill* has gone to the Abbey . . . I envision an Irish Film Industry eventually – the material is there but not the money . . . Did I send you any reviews of *The O'Neill*? It ran to packed houses in Dublin and was a large success. You had a hand in writing it – remember we discussed it one night at the Traverse. And your Constantine Maxwell book was an enormous help.

Mousehole is one of Cornwall's most picturesque fishing villages, and was also part of the St Ives art colony (in West Penwith). The poet W.S. Graham was living at Madron, nearby, and Hamish suggested Trevaskis make contact. He visited on Christmas Day 1967. Trevaskis describes Sydney and Nessa Graham as 'desperately poor, ill, hung-over, and starving. All they could offer me was a cold sausage, and all I could offer them was a few songs, after which Nessie sang me "The Broomielaw".' When Hamish wrote back he copied out several songs by Mary Brooksbank, including verses that Trevaskis immediately gave to one of his theatrical characters, describing him as 'really James Connolly and now on the stage of the Player's Theatre at Trinity College, Dublin!' He then informed Hamish of his plan to become a Cornish writer:

> Cornwall has so little by way of theatre and literature – quite unique for a Celtic people, isn't it? and so unutterably sad. Will I be Cornwall's playwright when I die? Made articulate by Ireland? The second play I'm doing is *Tristan and Iseult. Kilroy was Here* will be set in Manchester . . . .

And so it went on – brilliant ideas and exhaustion leap-frogging each other – until Trevaskis had a series of minor breakdowns. He left Cornwall for Bristol, London, Manchester: he moved from bed-sit to bed-sit, seeking out theatre companies, publishers and university courses. One letter to Hamish deals at length with the sexual abuse he had suffered in Homes, and it hints at the derangement that would finally overwhelm him. Hamish did what he could for Trevaskis but it was not enough.

Hamish also did what he could for Ireland, and the consequences were profound. Few people think of Hamish as even a bit player in the cultural, political and economic renaissance of Ireland but from childhood Hamish felt an Irish 'destiny'.[4]

In 1970 Edward Lucie-Smith edited the Penguin paperback *British Poetry Since 1945*. Lucie-Smith's introduction raises important points about recent Irish poetry:

> The Northern Irish phenomenon has been the most striking event in British poetry during the last decade and a half. In purely literary terms, the work of these poets is rooted in the Movement and the Group. It owes much to the fact that Philip Hobsbaum taught for a period at Queen's University, Belfast, and ran a discussion group there which was attended by (among others) Seamus Heaney, Derek Mahon and Michael Longley. But it is political and social circumstances which seem to have given the Northern Irish poets their real impetus – they found a subject (the condition of Ireland) and a way to write about it. Belfast seems to be the one place in the British isles where poetry has been able to take on some of the centrality it has in Russia, and indeed throughout Eastern Europe, and it has done so for not dissimilar reasons.

Why does Lucie-Smith make no mention of Hamish? He was active in the cultural and political life of Northern Ireland long before Hobsbaum enjoyed his short appointment at Queens, and throughout the second half of the twentieth century Hamish's cultural influence on Ireland must be adjudged far greater than Hobsbaum's. It appears his interest in the folk and in political activism has allowed metropolitan commentators like Lucie-Smith and academic historians like

4 The last 'Irish Joke' that he copied into his mother's recipe book (in 1928) is worth recording: 'The wife and I went to a football match. During the play a man next to us kept on shouting – "fifty one thousand men, fifty one thousand men!" "Fifty one thousand men", says I, "What's the idea of fifty one thousand men?" Says he, "Fifty one thousand men – so why did that pigeon pick on me!"'

Roy Foster to confine him to the margins. Hamish did not seek fame; he just got on with things.[5] On 15 October 1968 he wrote to Laura Simmons, wife of James Simmons, editor of *The Honest Ulsterman*:

> Just one criticism of the July number of The Honest Ulsterman – 'The Celts were the first settlers in Ireland . . . ' The Celts were *not* the first settlers in Ireland, and Dr Clancy should know better. Indeed, compared to the earliest settlers in Ireland the Celts are almost as much 'Nouveau riche' as the Danes, Normans, Saxons etc – who succeeded them. The art of the pre-Celtic inhabitants of Ireland is one of the glories of its history. One of the jobs of the 'Honest Ulsterman' might well be to get the record straight . .

The Irish magazine on which Hamish had the strongest direct influence was the *Broadsheet* edited by Hayden Murphy (February 1967–June 1978). Hamish first met Murphy in McDaid's Bar, Dublin, on 28 January 1965: he was then a student at Trinity College, just nineteen, long-haired, angelic, poetical and learning to drink. He was a member of a song-poetry group that called itself 'Dr Strangely Strange'. They felt themselves on the lip of a better Ireland. As artists, they felt it was their duty 'to throw-off the dust-jackets of a benighting Church, a censorious State, and all the inhibitions of Ireland's unnecessary, provincialism!'[6] Hayden inspired Hamish: his youthful idealism echoed that with which he himself had sought to 'free' Scotland twenty years earlier. Hamish saw Hayden Murphy and Brian Trevaskis, and thousands like them, as the shock-troops of a new Ireland that could do the world great good.

The following year Murphy travelled to Edinburgh to begin a lifelong association with the Scottish capital. In February 1967 the first *Broadsheet* was published and quickly recognised as a small but significant literary newcomer. Speaking about the *Broadsheet*, Murphy told me: 'I wanted it to be Irish and international, I wanted to look beyond Dublin and I wanted it to do the same.'[7] Despite limited funds and no infrastructure, these aims were realised. Earning his living as a cross-border journalist, Murphy remained in regular contact with Hamish and, in 1979, settled permanently in Edinburgh. One of his poems about Hamish is entitled 'Your Welcome':

---

5 On 22 October 1969 the folklorist Tom Munnelly wrote to Hamish: 'I'm pottering about with the idea of resurrecting the long defunct Irish Folklore Society . . . would you give a talk?'

6 Hayden Murphy, conversation with TN, 2006.

7 Hayden Murphy, conversation with TN, 2006.

It always begins with your smile:
Then the hand-clasp,
Each finger an embrace
Of knowledge delivered
With affection. Then
The embrace of comrade
Generosity with Brother Pleasure
At our meeting.
It is the warmth
Of knowledge heated
By the sure fire of intellect.
And, I hope,
Lit by friendship.[8]

Throughout the sixties Hamish was in irregular contact with the Guinness millionaire Garech Browne, owner of Claddagh Records in Dublin. Browne was a traditional music enthusiast and since 1962 had worked closely with Paddy Moloney of the Chieftains, the first Irish band to achieve international success. Encouraged by Hamish, Browne developed a plan to also promote Scottish poetry and, in the early seventies, a series of LPs of readings by MacDiarmid, Sorley MacLean and Hamish were produced – long before anything similar appeared in Scotland. In September 1972 Hamish set the framework within which he wanted his own work presented:

> Dear Garech . . . A great deal of my work is, or tries to be, genuine 'oral' poetry and song, and it is for this reason that I have much preferred to speak it or to sing it than to print it . . . I can assure you that this is not just purist bloody-mindedness on my part – what I have tried to do is to break away from print and create a kind of poetry which can be shared and recreated in the old style . . . and publication on gramophone records is closely allied to the whole process of circulation in folk clubs, student-parties, ceilidhs and the like . . .

Hamish's Claddagh LP did not appear until 1977 but when it did Hamish was well pleased.[9] Entitled *Freedom Come all Ye – the Poems and Songs of Hamish Henderson* it features the African band Atté, the Clutha, the Whistlebinkies (with Owen Hand), the Laggan, Dolina MacLennan, Andy Hunter, Alison McMorland and Willie Scott. The Scottish Arts Council, under the direction of Trevor Royle, contributed towards costs, and

---

8 Hayden Murphy, 'Your Welcome', unpublished.

9 In 1977 *Elegies for the Dead in Cyrenaica* was republished by Edinburgh University Student Publications Board, generously reviewed by Anthony Thwaite in the *Times Literary Supplement* 9 September 1977.

Hamish was paid £250. In a letter to Alex Scott of Glasgow University in 1972, Hamish had expanded his ideas about oralcy.

> Most of my Scots poetry (or songs) are really meant to be *heard* rather than read, and I have been very interested to observe what has happened to them when they have entered the maelstrom of the present revival . . . The fact is they are conceived and executed as *oral poetry*, and this sometimes means, I'm afraid, that their poetic texture may be a little thin. You see I am always thinking of the potential collaborator, and so I have to give him leeway. Sometimes it does pay off: for example, the version of my Highland Divs Farewell to Sicily, printed in 'Ballads of WWII' is a lot better than what I originally wrote – thanks to several unknown jocks. Sometimes it hasn't worked . . . The best way to present my work would certainly be on a record . . . Sicily has been recorded over thirty times . . . I have a contract with Claddagh Records (in Dublin) . . . I do not want to assert my claim in front of others – but I am acutely conscious that, of all the Scottish poetry to be issued or spoken by Claddagh, mine is probably the only contribution which is conceived *primarily* as oral poetry.

The British folk newspaper *Folk News* certainly liked what Hamish had done, Karl Dallas reviewing the Claddagh LP with brotherly gusto:

> It is hard to over-praise this magnificent record . . . not only is it a superb testament to a man who – as poet, folklorist, polemicist, political man of action – has made his mark on several countries as well as his native Scotland but it shows that the creativity of this man is still in full flood . . . It includes some of the finest singers in the Scottish revival and one traditional singer – read the sleeve-notes by Thomas Crawford – to a master of almost Leonardo-like virtuosity. My disappointment is that the record contains so little singing by Hamish – he is not much of a singer by any critical standards, including his own, but nevertheless there is a vigour and charm in his own rendering of his own songs which is completely unduplicated by any other singer, however superior in tone or technique . . . one senses the deep conviction that inspired him in the first place – his inevitable phrasing points up the discoveries within the lyrics.

That summer Dallas conducted two interviews with Hamish (published in *Folk News* Vol. 1, Nos 6 and 7). Reviewing the record in the *Scotsman* (22 October 1977), Alastair Clark described Hamish as the man who had taught him 'to feel the music' and demonstrated the folk tradition to be 'a living thing':

> These are songs of protest, songs of revolution, but, most of all, songs of love . . . The most haunting performance among the songs comes from Atté, a group of South African blacks living in London. They make a superb job of the 'free Mandela' song 'Rivonia', presenting it in African call-and-response form with Zulu phrases . . . And how naturally the phrases of 'The Gillie More' come thrusting from the lips of Willie Scott the Border shepherd. It is as if Hamish had written the song for him. Alison McMorland, too, gets completely inside 'The Flyting o' Life and Daith,' and no composer could hope for a better exposition than this.

Such reviews encouraged Hamish to hope that the record might hit 'the big time'. In December 1977 he wrote to Claddagh: 'If Paul McCartney's "Mull of Kintyre" – by no means a bad song – can reach the top of the greasy pole, it seems to me by no means impossible that the Whistlebinkies' "Banks of Sicily" might do the same – not to mention Atté's "Rivonia"! Why not get cracking and produce a single of these two?' Unfortunately, the greasy pole proved slippery, and sales of the Claddagh record remained low. As usual, Hamish's reward was the illumination of others: in April 1979 he received this letter from Jim Reed of Skipton, Yorkshire:

> I have listened to your record repeatedly and without disturbance. I had not thought to be so moved, nor to find myself, alien that I am, so in accord with your feelings about Scotland and with what I see Scotland representing in the wider world.

In October 1989, after attending the Cork Film Festival, Hamish spent a fortnight holidaying in the west of Ireland. When he got home, this letter was waiting for him:

> Dear Hamish . . . What a chance? I heard you speaking on 'Clare FM' this morning! I'm almost in Mayo – I should have left the house long before! . . . Anyway I felt I ought to let you know not only how pleased I was to hear you, but how glad I was that the people of Clare heard the very fabric of Scotland so warmly represented . . . It is amazing how that fundamental bond between Scotland and Ireland shows through when you least expect it.[10]

10 Letter to HH from Mark Wringe, University College, Galway.

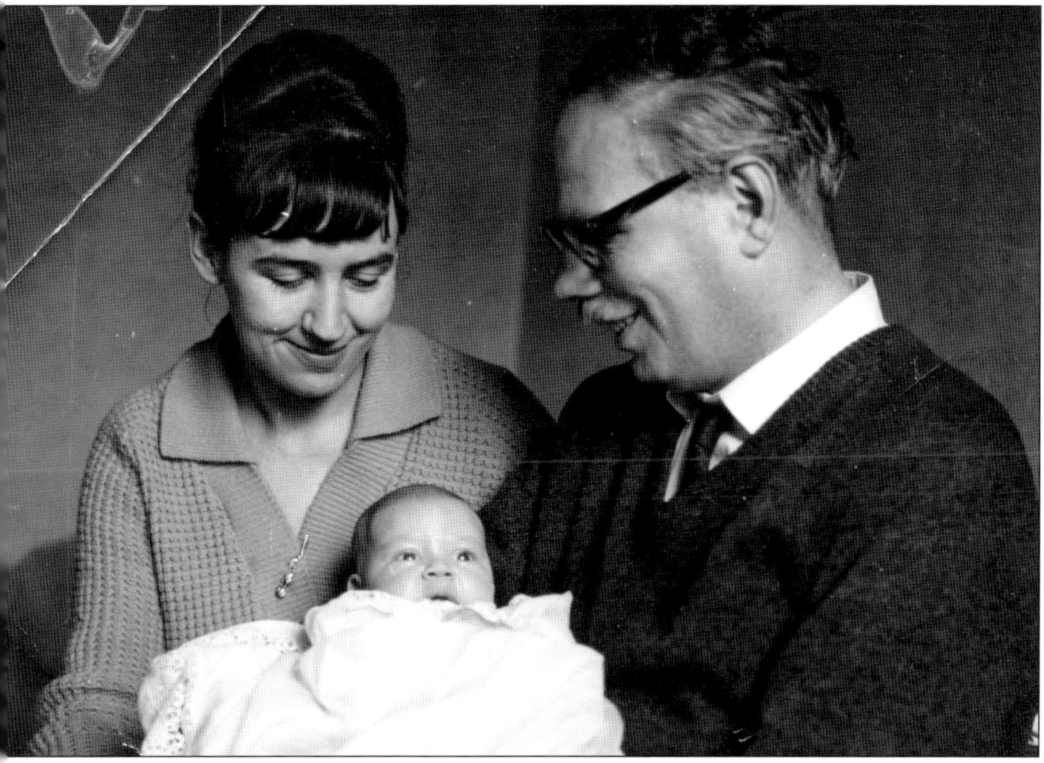

Katzel and Hamish with their firstborn child, Christina, Edinburgh, 1963 (KH).

School of Scottish Studies colleagues Bill Nicolaisen and Donald Archie MacDonald with Hamish in Athens, 1964 (KH).

The author Timothy Neat, filming *The Edge of the Forest*, January 1967, three months before he met Hamish for the first time (Photo: John Jones; TN).

The Padstow Obby Oss and Mayday Dancers, Cornwall, 1967 (Photos: Barry Herbert; TN).

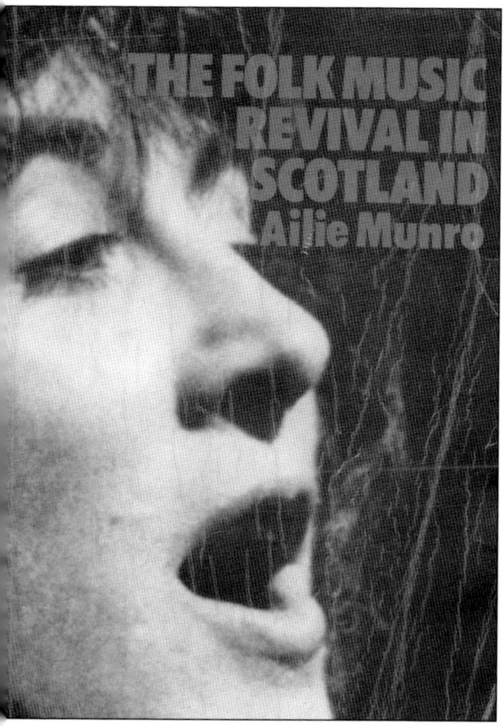

'olksinger Alison McMorland (1970) eatured on the cover of *The Folk Music Revival in Scotland*, 1984, by Ailie Munro Photo: John Harrison; TN).

The border shepherd and ballad-singer Willie Scott, c.1970 (SSS Archive; KH).

laswegian songwriter, singer and political ctivist Matt McGinn, 1967 (KH).

Hamish with folksinger Ray Fisher, Edinburgh, c.1970 (KH).

Pete Shepheard, instigator of the Blairgowrie Folk festival with the ageing folk stalwarts Davy Stewart and Jimmy McBeath, 1967 (KH).

Inverness Folk Festival 1969, Billy Connolly chatting with Gerry Rafferty, Hamish, Hamish Bain, Jean Redpath, Archie Fisher, Finbar Furey, Aly Bain, Tam Harvey, Derek Moffat; and Cyril Tawney, Eddie Furey, Tich Frier, Andy Ramage, Ian McCalman (AB/KH).

The Henderson family, 1975: Katzel, Tina, Janet and Hamish (KH).

Hamish with forester and ballad singer Willie Beattie, at Hermiston Castle, 1979, during the shooting of the film *Tig! For the Morn's the Fair Day* (TN).

Hamish at work and play, Edinburgh and Padstow (KH).

Hamish embracing his School of Scottish Studies colleague John MacInnes, and university friends, Edinburgh c.1980 (Photo: Jack Fisher; KH).

Hamish at a CND demonstration in Glasgow, c. 1972 (TN).

In 1977 Claddagh Records, Dublin, issued a Hamish Henderson LP entitled *The Freedom Come a' Ye*: his Nelson Mandela song 'Rivonia' was recorded by the South African Group Atté, in London. Here he celebrates with two South African friends (DM).

Dancing at Dry Drayton, Cambridge, 1980. Hamish insisted that the BBC television documentary *The Dead, the Innocent* (about his war experiences) should be 'framed' by a plea for peace and an exploration of the 'rare' necessity for war (KH).

Hamish talking with Holocaust survivors, Dry Drayton, 1980 (KH).

Singer and folklorist Jo Miller graduating from the School of Scottish Studies. Hamish is administering the *coup de grâce*. Dr Margaret Mackay looks on with pride, 1984 (Photo: Jo Miller).

Duncan and Linda Williamson with Betsy and Tommy, in their 'gelley', Lochgilphead, 1984 (Photo: Glasgow Herald; TN).

The Kirriemuir Folk Festival 1984: Hamish in his element (Photo: Ed Miller; KH).

Hamish with his lifelong friend Dolina MacLennan, singer, actress and television producer (TN).

The poet Tom Scott, a drawing by American sculptor Brad Graves, 1992 (TN).

Harry Erskine, the Langholm Spade Carrier, crosses the Ewes with Common Riding enthusiasts, 1985 (Photo: Timothy Neat).

Hamish and Eddie McGuire (with The Whistlebinkies) perform 'The Freedom Come a' Ye', for John Cage, at the Fruitmarket Gallery, Edinburgh, 1984 (Photo: Shaun Hudson; EM).

Hamish in conversation with Antony Burgess, Venice, 1988 (Photo: Timothy Neat).

Hamish serenading his fellow interpreter, Mary Acheson, during filming of *Play Me Something*, Venice, 1988 (Photo: Jean Mohr).

'talian actress Lucia Lanzarini and Fife welder Charlie Barron dance to Hamish's 'mouth nusic', the Guidecca, 1988 (Photo: Jean Mohr).

Hamish relaxing on a gondola during the shooting of *Play Me Something*, 1988 Photo: Jean Mohr).

Hamish arguing the case for Antonio Gramsci in the Sezioni of the Partito Comunista d'Italia (Communist Party of Italy), Guidecca, 1988 (Photo: Jean Mohr).

NINETEEN

Nationalism, Gay Rights and the Scottish Labour Party

What the Reformation did was to snuff out what must otherwise have developed into the most brilliant national culture in history.[1]

Fionn MacColla

The Scottish National Party revival of the late 1960s reawakened Hamish's interest in Scottish politics. Revolutionary activism, however, was a thing of the past: now the culture would lead the politics. When Donald Stewart (SNP) won the Western Isles by-election of 1970, Hamish congratulated him in an enthusiastic letter, requesting that he stand by his promise 'to keep the Home Rule flag flying, to fight for peace and continue opposition to the British arms trade with South Africa'. In the spring of 1970 Hamish worked to establish the Leith People's Festival (with Labour Councillor Sandy Ross and the writer Tom Buchan) as 'a new alternative to the Edinburgh Festival'. He also accepted nomination as a member of the Scottish Arts Council (SAC) committee responsible for the distribution of grants to literary publications and conference organisers. Douglas Eadie, literary assistant at the SAC, remembers Hamish speaking in support of the short-lived magazine *Scottish International* (1968–74). 'He also asked us to support attempts to honour the German poet Heinrich Heine, by backing a campaign to have the University of Dusseldorf renamed after Heine. This confused several members of the committee!'

When six Basque nationalists were sentenced to death in Spain, Hamish wrote to the Spanish Embassy. In January 1971 the Chargé d'Affaires wrote back: 'Dear Sir, I refer to your petition for clemency and am pleased to confirm that the head of the Spanish State, using his prerogative of mercy, has commuted the six death sentences imposed upon the terrorists brought before a Burgos Court on a charge of murder . . . I take this chance of enclosing some notes on the case . . . Manuel Gomez Acebo.'

August 1971 marked the bicentenary of the birth of Sir Walter Scott, and Hamish was invited to speak at an international conference held in Edinburgh. Hamish notes: 'Reread eleven Scott novels, re-explore *Minstrelsy of the Scottish Border*, read the criticism.' His lecture was

---

1 Fionn MacColla, *At the Sign of the Clenched Fist* (Edinburgh 1967).

entitled 'Scott and Folksong' and it was probably his last 'academic *tour de force*'. He was also responsible for the conference ceilidh and constructed a programme that affirmed the connections between the folk tradition, Scott, Scottish literature and contemporary Scotland. Traditional singers like Willie Scott and the Stewarts of Blair performed alongside young Revival singers like Jean Redpath, Isla St Clair and Jimmy Hutchison.

On 8 September 1971 – as usual ahead of the game – Hamish helped organise one of the first major demonstrations against Mrs Thatcher (then Minister of Education) during a ministerial visit to Edinburgh. Shortly afterwards, when closure of Upper Clyde Shipbuilders was announced, Hamish offered his support for the various 'Work-ins' that followed. He spoke to the Joint Shop Stewards Committee, sang at support rallies, applauded Jimmy Reid, and on 27 December sent a cheque for £14.95.

In September 1972 Hamish was a sponsor of the Indochina Solidarity Conference organised in London by Terry Smith of Pentonville Road. In December he supported the Federation of Student Nationalists in their campaign to preserve crofter rights on the Strollamus Estate on Skye. In February 1973 he joined a demonstration of three thousand people supporting Clydebank Town Council's refusal to implement the Government's new Rent Act. Morris Blythman sent him a newspaper report, 'Clydebank says "No to Rent Act"', and a letter:

> Dear Hamish, I was down there at Clydebank for the big Rents Demonstration last month, selling the John MacLean pamphlet – 'Remembering John MacLean' by Harry McShane – and by a huge coincidence the Trades Union Centre Choir inside the hall started singing 'The John MacLean March', and it was being carried outside by loudspeakers. I kept my slogan, 'John MacLean – the man who led Scotland's greatest rent Strike' but added, 'John MacLean – the man they're singing about' – and it was like magic, the last few were literally snatched out of my hands. It was certainly a great compliment to the singers and the song! This power of culture in politics – perhaps it's not exaggerating too much to say that MacLean has made a 'comeback' via Nationalism, Poetry, Drama, and Song.

When the Chilean government of President Allende was overthrown in a military coup in 1973 (orchestrated by the CIA), Hamish became a founder member of the Edinburgh Chile Solidarity Committee. He was soon speaking, writing, singing and fund-raising across Scotland. He formed a close bond with a young exiled musician, Carlos Arredondo, and the two remained friends for many years.

In February 1974 Hamish joined a demonstration against admission charges to the nation's galleries and museums. A *Scotsman* photograph shows him shoulder to shoulder with John Smith MP and Gordon

Brown. Hamish argued that such charges penalised the poor and 'were actually illegal because they frustrated the principles on which the Vaughan and Torrie bequests to the National Gallery of Scotland were made'. Later that month he joined Ruth McQuillan (a loyal supporter of Hugh MacDiarmid) in the campaign to save Langholm's historic Victorian Library from closure. In July, at an Edinburgh meeting of the National Council for Civil Liberties, Hamish spoke about 'Gramsci and Liberty'. In October, he addressed the Bertrand Russell Peace Foundation, attended a meeting of Amnesty International in St George's West Church, Edinburgh, and began a long acquaintance with the Rev. Paul Oestreicher. He notes:

> Myth with a Kirk – the central tawse of Scotland.
> Root paradigms = cultural translations of genetic codes.[2]

After the legalisation of homosexuality in Britain in 1967 the moral and cultural boundaries surrounding gay rights became a matter of increasingly open debate. Prejudices and taboos, however, remained strong, and the issue aroused antagonisms much fiercer than those associated with similar debates about recreational drugs. Hamish had sympathy for drug-takers but was personally opposed to the use of any mind-altering drugs. His attitude is encapsulated in this event remembered by Katzel.

> Hamish brought back a group of young musicians – including a young Polish man, known to be associated with a 'Madame' from Danube Street. It was 1969. We discussed drug-taking and he told me he could get me 'any kind of drugs you want'. Hamish overheard what was going on. He didn't do anything – other than keep a weather-eye on proceedings – but, when the party was over, he announced, with his iron temper hardly controlled: 'Don't you dare! Drugs will never come into this house!'[3]

Things were very different in his attitude to homosexuality. At home, at school, in the orphanage, at Cambridge, in the Army, Hamish knew male friendship to be one of the great boons of life. If friendship between men sometimes became love – arousing spiritual, emotional and physical consequences – so be it. Love was the summit of human being – and not to be divided. Any idea that love could be separated out by legal niceties, controlled by imprisonment or beatings, was anathema. Hamish himself never lived 'a homosexual lifestyle' but, lifelong, he loved men as he loved women and children, and accepted homosexual love as a fact of life. He saw post-Victorian Britain's 'legal obsession' with same-sex relationships

---

2 HH, unpublished notes, Henderson archive.
3 Katzel Henderson, conversation with TN, 2007.

as a historical aberration and a form of hypocritical brutality. In 1970 his friend Dougie Moncrieff sent him a card from London, quoting Somerset Maugham: 'People starting with the idea that certain things are right and are the Law, come to believe that others are right because they are the Law.' Hamish noted:

> The a-historical cannot imagine contemporary history being made. The hatred of the lumpen-bourgeoisie for the creative individualist – whose actions are beyond them and a threat to them – is as spiritually corrosive as it is institutionally enshrined.

In 1972, in response to a public outburst of 'homosexual high-horse-ism', Hamish joined the ongoing debate with a long letter to the *Scotsman* in which he asks:

> Can there be another subject on earth about which more nonsense has been written . . . People who talk about 'bastions of morality' all too often turn out themselves to be merely bastions of prejudice and outmoded myth and tabu. The sexual tabu which the Reverend Malcolm H. MacRae wishes to uphold surely has about as much relevance for us in this country today as the Hindu tabu on the eating of beef or the Jewish tabu on pork . . . Here and there you get 'the auntran guid ane' but in the main they are just the same old pack of self-elected elect who see sex as one of the comparatively few areas where they can still have the occasional field day, doing their self important thing and interfering with other people's lives.

This bold public statement stimulated a healthy response. One postcard came from Whitehaven, Cumbria: 'Dear Mr Henderson, Thank you for your courageous letter in The Scotsman of today. As someone who has suffered from the misunderstanding you write of . . . I can only applaud and admire your bravery. Though in my experience I can only say that privately I have met only sympathy from clergy – one using his influence to protect me from being sacked on anonymous information. Thank you on behalf of so many, I.S.' Two more ambiguous letters arrived from a man named Anatole James. It is not clear whether these were innocent enquiries from a genuinely gay man or whether James was one of the team of *agents provocateurs* paid to 'draw' Hamish on to criminal ground. Anatole's prime interest was in lowering the male 'age of consent'; he writes:

> I came to live in Edinburgh in 1945 . . . It seems to me that the proportion of homosexuals in Scotland, in proportion to the population is high. As to whether or not it is a good thing to legalise homosexuality in a small way, is, I think, debatable. The whole thing wants to be just as legal as heterosexuality and in just the same set of

circumstances. As I have already stated the age of consent for boys and girls should be 14. But this will take a lot of bringing about.

Hamish replied on 26 September, with courtesy but keeping his distance:

> Dear Mr James, Thank you for your letter. I'm afraid I'm a bit sceptical about attempts to associate sexual preferences or mores with groups or communities as big as Scotland. I once had a conversation with a Milanesi journalist – a real male chauvinist if ever there was one – who assured me, over a bottle of vino, that 'all Germans are paederasts'. When I reminded him of the many references to homosexuality in Latin and Italian literature he got quite annoyed. '*In Italia queste cose si nascondono*' . . . A few years ago, during the course of a conversation with Hugh MacDiarmid, about the period of the Reformation in Scotland, I mentioned the contemporary rumours about the homosexual affairs of both Darnley and Bothwell. MacDiarmid's reaction amused me – he said: 'But homosexuality has never been a Scottish thing!' I said that in my opinion homosexuality was a natural human thing, and that there was probably neither more nor less of it in Scotland than anywhere else.

With that Hamish terminated the correspondence. He was wise to do so. A word of support for the position Anatole James was soliciting could have exposed Hamish to exacting punishment. James was a subversive character. Andrew Hood, the former letters editor of both the *Scotsman* and the *Glasgow Herald*, has done some research into his background. James played a role in the Mass Observation Public Survey, offered evidence to the Wolfenden Committee in the 1950s and, as a renowned heavy drinker on the Edinburgh gay scene, got himself involved in a number of scrapes with the Edinburgh police and the Intelligence Services. He lived in Chester Street, Edinburgh, and in the sixties got himself imprisoned for a 'homosexual offence' (a rare event in Scotland). There is no evidence that James wished Hamish well but plenty to suggest that his sexual libertarianism was allied to flagrant anti-Semitism and the appetites of a number of his associates in the highly prestigious Monday Club (in London).

When the International Gay Rights Congress organised an important meeting in Edinburgh in December 1974 Hamish made his presence obvious. He was now concerned by use of the word 'gay'. Was it the right word to define homosexuality? He thought it was not. Not least because the word appears in 'The Freedom Come a' Ye' ('A' they rogues that gang gallus, fresh and gay'): he did not want his song hi-jacked by the Gay movement. He notes:

> It is clear that the word 'gay' has become a genuine linguistic irritant and it would be great if we could find a solution to the problem . . .

> Luckily there does seem to be a practical and pleasant solution which should be acceptable to all parties. The French already use 'gay' – spelt like that – as a synonym for homosexual. Why should we not return to the compliment and spell gay (meaning homosexual) gai? . . . Gai has an elegant, rakish, and even genuinely gay look about it; it is inconceivable that such a word could offend any sensibilities, indeed who could not be seduced by a word that signifies (according to Larousse) '*qui a de la joie, qui inspire la joie*'.[4]

The word 'gay' had, however, already gathered unstoppable momentum, and Hamish bowed to the force of the folk process in action. Grudgeless he spoke to the conference with his usual directness:

> Homosexuality is one of those things that poetry can tell you more about than prose – the reason being that homosexuality is one aspect of human love – and Freud himself remarked once that his work was only an imperfect prose description of what the poets sing.
>
> Homosexuality being one way of expressing human love – and of giving pleasure – should be regarded as a boon and a blessing, something of great *value* – and that's the reason why the traditional and legal attitudes to homosexuality are not only stupid and criminal but positively obscene.
>
> Sexual revolution – as Norman Mailer has said – 'is the most meaningful and natural revolution of our time', and must be kept going. St Just once said that those who make revolutions by halves – fail; and you must not underestimate the power of reaction. Victorian attitudes in Scotland are deep-rooted and horribly Philistine. The size of the homosexual 'underground' minority is large and has had to keep its head down too long . . . Way back in 1952 I organized contributions to the poetry magazine *Lines Review* from Cavafy and Stefan George and the editor, Alan Riddell, a good friend of mine, refused them . . .
>
> The Scots record, however, is better than the English, historically. We have never had the odious blood-sacrifice field-days that they have – with Oscar Wilde, Lord Montague, Peter Wildeblood etc. Scotland has had but one homo-sexual martyr – though he was not martyred by us but the British Army – Sir Hector MacDonald. This event is mentioned by Gide in 'Corydon' . . . One of the baleful results of the straight attitude to homosexuals has been the formation of power-hungry political pressure groups – usually on the

4 HH, unpublished notes, Henderson archive.

> outer fringes of Right-wing politics – which has sometimes been para-military and always bloody-minded. The most famous of such groups were the leaders of the SA or Brownshirts in Hitler's private army . . . Hitler got rid of them in the 'night of the longknives' but – *they* – had prepared the way for murder . . .
>
> . . . Bisexuality is much more common than some gay activists and a great deal of 'straight' society seems to think. Anyone who has been in an army overseas, for years – as I have – can testify to that . . .
>
> 'Homosexuality': Shakespeare and Michelangelo look with sympathy / Hitler and Stalin found it repellent: Lorca's 'Ode to Walt Whitman' expands these ideas. End with the words of Roy Campbell, 'Power to all our friends – and I mean – *all* our friends.'[5]

Hamish had a lifelong antipathy to Lord Reith (first director general of the BBC and a Minister in Churchill's War Cabinet), a didactic Presbyterian opposed to many of the causes Hamish espoused. When the *Reith Diaries* were published in 1975, Hamish read them with appalled fascination. On seeing a review of the diaries by Max Beloff, Hamish noted, 'What a horror was this man, "Reith, or Death of a Salesman".' He then continued:

> There is something of the Quisling manqué about Reith. British Dictator. Whatever his own professions of belief, and his diaries often give me the feeling that he was blaming the Almighty for letting *him* down, it is hard to believe that the epithet Christian should be applied to this man – a man with such obvious capacity for hatred and endlessly prolonged vendettas. To have expected Reith to have turned the other cheek would be the equivalent of suggesting a vegetarian diet to a man-eating tiger. It is rare to find a diary every page of which increases the reader's loathing of the writer.

John Reith, a very tall war hero from Aberdeenshire, might be described as 'an Old Testament Hamish', and there was an element of jealousy in Hamish's detestation of 'Lord Reith of Magisterial Reputation'. The two men represented two poles of the Scottish character – didactic authoritarianism and poetic humanism. In the seventies, the Reithian view remained overwhelmingly attractive to the British public: for example, whilst the *Reith Diaries* were flying off the shelves, Hamish's *Prison Letters of Antonio Gramsci* mouldered like stale buns. The story of how these translations were, finally, published is important – not least because of the part

5 HH, unpublished lecture notes, Henderson archive.

played by the young Gordon Brown. Whilst a postgraduate student at Edinburgh, Gordon Brown was elected President of the Student Union and, later, Rector of the University (1973–75). As such he had considerable powers and set up the Edinburgh University Students Publications Board (EUSPB). Its first publication was the *Gramsci Letters*.

Tom Nairn was also involved in this project. Tom Nairn – that rare and priceless commodity: an independent Scots intellectual – first contacted Hamish in 1959 after reading E.P. Thompson's magazine *The New Reasoner*. They shared political and cultural interests, and a lifelong friendship was established. On 21 December 1966 Hamish wrote to Nairn, in the hope that he might oversee the completion and publication of the *Gramsci Letters*: 'I am absolutely sure that there is no person in Britain better fitted to complete the work on the letters than you . . . The translation would appear as a 50/50 effort and the financial arrangements would be fixed accordingly . . . What do you say? The letters must be published.' This letter is evidence that, by the mid sixties, Hamish felt himself incapable of completing a major intellectual or creative project on his own. His problems were three fold – the demanding breadth of his commitments, the lack of funds and practical institutional support (secretary, researchers, sabbaticals, etc.), and his increasing dependence on alcohol. Tom Nairn gave Hamish help and advice but lacked the resources to get the *Gramsci Letters* published. It was Gordon Brown who made things happen.

The Prison Letters of Antonio Gramsci by Hamish Henderson were published in 1973–74 in three consecutive issues of the *New Edinburgh Review*, with illustrations and a major appreciation by the Welsh academic Glyn Williams. Unfortunately Glyn Williams had purloined a good deal of his information from a PhD thesis being prepared by an Edinburgh student! The student in question wrote to Hamish on 20 April 1974:

> Dear Hamish, I've been reading your translation of *Gramsci's letters* in the NER, and writing to say how splendid I think it is . . . [however] I'm having a first class row with Glyn Williams – who has plagiarised much of my Ph.D. thesis for his NER article . . . The man must be an utter shit. Anyway, since this no doubt will become public soon, I want you to know the row is between me and Williams – and that I think your stuff is splendid.

It was frustrating news, and the public critical response was minimal. The English communist historian Vic Gammon wrote to say that he believed, 'both Gramsci and you might have been better served by a more rigorous publisher: the editor I fear was not at his best in Organisation and Method – a general defect of the ultra-left, with its Anarchist spiritual ancestry – one has to have been through the old Party mill to appreciate Organisation.' The Scots composer Ronald Stevenson wrote:

> Dear Hamish, I've read your Gramsci translations on the bus, in the bath, in bed – I haven't been able to put them down! They are superb. Many congratulations and thanks . . . Can you very kindly make me a taped copy of the splendid Sardinian song? I'd like to base a composition on it.

The launch of the first issue took place in Sandy Bell's bar in November 1973. Hamish introduced me to Gordon Brown. He was long-haired, coy and keen to return to work! Glyn Williams was dwarfish, very intellectual, very Welsh and with wonderful hair like Einstein's. The publication was toasted, one or two brief speeches made. Hamish was euphoric. His eye fell on me and he asked me to speak. As an incomer taken off-guard, I spoke awkwardly:

> I am delighted to be here – to join in these celebrations – and I salute the translator of these marvellous letters. I have just come down from Dundee – where I work as an art historian. I've only been there a few months but, as you would expect, Hamish Henderson was there before me. At my interview, last May, the chairman of the interview panel was Professor Drever, Principal of the University. Suddenly he said, 'Mr Neat, I see you know Hamish Henderson!' 'Yes', I said, 'he's the only man of genius I've ever met' . . .

At this, Hamish guffawed and shouted out, 'And they still gave you the job!' It was a joke and great laughter erupted. This gave me a chance to wind up: 'Yes, they did! And I reiterate that now. Here's to Antonio Gramsci, and here's to Hamish Henderson!' The whole bar was soon thunderous with song and good humour, and Hamish drank a great deal in a very short time. At closing time the remnants of the party pitched out into Forrest Hill road. Bracing ourselves against the cold, it was suddenly apparent that only three of us remained – Hamish, Dr Slavka Sverakova and me. She, a Czech émigré, was sober as a judge and suggested we find a place to eat. As she did so, Hamish lurched away up the Forrest Hill Wynd and was violently sick: half a minute later he rejoined us, totally refreshed. We then crossed the road for an extended lunch in an Italian restaurant.

Hamish's vomiting is worth analysis. Only twice in our thirty-five-year friendship did I see him vomit. He had drunk heavily on both occasions but both vomitings were triggered, I believe, by intense emotional ideological recognitions – not alcoholic excess. He vomited following that 'sacred moment' when the *Gramsci Letters* were finally published. A great weight had fallen from his shoulders. It was the kind of thing that witch-doctors and shamans do – going into or coming out of a trance.

Once the Gramsci project was finished Hamish had no major creative project to excite his mind, and by autumn 1974 his physical health and spiritual confidence reached a low point. By chance I visited him the night before he was struck down with a bout of pneumonia that almost killed him. Having been invited to the opening of the annual exhibition of the Scottish Association of Artists, at the Royal Scottish Academy in Edinburgh, I suggested we attend together. He had a bad cough and his back was playing up. He told me he was booked on the night sleeper to London and was to be manipulated by his chiropractor, in Harley Street, next day. At the show, two things proved memorable: the 'searing' blue eyes of the painter Ian McCulloch and Jack Knox's account of the speech MacDiarmid had made when he accepted nomination as Honorary Professor of Literature at the Academy. 'I accept this honour', he said, 'not because this institution is Royal, not because it is an Academy but because it is Scottish!' Having waved Hamish goodbye at Waverley Station I heard nothing for weeks and it was New Year before he told me the full details:

> I had a terrible journey. I hardly slept. When I got out in London; it was as though someone was drawing a scrubbing brush up and down my lungs. I couldn't breathe. I knew I was seriously ill, so I ordered a taxi to take me straight to St Mary's Hospital, Paddington. It was a place I knew and I thought, if I'm going to die in London, I'll die above the streets William Blake was wont to walk. They diagnosed me with pneumonia and kept me in for two months! Eddie Linden and John Waller came to see me. I hadn't seen Waller since Cairo, in 1943! He was a good poet. In turns we entertained the whole ward![6]

On 14 November 1974 Gordon Brown wrote to Hamish:

> Dear Hamish, I have been sorry to hear of your illness and your confinement in St Mary's Hospital . . . You have been working so hard for so long a period of time, without being fully able to take care of your health, that you have fallen ill – so I hope that your spell in hospital will bring you back to your strength and fullness . . . I fully understand that you will not be able to complete that article for the Red Paper – and please do not feel worried about it. We will lose much without your contribution – but it is far more important that you recover your health. Yours aye Gordon.

Brown's reference was to the EUSPB publication, *The Red Paper on Scotland*, a heavyweight paperback scheduled for early 1975. Hamish had been involved in the project since its inception and, in March, Brown had written explaining his plans for 'A Red Paper on Scotland, whose aim is to sketch, analyze and comment upon, from a left-wing point of view,

---

6 HH, conversation with TN, 1975.

the live elements of the Scottish radical cultural and political tradition . . . it is intended as a speculative document, which attempts to correct the futile dichotomy between nationalism and internationalism . . . and to question the social and economic prospects for a socialist Scotland . . . Following our talks – I would hope that you can contribute an article on Oral Tradition, including, if possible, discussion on the significance of the Scottish Renaissance.' The *Red Paper* appeared in February 1975. Hamish wrote immediately to Tom Nairn commending his long article on 'Old Nationalism and New Nationalism':

> Dear Tom, I congratulate you on your first-rate contribution to the 'Red Paper' – an outstanding (or stickin' out) piece of work, in my opinion. The only qualification I would make is that which Brendan Behan made to me one morning (after the night before) in his parents' house in Kildare Road, Crumlin, when we had spent hours talking about the woes of Ireland, and I had come out with a particularly savage crack about Ireland's voluptuous self-inflicted necrophily – 'Don't burn our shit-house down!'

The Red Paper on Scotland exposed many of the issues dividing the Labour Party in Scotland and undoubtedly played a part in the decision to set up a new Scottish Labour Party (SLP) on 18 January 1976. The Party's aims were radical but far from revolutionary; its defining policies were a clear commitment to Scottish Home Rule and socialism. The leading professional politicians in the new party were Jim Sillars (Labour MP for South Ayrshire), John Robertson (Labour MP for Paisley) and Alex Neil (senior Labour Party researcher in Scotland), plus John McAllion, Maria Fyfe and Colin Boyd (later to become Lord Advocate). Hamish had been promoting SLP type policies for forty years but had no direct involvement in launching the new party. However, once it was operative he became a leading activist. David Ross (Highland correspondent for the *Herald*) describes events:

> I joined the Scottish Labour Party at its inaugural meeting in the Grosvenor Hotel Edinburgh. I was a student and subsequently involved in organising the first SLP meeting at the university's David Hume Tower. En route I called in at what we used to call 'the Alexander Bell Institute of Non Specific Studies' – Sandy Bell's – to collect my friend Scott Brady. Hamish was standing near the door. He offered me a drink, but I said I couldn't as I had to go off to a meeting. He asked what the meeting was about and I told him. I then asked if would like to come along. He thought for a second, raised his glass of Jura in the manner of a toast and said 'Why not, I haven't joined a political party in years.'

> He was then elected chairman of the Edinburgh branch. It was quite a branch, with the journalists Neal Ascherson and Rory Watson, the political philosopher Tom Nairn and Sorley MacLean all members. Hamish took the whole thing very seriously indeed. We used to have committee meetings up in the School of Scottish Studies, and he would organise wonderful ceilidhs. There was one at the Edinburgh Trades Council which resulted in us all being thrown out early. Hamish and a piper led us out into the night air, as he speculated that our early expulsion was part of the Labour Party's dirty tricks campaign.[7]

From the start the SLP was the victim of Labour Party in-fighting and the historical antagonism between nationalists and socialists. These differences of opinion were expertly nurtured by the Intelligence Services and fear of extremism was soon the order of the day. In October 1976 the SLP leadership announced that any SLP member 'associated' with the Internationalist Marxist Group would be expelled. They were, and by the end of the year the Scottish Labour Party was a degenerate rump. On 15 November the *Scotsman* reported the party's implosion:

> Jim Sillars said there was no chance of reconciliation . . . this after an impassioned plea from the 'Elder Statesman' Mr. Hamish Henderson, of the Edinburgh South, SLP branch. He said the time had come to end the name calling, and unite against the enemies of socialism. Mr. Henderson's motion, for moves towards an 'amicable and democratic resolution of differences' [was passed, but] . . . congress upheld by 569 votes to 212 the suspension of 12 delegates – accused of dual membership, or close links with, the International Marxist Group.

Hamish's disappointment at the turn of events is evident in this letter to Lindsay Paterson of Tain (then a postgraduate student, today a distinguished Professor of Education):

> Dear Lindsay . . . You refer to the 'rather unfortunate 1st Congress of the SLP'. That's surely the understatement of the decade. It was a truly awful experience; I didn't recover from it for weeks. Somebody had persuaded the even more unfortunate Jim Sillars to commit Hari Kari, and disembowel his promising infant at the same time. I did my level best at the resumed conference in Stirling – at which, incidentally, the International Marxist Group comprised a very small minority – to heal the disastrous breach with a very moderate motion of reconciliation that I proposed and which was carried

7 David Ross, email to TN, 2009.

> unanimously. At the same time I wrote a private letter to Sillars urging him to meet us halfway on this vital issue. I got no reply – although not long previously I had chaired a successful meeting he addressed in Edinburgh and had devoted a hell of a lot of time trying to build up the SLP. I thought then and I still think that bad manners reflect worse politics . . . Now the only hope of retrieving something from this shambolic situation is to keep some sort of dialogue going . . . I have no doubt that there were one or two agents of the enemy there (and I don't mean the IMG) to both the left and right of the SLP (and it is plain to everyone that due to Sillars' neurotic fears they enjoyed spectacular success) . . . You will understand the feelings of regret, fury and frustration this has unleashed in me. But, looking at your letter again I see that you are asking me about the folklore of Easter Ross . . .

Whilst the SLP was destroying itself Hamish found a level of satisfaction in the politics of practical usefulness, by taking up the cause of Jamie MacDonald Reid. Reid was a young Gaelic-speaking Canadian bagpiper, Highland dancer and folklorist who had suffered years of harassment by the British immigration authorities. Born, by chance, on the US side of the Canadian border, Reid had in the mid sixties become eligible for the US Vietnam Draft. Returning 'home' to the Scotland of his parents, Reid was declared an alien and ruthlessly pursued by the UK authorities. In the end he found sanctuary in Yugoslavia where he learned the Balkan languages, the Balkan bagpipes and became a leading authority on Eastern Europe folk culture. When the Vietnam War ended, Reid returned to Scotland and requested permanent residential status. Again the authorities moved against him. In 1976 Reid brought things to a head when, with the support of Hamish, Neal Ascherson wrote an article for the *Scotsman*, drawing attention to his case. Here was a young Scot – with talents galore – being hounded from pillar to post by civil servants, in Croydon, who knew nothing about him and cared naught about Scotland! The story became a *cause célèbre* and the biters found themselves bitten. When the case came to court Lionel Daiches offered his legal services and Hamish acted as Reid's prime witness. Press photographers were alerted and on the opening day Daiches arrived pushing a wheelbarrow stacked high with ancient tomes dealing with every aspect of the Act of Union and the history of Scots Law. Within a few minutes the two 'civil service brains', sent up from the Home Office were sent packing – denounced as 'unqualified to operate in a Scots courtroom'! Subsequently it was announced that only the Secretary of State for Scotland, not the British Home Secretary, could deport Scots like Jamie MacDonald Reid, or anyone else domiciled in Scotland, from Scotland. At the celebrations Hamish needed little persuasion to sing his Knoydart ballad:

. . . Then up spoke the men of Knoydart:
'You have no earthly right,
For this is the land of Scotland,
And not the Isle of Wight.
When Scotland's proud Fianna,
With ten thousand lads is manned,
We will show the world that Highlanders
Have a right to Scottish land . . .'[8]

On Sunday 22 April 1979 Hamish helped organise a commemoration service in remembrance of the Highland mutineers executed at Leith in 1779. It was the first such celebration and took place outside the Trade Winds Hotel, between Bernard Street and Tower Street. Dolina MacLennan, representing An Comunn Gàidhealach, led the tributes.

When, one month later, on 18 May 1979, Mrs Thatcher drove into Downing Street (to quote St Francis and begin seventeen years of Tory rule at Westminster) Hamish knew the battle continued. Within hours he was writing to a friend: 'The Conservative Victory means that we have to return to manning the redoubtable barricade – though I've been ill again, and am a lot weaker now. However, I'm ower thrawn to give in to the "Auld Enemy" without a gallus ramie.' It was the big issues that excited him but he was more than pleased to receive, on his birthday, 11 November 1979, a letter from two of his old Highland admirers: 'Greetings from two Arisaig dancing ladies, one of whom you escorted to a dance in carpet slippers – they are still living, and still in the same place.' It was an invitation no aging singleton could refuse. The following year, the Larach Club of the University of Glasgow gave him Honorary life membership. Not to be outdone, the Helmsdale Community Council asked him to become Chieftain of the Helmsdale Highland Games. He was also pleased to accept a seat on 'the Marrell, West Helmsdale, Gartymore and Portgower Common Grazing Committee'. He was a Land Leaguer at last.

8 'Ballad of the Men of Knoydart', published in the *Collected Poems*.

TWENTY

Branching Out into Film, Theatre and Television

Delays? We could never do without 'em.[1]

HH

Hamish was not an avid cinema-goer but was highly conscious of the power of film as an art form. At the Edinburgh People's Festivals he advanced the idea that film and television should have a role in modern folk collecting. The School of Scottish Studies did not develop 'a documentary arm' until much later but by 1960 Hamish was regularly on call as a historical and cultural advisor to film-makers and TV companies. In 1968 Horst Film of Munich employed Hamish as an adviser on a documentary about Scottish traditional music. Hamish decided that filming should centre on Blair Atholl and feature a mixture of traditional and revival singers. A spectacular live show took place in the great hall of the castle, abristle with weaponry, armour and tartan. After that it was on to Clydebank, where piper Andy Hunter showed the German public another side to Scots history and song. In 1971 the film director Sam Peckinpah used the pipe-tune 'Farewell to the Creeks' (on which Hamish had based his song 'Banks o' Sicily') as the musical background to the murderous finale of the film *Straw Dogs*, set in Cornwall. Peckinpah had previously worked with Paddy Moloney of the Chieftains, so it may have been Moloney who suggested 'Hamish's tune'. Hamish had hopes of big royalties, but was disappointed when the royalties went solely to the widow of the tune's composer (Pipe-major James Robertson of Banff) because the tune was played without Hamish's words.

It was another film, also shot in Cornwall, that first drew Hamish and me together. The year was 1967. I was a final-year student of Fine Art at the University of Leeds. With £27 in hand I had 'returned to Cornwall' to make a documentary about May Day in Padstow as my last course project. Hamish was there to make tape-recordings. He had attended in 1965 and become an *aficionado*, as is clear in a letter from Vic Gammon in May 1974:

---

1 Hamish's opening remark in the film *Play Me Something* (1989).

> Dear Hamish, I am writing an article I have been asked for on the history of Dancing from the Marxist point of view. I would like to include a mention of the Cornish Festival you were telling Edward Thompson and me about some time ago, and to quote you saying that you had never seen, even in Africa, any dancing that looked so ancient.

Mayday is a summer festival celebrated all over the northern hemisphere but the ceremonies in Padstow retain an ecstatic, Palaeolithic communality that Hamish recognised as archetypal. As an event he liked to compare it with the bull-running in Pamplona, the Palio of Siena and the great Panathenaic Procession in Ancient Athens. Winter is put aside, death addressed by living flesh, the mystery of fertility and the urge to display given form – as the whole town dances beneath the Maypole. Reporting on the festival to the School of Scottish Studies in 1965 Hamish wrote: 'It falls to the young men of Padstow, to become, in turn, the formidable black beast – and to dance as the "Oss" for twenty minutes or so (you can't dance much longer, however muscular you are, under the weight of the black tarpaulin regalia).' In 1967 he reported: 'In Padstow, I joined forces with a party from Leeds University who were making a sound and film record of the event. In exchange for information and the provision of contacts they agreed to give me copies of their recordings. This allowed me to move more freely amongst the participants . . . The Leeds tapes are a valuable addition to our archives.'

In reality, Hamish was pleased to make use of these 'Leeds recordings' because he had few of his own. He had spent half of his Mayday in the Padstow Police Station. As a fertility rite the Obby Oss draws young women and the infertile from miles around. It also draws the halt and lame. They follow the dancers in the hope of a cure. So there Hamish was in the thick of it, dancing with the girls and the lame, when the crowd found itself being parted – from behind – by a car pushing forward in an attempt to leave the town. Like many others, Hamish stood his ground. Later he told me what happened:

> Why should the dancers make way for this car! It was a Jag, with a wealthy farmer at the wheel! But Mayday is Mayday! Naturally, people were loath to move – and so was I, and so was this young cripple beside me. Well, this car pushed forward and this cripple – on crutches – fell to the ground. As he was hitching himself back on his crutches – the car came forward again. So, he swung his right crutch round against the car door! Bang! Whereupon the driver jumped out and knocked the cripple to the ground! That was enough for me. I stepped forward and told him, 'I'm making a citizen's arrest! I'm holding on to you till the police come. We're not having this – on

> Mayday – not in Padstow.' And that's what I did. And the Mayers stood with me!

Consequently, Hamish spent three or four hours at the police station explaining his actions. 'By the time I was free I wanted nothing but to join-in with the Mayers – and enjoy life!' It was at five to twelve that evening that I met Hamish.[2] We spoke late into the night. Next day I headed back to Leeds to complete the film whilst Hamish wandered on through Old Cornwall. First he visited Gwennap Pit, the great druidic, Wesleyan open-air theatre near Camborne, then Helston for the 'Furry Dance' the following week. There he watched Alison McMorland, dressed as Maid Marian, lead children through the houses of the town on Helston's great day (Alison was a local primary teacher). Three years later Alison returned to her native Scotland to become one of the great singers of the Folk Revival and one of Hamish's closest friends.

In April 1968 I was appointed Youth Leader and Art teacher at Lendrick Muir School in Perthshire. Hamish soon asked me to show the film *The Merry Morning of May* at the School of Scottish Studies. It lacked synchronised sound and displays the weaknesses of most student documentaries, but Hamish was delighted with it: 'It captures the spirit of the day.' After the showing, it was off to Sandy Bell's and then on to the West End Hotel till five in the morning. John MacInnes, Donald Archie MacDonald and Emily Lyle from the School were with us, and a young man from Harris sang Gaelic songs.

Hamish was also in demand as a theatrical consultant. Requests were often small scale; for example in 1971 Barrie Hesketh, of the Little Theatre on Mull, requested help with 'the pronunciation of Edinburgh accents – Morningside and Working Class', but Hamish's work with Bill Bryden and John McGrath, two of Scotland's outstanding modern theatre directors, was of long-term significance.

Bill Bryden was born in Gourock and grew up in Glasgow. After a short spell as a director at the Royal Court Theatre in London, Bryden returned to Scotland in 1972 as Associate Director of the Royal Lyceum in Edinburgh. Many of his subsequent successes explored subjects close to Hamish's heart, and the two men kept in irregular contact for many years. In September 1972 Bryden wrote to Hamish: 'I would certainly like to read the play by John Gray when you have finished with it . . . Steeleye Span will have arranged payment for "Young Neil My Darling" [Hamish's song] with the PRS . . . Maddy Prior has your two volume "Jacobite Relics" which they used for research.' When Bryden returned to London in 1975 to work at the National Theatre his magnificent productions of the Yorkshire Mystery Plays used 'idiom

2 This meeting is briefly outlined in the preface to Volume 1 of this biography.

of the people' folksong – and Alison McMorland – to breathtaking effect.

Hamish's influence on John McGrath and the 7:84 Theatre Company was more direct, most notably with McGrath's production of *The Cheviot, the Stag and the Black, Black Oil* (1973). In March 1972 John McGrath writes:

> Dear Hamish, I would just like to thank you again for the Donald Sage book [written by an ancestor of Hamish's father's first wife] which we shall not only treasure, but also use to great advantage in the play. Also for your support and encouragement which mean a lot to us. After all, we are only popularising in a fairly simple-minded way a lot of the hard work you and others have done over many years. We are very touched and pleased that you felt so strongly about what we are trying to do. Thanks for the Brocket air [Ballad of the Men of Knoydart].

The Cheviot, the Stag and the Black, Black Oil was an entertaining all-singing, all-dancing travelling show that aimed to change political thinking and the nature of theatre in Scotland. The play's subject was the continuing subordination of the Highland population, North Sea oil and the poetry of community. It was conceived as a many-faceted work of 'participatory theatre' and a counter-thrust against the tartan terrorism portrayed in Douglas Hurd's novel (and TV drama) *Scotch on the Rocks*. When the Principal of Edinburgh University joined the historian John Prebble in describing *Scotch on the Rocks* as a work of genius, Hamish wrote to the *Scotsman* in real anger (25 October 1973):

> Is it possible that anyone can actually believe that *Scotch on the Rocks* is a work of genius? This fantastic suggestion is grotesque . . . If Mr Prebble wants to see a play which really has something to say about Ullapool and to the whole Highlands . . . and has, in addition, satire and song galore, let him pay a visit to John McGrath's *The Cheviot, the Stag and the Black, Black Oil* which opens at the Royal Lyceum Edinburgh on 19 November . . . He will find it as good artistically as *Scotch on the Rocks* is execrably poor.

When *The Cheviot, the Stag and the Black, Black Oil* became the subject of a major BBC television broadcast in the summer of 1974, Wilfred Taylor used his 'Scotsman's Log' to attack both the play's subject matter and theatrical style. On 14 June 1974 Hamish replied with this letter:

> Taylor suggests that 'it would be dramatically far more exciting to cast Patrick Seller in a favourable, heroic light', and adds 'originality

> and unpredictability in the theatre are never lightly to be missed.' It would be quite possible, I suppose, to write a play in which Burke and Hare were portrayed as intrepid pioneers in the field of medical research . . . Highland folk tradition however is solidly behind John McGrath in the matter of Patrick Seller . . .

The Cheviot, the Stag and the Black, Black Oil made thrilling television, but the enthusiasm the show engendered in village halls and makeshift theatres across Scotland was phenomenal. Foot-stomping delight transmogrified into ceilidh dances that merged into weddings and one-night stands still well remembered.

In 1974 Hamish arranged for my Padstow film, *The Merry Morning of May,* to be shown at a folk conference in Aberdeen. There he introduced me to Charles Parker (the documentary broadcaster) and arranged a meeting with John McGrath on the opening night of his new play *The Game's a Bogey*. Later that year I made a film with first-year students of architecture in Dundee, for which Hamish supplied excellent recordings for the soundtrack. When it was finished, he asked me about my next project. I suggested we collaborate on a film about the Travelling People. We were in Sandy Bell's bar, beneath the proscenium arch, and within hours the bones of our first serious collaboration were laid out. He declared that the film should be entitled *The Summer Walkers*. It was agreed that he would supply contacts and access to the SSS sound archive, I would supply film-stock, shoot the film and edit the film. It was a primitive informal arrangement. We had no funds and no capacity to shoot with synchronised sound but the project quickly moved forward. I began filming in Perthshire and Fife in the winter of 1975 and we then travelled out together to Kintyre, lodging with Dr Julian Toms and my sister, Mary, at Muasdale. This provided a base camp for filming Duncan Williamson's family at Lochgilphead – gathering shellfish and making willow-wand baskets. We also filmed the Townsleys at Clachan, who went after rabbits and hazelnuts, and made a heather besom. They lived in an old bus, a bow-tent and a collection of chicken sheds, at Holme, above West Loch Tarbert. Visiting the Townsleys at bluebell time, Dr Toms found the campsite signposted 'Holme Sweet Home': on a scrubbed wood table by the bus – amidst a sea of bluebells – stood a milk bottle full of bluebells and beside it a small white towel laid out for him to wash his hands.

After that we went up to Sutherland to film the remnants of the Stewarts of Remarstaig. Only Essie Stewart, married to Eddie Davies the pearl fisher, remained on the road. We arranged to meet them at Grantown on Spey in August 1976. By the time we arrived, they had moved on. We found instead the Macmillan brothers, two Morayshire Travellers, camped on an island in the middle of the river Spey, living a lifestyle almost indistinguishable from that of their Palaeolithic ancestors: by their camps, stacks of river mussel shells stood on middens of shells dating back perhaps thousands of years. Moving north we found the whole Davies family – mother, father and four children – knee-deep in the river Naver, fishing for pearls. Their ex-army bell-tent was set out beneath the near perfect pyramid of Ben Klibreck, the spreckle-sided mountain that stands guard over what Hamish liked to call 'the great Cleared Strath'. And beneath the cloudless skies of August 1976 we filmed timeless, idyllic scenes.

The Summer Walkers was completed in 1977. It is 53 minutes long and features numerous excellent Traveller songs. I wrote the commentary. Hamish asked for no significant changes but inserted three sections that broaden the range of poetic reference, including a verse from Yeats's poem 'In Memoriam Major Robert Gregory'.

When the film was finished it was captioned 'A film by Timothy Neat and Hamish Henderson'. I had done 90% of the work on the film but Hamish had made an invaluable contribution. This acknowledgement pleased him and affirmed our collaborative partnership. Shortly afterwards, Hamish announced: 'Tim, your next film will be entitled Hallaig,[3] and explore the poetry of Sorley MacLean.' I knew Sorley's daughter, Ishbel, but not MacLean, and I had no Gaelic. It was a tall order, but a thrilling prospect, and within seconds I committed myself to a film that would become a six-year obsession. In 1978 at the funeral of MacDiarmid, Hamish introduced me to MacLean and his wife Renee. We got on very well. He gave his support to the idea of a film. I told him this film would be made within a properly professional framework. Later, looking for funds, I encountered both a lack of interest and fierce hostility. The BBC suggested it was an impossible project: 'MacLean ummms and ahhhs in a manner that makes him an impossible documentary subject!' My reply, that MacLean was a poet of genius with a magnificent bardic voice and a mesmerising intensity of character, fell on deaf ears. *Hallaig* consequently became a marathon slowed by a series of interventions.

For example, at MacDiarmid's funeral, Hamish and I also fell in with Arthur Elliot, who suggested we make another film entirely, about the Langholm Common Riding. Arthur's father, Walter Elliot, had 'Cried the Langholm Fair' for forty years. Arthur was a great Common Riding enthusiast and first assistant to the Langholm Spade-carrier. Hamish had recorded them both and had long championed the Langholm Common Riding – like the Padstow Obby Oss – as one of the great folk spectacles of Europe. Consequently it was decided that our next film would be a documentary about the 1979 Common Riding in Langholm. It could be made for a few hundred pounds. *Hallaig*, which would cost thousands, would have to wait.

Langholm's Common Riding dates back to 1759, but the Fair is part

3 Sorley MacLean's poem 'Hallaig', originally written in Gaelic, describes the loss and memories of a Highland community on the island of Raasay.

of summer festivities from pagan times. Hamish gave the film its title, *Tig! For the Morn's the Fair Day*; I added a subtitle, *The Langholm Common Riding 1979*. In the end we worked with a budget of £1,500, with technicians from the University of Strathclyde shooting the scenes that needed synchronised sound. Commentary was read by Hamish and Arthur Elliot, and the film includes a long sequence of Willie Beattie, a local forester, singing the border ballad, 'Johnnie Armstrong's Last Good Night'. That year Tommy Morrison proved himself a superb Cornet, leading 270 horsemen and women up the Kirkwynd at a thunderous gallop. The finished film proved very popular in town. Arriving at the Buccleuch Hall on Friday 6 June 1980 for the film's first showing, we found a queue stretching twice round the hall, and the film had to be shown twice back-to-back. Thirty years later, Common Riding enthusiasts still view battered video copies of the film with veteran pleasure.

For a year *Hallaig* languished in the doldrums, but in the autumn of 1979 something marvellous happened. We had discussed the *Hallaig* project at length with Keith Alexander (Head of Arts programmes at BBC Scotland), and Keith decided he would make a major film, not about MacLean but about Hamish and his war experiences! The idea went down well in London, and Hamish suddenly found himself the central figure in BBC Television's Armistice Day plans for 1980. On 4 January Hamish was on a plane to Rome to begin filming. It was his first visit since his expulsion in October 1950 and his arrival caused quite a stir.

Hamish made this note: 'Interviewed by Italian Television I was accorded treatment that seemed incongruous for a former deportee. The interviewer, referring to my expulsion, asked where my basic allegiance lay. I told him my allegiance – my allegiance of the heart – was to three of his fellow countrymen: Gramsci who seemed to me to have had the most amazing polymathic mind I had ever encountered; Dante who had written the poetry I most often return to; and Galileo who, beset by the bigots and "big brothers" of his time, had said in effect: "to Hell with you – it does move!"'[4] On 9 January, as Hamish and the crew flew on to Egypt, Amleto Micozzi (Hamish's long-time Roman friend) wrote to Keith Alexander: 'Tell Hamish he has in Rome a *Salvific* power. 1) I did not see my old friend Fausto so eager to speak – for years – as he was before Hamish. 2) Just the same thing happened to my son, Simone. 3) Piero Nelli rang me the morning after to thank me for introducing him to such a wonderful person as Hamish.' On 19 January Hamish wrote to me from Alexandria:

> The filming in Rome and Sicily went fine, and now we're based on Alex, 'doing the desert war'. It all seems like a dream. Heaven knows what the finished film will be like . . . On the way to Alex we stopped at a Bedouin settlement, and did some filming there. The number of

4 HH, unpublished notes, Henderson archive.

> Bedouin still travelling around has decreased steeply since the war, apparently; these folk were living in a sort of shanty town and they were cultivating the land between the coast road and the desert. Herds of sheep and goats – it looked like an illustration to a child's New Testament . . . At the Italian war memorial we saw a bloke with a superb Bedouin face – hawk nose, piercing eyes, he looked liked an illustration to the Seven Pillars of Wisdom . . . Tomorrow we're going to film the *3rd Elegy (Leaving the City)* on the outskirts of Alexandria. I couldn't resist sending you this Shepheard's Hotel envelope, although we left Cairo last week. The Latin inscription reads: 'He who drinks Nile water once will drink it again.'!

Returning to Scotland, Hamish and Keith Alexander soon found themselves involved in disagreements, and editing dragged on for many months. With regard to the content of the film, two issues divided them. Alexander wanted a story, theatre, the drama and imagery of war. Hamish was determined to contextualise the particular war *he* had fought. He wanted the reason why the war had been fought to be addressed: 'peace and well-being' understood as the only rationale for killing. Secondly, their ideas for the film's title differed. Alexander wanted *Keep Listening for Reveille*, the last sentence in the 'Ninth Elegy'.[5] For Hamish this was wrong both in feeling and logic. He wanted the title to be the last words in the 'First Elegy', *The Dead, the Innocent*. After threatening legal action and/or withdrawal from the film, Hamish won both battles.

The film begins with low-key footage of ex-Second World War refugees and holocaust survivors, gathered at a reunion on the lawns of the Dry Drayton Rectory. White-clothed tables were spread with food and wine. The sun shone down through the trees, and Hamish insisted that all who could should dance on the green, in a ring. He himself led the dance, everyone linking hands, circling first and spiralling out amongst the shrubs and flowers. His friend Sue Ryder was there; her husband, Group Captain Sir Leonard Cheshire, had observed the atomic bombs dropped on Japan in 1945. Thus *The Dead, the Innocent* got off to an unmilitary and undramatic start but Hamish – as poet, moralist and man – would have no other.

On 22 October 1980 Hamish wrote to his friend Paddy Rattray of Blairgowrie: 'I'm not sure if I told you about this programme, which was partly filmed in North Africa and in Italy, and which has been held up because of a number of artistic disputes between me and the producer. However, we've got it all ironed out now – to my satisfaction, more or less.' The editorial arguments had, however, been debilitating and if one listens carefully to Hamish's readings in the film a level of deflation in his voice is recurrently traceable. When broadcast, the film was widely

---

5 From HH's *Elegies for the Dead in Cyrenaica* (John Lehmann 1948), republished by Polygon (2008).

received as a triumph. And Hamish – despite physical awkwardness, huge new false-teeth, and a hot-brown tweed jacket that didn't suit him – was recognised as a deeply sympathetic character and a poet of profound understanding. The sequence leading up to the singing of 'Banks o' Sicily' is especially moving, and the programme confirmed Keith Alexander's reputation as a major Scottish broadcaster. Indeed within a short while he was promoted to a senior post at BBC Television in London. The letters of congratulation sent to Hamish meant a great deal to him. He saw them as part of the 'folk process': his poetry, the film, the letters – all part of a single organic reality:

> *Arnold Kettle, Milton Keynes (communist literary academic):* This is to thank you from the bottom of my heart for your marvellous television programme. I found your evocation and testimony so moving . . . You were speaking for our generation and said things that need saying again and again.

> *David Hammond, Cregagh, Belfast (lecturer and long-term communist friend)*: Your programme was a marvellous occasion . . . When I start to congratulate you I realise I am really congratulating you on your life and I realize then that that's a measure of how good the programme was. I was very moved by it all, by the way you were able to evoke those scenes of years ago, how you valued them, how the hero names were your proud possessions. Your speech was beautiful and effortless, direct and simple and it grew out of the rightness of what you were saying . . . Filmically – the programme was not all that good. I thought a better director and cameraman might have enhanced you – I'd like to have seen a bit more of the landscape you were inhabiting (and soldier's faces). The compelling moments were when you just faced the camera and talked. It was magnificent and unforgettable and I was proud that I knew you.

> *Sue Ryder (Founder member of the Mission for the Relief of Suffering):* Dear Captain Henderson, How kind of you to write and tell me personally about your excellent film – no words of mine can describe how moved I felt. It was a great pleasure, and indeed a privilege for us to cooperate with you.

> *Betsy Whyte, Montrose (Traveller)*: We had no idea of the extent of your war activities, and I could almost feel with you the deep emotions and nostalgia you felt on seeing those places again . . . You have a beautiful voice. So pleasant to listen to, and I was thrilled to hear you using those words (hotching) and (hunkering) in such an intellectual programme . . . Bryce was enchanted too – it gave him such pleasure to say to his friends 'I know Hamish'.

The media and critical responses were less generous. Robin A. MacWhirter felt impelled to write a letter of complaint to the *Scotsman*, criticising its reviewer, Stanley Eveling, for turning his back on an important programme: 'On Saturday [Mr Eveling's] TV review devoted three columns to *Dallas* and *MacKenzie* . . . *The Dead, the Innocent*, Mr Eveling dismissed thus: "Robert Graves and Hamish Henderson, two poets featured this week – both brave, decent poets – and I have absolutely nothing to say about either of them." It's a pity Mr Eveling is stirred more by Sue Ellon (who gets full coverage twice a week) than Hamish Henderson (who is introduced to the Television screens once a decade).'

During 1980–81 the *Hallaig* project advanced slowly. I made regular trips to Skye and Raasay to film the landscape and develop ideas with MacLean, but without funds everything remained on hold. John MacInnes joined us as a Gaelic consultant and presenter. Keith Alexander at BBC Television continued his tentative interest. The Scottish Arts Council offered a small development grant then withdrew its support. Finally, Alexander agreed to finance the film if I accepted the role of script-writer and the proposed one-hour film become a 27-minute television arts documentary directed by Alexander's assistant Eleanor Aitken. I accepted Miss Aitken but insisted that the programme be 'fifty minutes or nothing'. The BBC then withdrew and, as if by magic, the film took off at a run. The School of Scottish Studies and the Duncan of Jordanstone College of Art remained loyal to the project, the film-makers Murray and Barbara Grigor offered production support, and the Alva Film Workshop – a cooperative in Clackmannanshire – volunteered to produce the film if it was edited in Alva. The Workshop directors, Bill Burrows and Russell Fenton, then organised funding from the EU Minority Languages Fund, Urras an Eilein (Skye Trust) and the recently established Scottish Film Production Fund. The film soon had a budget of £17,000 and most of the filming took place in February 1984. Seamus Heaney agreed to introduce Sorley, and Iain Crichton Smith replaced John MacInnes as reader of the commentary. Mark Littlewood took charge of synchronised filming and, far from 'ummming and ahhhing', Sorley MacLean emerged as a star, galvanising friend and foe with a riveting performance face to face with the camera.

Hamish's role in *Hallaig* was 'hands-off', but crucial. He initiated the film and set the general intellectual parameters. He also supplied his personal copy of an illustrated booklet of Spanish Civil War Songs for use in the film, and made new recordings of Glasgow veterans of the International Brigade singing 'The Battle of Jarama'. As editing moved towards completion, Hamish 'inspected' the film. A few days later he wrote to tell me about the tape-recordings he was digging out of the School of Scottish Studies archive for inclusion in the final sequences of the film (23 June 1984):

> Dear Tim, I've just been listening again to Marietta MacLeod's marvellous *Oran Mor*, and was again struck by its peculiar appositeness in the context of the film. Indeed, it should immediately precede Somhairle's Gaelic 'Hallaig' [in fact it concludes the poem and the film] . . . Anyway, Tim, I've no doubt now – seeing what I've seen – that this film will be your masterpiece. As Burns wrote of James Johnston (printer of *The Scots Musical Museum*) – 'only go on, and you will be immortal'![6]

Hallaig was premiered at the Edinburgh Film Festival in August 1984, the French Institute hosting a reception. Nella Doran (nee O'Shea), the woman who inspired many of Sorley's early poems, came over from Ireland to join in the celebrations.

After the showing, Hamish and I ended a long night at the flat of Norman MacCaig, with John MacInnes. We enjoyed a splendid Enlightenment evening until the dawn came up – and I came away thinking that the stories of the great antagonism between Hamish and MacCaig were exaggerated. A day or two later RTE (Radio Telefis Eirann), in Dublin, phoned me at midnight to 'demand' that Ireland see the film. They offered £3,000, and everything was agreed in two minutes flat. In March 1985 the film was screened at the Celtic International Film and Television Festival in Brittany. Brian Wilson (the future MP) was there and wrote in the *Herald*: 'When the Gaelic version of a film, about one of Europe's greatest poets, is complete, Neat – Cornish by birth – will have been responsible for the only substantial Gaelic documentary in history. That is how tenuous the Celtic film industry is.'

The catalogue of *As an Fearran* (From the Land), an exhibition staged at the Royal Scottish Museum, took up this theme, describing *Hallaig* as 'not only a fine film and a marvellous tribute to a remarkable man, but an artistic indictment of the prevailing philistinism of our Scottish broadcasting companies, all of whom have signally failed to produce this kind of film over the last twenty years'. When *Hallaig* won the Pascoe McFarlane Documentary Award for best film by a new director it also won a showing on Channel 4 Television: Michael Kustow scheduled it for early evening on Christmas Day 1985. The Alva Film Workshop earned itself £5,000, and interest in *Hallaig* stimulated a campaign – led by writer P.H. Scott and Hamish – for Sorley MacLean to be nominated for the Nobel Prize for Literature. The nomination went forward but the Prize would be Heaney's.

---

6 Letter from HH to TN, TN archive.

One by-product of Hamish's involvement in *Hallaig* was a meeting with the Franco-Scottish poet Kenneth White. When Hamish knew the film was to feature at the Film and Television Festival in Brittany in the spring of 1985, he asked to accompany me. Having renewed acquaintance with the Breton folklorist Claudine Mazéas, Hamish was soon announcing, 'Tim, our next film must be about Brittany and open with "The Seige of Guingang" played by Georges Cadoudal on the Breton pipes!' Next day, I too visited Claudine and she drove us out to see Georges Cadoudal and his wife on their farm. He was out mushrooming but when he returned took up a commanding stance in front of a great open fire. From the mantelpiece a short curtain of white Breton lace hung down. The black chimney-piece, the red jumper buttoned at the shoulder, the lighted face: it was a scene for Georges de la Tour. He played the pipes and then it was cider, ham, calvados and talk of Tristan Tzara. Things were so good that Hamish decided he would return in the summer – with his daughter Janet – to holiday with Claudine. It was during this stay that Claudine arranged for Hamish to meet her new neighbour, Kenneth White.

White had been appointed to the Chair of Twentieth Century Poetics at the Sorbonne in 1983, and Claudine was keen that these two distinguished 'Euro-Scots' should meet. (White had won the Prix Médicis Etranger in 1983 and would win the Grand Prix du Rayonnement later in 1985.) However, White's reputation seems to have made Hamish uneasy. From Brittany, he sent me a postcard that begins, 'By Tre, Tre, Tre and Tre again, / Thus shall ye know the Cornouaille men!' and ends, 'Claudine Mazéas has invited Kenneth White and me to dinner tonight: I have to admit, I'm viewing the prospect with somewhat mixed feelings!'

Whatever the reasons for Hamish's apprehension, a detailed account of their evening at a restaurant on the North Breton coast, with a lighthouse blinking in the distance, appears in one of White's books published fifteen years later, *House of Tides* (Polygon, 2000). A chapter entitled 'Echoes of Scotland' is based around 'Donald Donaldson, of the School of Scottish Studies in Edinburgh'. Anyone who knew Hamish will recognise, in slightly caricatural form, the physical portrait:

> Donald Donaldson turned out to be about seven feet tall, ruddy-faced, with four strands of very white hair on a shining skull, the foremost of those strands continually falling over his brow. He looked a bit like a retired major of the British army – till he'd give one of his great gumsy laughs (he has not a tooth left in his gub), when he looked like a hilarious demon. A habit of his when he was speaking was to make a gesture over his heart with his right hand, as if to say that all he was saying was straight out of that ilk . . .

The portrait White then develops is, in my view, unsympathetic. However, as we have seen, Hamish was often misunderstood, and recurrently the subject of a level of ridicule. The shamanic personality that inspired so many ordinary people irritated a number of his intellectual and establishment contemporaries. One reason for this may be that he was an instinctive thinker. This was a characteristic he shared with the Dutch ethnologist and Nobel Laureate Niko Tinbergen:

> he hated jargon and long words: his exposes were put in clear and simple language . . . it helps to be a daring fighter but the ability to win cooperation from absolutely everyone who can help you is what really counts . . . he was a populariser . . . 'I have not made any "major discoveries". What I have been acknowledged for is a method of approach . . . I worked initially rather on my own, driven by some non-rational urge which I identify with that of the born hunter who wants to understand and outwit his prey animals – my recognition of a problem, and my flashes of insight towards a solution have always come intuitively.'[7]

---

7 Hans Kruuck, *Niko's Nature: A Life of Niko Tinbergen and His Science of Animal Behaviour* (Oxford University Press 2003).

TWENTY-ONE

Hamish Henderson No OBE

Saskatchewan is caught in the grip of an arctic front. Regina is covered in a blanket of snow. The windows of our house are painted in frost . . . at 08.47 hours the radio announces – one Hamish Henderson of Edinburgh has publicly refused an OBE over the Nuclear issue . . . I cannot believe my ears! Within an hour the news will be rebroadcast in Alberta and within two, in British Columbia, the Yukon, and the North West Territories . . . I phone my friends.

Professor Jim McCrorie, Regina[1]

During the early 1970s Katzel Henderson found herself in an increasingly impossible situation trying to bring up their two young daughters in a household in which Hamish's work and lifestyle caused continual disruption to domestic stability: when would Hamish come in, how many friends would he bring, would they stay up talking into the early hours of the morning, would they expect food? In 1975 Katzel moved out of their top-floor flat at 20 Melville Terrace and into the tiny top-floor flat that she had bought, across the road, at number 22. She took the two girls with her. It was a painful time for the family but, in the long term, things worked out reasonably well for all parties; the arrangement might be described as modern and sensible. From his flat, Hamish could see the girls at their window and would wave to them; he also made regular visits for Sunday lunch. The girls, aged twelve and nine, adapted well, and Katzel started work at Jenners department store in Princes Street. The conditions in their tiny flat were cramped, and cash was in short supply, but they came through. For some years Hamish struggled to re-adapt to a bachelor-type existence and, although racked with guilt, he blamed Katzel for deserting him! She, however, continued to care for him, and their separate lifestyles enabled Hamish to pursue his literary, cultural and political interests much as before.

Throughout the 1980s, with Margaret Thatcher in Downing Street and Ronald Reagan in the White House, Hamish saw peace campaigning as a permanent necessity. In particular he supported the Campaign for Nuclear Disarmament and the Women of Greenham Common. On 16

1 Letter to HH, Henderson archive.

January 1980 he helped set up a ceilidh for 'Parents against Torness', to raise funds for those opposed to the building of a nuclear power station within twenty miles of Edinburgh. Up to the oxters in these pursuits, Hamish was surprised in late December 1983 to find a letter from 10 Downing Street on his mat. Opening it, he found himself being offered an OBE. In great excitement he tore the letter up and flushed it down the lavatory. He then phoned Katzel to tell her the news. She rushed over, but the letter was long gone. 'I did, however, manage to rescue the envelope from the wastepaper bin and it was lucky I did,' she told me. 'Ten years later, Hamish sold it to Ross Roy at the University of South Carolina!' Hamish was furious about the offer of an OBE. He wanted no bauble from any nuclear-armed Tory Prime Minister, nor would he kneel before any Hanoverian monarch. He sensed this honour to be either far too much, or not enough. If he was a man to measure with Montrose (or even Lord Brocket!), he deserved much more than an OBE. If he was a traitor/terrorist, to measure alongside Wallace or Thomas Paine, he deserved imprisonment or execution! With his usual courtesy, he wrote to 10 Downing Street:

> Please inform the Prime Minister that in view of the fact of her suicidal defence policies – organised in collusion with the Americans and their trigger happy President – putting at risk the continued survival of the human species on this planet, I cannot see my way to accepting this honour.

Hamish was soon wondering who had put his name forward and why? Was the Honour an attempt to buy him off? Was it a ploy to discredit him in the eyes of his radical followers? Eddie Linden has told me that it was he who had put Hamish's name forward to the committee of the Poetry Society in London but – whatever the mechanics – Hamish had no time for a class-ridden Honours system and he decided to exploit the God-given opportunity he had been given. That evening Hamish phoned his friend Lorn Macintyre in Edinburgh with the suggestion that here was news that might be passed to his brother, Kenny Macintyre, BBC Scotland's political correspondent. First thing next morning the Scottish news headlined the fact that Hamish Henderson had refused an OBE. By eight a.m. however, senior managers had phoned in, and the Henderson refusal was never again mentioned in BBC newscasts. After that Hamish contacted various friends to discuss further 'media tactics'.[2] Joan Lingard, novelist and children's author offered practical advice: as chairwoman of 'Scottish Writers Against the Bomb' she suggested that they, jointly, orchestrate the contro-

2 When he phoned me I told him about a rhyme I'd seen on the wall of a Cornish pub: 'She offered her honour, he honoured her offer / And all night long it was honour and offer!'. 'Now, we don't want any of that!' he said.

versy to advance the anti-war and anti-nuclear causes in Britain. When the press came calling, Hamish stated:

> I am not going to be bought-off by any honour offered by a British government advancing policies that I have spent my life opposing. This government has implemented cuts in expenditure on health, social deprivation and education. The Prime Minister's educational policies are endangering not only the operational efficiency of the School of Scottish Studies but its very existence within the University of Edinburgh – the Prime Minister's suicidal defence policies . . . are a danger to the world.[3]

Public refusal of a State Honour was rare at this time, and the establishment's response to Hamish was cold distain. The Scottish public, however, acknowledged Hamish's boldness with delight and, at the end of January 1984, the listeners of BBC Scotland voted him 'Scot of the Year'. Monsignor Bruce Kent came north to share a CND platform with Hamish at the Netherbow Arts Centre in Edinburgh, and a flood of letters came in. Taken together, these letters create a poetical group self-portrait of radical Britain in the post-Falklands period.

> *Tom Leonard (Glasgow):* What particularly pleases me myself is that having 'broken protocol' (!) as the Guardian puts it you have refused to be party to the damnable ubiquitous and silent laws of Nudge Nudge, Wink Wink that keeps the British state apparatus working so efficiently. *That's* what they'll hate you for – breaking that!

> *Sir James Graham, Bt. (Bedford)*: I agree most strongly with every word you said. Mrs Thatcher has degraded herself from leader of a supposedly independent state to something like President Reagan's gun moll . . . I am a baronet and was educated at Eton and Oxford – your supporters are not limited to students – Trotskyists/anarchists/fellow-travellers and I hope most sincerely that you will have another chance to strike another blow for peace and sanity.

> *William Wolfe (SNP President):* Let
> what can be shaken
> be shaken
> and the unshakable
> remain . . . (H. MacD.)

3 HH, unpublished notes, Henderson archive.

Hamish, brother! Congratulations on your rejection of a 'Brit' honour. Ever since I was first moved by hearing you in the Kirk Assembly Hall, on the launching of MacCormick's Covenant, my regard for you has been high and unqualified. My faith in you all these years has now been clearly justified.

Tom Nairn and Christine (St Monans): How much greater an honour to be an 'OBE – refused' than just another initialled-name sycophant of the Imperial Cadaver!

Adrian Mitchell (London): Congratulations on turning down her 'honour'. You're deeply honoured in the hearts of thousands and thousands of friends and people who love your poetry.

Geordie and Catherine McIntyre (Glasgow): It's been said everybody needs a hero or heroes. Your words, above all, your actions, make you one of ours.

Una MacLean (Edinburgh): I want to offer you my congratulations on your public spirited rejection of the OBE. To hear your voice booming over the airwaves this morning restored my faith in human nature. A grand three-fingered gesture.

John Aitkenhead (Kilquanity): Well man, Hamish, more power to your elbow, what a blow you have struck for us all on the earth, and for Scotland.

Federation of Student Nationalists (Kirkcaldy): Congratulations on refusing the OBE and thus asserting your opposition to this kind of corrupt patronage. Our conference has decided to award you the position of Honorary Vice-President of the Federation. We would be honoured if you accept this offer . . . Yours for a Scottish Socialist Republic – Kay F. MacLeod.

Kay Goodall: 'Don't worry you don't know me . . . I'm a student (but I know) even the most famous or experienced of us lose heart and feel isolated sometimes – in case you ever feel exhausted or pessimistic – I'd like you to know that there are people who admire you and your commitment, who take heart from your sustained enthusiasm – keep on trying, if only because you give others a bit of extra spirit. Thanks.

Izvestiya/Novosti, the Soviet news agency, sent two reporters to Edinburgh to interview Hamish; he was pleased but a little wary. He notes: 'Both men obviously wanted me to give anti-American statements, and I obliged to the extent that I said, "Reagan is the biggest single menace that the world is facing at the present moment." Later I made a prepared statement:'

> I'm totally against all nuclear weapons, Yank, British and Soviet. Every power has an awesome responsibility in the face of humanity. If I were a Soviet citizen I would probably be making the same sort of protest as I have made here, and I wonder where that would leave me . . . But I'm a Scotsman and therefore a British citizen, and so it's our scene I'm directly concerned with. Here, our greatest threat is the miserable subservience of the Tory government to one of the most dangerous men who have ever in history held a high government office, namely Ronald Reagan. He more than anyone else in the world is in a position to do us all in – the British, the Yanks, the Soviets – as well as all the inhabitants of the globe – for once a nuclear war started it couldn't be limited in scope; it would be bound to escalate, and this would literally be a death sentence to us all.

On 1 February 1984 the *Morning Star* used the announcement that Hamish had been voted 'Scot of the Year' as an excuse to profile him as one of its long-time heroes:

> It is an indictment of our capitalist society, which so successfully muffles the voice of protest and challenge, that many in England, and even some in Scotland will ask, 'who is Hamish Henderson?' . . . We should celebrate the election of Hamish Henderson as "Scot of the Year" and carry forward the message of his epic song 'Freedom Come a' Ye' . . .

TWENTY-TWO

The Hugh MacDiarmid Memorial Sculpture in Langholm

Man can embody truth but cannot know it.
W.B. Yeats

Hugh MacDiarmid died on 9 September 1978. His relationship with Hamish remained uneasy till the end but the hatchets had long been buried and on many issues the two men now agreed disputatiously, rather like father and son. A letter Hamish wrote to his crotchety old guardian James Maclaren, from the North African desert in 1942, explains the psychological imperatives that drove this bonded antagonism:

> The most satisfactory relations of life must be between people who have loved each other in the past. Relations between them can never again become quite colourless and 'normal'. However much each of them might desire it. It's possible they may be lastingly estranged, much more likely they will maintain ambiguous friendship. This must happen in marriage.

On 2 March 1975 Hamish replied to a note from MacDiarmid with these reminiscences: 'Dear Chris, Your reference to D.S. Moncrieff [Hamish's communist friend in London] carried my mind back to that fantastic evening we spent in his flat in 1952; and if you remember, his wife Queenie gave birth to a son on the strength of it – the son being eventually christened Diarmid Hugh! This Diarmid who has written the odd poem has now married an Algerian Arab girl, and their progeny will no doubt be the very embodiment of the East–West synthesis.' Hamish subsequently joined the campaign to get MacDiarmid elected a Freeman of the burgh of Langholm, and on 13 January 1977 wrote a long letter to the *Scotsman* praising 'the Muckle Toun' and suggesting that it glory in the fact that MacDiarmid had written, 'Langholm remains my touchstone in all creative matters.' He also suggested that the 'immortal poet' be invited as a special guest at the next Common Riding, to coincide with his eighty-fifth birthday.

MacDiarmid died the next year, his funeral taking place on 13 September in Langholm. I drove Hamish there in the company of the poet

Hayden Murphy and Timothy O'Keeffe (joint editor of *The Complete Poems of Hugh MacDiarmid*). It was a day of gentle drizzle and mist-shrouded hills. Valda Grieve stood above the open grave, orange hair aflame amongst the dark coats and trees. Norman MacCaig spoke of MacDiarmid: 'He would walk into my mind as if it were a town and he a torchlight procession of one, lighting up the streets of my brain.' Valda dropped one little white rose on to the coffin. 'This is for you, Chris', she said. Hamish, stiff with standing, asked me to pick up a handful of earth which he then tossed forward on to the oak of the coffin.

At the reception in the Eskdale Hotel, a great wake unfolded. As John MacInnes recited his latest, very long Gaelic poem a thunderstorm broke. We set off homeward as darkness began to fall, Hamish insisting we detour north, via the cemetery at Crowdieknowe – the burial place of many of MacDiarmid's ancestors and subject of his dramatic poem 'Crowdieknowe'. The rain was teeming down as we splashed our way into the graveyard. Tim O'Keeffe and Hayden Murphy shared an umbrella to ensure that, if the lightning struck, Hamish would live to tell the tale! The grass was a livid green; Hamish selected a large lichen-encrusted gravestone and, flinging one arm back, declaimed to the heavens:

> Oh to be at Crowdieknowe
> When the last trumpet blaws,
> An' see the deid come loupin' owre
> The auld grey wa's
> . . .
> An' glower at god an' a' his gang . . .[1]

With MacDiarmid dead, plans to honour his memory gathered pace. The University of Glasgow set up a committee to assess possibilities. Hamish was invited to join a similar Scottish Trades Union Congress (STUC) committee. The university committee proposed that a MacDiarmid Chair of Scottish Literature be established in Glasgow, but nothing happened. The STUC committee achieved rather less. Consequently, after a year, Hamish and I began to discuss what we could do. By chance, in 1980 I was elected convenor of the Scottish Sculpture Trust (SST), a charitable body dedicated to advancing sculptors and contemporary sculpture in Scotland. Barbara Grigor, a MacDiarmid enthusiast, had recently been appointed part-time administrator and, with the promise of £1,000 from the Scots-German film-maker Albrecht Lauder, that autumn we launched plans for an international competition for a Hugh MacDiarmid Memorial Sculpture in Langholm.

Some people did not like the idea of a MacDiarmid memorial, and

---

1 Hugh MacDiarmid, 'Crowdieknowe', published in the *Complete Poems* (Martin Brian and O'Keeffe 1978).

Border Television, in Carlisle, latched on to any opposition they found. Introducing the memorial project on the evening news, the newscaster started with this question: 'Mr Neat, wasn't Hugh MacDiarmid far too communistic, too nationalistic and too atheistic for the people of Langholm to want to have anything to do with him?' The interview was then 'illustrated' with a selection of metal sculptures exhibited by the SST, giving the impression that a heap of scrap-iron was about to be placed on the border hills above Langholm. Battle was joined, and a lively correspondence erupted in the local newspapers. One letter denounced MacDiarmid as a self-confessed squirrel killer and quoted his poetry to prove the point! Fortunately, as the makers of the film *Tig! For the Morn's the Fair Day!* Hamish and I had a good number of supporters within the Common Riding fraternity, and the Langholm MacDiarmid Committee was soon fighting its corner. Robert Burns was drawn into the fray, and Hamish invited to deliver the 'Immortal Memory' at the Langholm Burns Club supper on 23 January 1981.

I drove him there and Hamish used his speech to pave the way for MacDiarmid's homecoming. He began by 'questioning the idolatry that surrounds the Burns Cult'. He related it to the idolatry surrounding so much organised religion, stating: 'If Christ is looking down on the thousands of Burns Suppers being celebrated around the world this week – he will probably be saying, "I know what you're feeling mate: I went through it too!"' He argued that there is something inherently repellent about all organised cults and that 'sanctification' leads to fossilisation. 'Real poets, like Hugh MacDiarmid, expect to be criticised! As you know, MacDiarmid attacked the Burns cult with savage irony. It wasn't Burns MacDiarmid attacked, it was the hypocrites who have taken him – in their various attempts to remake him – in their own image.' Hamish asked his audience to look at the true genius of Burns and the reason why he remains so important to his countrymen.

> Why this special relationship of a poet to his country? There is nothing similar in other countries, this celebratory night. Portugal and Camoes? No. Italy and Dante? No. There is much love, of course, but no Night. England and Shakespeare? No. William Blake? His political, moral and sexual standards were very similar to Burns – but no supper – not even jellied eels have been eaten by his London followers!
>
> There is a Burns phenomenon. It is very Scottish – but it spans the world from Buenos Aires to Peking . . . Auden admired him as 'the vertical man' – Burns was a man of robust common sense, virile courage, spunk and independence: his free, spiritual honesty in matters of sex – are all lead-ons for us . . . And I celebrate his keen satirical spirit – which waded into the shams and dishonesty of his

> days. Make no bones about it, Burns was a radical and a revolutionary. He was a paid-up member of The Friends of the People. Goethe greatly admired him . . . However, the poet Burns resembles most is Lorca – the great Spanish poet murdered at the very beginning of the Civil War in Spain. Both were men of passion. Both died young. Both 'embodied' the folksong of their countries. Both 'remade' folksong, both were anti-authoritarian. . . . At the Burns grave in Dumfries, Keats celebrated 'the great shadow of Burns' . . . As we should, in these coming years, celebrate Dumfriesshire's other immortal poet – Langholm's Hugh MacDiarmid . . . We have heard great Burns' songs this evening. His songs are Immortal: Burns' songs represent an act of national pride, a patriotic effort to preserve the characteristic culture of his homeland, to protect it from the myriad negative consequences of Scotland's loss of independence – and so – I toast the Immortal Memory of Robert Burns.[2]

Six days later, on 29 January 1981, the Hugh MacDiarmid Memorial Sculpture project was formally launched at the Staff Club of the University of Edinburgh. Valda Grieve and Norman MacCaig were there. The Langholm MacDiarmid Committee was there. Hamish demonstrated *port a beul* (mouth music) and Duncan Williamson swept Naomi Mitchison off her feet – swinging her around the Staff Club in a spontaneous Schottische that belied her eighty-five years. Knowing that the great institutions of Scotland had failed to raise any significant funds for the MacDiarmid Memorial project, the SST announced that it would target students, the disabled, the unemployed, poets, artists and the poor, and that it would make the process of fund-raising as important as the fund itself. Thus, even if no money was raised, we would have had a good time.

The main campaign began on 11 February when students at Duncan of Jordanstone College of Art in Dundee organised an auction of artworks by themselves and others. The event raised £1,027. In April, Barbara Grigor organised a second auction at the Third Eye Centre in Glasgow. Valda Grieve donated 'a gold banded pipe given to Sir Harry Lauder – inscribed from Rotary Club – given to Chris Grieve who smoked it regularly'. It made £300. I shared the auctioneering with the Glasgow comedian Chic Murray. MacDiarmid's only landscape drawing – done in the Shetlands – was bought by Dolina MacLennan. It was a memorable night with all the buyers reconvening at the house of Michael and Deidre Grieve in the West End.

Meantime a letter-campaign was reaping rewards: on 10 February Hamish sent me a cheque from Bert Davis, editor of *The Age of MacDiarmid*, and a letter from Alan Lomax:

---

2 HH, unpublished speech notes, Henderson archive, and TN's notes taken at the event.

> Dear Hamish, Thank you so much for sending me the note about Hugh. In my mind he can never die. It seems to me the best monument to him would be an open piece of heathland, like the one in the picture on the leaflet, a place where all Scots could do as they pleased, unchecked and untrammelled by the police and the authorities and surrounded by engravings of MacDiarmid's poems. Even better, why not put his poems on broadsheets and make them available for nothing at every bookseller and newspaper kiosk. He must be made as popular as Burns and as the ballads. I enclose $15.

The Scottish universities at last got their act together and raised £26: £20 from the University of Dundee and the rest from the University of Glasgow (after what we learned was a long and impassioned discussion!). A raffle at the SNP's Annual Conference in Aberdeen raised £73. The campaign finally raised around £10,000, including personal donations resulting from the leaflets. With Scottish Arts Council support, the final tally was £20,000.

The Memorial Sculpture itself was selected as the result of open international competition, with over two hundred entries. Initial judging took place at the Talbot Rice Art Centre at the University of Edinburgh in November 1981. The committee selected a shortlist of five from which, on 1 May 1982, Jake Harvey from Kelso was selected as winner. His sculpture, of bronze and corten steel, takes the form of a giant, abstracted, open book full of images from MacDiarmid's poetry and the border landscape.

The competition encouraged a number of foreign artists and writers to visit Scotland. Two struck up interesting relationships with Hamish. One was the American sculptor Brad Graves, a Vietnam refusnik who developed a strong interest in the Pictish stone-carving tradition and worked intensively in Aberdeenshire and Orkney – where he became a Scots song enthusiast with a high regard for Hamish's poetry. The other was the writer John Berger, who in 1981 began a series of collaborative projects in Scotland. In November 1981, following his 'jury service' at the sculpture competitions, Berger participated in a colloquium in Dundee entitled 'The Making of Art in Small Countries', sharing the platform with John Byrne, Liz Lochhead and the Stewarts of Blair. In May 1982 he lectured at Glasgow School of Art and the University of Edinburgh. During a weekend with Barbara and Murray Grigor at Inverkeithing, Hamish joined us for dinner. John talked, Hamish sang, we play charades. As the party was about to break up, Hamish sang the Obby Oss song. As the 'death-dirge' began, we both went down under the table, ritualistically pawing each other like animals, then to the words 'With a merry ring adieu the merry Spring' . . . we rose, hands in the air, to dance and sing the rest of the song. Berger's Russian friend Nella Bielski was delighted. Hamish gave Berger a copy of his *Elegies for the Dead in Cyrenaica*. Two years later, in 1984, Berger published his brilliantly original book *And our Faces, My Heart, Brief as Photos*, which carries telling echoes of his time in Scotland.

Jake Harvey worked on the MacDiarmid Memorial for three years. The Duke of Buccleuch gifted the site and in March 1985 a request for planning permission was presented to Dumfries and Galloway Regional Planning Committee. Permission was refused. On 7 March 1985 the *Glasgow Herald* reported my statement: 'This must be seen as a national disgrace. We are not talking about planning permission for a garage or shed but a memorial to a major national figure made by a major Scottish sculptor.' The *Scotsman* headlined the affair 'National Disgrace', Scottish Television gave the story excellent coverage and the local newspapers came out strongly for the memorial. Taken aback, the Planning Committee justified its decision by stating that it had received 'five complaints' and that one member of the committee had 'opined that the memorial might disrupt the view'. This was Councillor Robinson, an English pig farmer, who added salt to the wound by describing the sculpture as 'no better than an Oxo hoarding!' The poet William Neill, a Dumfriesshire man, then penned two ripostes to the press – one in English, one in Scots. The second was entitled 'Wha Jeedges Pigs, Jeedges Sculptures Tae':

> Ma hert fair stouns wi scunner
> At puir Scotland's latest hap:
> For they'll hae nae sculpture yonner
> On the lang toun's braid hill-tap,
> Syne a wheen wee dounce doonhamers
> Hae damned yon brawlik plan . . .
> Led by the neb in chaumers
> By a fermin Inglishman . . .[3]

A letter published in the *Times Educational Supplement* (Scotland) asked why Scotland's universities remained silent as the debate unfolded:

> Does higher education deserve any state funding at all? What are the departments of English and Scottish literature up to? What do the educators of tomorrow's planners have to say? Nothing. Who and what do these people represent? They live on the shoulders of giants and all they do is admire the view and their own good fortune. They are a disgrace . . . Contrast official treatment meted out to MacDiarmid since his death with that offered to Jean Paul Sartre in France! One finds himself rejected by a Regional Planning Committee, the other publicly mourned by a conservative president,

3 Published in various local newspapers in south-west Scotland.

Giscard D'Estaing – on foot at the head of hundreds of thousands of French citizens.

Three months later the SST submitted a second planning application, for a new site nearby, and began organising a public demonstration to coincide with the meeting. On 25 May 1985 Hamish wrote to me: 'I'm all in favour of a "show of force" at Dumfries on 4 June. Do you think it would be a good idea if I wrote a letter to the Scotsman nearer the time, to gather the clans?' After contacting various speakers, singers and musicians I wrote to the Dumfries Police requesting permission that supporters of the memorial might gather in the town on Planning Day. They agreed that we could hold 'a demonstration at the Bandstand in Dock Park – assembling at 12.00 and dispersing before 24.00 hours'.

A hundred of us set off from Dundee and Edinburgh by coach on the beautiful summer's morning of 4 June and when we arrived in Dock Park a crowd soon gathered. The introductory speeches lasted from 12.30 to 13.00, then having announced we would reassemble at 14.00 it was either *le déjeuner sur l'herbe* or off to the pub, Hamish heading for the Globe Inn (where Burns had spent many happy hours). The memorial application was scheduled last on the agenda but, when councillors realised the seriousness of the situation the town was facing, it was moved to the top of the agenda and passed, unanimously, in thirty seconds. Our observer at the meeting, Murray McNaught – recent winner of the Dundee Marathon, and well prepared in running kit and a red bandanna – noted the facts on a scroll before setting off on a historic run through the streets of Dumfries. Some say he ran too fast, others that it in his excitement he took a shortcut but, as McNaught sprinted from beneath the dark shade of the trees into the sunlight and the bandstand loomed before him, he realised there was nobody there – just a few mums with toddlers and a handful of students drinking cheap wine! Undaunted, he unrolled his scroll and read out the news. As a feeble cheer went up, the television crews arrived – desperate to capture the moment they had missed. One reporter had the idea of asking McNaught to do his run, and read his scroll, a second time. This he did – and a crowd of about seventy, including Hamish, cheered when the news went round, 'The MacDiarmid Memorial will rise above Langholm!'

After that a party broke out. The demonstration became a celebration. Before the coaches returned to take us home, the Dundee students dunked me in the Nith. Hamish was euphoric. He sang the whole way back to Edinburgh, and next day sent a letter and package of cheques: 'What a great day! And what a glorious spree! . . . A few stragglers (of greetings and messages) continue to come in, of which the enclosed is a sample . . . The School was delighted to hear news of the victory – we've just been out celebrating in Sandy Bell's. Cheers Hamish.'

On 11 August 1985 the Memorial was unveiled by Valda Grieve, in front of a crowd of four hundred people on the open hillside above Langholm. A ferocious storm was in progress. Short speeches were shouted. Red flares rocketed into the clouds. The two largest Saltires ever made (up till that time) were pulled down like torn rigging and the sculpture revealed to sustained whoops and applause. The Langholm Pipe Band then sounded the retreat to the hall of the Eskdale hotel, having 'lionised' a crate of Glenfiddich! With proprietorial rectitude the management of the Eskdale Hotel refused to allow Valda Grieve in, unless she left her dog outside. She refused – so the whole event had to proceed without its 'honoured guest'. But it was great. Sorley MacLean stole the show with an oration, a panegyric, in honour of the immortal poet:

> In conversation during MacDiarmid's life-time I more than once referred to him as the best living poet in Europe, and I have said as much, though not in the same words, in print. It is not that I have ever set myself up as a judge of the poetry of Europe. For one thing I could not set myself up as a fit judge of the poetry written even in Wales or Ireland because I do not know Welsh at all and do not know Irish well enough to be a judge of its poetry. And there is no other European language that I know well enough to be a judge of its poetry. Therefore, to say or have said that MacDiarmid was the best poet of his time in Europe means only that I could not imagine a better poet than the poet of 'Sang Shaw', 'Pennywheep', 'A Drunk Man Looks at the Thistle' and many more things that were written by MacDiarmid. So I let it stand and say again: 'MacDiarmid was the best poet of his time in Europe'.
>
> . . . Christopher Murray Grieve had a sensibility that was and is beyond words, and with that a courage and spiritual ambition that made him live a life of material poverty in order to have no trammels on his visionary spirituality. He was the kind of man who was at once a philosophical materialist and a moral idealist of idealists, and to me at any rate that is the most admirable of men . . . 'Our soul has felt him like the thunder's roll' and he has taught my generation, and I daresay many of this generation too, not a little, but mountains and mountains of things about the human spirit.[4]

When Hamish got home late that night he was exhausted. Hung-over, in the 'dull aftermath of poetic experience', he sat down and wrote this angry letter to the chief executive of the construction company then renovating the communal stairwell of his flat at 20 Melville Terrace:

---

4 Sorley MacLean, Speech notes on the occasion of the unveiling of the MacDiarmid Memorial, TN archive.

> Dear Sir, When I got back from Dumfriesshire today, I expected to find the mess on the stair and around the door cleared away – and the stair washed. Instead I find a fly crawling over the unsightly yellow gobbets of dried sour milk which surround what is now obviously an indelible stain. It is now five days since I told you about the mess around the door. You twice assured me it was going to be cleared up, but nothing has been done. Have you any explanation for this scandalous neglect? The people who drove me back from Langholm commented that the stair needs an application of disinfectant, as well as a wash.

Thus the greatest literary relationship of Hamish's life ended with the bang of fireworks over the eternal hills of the Border and a whimper on an Edinburgh stairhead.

TWENTY-THREE

The Tree of Liberty and *Play Me Something*

Handsome boy, beautiful Druid's son.
Tell me, my handsome one;
What do you want me to sing to you?
HH[1]

At the beginning of December 1985 the singer Jean Redpath phoned to tell me she had enjoyed a viewing of *Hallaig* and suggest that my next film should be about Serge Hovey, the American musicologist and Burns scholar. She told me that Hovey had multiple sclerosis and had spent the last eight years bedridden on a breathing machine so, if the film was to be made, 'it needs to be made now'. I contacted Hamish to let him know, and on 12 December he wrote: 'Dear Tim, The Serge Hovey idea is a winner – we must talk about it soon . . . ' By January 1987 a major 73-minute documentary film, *The Tree of Liberty – The Songs of Robert Burns, sung by Jean Redpath, researched and arranged by Serge Hovey*, had been completed.

It was in the late fifties that Hovey became obsessed by the poetry of Burns. In the early sixties he decided to do systematic research into all the songs attributable to Burns, make modern arrangements for them, and record them on twenty-four LPs. In 1969, on his second visit to Edinburgh, Hovey met Hamish and the two men began an inspired relationship. Five years later, when Hovey asked Hamish who could sing all the Burns songs best he answered 'Jean Redpath'. In 1976 the first of the Hovey–Redpath LPs was released by Philo Records of New Hampshire. Ten years later, in February 1986, I was knocking on the door of the Hovey House in Pacific Palisades, California, to begin filming *The Tree of Liberty*.

Hovey's wife, Esther, took me through to the bedroom where Serge lay surrounded by books and the technology of modern medicine. He was paralysed but his eyes could move, and one elbow. Tended by his Mexican nurse Ruben, he looked like a Pharaoh. Hovey had been brought up in the exotic Hollywood of the thirties: the family circle included the writers Jack London, Thomas Mann, D.H. Lawrence and

1 Breton folksong translated by HH from French text 'The Druid and his Disciple', published in *The Armstrong Nose* (Polygon 1992).

the actor Will Rodgers; at the age of five it was George Gershwin who had selected his Steinway grand piano. He later studied music with Arnold Schoenberg and Hanns Eisler. In 1947 he worked as composer/ director of the music for the first staging of Bertolt Brecht's *Galileo*. Driven out of Los Angeles during the McCarthyite purge, Hovey moved to New York, becoming one of a brilliant group of composers (Aaron Copland, Leonard Bernstein, Elliott Carter, Alan Lomax, Pete Seeger) attempting to create 'new music for the American century'. Gradually, Hovey began to find Scots music the most exciting of all America's immigrant musical traditions and soon saw Burns as a genius comparable to Michelangelo and Shakespeare. When Hovey met Hamish he found himself welcomed into the House of Scotland. After his third visit, in 1972, Hovey wrote:

> Dear Hamish . . . The entire level of communication between THIS composer and Scotland rose precipitously the instant I entered the doors of the School of Scottish Studies – oscillating between the Conference Room and Sandy's Bar, with a little time out for some pretty lively theatre, I felt that the doors of Scottish culture, which until then had been open a gingerly crack, suddenly flew wide open and I felt welcome. After all these years of relative isolation on these Burns songs, this was a stunning experience . . . You spoke of not taking Burns uncritically as a standard of Scots song, referring to the simple but profound fact that one individual, however much a genius, has but a partial, prejudiced view. One has to look further than Burns to attain a balanced, panoramic, social view (like the spectacular view atop Stirling Castle) of the whole of Scots song! . . . You brought up your strong feeling that many Scots songs, especially the old 'Child' ballads, do better with no accompaniment . . . [but] when *I* take particular pleasure precisely in creating accompaniments for *Burns* songs, I may be doing something valid and *part of the folk process* – as you kindly suggested . . . I am building up a Scottish-American approach – separate to the unadorned, pure melody that you seem to wish to define as the quintessence of the National Scots musical idiom: – and this distinction must be kept straight . . . I have always felt, and still feel, that no one can write 'world music' and that the fashionable current 'world' style practised by Stockhausen, Berio, Cage etc. is no universal language. Though often genuinely experimental and exceedingly interesting it is parochial indeed . . . My interest has been in Jewish Americana and Afro-American music – now the interest has switched to Scottish–Americana. Not that the English have not contributed to American music, but when I hear a fine, slow lyric by Charles Ives, or even Aaron Copland, I think they are echoing old Gaelic airs. Many hymns and Negro spirituals have this association in my ear. There's no question of the strong Scottish

> musical heritage in the Appalachians (mis-named 'English' by the otherwise capable Cecil Sharp) . . . Scottish melodies are organically, deeply related to American musical scenery. Thus, working on the 'Robert Burns Song Book' fits in perfectly with my aims as a composer.

After Hamish had put Hovey in contact with Jean Redpath in 1973 the Burns recording project progressed well. In March 1975 Hamish writes:

> Dear Jean, I was delighted to hear from you, and am glad to know that your mighty Burns project goes forward well. Serge has written to me and I shall certainly write an enthusiastic letter of recommendation for him. Also a eulogy of yourself – if I can stop the adjectives soaring up into the empyrean! . . . Our record of big ballads – 'The Muckle Sangs' – has just appeared . . . Jeannie Robertson has a glorious rendering of the 'Gypsy Laddie' on it. Unfortunately she never heard the completed record, as you no doubt know, she died a month ago. Her death hit me hard.

In 1976 Hovey wrote to Hamish: 'At last, the first of the Redpath–Hovey records emerges! Now we have created a true Scottish–American sound? Would have liked to have created work closer with you . . . Perhaps it will be possible with record 2.' The brevity of that message is evidence of Hovey's loss of muscular control as MS began to destroy his body's nervous system, but his musical insights seem to have intensified as his physical capacities deserted him. When *The Tree of Liberty* was shot in 1986, five LPs had been completed, and number six would be made as part of the film.

My first title for the film was *The Silver Tassie*. Hamish was keen that it should be entitled *As I cam by Crochallan*. Then, whilst attending the planting of a Tree of Liberty in the Perth Road, Dundee, I decided that *The Tree of Liberty* should be the title. When I phoned Hamish to tell him, he burst into song:

> Wi' plenty o' sic trees, I trow,
> The warld would live in peace, man.
> The sword would help to mak' a plough,
> The din o' war wad cease, man.
> Like brethren in a common cause,
> We'd on each ither smile, man;
> And equal rights and equal laws
> Would gladden every isle, man.[2]

2 Robert Burns, 'The Tree of Liberty'.

Hamish's to-camera contributions to *The Tree of Liberty* were filmed in September 1986, in the conference room of the School of Scottish Studies and in Sandy Bell's bar. His identification with both Burns and the Hovey–Redpath enterprise is evident in the statements he made:

> In his own lifetime attempts were being made to cut [Burns] down to size and obscure his message. William Blake, in many ways Burns' true soul-mate, put it very well when he wrote: 'A man's worse enemies are those of his own house and family', and it is among the Scots that one has to look for his most deadly enemies and insidious false friends. He was up against pre-potent Calvinism in other words . . . How is it possible to rescue this poor painted, cosmeticised cadaver of a dead poet from the ghastly mess in which they've laid him? Can it be done? In my own opinion, triumphantly, the answer is yes – and the key is the song, and specifically the great song complex on which Serge Hovey has been labouring and devoting so much selfless love . . . Burns knew that he was fulfilling and not betraying his own genius by devoting himself to the largely anonymous song culture of the Scottish people . . . The magic of Serge Hovey's arrangements, for me, is that while they draw on a tremendous, complex, rich tapestry of musical research and experience, they preserve and glorify the native features of Scots music. And in doing so they do due honour to Burns' marvellous achievement, round and fill-out all he wanted for Scots traditional song and his own part in it.

When the film was premiered on television on Burns Night 1987, Hamish was speaking at an Edinburgh Burns Supper and missed both the Grampian and STV broadcasts. He finally viewed the film on Channel 4 on 29 January – phoning to describe it as an 'immortal film'. A day or two later he phoned again to say that that the BBC reviewer on *Kaleidoscope* had criticised the film as 'pretentious and sluggish'. On 2 February he wrote with better news: 'Dear Tim, Tom Nairn and Douglas Eadie came in to see me today about the Gramsci film – they're using my translations of the prison letters. Both were singing the praises of *The Tree of Liberty*. "Wonderful film" (Tom). "Superb film" (Douglas). Indeed, Douglas said it was the only film with a Scottish interest that he wished he had made himself. This sounded like genuine praise! – So the consensus is building up.'

The *Glasgow Herald* commended the film as 'something to make us jump out of bed – an original, moving and obliquely charming film about the liberation of Robert Burns. Jean Redpath's version of Auld Lang Syne reinterpreted by Serge Hovey was a thing of pure spine tingling beauty.' Michael Kustow, Arts Commissioner at Channel 4, described it as 'a film at once complex and sublime'. Billy Connolly wrote to Barbara Grigor, the film's producer, 'I loved it, the film, the music, Jean and Hamish, their line on Burns.' The Hoveys themselves were also pleased:

> *Serge Hovey*: The film is exciting beyond words. The green man is not the only facet that is haunting. The entire production weaves a spell around the viewer. The nature scenes are just right. Hamish looks and sounds marvellous.
>
> *Esther Hovey*: You have created a film in which the concept of dialectics rises to new artistic heights. The sadness of Serge's dependence on the breathing machine is somehow connected to the beauty of nature's cycles. The continuity and recreation of traditional expressions into modern forms is a recurring theme beautifully demonstrated in nature, in the recording studio, the wonderful comments by Jean and Hamish.[3]

In May 1987 *The Tree of Liberty* won Best Documentary at the Celtic International Film and Television Festival in Inverness. The awards ceremony took place in the Eden Court Theatre with Hamish seated quietly at the back of the stalls – already deeply involved in a new project, a drama-documentary about Antonio Gramsci, being made by Pelicula films for Channel 4 Television. He was the film's starting point and consultant. It was premiered at the 1987 Edinburgh International Festival and following its television showing Hamish took part in in a one-hour live discussion about Gramsci and his contribution to twentieth-century culture and politics, on Channel 4.

The following year I began work on a feature film, *Play Me Something*, with John Berger. Hamish was soon dropping hints that he hoped to be involved: not least because the film was about storytelling and set on the islands of Barra and Venice. Consequently, when the Scottish Film Production Fund offered funding for a research and development trip to Italy, Hamish joined the team – as Italian interpreter.[4] We left Scotland on 17 March 1988 for a three-week trip to Italy – driving via Paris, Geneva and the Haute-Savoie. En route we stopped for a day in Versailles[5] before finding ourselves lodgings in a dilapidated hotel in Bonneville, Haute-Savoie, just a few miles from John Berger's house at Quincy. Unfortunately Hamish and Berger's American wife, Beverley, did not get on. An argument about the IRA flared up and, for a moment, I

---

3 Letter from Esther Hovey to TN, 1 February 1987.

4 In the end the film had three interpreters: Hamish, my daughter Mary and David Kerr (from Urbino).

5 To further our plan to make a documentary film about Ian Hamilton Finlay's commission to 'design' the French Government's memorial for the Bicentenary of the French Revolution – see Chapter 25.

foresaw *Play Me Something* running like blood into the sewers of history. Hamish and Berger behaved, briefly, like two bulls in an orchard after a winter in separate stalls. When Berger left the room, Hamish said quietly, 'Tim, he's a bit of poseur!' When Berger played Tom Waits on a tape, for possible use in the film, Hamish bridled at the folk-mannerisms underpinning that magnificent voice. But, when Beverley flew off to tend her dying mother in Washington, and the grappa began to flow, the tensions fell away. Indeed, as John and I worked on the script, it became apparent that Hamish should be integrated into the creative core of the film, as one of our actors. Berger then wrote Hamish into the film as the island's electrician: an old singer, who, arriving at Barra airport by horse and cart, conjures a storyteller (and the film) into being – like a modern Prospero.

Years later, reading through Hamish's war diaries, I came upon a passage that mysteriously prefigures the central storyline of *Play Me Something* (based on a Berger short story in his book *Once in Europa*). After bloody fighting on the Sangro Front in January 1944, Hamish made these diary jottings. First, he quotes Henry James: 'The Venetian's easy surrender to the senses is the sign of an unconscious philosophy of life – the philosophy of a people who have lived long and much, who have discovered no short cuts to happiness, and no effective circumvention of effort.' Then he adds these words of his own: 'Out of this war, out of the suffering of Scotland across the ages, we can build our cairn – a civilisation as beautiful, as different as Venice and Barra.' Those two quotations encapsulate the essence of the ideas John and I had presumed to explore in *Play Me Something*, before Hamish joined the team. His 'inspiring presence', however, did not end there. Once he became part of the production team he made a second crucial contribution to the film by grounding it in the actuality of Scottish and Italian history, and by giving substance to its mystical elements.

After five days in Quincy, we drove in high spirits to Geneva to pick up Jean Mohr – our Swiss photographer – and head south through the Mont Blanc Tunnel. Arriving in Venice, we began our search for two actors who would pose as our film lovers. 'Marietta' was a young communist who worked in a chemist's shop in Mestre, the industrial port of Venice; 'Bruno' an unmarried Alpine peasant, in his early forties. That a Bruno was difficult to find in Venice came as no surprise but that Venice contained no Marietta willing to take off her clothes before an ageing Swiss photographer almost flummoxed us. With the Easter weekend approaching, we phoned the Academmia Vittorio Gassman, in Florence; they said they had plenty of actors. So, leaving Jean Mohr in Venice, we set off for Tuscany. We spent the night in Padova, very close to the Cathedral of St Anthony. In the morning we visited the Scrovegni Chapel to see the Giotto frescoes that Hamish had viewed with the artist Angelo Savelli in 1949. Then in mist and driving sleet we crossed the Apennines, arriving on the south bank of the Arno to see Florence effulgent in afternoon sunshine. We booked into the Hotel San Remo, and from the bedroom window Hamish spied a blue plaque on the opposite wall. It was a memorial to Lt Hugh M. Snell, of the Scots Guards, killed 4 August 1944, on the Via Lupo.[6] That evening we drove up to the Piazza Michelangelo to look out across the city that Hamish had helped liberate forty-four years previously.

Next day, Easter Thursday, we rushed to the Gassman Academy. Like Venice, Florence had no actor who looked like a Bruno, but there were three possible Mariettas – one in Bologna, one in Milan and one in Turin. Knowing now that we would find no Bruno in Italy I phoned my old friend Charlie Barron, a farmworker in Fife. He agreed to be our 'mountain peasant' and arranged to fly to Venice the following Tuesday. Early on Good Friday we drove north, Hamish singing partisan songs, translating as he sang. Our actress in Bologna, Lucia Lanzarini, lived high in a block of flats, on the Via Antonio. As soon as she had unchained the door we knew she was the one. We ate lunch with her, paid her £500 and arranged to meet her in Venice. After that it was north to Treviso to begin our search for Bruno's 'village in the mountains'. On Easter Saturday we drove into the Dolomites – snow, great towers of limestone rock, mist – and, suddenly, we glimpsed it, a 'doon tummelt clachan'[7] suspended on a great cliff disappearing in cloud. We left the road. Now our old Saab came into her own and – with stones flying – up we went into a farmyard that was a dead-end. A farmer appeared at a door. His name was Enrico Penzo and before long he was standing with one leg on a boulder, pointing out the scars where German bullets had exited his calf. Enrico was an ex-communist partisan, severely wounded in the last months of the war. Within minutes he and Hamish were comrades-in-arms, roaring with laughter. We were invited into the house where, around a great kitchen table, the women were rolling out a gigantic piece of pasta – a metre square – preparing a feast for Easter Sunday. Jugs of vino were brought out. Italy, Scotland, the partisans were toasted. Hamish explained: 'We have come to this place in the mountains to make a film about a man called Bruno – milking his cows.' Enrico smiled: 'This is the place! Bruno is down in the cowshed, now! Milking, at this very minute. He lives up in the village, above us – all alone since his mother died, ten years ago. He comes down here to do the milking.'

In Berger's story the fictional Bruno also lived alone: 'Yes, I've lived alone for eight years. A fifth of my life.' Thus it was with an unusually strong sense of purpose that I followed Enrico to a small stone byre – and there was Bruno! His head nestled against one of two beautiful white

6 When he returned to Scotland, Hamish spent several months searching out Snell's living relatives: he found one surviving sister, Riccia Snell, and he wrote to her.

7 Doon tummelt clachan: ramshackle village.

oxen; he was just finishing milking, and the bedding on which the cattle stood was dried beech leaves, exactly as described in the story. There was also a tethered calf, and a white plastic bucket glowing softly in the dark. When I'd finished filming, Bruno shook my hand shyly and set off up the track that zig-zagged the cliff to his village. He was in his early forties and the village's only inhabitant. Meantime, a ceilidh had broken out in the farmhouse. Hamish was singing, and by the fireplace Enrico's mother, Maria Magdalena, sat in evident rapture. She was ninety-three. When Hamish sang 'Il Cacciatore' she bounced with delight. When he sang 'La Pastorella' she burst into tears, saying: 'I never thought I'd live to see the day!'

On Easter Tuesday we reassembled in Venice. Jean Mohr now had two days to photograph 'the lovers'. On the island of Giudecca we found an old grey gondola where the couple's 'love-making' took place. A wonderful sequence of photographs shows Bruno and Marietta dancing on the quayside. It was Hamish who supplied the music – *port a beul* – and how they danced! After a trip in a gondola to photograph Venice from the water, we raced west up the great flat valley of the Po – until the police stopped us just north of Turin. Hamish said, 'Pretend we don't speak Italian.' I got fined 10,000 lira. We reported our experiences to John Berger, delivered Jean Mohr safely home, hurtled on through France and back home.

That summer *Play Me Something* was awarded a British Film Institute grant of £270,000 and it blossomed into a 35mm feature film for the cinema, with production controlled by a young Scottish graduate of the National Film School, Kate Swan. In September she led a small professional crew back to Venice, with Chris Cox, our cameraman. Hamish again came with us as our chief translator. Our prime task was to film the Festa de l'Unità on Guidecca, as background to our love story – already photographed in black and white by Jean Mohr.

From Venice we moved to Treviso to spend a day filming in the Dolomites. Returning to San Antonio we learned that Maria Magdalena had died a few weeks after our visit. Hamish resumed his friendship with Enrico Penzo, and began a correspondence that went on for years. After filming shepherds moving thousands of sheep over the Pass of Pasubio, we flew back to Scotland on 11 September. Three days later the full film team (including actors) met in Oban to sail out to Barra. We had four days for rehearsal and five days for filming. Actress Tilda Swinton got rehearsals going on the boat. Because filming was to be done in the waiting room of Barra's working airport things were far from simple. Our actors were a mixture of professionals, amateurs and friends but Tilda Swinton proved a wonderful catalyst and John Berger emerged as a compelling storyteller. Margaret Bennett, a friend and colleague of Hamish's at the School of Scottish Studies, played the part of the island's schoolteacher; Liz Lochhead, poet and playwright, played a pregnant mother about to fly off to the mainland; Stewart Ennis played a Barra motorcyclist flying to Glasgow to watch Celtic play Hearts at football. Hamish, the island's 'electrician', arrives with a television set to conjure John Berger off the beach to mesmerize passengers awaiting a plane. *Play Me Something* is an unusual film. Its strengths and weaknesses are neatly summed up in a postcard Hamish sent to the poet Hayden Murphy:

> Dear Hayden, . . . believe it or not I'm acting in a film called 'Play me Something' which is based on a short story by John Berger, and has been partly shot in Italy (Venice and an Alpine village) and partly on the Isle of Barra. The director is Tim Neat, who made 'Hallaig' and 'The Tree of Liberty' and he has turned John Berger's short tragic idyll into a beguiling fairy tale . . . it will be a great success – or I dread to think. However, I'll keep my fingers crossed.

As an actor, Hamish sometimes struggled on set. It took eleven takes for him to coordinate actions and words for the scene in which he 'toasts' the storyteller near the beginning of the film. Afterwards Hamish remained disconsolate until, having returned to the Barra Hotel, he fell in with a Canadian who announced that his favourite Scottish song was 'Banks o' Sicily'. So Margaret Bennett said, 'This is the man who wrote it! He'll sing for you, won't you Hamish?'

On set, Berger and Hamish in general stimulated each other. Between takes, Hamish sang almost too incessantly, but Berger was thrilled to feel the film's *raison d'être* underpinned by so real and ancient a phenomenon. When editing began, both men contributed to the soundscape of the film. I was keen to create a blend of the musical traditions of the Atlantic and Mediterranean, and everything gelled when Hamish suggested Jim Sutherland as the man. A Highlander who had started work at the Dounreay Nuclear Power Station, Jim Sutherland was a close friend of Carlos Arredondo from Chile: together they had developed a highly original blend of Celtic and Latin music, which Jim constructed into a soundtrack of poetic power and psychic force. With sitar and trombone, the film's protagonists are recurrently summoned to the screen and, as the end-titles reprise the narrative, Margaret Bennett sings 'The Cave of Gold' in Gaelic: a song that embodies the film.

Play Me Something was premiered at the Berlin Film Festival on 17 February 1989. Hamish was there as our German translator. For some reason the Festival programmers had scheduled our film to follow a short, very violent English film entitled *The Broken Spine*. Consequently, when the curtains drew back and *Play Me Something* began with a black and white close-up of the two hind feet of Bruno's cow, standing on beech leaves, the relief was palpable. In July 1989 *Play Me Something* was shown at the Barcelona International Film Festival and won the Premio Europa. At 200,000 euros it was then the largest film prize in the world.

Play Me Something also delivered a new group of friends to Hamish. Stewart Ennis wrote him regular letters, and the young amateur actress Alison Carruthers, who 'arrives' in the film on the back of Hamish's cart listening to her transistor radio, adopted him as a kind of grandfather. After emigrating to Canada she wrote to him in November 1989:

> I'm so happy to hear about 'Play Me Something', Tim was ecstatic (you know what I mean), his letter was full of poetry; time was 'hammered out in sheets and copper curls'. I don't know if that's a reference to me, but lovely images. It took me a while to work out his meaning in his parting line, but it's something about 'as snow melts in water, I say goodbye', beautiful . . . it cheered me up. He does manage to write a lot and say little doesn't he? Happy birthday Hamish – we Scorpions should stick together!

There had been a dozen Scorpios on the Barra shoot, including Hamish and John Berger, Margaret Bennett and Tilda Swinton, and it is a letter from Tilda that sums up the strangely numinous coming together – of poetry, people, places and things – that *Play Me Something* was:

> Where would we be without magic, Tim? Without miracles? And without souls to share them with? . . . My life is revealing to me daily the miracle of the resilience of the human soul. I never wanted to tell you this, but just before we made *Play Me Something,* something very, very sad and dispiriting had happened in my life – a death – that our time on Barra was the first steps away from – the first breath forward. Since then, so wonderfully set up for recovery by our truly heart warming time on the isles, my months have been unravelling accordingly . . . Human Spirit! *Play Me Something* will always be precious to me for its liberating and life enhancing luminary: but especially as a lesson in, a confidence in, the power of the communication of souls – coming at such a time – uniquely dear.

TWENTY-FOUR

Brittany, *Journey to a Kingdom* and *The Traveller Roads*

Catharsis: *Greek for 'purging' or 'cleansing'.*
From the Greek katheiro, *'to rid the land of monsters'.*[1]

Following my introduction to the Breton folklorist Claudine Mazéas, in March 1985, Hamish, Claudine and I began planning a series of collaborations: most notably a film to be entitled *Deep Song of Armor*, a study of Breton folk culture seen from a Scottish perspective. Hamish loved Brittany, had a huge admiration for Claudine, and was keen to bring his vision to bear on this ancient heartland of the Celtic world. Claudine Mazéas was very like Hamish. In her youth she had ranged the countryside collecting traditional songs, music and oral law. Her ancestry was part French, part Jewish, part Breton but her loyalty was very much to Brittany and the old Celtic World. In the 1930s her father, Goulven Mazéas, had published a book entitled *Social-Fédéralisme*. It advocated a socialist, federal future for Brittany. The book was sold under the slogan: 'Capitalisme? NON! Collectivisme? NON! – SOCIAL-FEDERALISME – Expression occidentale du *Principe Socialiste*.' During the war the Mazéas family was arrested by the Gestapo. In Paris, Goulven Mazéas was interrogated by a Nazi Commander whom he had met previously at an international Socialist Youth Camp: consequently the Mazéas family was sent not to a concentration camp but back to Brittany. There Claudine lived the life of an outsider in her own community. She was big, she was strong, she had a wonderful ear for music, and throughout her twenties she cycled around Brittany in search of musical genius. One of her great finds was Madame Bertrand, a shoe-maker's wife, an old woman who combined the qualities of Edith Piaf and Jeannie Robertson. Like Ailidh Dall, Madame Bertrand always began with her oldest song, 'Skolven'. It was fifteen hundred years old. Hamish told me, 'This is the song that should follow "The Siege of Guingang" in the Brittany film.' Like Hamish, Claudine was also a great champion of young tradition bearers.

---

1 HH, notes, Henderson archive.

In the fifties she had been thrilled to learn of the work being done at the School of Scottish Studies and began to believe that it was in Scotland that the Celtic tradition retained its greatest artistic quality and integrity. By the 1980s when she met Hamish she was more than ready to fall head-over-heels in love not just with Scots music but with the man she called 'the greatest druid of the Western World'. Claudine lived alone at Guingamp, in a modern house on the edge of a small ravine, to which gnarled oaks cling in filigreed splendour. She believed she had divining powers. She liked to call herself a witch and deferred to her cat, 'Monsieur le Directeur', when in intellectual doubt. Holidaying in Roscoff in 1989 she wrote to tell me, 'Monsieur le Directeur is here too! I wished he would see the sea once in his life . . . ' Claudine's many letters to Hamish, and to me, throw a vivid light on her very Celtic psyche:

> *April 1989:* Dear Tim, Is it really filming you intend . . . I should tell you that summer is not the good time to meet [to film] my own beloved country (too much people near the coast – too many leaves on the trees – too much green over the landscape) . . . Forgive me! That is my feeling . . . autumn and winter are better (and the tourists gone) . . . [The film] is so near my heart and your questions awake so many remembrances that I could write pages and pages answering you. I feel it is a handicap to know so little about 'cinema' . . . I am not a scientist but I feel as an artist (I try to say that I have always been near poets and artists) . . .

> *August 1989:* Dear Tim and Hamish – I understand that your aim is to find money, and that can explain my feeling, very uncomfortable feeling, that you are running too quickly without real Breton bases. Such as someone who has 'love at first sight' – but please, is it really impossible for you to meet me and Donatien [Laurent] as soon as possible, the soonest the best? He has the 'Barzaz Breiz',[2] he has the working notes of La Villemarque, he has collected more than twenty versions of the Druid and his Disciple. He speaks perfect English, drinks whisky, meets Irish people, he makes love to his wife and so on . . . He is not only a searcher . . . he met Hamish some years ago.

Unfortunately, by November 1989 the co-production arrangements with which we had hoped to make the Breton film (as one of a series of six Celtic films) were collapsing. The early leaders of Channel 4, Jeremy

2 'Barzaz Breiz' is a collection of Breton bardic poems by La Villemarque, a nineteenth-century Breton folk collector. Hamish became interested in him and translated some of his works, notably 'The Druid and His Disciple'.

Isaacs and Michael Kustow, had been replaced by new brooms, and the economic recession was biting. On 15 November 1989 Hamish wrote to Alistair Moffat at STV in an attempt to save our sinking ship:

> As you know, I have been working closely with Tim Neat in constructing the set of six programmes on various aspects of Scottish culture which STV hoped to commission in association with C4. Tim's deeply imaginative project seemed – and seems – to me of quite exceptional interest; I'm quite sure that taken together, these programmes would make a major and quite out of the ordinary statement about Scotland and the Scottish people. I regard it as a privilege to have been asked to collaborate with Tim in making them.
>
> Consequently, you can well imagine the dismay I felt yesterday when Tim informed me that all the programmes but the one on Ian Hamilton Finlay were unlikely to be made, because of the limitations on the C4 Arts Budget. A great opportunity is in danger of being lost . . . The irony (for me) is that Polygon has recently approached the School with a view to publishing six (or more) books based on its work, and – as a member of the small committee the School has set up to examine this idea – I was about to suggest a series of books based on these programmes . . . Tim has just gone off to Paris to see Yves Abrioux (author of the major book on Finlay); he's also going to Brittany to gather fresh material for the 'Blue Donald and the Horseman's Word' programme. (We're very lucky, incidentally, to have the cooperation of Claudine Mazeas, one of the most brilliant of European folklorists.)

In 1991, following his annual trip to Padstow, Hamish crossed to Brittany to see Claudine. On 5 May he sent me a card: 'Claudine is in fine form – we listened to some of her tapes last night – including the Morven brothers, singing Breton *puirt a beul.* (She's annotated Luzel's versions of the Druid and his Disciple – references to the ship with wine in the hold – with the words Blue Donald!) . . . ' And so things were to continue for the next ten years. Various television companies requested synopses but seemed unable to commit themselves to a foreign project.

Desperate circumstances necessitated desperate measures: so in 1993 I put film-making to one side and turned to book-writing. In 1994 my book *Part Seen, Part Imagined – Meaning and Symbolism in the Work of Charles Rennie Mackintosh and Margaret Macdonald* was published. Two years later *The Summer Walkers – Travelling People and Pearl Fishers in the Highlands of Scotland* came out. Hamish features prominently in *The Summer Walkers*, and Claudine gets a mention. She was thrilled and subsequently asked me to arrange for her great collection of Breton folk recordings to be bequeathed to the School of Scottish Studies in Edinburgh. Hamish set up a meeting between me and the new director of the School, Professor Sandy Fenton. He told me he saw little point in Edinburgh acquiring a Breton musical archive, but put me in the hands of Dr Margaret Mackay, who suggested that the proposal should be welcomed if a copy set remained in Brittany. However nothing happened. In 1999 I wrote to Claudine to tell her of my plans to write a book based on Hamish's Horseman's Word researches. She wrote back on 30 May: 'Dear Tim, Imagine – when I received your letter I thought I knew nothing about horses – and now books are "flying" unto me and recognitions. "Things" there are I can tell you . . . so good to think that between us and our two countries there will be magic, druidic links – that makes good to my heart.'

In March 2002, I phoned Claudine to tell her that Hamish had died. She asked the hour of the funeral service. When I told her two o'clock on Friday 15 March, she said: 'I will go out – with Georges Cadoudal – into Highlands of Brittany and he will play "The Siege of Guingang"! We will be with you, and with Hamish.' Later, I sent her a selection of the newspaper obituaries and the eulogy I spoke at the funeral, which mentioned both her and Georges Cadoudal. She phoned to say how proud she and Georges Cadoudal were to have been part of the ceremony. Within a few days she was dead.

* * *

Journey to a Kingdom was a one-hour documentary produced by Grampian Television in 1991. The man who triggered it into being was Jim Sutherland, the musician who made the soundscape for *Play Me Something* in 1988. By 1990 he had become a regular composer for the BBC and other television companies. At a meeting with Ted Brocklebank, Head of Documentaries and Features at Grampian Television, Sutherland suggested that Hamish's life was well worth a documentary, and that I was the man to make it. Brocklebank, a former journalist with the *Scottish Daily Express* (now a Conservative MSP), responded positively. He commissioned a programme about Hamish in which Scots song and the North-East would feature strongly. Within six months, *Journey to a Kingdom: Hamish Henderson returns to the North East of Scotland* had been completed. We filmed on location in Edinburgh, Blairgowrie, Glenshee, Aberdeen, Mintlaw and Maud. Many of Hamish's musical associates feature: Martyn Bennett, Peter Hall, Jane Turriff, Lizzie Higgins, Joe Innes, Robert Lovie. Piper Tom Smith of Turriff, who had served with Hamish at Anzio and in Rome, played live to camera, whilst fine old recordings of Jimmy MacBeath and Jeannie Robertson brought the past to life.

It was Hamish who chose the programme's title, *Journey to a*

Kingdom.[3] He knew this was likely to be his last opportunity to address his countrymen publicly, and he consciously set out to round out his life in this film. I suggested that he finish the valedictory poem that I knew he had been working on for many years for presentation in the film. This he did. The poem's title is 'Under the Earth I Go'.[4] It opens with a four-line 'Druidic riddle' that Hamish had collected from Andra Stewart of Blairgowrie in 1955. It then goes on to celebrate springtime and Mayday in Padstow, looks death in the face, affirms the necessity of communal action, celebrates the renewal of Scotland in his lifetime, exults the power of art and the joy of living, before ending with an old folk rhyme from Aberdeenshire that speaks of the daily darg that is the common lot.

Under the earth I go
On the oak leaf I stand
I ride on the filly that never was foaled
And I carry the dead in my hand.

There's method in my magic!

Seeing I have passed my sell-by date
And will no doubt be hanging up my clogs quite soon
I have come back to Padstow to dance – to dance!

Doddle of drums on a May morning
Slash of sunlight on hill and harbour
High-jacked greenwood louping along the quay.

To hell with aunt Ursula Birdhood
And her old yowe dead in the park
While my love lives, I'll dance with the Mayers
Teasing the Old Oss till there's new life in him
Chasing sweet lusty Spring with pipes, goatskin and bones.

Sunshowers over the estuary
Cormorant black on the pale sands yonder
Taste of dank earth on my tongue

---

3 Hamish chose the same title for his 'last' film as he chose for his first 'big' poem: 'Journey to a Kingdom' (1935–40).

4 Arnold Rattenbury, an English poet who knew Hamish in the forties, has stated (*London Review of Books* 23 January 2003) that this poem was written in the 1950s and that he heard it recited by Hamish on a train in the 1970s. Hamish 'collected' the opening and closing of the poem in the fifties but Hamish worked on this poem – in Cornwall, Brittany and Scotland – during the 1980s and completed it in 1991.

Trembling oak-leaves coortin' the Sun
And the twin dragons, Life and Death,
Jousting thegither under the Maypole.
Change elegy into hymn, remake it –
Don't fail again. Like the potent
Sap in these branches, once bare, and now brimming
With routh of green leavery
Remake it, and renew.

Makar ye maun sing them –
Cantos of exploit and dream
Dain of desire and fulfilment
Ballants of fire and red flambeaux . . .

Tomorrow, songs
Will flow free again, and new voices
Be borne on the carrying stream

Asleep in Spring sunshine
Cornish riverbanks
Flower again!

Back in Fyvie's lands
I'll say fareweel wi' the plooman's week:

Soor Monday
Cauld Tysday
Cruel Wednesday
Everlasting Thursday
On Friday – will ye n'er get duin!
Sweet Setterday, and the efternuin
Glorious Sunday – rest forever. Amen.

In October 1991, I sent the poem to John Berger. He sent back a note for Hamish: 'Dear Hamish I love your poem! I read it out loud – it has such breath in it – wherever there is an ear that I like the look of. If such a poem grows out of half a lifetime – It's worth it – what an example you give us.'

When *Journey to a Kingdom* was broadcast in March 1992 Julie Davidson, in the *Herald*, described it as

> not only an adventurous piece of film-making but a celebration of the region where Henderson has mined his richest seams – the north east . . . Neat's film and Henderson's narrative were muscular. They showed 'a dour, even an intransigence' in the north east character,

> 'counter-balanced by a rich vein of poetic imagination and sensibility'. We saw faces that looked as though their clay had been roughed up by the plough, heard singers of ballads howked from the spare and hostile landscape. It is harsh, the north east, as well as beautiful. And it has never asked for any hand-out.

The writer Pat Gerber (wife of Glasgow's Compass Gallery director Cyril Gerber) wrote:

> Dear Tim Neat, Your film about Hamish Henderson was the best piece of television I have ever seen . . . Hamish and dozens of other people well-known and unwell-known, have helped me a great deal with a book I have been working on for the past four years . . . it deals with all the history, myth, legend and mysteries surrounding the Stone(s) of Destiny . . . I'd like to ask you if you'd be interested in making a film about it . . . Since I saw your film – THAT is the way I see it – the collage effect, the visual jokes, the beautifully deep and thorough treatment of the subject. A Stone is clearly not a *character* like Hamish, but you'd be amazed at the characteristics this one has collected over the centuries . . . Meantime, I can't wait for your next film.

As a by product of *Journey to a Kingdom*, Grampian commissioned Jim Sutherland to create a sound-tape cassette of a selection of Hamish's songs and poems. Hamish entitled the tape *Pipes, Goatskin and Bones*.

* * *

The following year, 1994, Hamish featured in what would be our last film project – *Rathad nan Ceard,* a 27-minute television programme commissioned by Alistair Moffat for STV in Glasgow. Funded by the Gaelic Television Council it retraced the journey Hamish made to Sutherland with the young Norman MacLean in 1957. As a native Gaelic speaker, Mod medallist (as both piper and poet) and the best comedian in the Gaidhealtachd he was the ideal man to 'carry Hamish' though the programme. The idea was that the two men would drive north from Edinburgh for a meeting with their old friend Essie Stewart and enjoy some adventures en route. To save money it was decided that Norman would drive Hamish in my old 'tinker-looking' bee-keeping truck (a Volkswagen Caddie). The trouble was, Norman was still subject to a drink-driving ban! Luckily the Highland police were looking the other way and we put the van on a flatbed lorry driven by Charlie Barron (who played Bruno in *Play Me Something*) where necessary. Shooting started on 18 September at the Baiglie Inn in Fife. Hamish joined us at Dalwhinnie, and the following day Norman drove him north up the A9. They chatted in Gaelic but Hamish's 'windows of coherence' were now sometimes very short and the performance was not what we had hoped for. However, Eddie Davies the pearl fisher was soon discoursing on the facts of his ancient occupation with all the eloquence of Wordsworth's leech-gatherer. After this Norman and Essie Stewart journeyed west to visit old camping sites and explore use of the *Beurla Reagaird* (the secret cant-language of the Gaelic-speaking Travellers, first recorded by Hamish in 1957), whilst Hamish drove north with Gordon Stewart who, as a boy, had acted as the eyes and support of old Ailidh Dall. Then, beneath sunlit peaks of Ben Hope and Ben Loyal, the two separate parties met up at the Kyle of Tongue. Here they were to ceilidh with the Williamson clan. Unfortunately Alec John Williamson's very elderly aunt Katie, matriarch of the Ross-shire Williamsons, died suddenly. Consequently, Alec John announced that he and his family would have to withdraw from the film: 'Indeed, we cannot appear on television whilst we're in mourning. None of the Williamsons can have anything to do with any film for years to come. I don't think we'll ever get over the death of Katie.' Returning to Glasgow to lick his wounds, Norman decided to take a break – spend his fee on whisky – and disappeared. Two days later Alistair Moffat, Chief Executive of STV Enterprises wrote to say that the 'rushes' looked good but that Hamish would have to be removed from the film – that his Gaelic was poor, that we would be pilloried by the press and the Gaelic Television Committee. I was shaken but wrote back to say that Hamish must remain in the film because he was the prime subject. Moffat sent a conciliatory reply but demanded that I create an alternative structure without Hamish, in case 'good editing' could not solve the problems. Two months passed. Suddenly Norman re-appeared, Alec John Williamson decided to shorten the period of mourning for Katie Williamson, and Moffat agreed that Hamish could remain in the film.

At the end of November the film crew reconvened, in a mud-floored eighteenth-century barn in Strathdearn, for the ceilidh that is the climax of the film. Willie MacPhee arrived on the dot, resplendent in full Highland dress with pipes akimbo; his wife Bella, bedecked in red tartan, looked equally magnificent (fresh from a summer on the Perthshire steppe). Alec John emerged as a peerless *fear an tighe*; Norman MacLean and Essie Stewart led the dancing like lovers; Ian Stewart brought his band from Blairgowrie; and James Stewart came from Alford – to sing the kye hame. An open brazier roared, a collie joined in the dancing and Hamish presided with bardic contentment. In 2006 Norman recalled, 'of all the television programmes I've made it's *Rathad nan Ceard* that the Gaels remember and ask me about.'

Over the previous decade Alastair Moffat had been a loyal supporter of my work but things now fell apart. *Rathad nan Ceard*, like *Journey to a Kingdom*, appears to have been blackballed from getting a screening at the annual Celtic Film and Television Festival. This probably dates back to 1989 when Neil Mitchison (Scottish juror at the Brittany Festival) informed Hamish and me that our work wasn't Celtic and would court exclusion in future. To add to our woes, in late 1994, the STV finance department began a bad-tempered exchange with Hamish over money. They claimed that he should have been paid £300 (for his screen performance) plus £200 for use of archival photographs but, by mistake, he had been paid £725. They demanded that he return £225. Hamish did not reply. When he received what he interpreted as a threatening letter he decided he would not return a penny. STV then asked me to sort out this recalcitrant rebel. On 12 January 1995 Hamish wrote to me: 'Dear Tim, I'm very grateful to you for ironing out this stupid problem about the money – although it seems rather poor that you should even have to do so. Should I get an agent at long last? Robert Burns didn't have one . . . but the times, they are a-changing!' *Rathad nan Ceard* was broadcast on 5 March 1995, first on STV and then on Grampian. And that was the end of our film careers.[5]

5 Between 1988 and 1998 over one hundred of my programme proposals were rejected by the Scottish broadcasting companies. Hamish was involved in about one quarter of these. It was our failure to make programmes about Brittany, and the young Hugh MacDiarmid, that frustrated him most.

TWENTY-FIVE

The Carrying Stream: New Friendships and New Beginnings

Come drink and love with me my lad
Come sport with garland o'er your eyes
With me be mad when I am mad
With me be wise when I am wise

HH[1]

As Hamish grew older, he increasingly saw his role as an educator as key, and his wish to nurture young people became his prime creative concern. During the 1970s and 1980s he was proud to see a new generation of students and music-makers taking his message to the world.[2] One was Freddie Freeman. Brought up in Cincinnati, Freeman came to Edinburgh in the early 1970s determined to make an impact on the Scottish folk scene. From 1974 to 1981 he lived in a flat opposite Sandy Bell's bar in Forrest Road. He was married and enrolled at the School of Scottish Studies to begin a doctorate on eighteenth-century Scottish humanism and the poetry of Robert Fergusson. Professor John MacQueen was his supervisor but it was Hamish who changed his thinking and his life:

> I was already interested in the poetic power of the Scots language but Hamish got me interested in the outlandish contribution made

1 'Greek Drinking Song', written by Hamish, aged fifteen, published in the *Alleynian*, October 1935.

2 Jo Miller, who joined the School of Scottish Studies in 1986 as a postgraduate student, can be seen as a classic example of Hamish's influence as an educator. Whilst she was a student, Miller became part of the Scottish folk scene as both a traditional singer and a revivalist (with the Whistlebinkies). In the early 1990s she began teaching at the Royal Scottish Academy of Music and Drama in Glasgow and helped design the Academy's new degree courses in Scottish Music. She then acted as a consultant on the new Folk and Traditional Music courses being set up at Newcastle-upon-Tyne, and helped Scotland's National Centre of Excellence in Traditional Music at Plockton High School in Wester Ross into being.

> to Scots culture by Scotland's Episcopalian minority. One day we were in a café. He said, 'The whole Scottish tradition looks upwards to Fergusson and downwards from him, in many respects.' He also told me a story about a visit to the West of Scotland. A discussion became heated. A man asked Hamish what religion he belonged to. Hamish said, 'I'm a Pisky.' The man replied, 'Then I don't recognise you as a citizen of the same country!' . . . He was also a great practical help. Excited by one of my thesis chapters, Hamish phoned MacDiarmid and, within minutes, it was arranged that I would take the bus to Brownsbank and meet the man – face to face. The reason I stayed in Scotland was that the Enlightenment I was studying was still a living reality here. When my thesis was complete – and I'm almost shy to say this, Hamish said, 'Freddie, you're a hero of my people.'[3]

In the late seventies the Freeman flat became a memorable ceilidh house: 'Hamish would sing "Tail Toddle", Nancy Nicholson "The Cuckoo's Nest", I would play the pipes. We would first-foot Hamish at Hogmanay and he helped introduce Winnie and me to the Scots Jewish scene, to the Avrom Greenbaum Players, to the Daiches brothers. He liked to remember the children's birthdays, he liked to sing them lullabies [as he had done to his own daughters].' In the years following the Lockerbie air disaster in December 1988, Freeman initiated a series of benefit concerts in the Rex Cinema in Lockerbie: Fish, Dire Straits, the Battlefield Band and dozens of Scottish folk artists gave free performances. In 1992 Freeman wrote to thank Hamish:

> From the moment you spoke I forgot the hassles of Festival organisation and remembered and reaffirmed in my mind why it was so important to have you in Lockerbie. Poetry and song, as you rightly reminded us, belong to the people. They are part of a shared consciousness, something which brings back together and humanises the tribe. They reassert life (Lockerbie needs this) where disaster and apathy tear us to bits . . . You are one of the few in our culture who has not forgotten the tribal significance of Art. Without it, all we would be left with are pretty artefacts, academic dissertations, Arts Council back-scratchings . . . Through my involvement in three Lockerbie Folk and Rock Concerts and this Book Festival – Lockerbie has given me back a sense of purpose . . . Thanks Hamish again I am in your debt.

Freeman was now working on a huge project to see 'The Complete Songs of Robert Burns' presented on thirteen CDs (Linn Recordings).

---

3 Freddie Freeman, conversation with TN, 2008.

It complemented the Hovey–Redpath project (see Chapter 12) but Freeman's emphasis was on Scottish singers and Scottish bands. In 1995, Freeman worked in Swansea as director of its UK City of Literature and Writing Festival. Hamish took part in two major sessions, first, with Sorley MacLean and the singer Rod Paterson, second, with MacLean, Meg Bateman and James Kelman. The platform provided Hamish with a chance to bring Welsh audiences up to date with his memories of the poets Keidrych Rhys and Dylan Thomas. Since Hamish's death, Freeman has presented his work on CDs, on radio and in the theatre.

Hamish enjoyed an even closer friendship with Alison McMorland, the 'Maid Marian' he had glimpsed at the Furry Dance in Cornwall in 1967. Their musical relationship began in 1971 after Alison moved from Cornwall to York, and began to seriously re-immerse herself in Scots song. That year she won the Ladies Singing Competition at the Kinross Folk Festival with renditions of 'Skippin Barfoot through the Heather' and 'The Gypsy Laddies'. When she came down off the stage:

> Hamish swept me into his arms! He congratulated me. He sat me on his knee. He was euphoric but was soon wanting to know what I wanted to do. I told him I wanted to sing, that I was interested in collecting songs but what I wanted – was to sing! Soon I was coming up from York to stay with him and Katzel; and we would go to the School of Scottish Studies. We would select tapes, then he would lock me in and go off to Sandy Bell's. Then he would come back and take me up [to Sandy Bell's] – to sing the new songs! I was shy in those days but he'd say, 'Alison, you start – and a great hush will come over the whole bar.' And that's what would happen. He'd get me to sing 'The Colours Three' and 'The Cuckoo's Nest'.
>
> One day I was rushing from the School to catch the train when he chased after me – down the great stairwell – to give me a tape! It was 'The Sweet Lover's Ghost', collected by Sean O'Boyle. Why that song at that moment? My interest was in the mystical ballads. That song: it was *the* song. Thinking back on that moment still brings the tears to my eyes. What he did was uncanny and unforgettable. Later he did something similar when he introduced me to Lucy and Elizabeth Stewart. When I asked why, he said: 'You, after all, are out of this stable.' He saw something in me that I didn't see; he recognised then – what I have become. My work with the Stewarts of Fetterangus would become one of the big things in my life. Like Jeannie, Elizabeth is 'a singer sweet and heroic'.
>
> In the seventies I was interested in the Women's Movement and one day up in Sandy Bell's I sang Frankie Armstrong's song about

> the environment – 'Mother Earth'. Hamish loved it and got me to sing it three times, in the bar. Then, it was down to the School to record it. He told me the two most important political developments of our time were the Environmental movement and the Women's movement. He believed the importance of *the mother* – in the transmission of song, of language, of historical memory – was something the leaders of the Women's movement should recognise. When I told him I was going down to Greenham Common he made me promise I'd sing 'The Flyting o' Life and Death' and he encouraged me to make the song 'my own'. One thing I did was to put 'Life' in the major key, and 'Death' in the minor. Hamish set me up for my first LP, with Tangent Records. We worked together when I did a theatre show about the songs of Brecht. On his way to Cambridge – for holidays – he liked to stop over in York, with Tina and Janet, and stay with us. We would all go to the Cathedral, or wander around the Shambles. One day, in the gardens near the castle, Janet and my daughter, Katy, were playing amongst the trees and the flowerbeds: the sun was shining and I've often thought – life was perfect at that moment. In 1980 I came back to Scotland to begin my folklore work and my singing career. Hamish did so much for me and when he retired I used to go to the School to help him sort out his tapes and things like that but, very often, he would ask me to sing, and the bottle would come out. Some people think this is sad but I don't regret a moment of my life with Hamish.[4]

Alison's second husband is the singer and songwriter Geordie McIntyre. McIntyre first met Hamish in 1962, when he was a young Glasgow schoolteacher. Learning of his interest in political song, Hamish sent him a photostat of his booklet *Canciones de las Brigadas Internacionales*. Twenty-four years later, Geordie composed a song that Hamish would describe as one of the best of all the Spanish Civil War songs. Geordie had spent the day with Eddie Brown, one of Scotland's last Brigaders: 'Then, as the sun went down over the Campsie Fells we saw "the Sleeping warrior" disappearing gently into the darkness, and the words of the song started coming to me. Its title is "Another Valley".'

Apart from his wife Katzel, Hamish's closest woman friend during the last twenty-five years of his life was Margaret Bennett. Her mother was a native Gaelic speaker from Skye (recorded by the School of Scottish Studies in 1956), her father a piper from Glasgow. Crippled by polio, at the age of eleven she began keeping a 'Song Book' and became a singer and amateur folklorist long before she left school. While a student at

4 Alison McMorland, conversation with TN, 2008.

Jordanhill College of Education in Glasgow, she visited the School of Scottish Studies with the College Folk Club:

> It was a Saturday. It was Hamish showed us round the archive. He talked, he sang and took us up to Sandy Bell's and sang 'Rivonia', fist in the air. I was already hooked on the idea of a career in folklore but that day I knew I had seen what I aspired to. Later, I studied folklore at the Memorial University of Newfoundland: so it was the two great HH's, Herbert Halpert and Hamish Henderson, who made me what I am.[5]

In 1973 Ed Miller – at the University of Texas – wrote to tell Hamish: 'I have a lovely girl singer called Margaret Bennett from the Isle of Skye, here; studying Folklore at Newfoundland . . . ' In 1978, back in Scotland, Margaret wrote this letter:

> Dear Hamish, I wonder if you remember me? The last time we met was in the MacLellan Galleries in Glasgow at a memorial concert for Paul Robeson, which you chaired and at which I sang a couple of Gaelic songs. Margaret Bennett is the name . . . I recently wrote to the HIDB [Highlands and Islands Development Board] asking them about the possibility of their supporting a folk-collecting and documentary project in Skye – and here's where you come in . . .

By 1980 Margaret and Hamish were meeting at folk festivals and conferences all over Scotland. In 1984 Margaret applied for a lectureship at the School of Scottish Studies. Hamish strongly supported her and, in 1985, she was appointed on a three-year contract, which was later made permanent. Hamish saw her as the person best able to carry his cultural vision at the School. In some ways she reminded him of his mother. They shared some of their teaching. Margaret drove him to various folk festivals. He encouraged her as she researched and published a series of books on folk life in Scotland and Canada. Both made light of their physical disabilities and the disputes endemic in university life.

> One day we were crossing George Square – through the gardens – to a faculty meeting in the David Hume Tower. I was speaking about Sir Walter Scott and his use of 'tradition'. When I mentioned 'Glenfinlas', Hamish put his hand on my arm and started to sing. He sang the whole poem – there and then in the garden – seventy-seven verses! People stopped round us to listen. When he had finished, we walked on. I asked him where he got his tune. He said he'd made it

5 Margaret Bennett, e-mail sent to TN, 2008.

> up when he was a boy, to help him remember the poem. We were late for the meeting but I wouldn't have missed that moment for all the tea in China![6]

For Hamish, Margaret bridged the gap between Scots song and Gaelic, between academic scholarship and stage performance, between the domesticity of folk art and hauteur of national pride.

* * *

Pino Mereu, a Sardinian from Rome, was the last of Hamish's many close Italian friends. As a schoolboy Mereu fell in love with the British Romantic poets – William Blake, John Keats, Shelley and Robert Burns. As a young man it was folk music and Celtic song that took his fancy. In the early 1980s he bought Dick Gaughan's record *Kist o' Gold*. One of its tracks was 'Banks o' Sicily'. He thought it was the most beautiful folksong he had ever heard. In 1985 he wrote to Hamish, who responded immediately by sending Mereu copies of his *Elegies*, *Chapman* No. 42, and numerous back issues of *Tocher*. In 1986 Mereu published the first issue of his magazine *Kilmarnock Edition*. It was largely in Italian, deals with Celtic folk culture and uses Hamish as the measure of modern European culture. In 1987 Mereu visited Edinburgh and attended the premiere of the film *Gramsci*, as Hamish's personal guest. Later, in Sandy Bell's, Hamish introduced him to the Sardinian artist Renzo Galeotti. 'I soon realised that Hamish was a man who knew far more about the Sardinian and Italian heritages than we did!'[7]

In 1996 Pino approached the British Council in Rome with a plan to organise a festival of music, cinema, poetry and folklore entitled 'Meeting Scotland: Hamish Henderson and Timothy Neat'. After protracted negotiations the British Council announced that it was not prepared to countenance any such project. Pino writes:

> For me Hamish was a man of genius. Like Bela Bartok he believed that 'folk music is like a human being – it changes minute by minute'. Hamish's life is with us – his story, his poetry, his songs: the music he collected grows beside us as we grow. If you think about wars, emigrations, racism, unemployment, socialism, nationalism – you will find everything in his poetry, in his songs, in the words he spoke. Hamish's ideas are still fermenting in our consciences, his writings – like those of Marotto[8] and John Berger live on, like Gramsci's thought. It is incred-

6 Margaret Bennett, conversation with TN, 2008.

7 Pino Mereu, e-mail to TN, 2008.

8 Peppino Marotto, Sardinian shepherd, trade unionist, singer and poet, murdered at the age of eighty-two.

ible how Hamish's life captures the minds of the people, here, in Italy. I remember how he told me, many years ago, that one day I would sing a Sardinian song to the melody of *Banks of Sicily* and – when it happens 'it will represent a fusion of my two greatest loves – Scotland and Italy'. In one hundred years Hamish's great achievements will still be topical. Like Antonio Gramsci, Hamish is the life – that will be yet. So now I have started a new magazine, *Hendersonia*. When I decided that, I did not know that as a small boy he used the pseudonym – *Sidonia* (the fairyland of the *Sidh*).[9]

* * *

Although Hamish's influence was greatest in the world of folksong he also had an influence across a wide spectrum of the arts in Scotland. The career of the composer and music historian John Purser is one, perhaps surprising, example. Long regarded as an iconoclastic rogue, Purser has, in recent years, been commissioned by BBC Radio Scotland to present two radio series exploring *Scotland's Music*. Programmes were based on Purser's book *Scotland's Music* (Mainstream 1992 and 2007) and owe more than a little to Hamish. When Purser's book was first published the academic response was muted but Hamish was one of a much larger group who immediately recognised its profound importance. The two men had first met when Purser was an eighteen-year-old student, and Hamish wrote to congratulate Purser on the manner in which his book championed the many-coloured coat of Scots music. On 12 April 1992 Purser replied:

> Dear Hamish . . . I remember being impressed by your insistence that the tradition was a living one. The impression never left me, though I was confused by it at the time because my knowledge was through print not lips. Now I know better and can put that down to a distant memory of your own vivid enthusiasm as well as to the

9 Hamish's love for Italy is affirmed in a letter he wrote to me, 19 August 1982: 'If you need a Sherpa, just give me a ring . . . I had a splendid time in Italy – Pisa, Florence, Rimini. While swimming in that old sophisticated polluted Med, I suddenly invented APIVIL (the Association for the Promotion of Italian as a Viable International Language). Esperanto has had a hundred years, and has failed to make the high peaks, because it is an inorganic thought-up language . . . What is needed is a clear, regular, simple – well, comparatively simple – organic language like Italian. Spelling and pronunciation are a model of regularity. The verb is a bit of a bugger but you can't have everything. Above all a magnificient literature – who wants to read poetry in Esperanto? . . . Don't you think it's a great idea? We must have a joint launching of APIVIL in Edinburgh and Rome – preferably before the end of the year – And APIVIL is such a tasty euphonious acronym – boy, this idea has got everything!! (Don't worry – I'll wake up in a minute!)'

> wonderful burgeoning of music and song that you and others have done to bring to the fore . . . You may therefore imagine with what pleasure I read your kind letter . . . I have never worked so long or so hard in my life . . . and to be rewarded by appreciation from my peers is sweet indeed. The best reward will, of course, be when younger generations take up the work – which they show every sign of doing.

Hamish applauded the manner in which Purser had integrated folksingers like Jeannie Robertson and Duncan Williamson into the mainstream history of Scottish music and he became a vocal supporter of Purser's successful attempt to recreate the Pictish Carnyx as a working musical instrument (Purser worked with the trombonist John Kenny and craftsmen at the Museum of Scotland). Its very existence opened new horizons for both composers and musicians. Like Hamish, Purser believes that the creative new must build on the best of the past.

Via the folk band the Whistlebinkies Hamish made contact with the American modernist John Cage. This brilliant band emerged in the 1970s, and the band's flautist Eddie McGuire[10] was particularly close to Hamish. In 1984 the Whistlebinkies celebrated Cage's eightieth birthday at the Edinburgh Festival with a concert and exhibition at the Fruitmarket Gallery. McGuire asked Hamish to join them on stage for a piece entitled 'Music Circus for John Cage'. Hamish sang 'The Freedom Come a' Ye' and an impromptu 'happening' was soon under way, McGuire describing it as 'an untitled, uncaged piece in honour of the master'. The *Glasgow Herald* reported:

> . . . now and again it would sound chaotic, at other times – as when Judith Peacock was suddenly left singing Gaelic in a small pool of silence – the effect was hauntingly beautiful . . . Hamish Henderson said he'd heard nothing like it since wandering into a pub in the Highlands at one of the early folk festivals in the sixties and hearing the mingling of several fiddlers playing different tunes in the hubbub.

Meantime a brilliant new classical composer was appearing on the Scottish music scene, the young James MacMillan. MacMillan is a European Modernist but his accent is Scots, and the parameters that shape him owe much to Hamish. On 1 October 1987 MacMillan wrote to him from the University of Manchester:

> Dear Sir, I am a young(ish) Scottish composer who has been asked by the Edinburgh Contemporary Arts Trust to write a piece for

10 Today Eddie McGuire is regarded as one of Scotland's leading composers.

> a concert on 6 November at the Queen's Hall., and I would very much like to seek your permission to use a section of one of your great poems 'Freedom Come All Ye'. The bulk of the work will be a setting of Joseph Bovshover's 'Revolution' but I would like to use the final four lines of your poem 'And when MacLean . . .' as a hymnal-type coda and to give the work a Scottish political connection . . . The theme of the concert is 'The Revolutionary Spirit' and there are other works by Weill, Eisler, Rzewski, and Martland in the same programme. I am sorry for delaying to contact you but this idea was a late 'flash of Genius' hopefully, and I hope you approve . . .

Hamish did approve and he liked the fact that this 'student' should write about a 'flash of genius'.

The young musician to whom Hamish was closest in his later years was Martyn Bennett, only son of his dear friend Margaret. Born in Newfoundland in 1971, Martyn moved at the age of eight to the Highland village of Kingussie, where bagpiper David Taylor found a maestro on his hands:

> I have never seen anyone learn the chanter so fast. In his first lesson he mastered everything I gave him first time round . . . I arranged for him to have an old set of full ivory-mounted Henderson bagpipes – never did a wee boy's eyes open so wide as when he got his first shot of them . . . I often wondered about his natural – and uncanny – musicality.[11]

By the mid 1980s, Hamish became a kind of surrogate grandfather to the young protégé. In June 1985 he arranged Martyn's first gig when he got him a day off school to be piper at the MacDiarmid Memorial Protest in Dumfries (see Chapter 22). At the Royal Scottish Academy of Music and Drama (RSAMD) in Glasgow, Martyn quickly proved himself an outstanding piper, classical fiddler and composer. For a while he juggled his career options but then decided to be a Modernist – working with Scots tradition. Others had made similar decisions before – Annie Lennox, David Byrne, Runrig, Capercaillie – but Martyn's work has an artistry and creative energy that make it unique. By the late 1990s Martyn had a nationwide reputation, and when the Scottish Parliament was formally opened in 1999, the two composers commissioned to make the music were James MacMillan and Martyn Bennett. When, in addition, Hamish's old friend Sheena Wellington stole the show singing 'A Man's a Man for a' That' he had every reason to feel

11 Quoted in Margaret Bennett, *It's Not the Time You Have . . .* (Grace Note Publications 2006).

proud. Hamish was not invited to the Opening – he watched the ceremonies, alone, on television, but made no complaint at his exclusion. Glasgow treated him better, particularly the organisers of the Celtic Connections Festival.

In 1999, at the end of a concert in the main Festival Hall, Martyn hauled Hamish up on stage to shout to his adoring fans: 'Let us not forget the fireside. Human beings should be united. This is where it came from: Hamish!' Martyn was now unfortunately very ill with cancer. Soon he would lose the power to play both the pipes and the fiddle but, as he did so, like Serge Hovey, he made new music through other musicians, old recordings and synthesizers – in the studio. In despair, like James Macpherson on the gallows in 1700, he broke his fiddles. Then, again like Macpherson, he went forward to meet his death with pride and great courage:

> *Like a man for long prepared, like a brave man,*
> *like to the man who was worthy of such a city*
> be glad that the case admits no other solution,
> acknowledge with pride the clear imperative of action
> *and bid farewell to her, to Alexandria, whom you are losing.*[12]

Martyn Bennett's last major achievement was his DVD *Grit*. It uses Hamish's recordings of Travellers, such as Sheila Stewart, to create timeless contemporary music and, during the last days of Hamish's life, he was greatly moved to have visits from Martyn who, despite great frailness, played his demo-tapes and discussed his latest ideas. The last letter Hamish wrote was to Martyn Bennett. After Martyn's death on the Isle of Mull, in February 2005, Brian McNeill, Head of Scottish Music at RSAMD, wrote: 'I am convinced that, a hundred years from now, Martyn will be spoken of as a great pioneer, a liberator of our tradition from pose and sham, narrow-mindedness and hypocrisy.'[13]

* * *

By the late twentieth century Hamish's influence on the media in Scotland was also significant. A number of Scots broadcasters studied with him at the School of Scottish Studies and many more now shared his cultural values. When Ishbel MacLean set off for Rome as a young art historian in 1973, Hamish insisted that she meet his wartime Italian friend Amleto Micozzi. Returning to Scotland Ishbel became one of the BBC's most innovative producers of schools' programmes. The television presenter

---

12 HH, Third Elegy, 'Leaving the City', *Elegies for the Dead in Cyrenaica* (Polygon 2008).

13 Brian McNeill, quoted in Margaret Bennett, *It's Not the Time You Have . . .* (Grace Note Publications 2006).

Kirsty Wark attended Hamish's lectures, and her feisty self-confidence and (early) anti-Thatcherism probably owe something to Hamish's promptings. The radio broadcaster Billy Kay (who studied modern languages at the University of Edinburgh) chose to attend lectures at the School of Scottish Studies simply to gain access to Hamish; he remembers:

> Hamish's presentations on Scots song were unforgettable – the word lecture doesn't convey what he achieved – you were aware that there was a warmth and a presence in the room as he ranged from Burns to the Ballads, often singing a verse or two himself but drawing in analogies from German and Italian culture and quoting from the great writers in those languages. It was Scotland the way it should be – proudly national yet completely and comfortably international. Quite apart from the pleasure of hearing him, Hamish showed me how to communicate directly with a live audience.[14]

As 'a native Ayrshire speaker', Kay quickly became the BBC's authority on the 'Mither Tongue' and, at a remarkably early age, was commissioned to work on the *Odyssey* series (1980–84), now regarded as a landmark documentary achievement in Scottish broadcasting. Hamish introduced the *Odyssey* series to readers of the *Radio Times* in typical style:

> In one of his prison letters the great Italian Marxist philosopher Antonio Gramsci refers to the 'unknown Italy' and contrasts the piazza 'with its shouting and vain glory, with the secret labyrinth that lies hidden from the outsider'; he even claims that the gap between what one sees and doesn't see goes deeper in Italy than elsewhere. It's a pity Gramsci never visited Scotland, for I'm sure the contrast between the garish outer wrappings and the goods it contains can nowhere be more grotesque than here. What Tom Nairn has called 'the vast tartan monster' wallows everywhere in the foreground, and yet, if you get past him, you become conscious of an infinitely complex amalgam of cultures, languages and traditions, the heritage of a country whose ethnic multiplicity has been one of the chief sources of its energy and resilience, as well as its vulnerability . . . It is this ethnic diversity, these differing and at times mutually antagonistic Scotlands that Billy Kay starts to unveil in his ambitious series *Odyssey* in January 1980. What is evolving is a new and highly interesting radio-art form which blends oral history with poetry, song and traditional music . . . it resembles the Ewan MacColl and Charles Parker radio ballads of the 50's but the

14 Billy Kay, conversation with TN.

> best of Kay's programmes seem to me to exhibit a quite distinct new identity.

Hamish was tutoring a 'hedge school of the airwaves', and esteemed broadcasters like Kenneth MacQuarrie, Iain Anderson, Bryan Burnett, Robbie Shepherd, Archie Fisher, Sheena Wellington, Rod Paterson, Adam Jack, Ruth Wishart, the various Macintyres and many of the Gaelic programme makers have all found shelter beneath Hamish's pelican-like bill. Indeed, by the mid 1990s, BBC Scotland, which had kept Hamish and his cultural vision at arm's length for so long, had become very much the kind of broadcasting company he envisioned in the fifties.

On the literary front, by the 1980s, a third generation of 'Scottish Renaissance writers' was making its presence felt. In May 1985 Hamish attended a Writers Festival in Paisley, noting meetings with Alasdair Gray, James Kelman, Alan Warner, Irvine Welsh, A.L. Kennedy, Duncan McLean, Janice Galloway, Jeff Torrington. In 1987 Hamish wrote a lively foreword to Freddie Anderson's *At Glasgow Cross and Other Poems* (Fat Cat Publications). In January 1990 James Aitchison wrote an article in the *Herald* entitled 'Young Poets', to coincide with the start of Glasgow's year as European City of Culture. It featured Carol Ann Duffy, Valerie Gillies, Tom Pow, Andrew Greig, Robert Crawford, Gerrie Fellows and Donny O'Rourke, and Aitchison uses Hamish as an exemplar: 'The retreat from artistry becomes obvious when one looks again at a poem like Henderson's *Elegies for the Dead in Cyrenaica*: – it may not be a great poem but in conception and execution it is a major one.'

The 1980s was the decade in which oral literature began making a real impact on the publishing world. In Scotland, the breakthrough was led by Hamish, supported by Linda Williamson, Dr Alan Bruford, Donald Archie MacDonald and Dr Peter Cooke – all at the School of Scottish Studies. Amongst the Scottish publishers, Stephanie Wolfe-Murray at Canongate was the great facilitator, and for once the Scottish Arts Council kept abreast of the new development. Hamish saw the new publications as the apotheosis of the 'Tinker Project' he had initiated in 1953 and he was delighted that the first big success was Betsy Whyte's autobiographical memoir, *The Yellow on the Broom*. A flood of Traveller books, plays and television programmes followed. On 21 October 1989 Hamish reviewed *Exodus to Alford*, by Stanley Robertson, in the *Scotsman*:

> One of the most astonishing and potent phenomena of the present day cultural scene is the emergence of gifted performers and tradition-bearers from the ranks of travelling people. Shunned and avoided by settled society, the travellers guarded their love of song and story almost as if it were a sacred charge, although this inherited treasury

remained a closed book to outsiders right up till the 1950s . . . in many ways the most intriguing figure of all is Jeannie Robertson's nephew, the author of *Exodus to Alford*, who has earned the title of 'master storyteller of the travelling folk'.

On 31 March 1991 Hamish reviewed Betsy Whyte's *Red Rowans and Wild Honey* for the *Weekend Scotsman*: 'Her second book, like the first, has the authentic bloom of the open air on it; it carries the reader to the very centre of a way of life which, although profoundly alien to most industrialised Western society, has a permanent appeal, validity and attractiveness of its own'. It was, however, Hamish's close friend Duncan Williamson who would make the major contribution to this rapidly expanding literary form. Essentially non-literate, Williamson wrote thirty books, and his impact on modern storytelling and children's publishing continues to this day.

One of Hamish's literary finds in the mid 1980s was George Gunn, a young North Sea roustabout from Caithness. Hamish was proud of his own Gunn ancestry, and the two men quickly allied themselves as kinsmen. Gunn wanted to leave the oil business and become a writer. Higher Education and the Open University were options, but Gunn chose self-education and 'apprenticeship' with Hamish. By the late eighties he had made himself a dynamic new voice in Scots poetry; by the mid nineties he was author of a string of plays and director of the Grey Coast Theatre Company, in Thurso. George Gunn's closeness to Hamish is evident in this letter, written to Hamish in the summer of 1988:

> Yesterday I was making my way down Glenshee from a couple of days communion in the mountains and I passed, hot and sweating, *Clach na Coileach*, the gathering place of the clan MacThomas – people close to your heart I think . . . It is one of the most beautiful rocks I have ever seen and so gentle – surrounded by its circle of pines. Just the place for a poet to take his rest. As I did, I was flicking through the best bits of 'The Green Fool' by Paddy Kavanagh – when lo! The very original pages of 'Ghillie Mhor' – my poem to you – fell out. So being a great respecter of symbol and ceremony I tacked them as best I could on to the rock of the MacThomas and said 'From a Gunn to a Gunn in the land of MacThomas. Luck on ye and from ye!'

The poem referred to is Gunn's 'Liberty Ode (for the Ghillie Mhor at 70)'.

> As I write this empires crumble
> can we blame it all on you
> Hamish Henderson?
> Russia, America, cracking open

in their different ways
like an old damp Gorbals tenement
Russia, where the wild wind of freedom
blows loud at last
America, a desert of rabid dogs
and the poor sleeping beneath their feet . . .[15]

Gunn's first collection of poems, *Sting*, with an introduction by Tom Scott, was published by Chapman in 1991. At least five of the poems appear to be about Hamish. And this may explain why: in 1995, Hamish wrote to Gunn asking him whether he might be prepared to carry his ashes to the summit of Ben Gulabin in Glenshee to be spread. George wrote back on 5 November: 'Dear Hamish, I received your letter this morning. I am very moved and deeply honoured that you have singled me out for the role of *leichenbegleiter*. Of course I will do it . . . but let us cheer up – this will be many years in the future! P.S. The Pictish Fighting Queen sends her love [Leslie Riddoch, Gunn's first wife].'

* * *

Hamish was always interested in the cultural dynamic of the theatre. In 1983 he encouraged the folk duo Maran and Shepherd to expand their careers on to the theatrical stage, helping them write their first drama, based on MacDiarmid's *A Drunk Man Looks at the Thistle*. After their first night at the Edinburgh Fringe, he noted:

> An inspired show – that has flowered over the spikes and jags of an incomparable masterpiece – I only wish the divine-diabolical genius H.McD. were alive today to view this true gallimaufry – musical, psychological, political, personal, satiric, goliardic. Burns suppers – Cockney pipers – the throwaway parts of the poem are deftly caught and sent cavorting. The sex symbolism grasped bold as brass – the Thistle stuffed into trousers 'where the zip is'. Inspector Wellbeloved: 'Thistles – why should they all be put inside?'

Perhaps the most brilliant Scottish theatre group of the 1980s was Communicado, led by Gerry Mulgrew. Hamish was involved from the beginning. In the late 1970s he encouraged Mulgrew's collaboration with Gerald Mangan at Edinburgh Theatre Workshop – where their Shadow-Puppet Theatre enjoyed a surprising success. Communicado was then established and between 1984 and 1988 won consecutive Scotsman First Awards at every Edinburgh Festival. In 1990 Mulgrew was commissioned

15 George Gunn, 'Liberty Ode (for the Ghillie Mhor at 70)', first published in *Cencrastus*, No. 36, Spring 1990.

to create a multimedia spectacular to open Glasgow's year as European City of Culture. Liz Lochhead wrote *Jock Tamsin's Bairns*; Karen Wimhurst and Steve Kettley directed the music; the painter Keith McIntyre was visual designer. It was a great success. Before the show opened, McIntyre made drawings of the major contributors to the production, including Hamish. In April 1990 McIntyre writes:

> Jock Tamsin's Bairns . . . I can never thank you enough for all the help Hamish; with the portrait, with the catalogue and 'as performed in the production *Quo Life*' . . . my eternal wish is that the *spirit* with which the company worked together can be explored and exploded no matter what medium of the arts we work in . . . To succeed, the synthesis of all the component arts had to make a language that was international in vision yet *unapologetically* Scottish . . . I sincerely regret we couldn't incorporate more of your own work – next time.

* * *

Hamish's prime involvement with film-making was as a collaborator with me on seven projects, but he was actively involved with other film-makers. In December 1979 he received this letter from the Central Institute of Information: 'We followed your advice and filmed at the College of Piping in Glasgow and then travelled to Dingwall to film John Burgess playing a pibroch at Tulloch Castle. The Japanese were delighted with the results and the programme has been expanded to 25 minutes.' In 1982 Hamish acted as a consultant to Pelicula when they negotiated their first major series for Channel 4, *How to be Celtic*. Subsequently he featured in the Scottish programme in the series *All Quiet On the Northern Front*. After this, Pelicula emerged as the leading independent television production company in Scotland. Its three directors, Mike Alexander, Douglas Eadie and Mark Littlewood, all got to know Hamish well. Initially, in the 1960s, Eadie had taken the MacDiarmid line in the folk/literature debate. But, after a spell in Italy, Eadie began to change his views, and any study of the subjects of the television programmes made by Pelicula between 1980 and 2008 shows how strongly Pelicula's success was linked to Hendersonian ideas.

In 1989 Hamish gave Lindy Cameron support for her plan to make a film entitled *La Passionaria*. In 1990 an American postgraduate student at the School of Scottish Studies, Barbara McDermitt, invited Hamish and me to join a project to make a film about Scots Traveller storytelling and Appalachian Mountain storytelling. Production was put in the hands of Milan and Sharma Herzog of California, but nothing came of it. During the late 1980s Mark Cousins,[16] while a student at Stirling University,

16 Mark Cousins is now a film writer, presenter and producer.

selected Hamish as his mentor and became a regular visitor to Sandy Bell's and Hamish's flat. His early work was influenced by Hamish, who made a major to-camera contribution to a documentary that Cousins made about Ian Hamilton Finlay's garden at Little Sparta. In January 1993 Hamish recorded two contributions for the RTE programme *The Pure Drop*. Later that year Les Wilson filmed an interview with Hamish for their STV programme *The D Day Dodgers* (celebrating the fiftieth anniversary of the liberation of Rome). When Ken Loach's film *Land and Freedom* was released, many of Scotland's old brigadiers made contact with Hamish to express their general disgust. John Dunlop writes: '*Land and Freedom* was certainly what the war was really about. But what was the film about? . . . One wonders what was the purpose of the film and why eight and a half million pounds was forked out . . .'

In May 1996 Hamish made his first and last full-length, one-man broadcast – on BBC Radio Scotland. It took the form of an interview with Robert Shaw. The original plan was that various acquaintances would speak about Hamish before he himself concluded the programme. The interviewees did well but Shaw found Hamish's youthful reminiscences so compelling that he decided to give the whole programme to Hamish. It might have been the start of a major autobiographical series but no follow-up programmes were made. This programme, if it still exists, should be rebroadcast because it was excellent radio and it stands as eternal evidence to the hundred opportunities lost by the BBC over the previous fifty years.

* * *

The visual arts were not Hamish's strongest suit but he won art prizes at school and retained an interest in painting, sculpture and architecture throughout his life. In the thirties he championed Picasso, in the forties Colquhoun and McBride, in the fifties the Palaeolithic artists of Altamira and Ian Hamilton Finlay. In the sixties a new generation of artists – John Bellany and Will Maclean are examples – began to address his vernacular interests with contemporary energies. Even Jack Knox's enthusiasm for still-life tradition can be seen to owe something to Hamish's demand that Scotland's artists paint where they stand. And, in retrospect, it seems likely that the appointment of Knox as Head of Drawing and Painting at Glasgow School of Art in 1981 triggered the emergence of the new 'Glasgow Boys'. For the first time since Fra Newbery's reign before the First World War, a Scottish Art School was at the cutting edge of worldwide developments. The high point of the group's decade-long success was the exhibition *The Vigorous Imagination: New Scottish Art* at the Scottish National Gallery of Modern Art in 1987. The painter who caught the public's eye was Ken Currie, a great John MacLean enthusiast, and when Hamish wrote a new introduction to his *Gramsci's Prison Letters* (Zwan 1988), he started by making reference to Ken Currie's work:

> One of the most striking pictures in the exhibition . . . was 'The Self-Taught Man' by Ken Currie. This – like another of Currie's pictures, 'Shipyard Poet' – shows a Clydeside worker with a book in his hand. The poet is holding his own manuscript notebook; the 'self-taught man', sitting at a table, with the dove of peace on a poster behind him and a notebook open in front of him, is holding a volume on the cover of which, plainly visible, is the name GRAMSCI. That a Scottish working class intellectual – a stubborn survivor in Thatcher's Britain – should be interested in Gramsci's political thought in the 1980s is readily comprehensible . . .[17]

Hamish attended the unveiling of Ken Currie's 'Clydeside Murals' at the People's Palace in Glasgow in 1987. The folksinger and collector Geordie McIntyre was there, and realised that no portrait of Hamish had ever been painted. Consequently, McIntyre organised 'a portrait of Hamish Henderson by public subscription': thirty-eight friends donated £10 each. He selected a young Glasgow-trained artist, Ruaridh Macleod, as painter (partly because Ruaridh's mother had been recorded by Hamish, on Skye, in the 1950s). Whilst it was still being painted Hamish wrote to me (5 October 1987): 'Rory's portrait of me has been in the wars – he came through from Glasgow with two friends to collect it; strapped it on to the top of a car, and set off back along the motorway. At some point they discover it's been blown off the roof of the car, and have to search for it! . . . and find it – in three pieces!' The reconstructed picture was presented to Hamish at the Riverside Club in Glasgow on 29 January 1988. Donny O'Rourke reported the event in the *Glasgow Herald*:

> Norman Buchan, in a robust and moving speech, put his old friend's contribution to Scots culture in clear, if sentimental perspective . . . Arthur Johnstone sent the John MacLean March ringing round the room . . . The regal, angel-voiced Flora MacNeil was in a form to match Hamish's . . . may his reputation as a poet and scholar catch up with his celebrity as our finest song writer.

Meantime, Hamish's friendship with Ian Hamilton Finlay had flared to a new intensity as a result of the campaign by Strathclyde Regional Council to force him to pay rates on 'the garden temple' that forms the centrepiece of his garden at Little Sparta, Dunsyre, Lanarkshire. In 1978 they declared it a commercial art gallery and demanded £9,000 a year. Finlay refused to pay or accept Strathclyde's definition of what

---

17 The exhibition catalogue, however, wilfully ignored the politics underlying the work of many of the New Glasgow Boys, and their closeness to the folk and literary revivals.

'art' is. The fifteen-year 'Battle of Little Sparta' began. It cost Strathclyde Region vast sums of money and a mountain of goodwill; Finlay lost his health, his marriage and his faith in institutional democracy. It was a black chapter in the history of regional government in Scotland. Like Hamish, Finlay would not separate his vision of life's poetry from the practicalities of life in society. With Greco-Roman rectitude he would die rather than submit to 'foreign intervention'. His enemies called him a fascist, a taliban, a self-righteous prick. When the battle was finally won, he declared, 'The Battle of Little Sparta is perhaps my greatest work of Art.' From the start Finlay saw the issue as a clash of ideas and values, and Hamish gave him full support. In June 1978 Finlay had stated:

> If you ask if life is more physically comfortable without battles, then obviously it is. One has to decide whether life is to be lived in terms of comfort – or something else. What has interested me in my life is the idea of purity. I will always fight so that it is easier for an ordinary man to say the true thing. Clausewitz, the Prussian militarist, said war was diplomacy carried out by other means. I believe that ethical battles are classical art carried out by other means . . . There's no principle in the world that says if you sit back and spectate, things will come right.[18]

Finlay's struggle became the subject of his art. Little Sparta became an artistic fortress. Postcards and booklets were distributed as visual ideas:

> When man obeys
> Without being presumed good
> There is neither Liberty or a native land. *(Louis-Antoine Saint-Just)*
>
> DEATH TO STRATHCLYDE REGION. *Ian Hamilton Finlay*

As the rates dispute rumbled on, another controversy blew up. In 1986, in collaboration with the French landscape architect Alexandre Chemetoff, Finlay was commissioned to design the French national memorial to commemorate the Bicentenary of the French Revolution. It was to be a 'philosophical garden' on the site of a ruined tennis court in Versailles, where the 'Oath in the Tennis Court' had been taken in 1789.[19] Unfortunately, accusations of anti-Semitism against Finlay surfaced, and after a vociferous newspaper campaign – across Britain, Canada, Belgium and France – the French government cancelled the commission. Hamish

---

18 Published in *Artwork*, June/July 1978.

19 In 1987 Channel 4 commissioned me to begin work documenting the project on film. In March 1988 Hamish and I did a 'photo-reconnaissance' in Versailles.

was adamant that he should be despatched to argue Finlay's case with President Mitterrand: 'We will speak in French. He was in the Resistance, I was with the Partisans. I have known Finlay for forty years – he is no more a fascist anti-Semite than I am!' On 26 April 1988 Hamish wrote to the *Scotsman*:

> The present day Vigilantes of Saint-Just have sprung into action in defence of Ian Hamilton Finlay, because he has been accused – incredibly – of being a sympathizer with fascism. As 'evidence' Finlay's traducers have pointed to his use of the SS symbol in his work *OSSO* (Italian for bone). This is as if one were to accuse Brecht of sympathy with the Nazis because he made use of the paraphernalia and rhetoric of Hitlerism in *Arturo Ui* . . .

On 30 April 1988 Finlay wrote back: 'Dear Hamish, Sue and I thank you from the bottom of our hearts for your wonderful letter in yesterday's Scotsman. Another Saint-Just Vigilante rang me at 7 o'clock to tell me about it! And what a superb story about Saint-Just and the Committee of Public Safety. Almost too relevant to be true.' Douglas Hall (director of the Scottish National Gallery of Modern Art) subsequently described Finlay's commission as 'probably the most conspicuous tribute ever paid by a foreign government to a Scots artist'. Michael Schmidt, editor of *PN Review*, described Finlay as 'a victim of his own independence, of the necessary clarity of his art, of the insistent simplicity of his good-faith and his belief that reason and dialogue are still properties of our artistic and political culture'. The French cancellation stood.

Towards the end of June 1993, whilst the Strathclyde rates debacle was still unresolved, Hamish and I drove out to Little Sparta to give Finlay an afternoon's encouragement. Finlay showed us around the gardens and the temple, 'despoiled by the Strathclyde bailiffs'. On 30 June Hamish wrote to the Scottish Arts Council:

> Strathclyde Region is suing Ian Hamilton Finlay over the 'Garden Temple' at Little Sparta . . . if ever there was a case where the Scottish Arts Council should exert its considerable influence on behalf of an artist of rare ability, this is it . . . In his Temple Garden he has created a work of art which is a place of pilgrimage for scholars, poets, sculptors and architects from all over the world. It contains the most famous examples of 'Concrete Poetry' to be found anywhere. I find it quite incredible – and intolerable – that an artist who has given so much to Scotland – and the world – should be harassed in this manner by short-sighted philistine bureaucracy . . . I do hope that the SAC will do its best to bring home to Strathclyde Regional Council that the action it has undertaken is endangering not only

the life and welfare, but also the creative achievements of a uniquely valuable Scottish artist.

The Battle of Little Sparta had one unexpected consequence: a long-term literary alliance between Finlay's son – Eck Finlay (poet, artist and publisher) and Hamish, which will be discussed in Chapter 28.

Embark on a garden with Vision but never with a plan.[20]
Ian Hamilton Finlay

20 Quotation from one of Ian Hamilton Finlay's many postcard artworks.

Sandy Bell's Bar, Edinburgh: Hamish with 'Sandy', 1989 (Photo: The Scotsman).

Folklorist and singer Margaret Bennett with the poet Liz Lochhead on Barra Strand during the shooting of *Play Me Something*, 1988 (KH).

Hamish and Alison Carruthers in a scene from *Play Me Something*, Barra, 1988 (Photo: Jean Mohr).

Hamish, like Prospero, 'singing' the film *Play Me Something* into being, Barra Airport, 1988. From the right, John Berger, Hamish, TN (director), Harvey Holton, Margaret Bennett (Photo: Jean Mohr).

The waiting room, Barra Airport; a pause during filming: Tilda Swinton, Hamish and Stewart Ennis (Photo: Jean Mohr).

The Hugh MacDiarmid Memorial, Langholm, sculpted by Jake Harvey of Maxton (Photo: Timothy Neat).

Hamish in his study at the School of Scottish Studies, c.1991. The painting, by Martin Rayner, shows the Langholm cornet charging up the Kirkwynd on Common Riding Day (Photo: Tricia Malley; KH).

Timothy Neat, Andy Hunter (academic, piper and singer) with Hamish in the library of the School of Scottish Studies, 1991 (Photo: Tricia Malley; TN).

Norman Maclean and Hamish on stage at the Wallace Tower, Aberdeen, during filming for *Journey to a Kingdom*, 1991 (TN).

Ian Hamilton Finlay, poet, artist and landscape gardener in the wilds above Little Sparta, Dunsyre, 1997 (Photo: Timothy Neat).

Hamish with the poet Valerie Gillies, Edinburgh, c.1997 (KH).

Hamish's two great Roman friends, Amleto Micozzi and Pino Mereu, 2004 (Photo: Timothy Neat).

John Purser (composer, musicologist and poet) walking the Cuillins with TN, 1999 (Photo: Francis Neat).

Hamish, with Karin Chipulina and Michael Law (Hamish's helper), enjoying the Day for Scotland, Stirling, 1992 (KH).

Hamish with his helper Paddy O'Neill celebrating with members of the Vigil for a Scottish Parliament, Calton Hill, Edinburgh, c.1995 (KH).

Serenading Scotland, dancer Ruth Frame and piper Graham Fenton make music at Findhorn, 2003 (RF)

Hamish, Katzel and Tina Henderson following the award of an Honorary DLitt by the University of Edinburgh, 1992 (KH).

Hamish amongst mourners at the funeral of Norman MacCaig, Edinburgh, 1997 (KH).

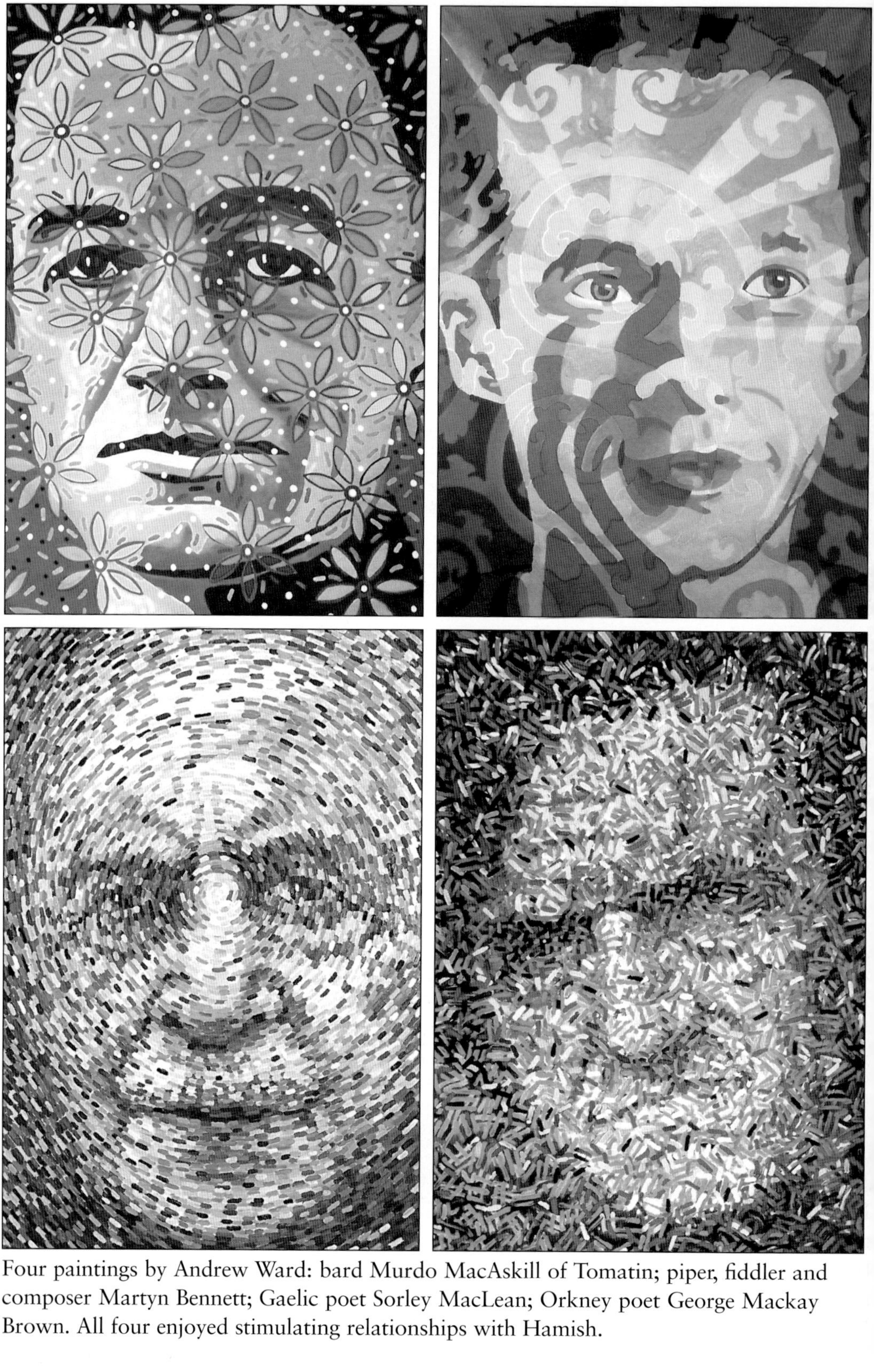

Four paintings by Andrew Ward: bard Murdo MacAskill of Tomatin; piper, fiddler and composer Martyn Bennett; Gaelic poet Sorley MacLean; Orkney poet George Mackay Brown. All four enjoyed stimulating relationships with Hamish.

Following the reopening of the Scottish Parliament, on St Andrew's Day 1999 members of the Vigil for Scottish Democracy ended their six-year protest on Calton Hill. Hamish lit the 'Beacon for Democracy' in an iron chalice constructed by apprentices from Govan. He then made a last, short public speech, supported by Ian Thompson and Dr Alistair McIntosh, and 'The Freedom Come a' Ye' was sung; Heather McMahon on bodhran (IT).

(*Above and facing*). Hamish in Provence, for the wedding of his daughter Janet Henderson to Olivier Hickman, Valréas, July 2000 (Photos: Reginald Hickman; KH).

May 2000, Hamish salutes the Padstow Obby Oss for the last time. Alison McMorland (at his left shoulder) is the pre-eminent singer of Hamish's 'The Flyting o' Life and Daith' (Photo: Geordie McIntyre).

Siohan Miller – singer of the new generation – listens to advice from the master, at the Stewarts of Blair Memorial Concert in Blairgowrie, May 2000 (Photo: Bill Innes; KH).

Cathal O'Connell of The Boys o' the Lough visits Hamish in the Grange Care Home, Edinburgh, November 2001 (Photo: Katzel Henderson).

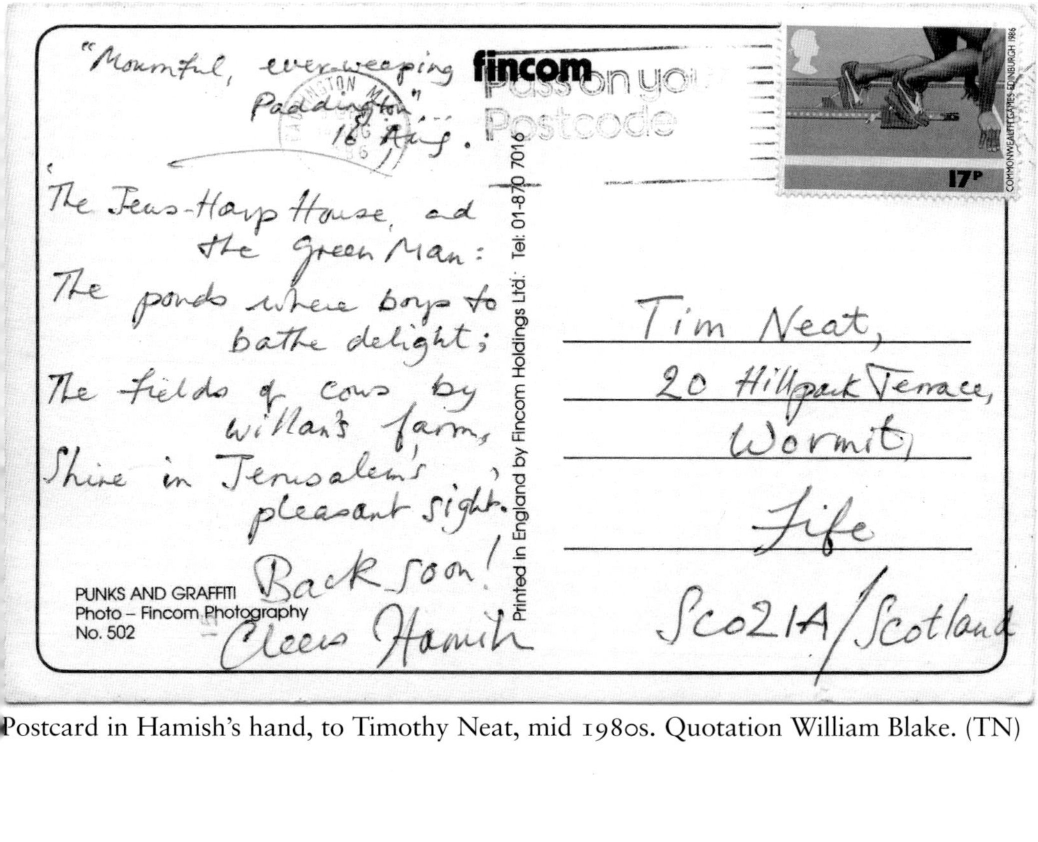

Postcard in Hamish's hand, to Timothy Neat, mid 1980s. Quotation William Blake. (TN)

The poets George Gunn and Angus Calder raise 'the Gramsci Banner', on Ben Gulabin above Glenshee, before the scattering of Hamish's ashes, 4 May 2002 (Photo: Timothy Neat).

Christopher Murray Grieve (Hugh MacDiarmid) digging peats in Shetland in the thirties (Photo: Valda Trevlyn Grieve; KH).

The last of a series of photographs taken three weeks before Hamish's death, on 8 March 2002 (Photo: Timothy Neat).

TWENTY-SIX

At the Forge of Old Age: Literary Achievements in the Later Years

Look! Is that only the setting sun again?
Or a piper coming from far away?[1]

'When you become *Anon*, you've arrived' was a phrase Hamish enjoyed, and he delighted in the knowledge that many of his songs were recurrently assumed traditional. 'Invisibility' had always been one of Hamish's cultural weapons, and the success of his silent 'underground methodology' is well illustrated by the little-known collaboration Hamish enjoyed with the historian Ted Cowan.

In 1979 – as he set out on what would become a distinguished academic career – Edward J. Cowan was commissioned to edit an alternative history of Scotland, *The People's Past – Scottish Folk, Scottish History* (EUSPB 1980). Cowan planned the book in collaboration with Hamish and, although the book is very much Cowan's, Hamish's contribution was important. Hamish wrote the opening essay, the keynote essay, and the poetical postscript that rounds the book out. On publication *The People's Past* was received with considerable enthusiasm and helped make Cowan's reputation. Today, Cowan is Professor of Scottish History at Glasgow University and his philosophical framework as a historian remains very close to that originally defined by Hamish.

Hamish's opening essay to *The People's Past* has an intriguing title: 'It Was in You that It a' Began'. What does this mean? As the essay unfolds we learn that this is a line from a song fragment entitled 'Vive la Republican':[2]

Vive la new convention
        Vive la Republican
Vive la America
        For it was in you that it a' began.

---

1 Hugh MacDiarmid, 'Lament for the Great Music', in the *Complete Poems* (Martin Brian and O'Keeffe 1978).

2 Information supplied by Hamish's School of Scottish Studies colleague Dr Emily Lyle working with the Gavin Greig Collection, Aberdeen.

In the essay Hamish links the song to the eighteenth-century revolutions in America, France and Ireland before revealing that the tune is Scottish ('Willie was a Wanton Wag'). He does not explain the song or this haunting line. Who is the 'you'? What was the 'it' that began it all? Was it the Fall of the Bastille, the 1798 Rising in Ireland? Was it Ancient Athens, Jesus Christ, the Magna Carta, the Scottish Enlightenment? Might 'it' be a reference to Scottish music, dating back to time immemorial? Is the 'you' revolutionary democracy, the republican ideal, socialism, the Folk Revival?

Hamish certainly salutes Republicanism in the age of the European Enlightenment. He also elevates the idea that 'the sang's the thing!', arguing that songs can embody the living energies of peoples, can make and break nations, rather as the Bible informs us that the world began with the 'Word'. He then quotes the great nineteenth-century Italian folklorist Countess Martinengo-Cesaresco: 'the ballad-maker only wields his power for as long as he is the true interpreter of the popular will. Laws may be imposed on the unwilling, but not songs.' He asks why Jacobite songs have lived so long in the hearts of the Scots, and argues that they voice enduring emotions that transcend the moment: that they have 'something of the rebel underground' about them – a rebel *élan* that gives them enduring appeal. He quotes Gramsci: 'That which distinguishes folksong in the framework of a nation and its culture is neither the artistic fact nor the historic origin; it is a separate and distinct way of perceiving life and the world, as opposed to that of "official" society.' This is the nub of his argument: in song, forgotten values can revive and a new consciousness be born. The essence of folksong grows like the Tree of Life, lives like the ideal of Liberty. Quoting Martinengo-Cesaresco again, he writes: 'Proscription does not kill a song. What kills it sometimes, if it is political, is the fulfilment of the hopes it expresses.' Thus, in defeat, the seeds of long-term human wellbeing are sometimes sown.

Hamish was writing in 1979, in the aftermath of Mrs Thatcher's overwhelming electoral success, and was affirming that now was the moment for 'song' to once again come into its own. And perhaps his inference is that he is the carrier: that he is the 'you' who carries the seeds of Scotland's song revival. Another major essay in the book, by Adam McNaughtan, is entitled 'The Folksong Revival in Scotland'. Having raised the spectre of Scotland's cultural and national need in the post-war period, McNaughtan writes:

> And the hour brought forth the man! Hamish Henderson. He worked with Alan Lomax on the collecting tours when so many traditional singers who were to become household names were discovered. With the late Calum Maclean he was one of the first apostles of the School of Scottish Studies. He wrote the Revival's finest songs – he arranged the seminal People's Festivals Ceilidhs . . .

In July 1979, Hamish went to Dundee to receive his first Honorary Doctorate. The prime mover was Professor Geoff Dutton, mathematician and poet, but arrangements were delegated to Dr Kamba, a visiting Nigerian lecturer in English literature. Because Dr Kamba knew nothing about Hamish he phoned to ask me if I would write his citation. After the ceremony, Professor Dutton wrote to Hamish, 'All you have done – and only you could have done it. It was one of those rare occasions when a university does what it should – and the pleasure at your graduation was unanimous.'[3]

On 29 November 1979 the Hellenic Society of Edinburgh and the Edinburgh Greek Students' Association invited Hamish to play a central role in celebrations marking the award of the Nobel Prize for Literature to Odysseus Elytis (the event is described in Volume 1 of this biography). The Edinburgh University Students' Folk Club was also resurrected that autumn by Donald Smith, a young PhD student and Church of Scotland minister from Glasgow. Today, Smith is director of the Scottish Storytelling Centre at the Netherbow, Edinburgh, and well used to the fantastic, but in 1979 he was more than a little surprised when Hamish – invited to re-open the Folk Club – asked Smith to 'disrobe' him in a small anteroom. Hamish said, 'Donald, if this folk club is to begin again – it needs to begin at the beginning' and nine robes were 'ritualistically' taken from his shoulders. Then, 'in utter nakedness Hamish strode out to announce that the Folk Club that he and Stuart MacGregor had founded in 1958 was reborn. It was an evening that changed my life.'[4] Hamish had again become Poor Tom leading his poor players – Jeannie Robertson, Jimmy MacBeath, Stuart MacGregor – back on to the life stage they had left. After this Donald decided his work as a minister would be that of a layman working directly with people and the culture of the folk.

From the late 1970s Hamish was spending a good deal of time as an unpaid consultant to the Salamander Trust, set up in 1976 by Victor Selwyn. Its aim was to conserve and publish the folk poetry of the Second World War. Selwyn had helped set up the original *Oasis* magazine, in Cairo, in 1943. He admired Hamish as the most significant poet to straddle the literary/folk divide. Eric de Mauny, Denis Healey and Spike Milligan also acted as consultants. The Salamander Trust published *Return to Oasis* in 1980, *From Oasis into Italy* in 1983, *The Voice of War* in 1995 and *More Poems of World War II* in 1996. Hamish insisted that the Gaelic war poets be given their rightful place as major war poets. One stimulating by-product of this project was a new friendship, with John Brookes. Brookes served with the Australian Army in Greece and North

3 In 1983 the poet, writer and historian Angus Calder, a long-time friend and admirer of Hamish's, arranged that Hamish be awarded his second Honorary Doctorate by the Open University, in Edinburgh.

4 Donald Smith, conversation with TN, 2007.

Africa and now lived at Castle Cary in Somerset. He had been ordered to hold the Pass of Thermopylae against the advancing Germans in 1941 and used his experience to write a poem, 'Thermopylae', which Hamish thought was wonderful:

> . . . I said to Blue,
> my Aussie mate, 'There was this famous chap
> Leonidas, he was the Spartan who
> defended it with just three hundred men
> against an army.' Bluey took a draw
> upon his cigarette. 'Well stuff 'im then!' . . .
> . . . I said 'They wore
> long hair, the Spartans, a visible proof
> that they were free, not helots, and before
> the battle they would gravely sit aloof
> and garland it with flowers.' Bluey spat.
> . . . With the sounds
> of planes we kept our heads down. After dark
> we dug slit-trenches neath the April moon . . .[5]

On 9 September 1985 Brookes wrote to Hamish:

> To have poetry published at all is an unexpected pleasure; to have someone like yourself taking the trouble to ring me up from far away and tell me it has made some impact seems miraculous, like a half forgotten insurance policy which suddenly produces an unforeseen bonus . . . The war poems (which my wife discovered in our 'glory-hole' under the stairs on seeing Victor Selwyn's advertisement asking for war poems in 1979) were all written in 1941 and all describe true incidents . . . There is a slight Scottish connection, in that the 2nd/5th battalion of the AIF in which I served was affiliated to the Gordon Highlanders – our piper being RSM McLellan.

John Brookes was soon offering his house at Castle Cary as a stop-over for Hamish on his annual pilgrimages to Padstow. There Hamish was introduced to Pam Pope, whom Brookes described as 'an artist, a witch and our local druid'. In the summer of 1987 she gave Brookes a number of four-leafed clovers and he decided to send one to Hamish, who forwarded it to his daughter Janet in France. Shortly afterwards Hamish fell and broke his arm. Learning of this Brookes writes, 'Dear Hamish, Very many thanks for your telephone call, it was stimulating to hear your enthusiastic old Scots voice again. Clearly your broken arm is the result of transferring

---

5 John Brookes, 'Thermopylae', in *Return to Oasis* (Salamander Trust 1980).

the protection that Providence offers to those who possess a four leafed clover from yourself to your daughter; evidently Providence takes little or no account of family loyalties. As a renewal of the insurance policy, I enclose two further clovers (one for yourself and one for Tim Neat) which Pamela Pope's witch-like qualities enable her to find to order.' Later that year, Eric de Mauny (one of the most distinguished BBC reporters of the Second World War) wrote to Hamish:

> I think you have had a letter from Victor Selwyn, asking if you would be prepared to take over as chairman of the Salamander/Oasis trust. I am writing now simply to add my own plea to his . . . It was great fun to meet you last year (at the Imperial War Museum for the launch of the Dent Everyman *Oasis Anthology*) after all these years, but there was little time for reminiscences – do come and stay at Val Gosse – we would love to see you. Yours ever Eric.

Hamish was about to retire from the School of Scottish Studies and declined the offer. However, as his retirement approached, he began, at last, to think seriously about publishing a new collection of his own poetry and this stimulated a brief surge of creativity. These notes on the paintings of William Blake show how vivid his imagination remained:

> As Dante and Virgil wend their way down the translucent tracks of Hell, as the Beasts of Revelation rear up above the multitude, tossing their multiple heads; as the sun boils over and the galaxies become alive with fumbling zodiac figures, Blake's achievement takes on a psalmist's rapture. There are meanings behind all he depicts – the rainbow lands, the complex rants and showdowns, his entire order of creation. So connoisseurship is certainly necessary, up to a point, the more you know about the works the more they signify. But the immediate, instinctive reaction is the best response. That's to say = Hallelujah, Hallelujah![6]

He also wrote a number of short poems, the best entitled 'Michelangelo, Painter':

> Christ and Stone wishes, lead his desire
> Through vein of coral or celestial nudes.
> Tomorrow's love will be rocks
>   and Time
> A breeze that comes sleeping through the branches.[7]

---

6 HH, unpublished manuscript, Henderson archive.

7 HH, unpublished poem, Henderson archive.

In 1985, Joy Hendry had suggested that she make *Chapman* No.42 a special Henderson issue and, to many people's surprise, Hamish had agreed. Raymond Ross and Adam McNaughtan wrote contextualising essays and a slim volume soon appeared.[8]

Indeed, once he was retired, Hamish began to publish quite a lot, particularly in partnership with the editor of the quarterly magazine *Cencrastus*, Raymond Ross. They had first met in the Meadow Bar in Edinburgh at the time of the Anti-Springbok demonstrations in 1969. Ross was sixteen. Following the failure of the Devolution Referendum in 1979, Ross decided that a radical, socialist magazine would be his best means of advancing Scotland's cause, and *Cencrastus* was established. It ran for the next twenty-five years. Ross was a forceful editor but it was Hamish's thinking that gave the magazine much of its character and quality: it mixed articles, poems, artwork and photographs in the grand European tradition. Ross earned his living as a freelance journalist, lecturer and playwright and he persuaded Hamish to write a series of biographical articles over a ten-year period, now republished in *Alias MacAlias* (Polygon 2004).

Over the years Ross had also suggested that Hamish edit a collection of his songs and poems. Hamish would reply, 'my commitment has to be to the oral tradition and the Folk Revival'. But one day, in 1998, when Ross renewed his offer, Hamish said: 'come round tonight'. Over the following eighteen months *Hamish Henderson: Collected Poems and Songs* was assembled and published by Ross's own company, Curly Snake, in 2000. It has a short introduction by Ross and contains one hundred and fourteen poems and songs. The cover, by Fred Crayk, is a drawing of a calloused hand grasping a spiky, moth-like, resurrectional thistle. The book was launched at the Scottish Storytelling Centre. Sales and critical responses were minimal but it is an important book.

In 1990 Alec (Eck) Finlay joined the small group of editors and publishers advancing Hamish's work. By this time, Finlay's father, Ian Hamilton Finlay, was represented by a prestigious German art gallery, which provided him with the financial, artistic and technical help he needed. Hamish, however, remained in desperate need of intellectual and editorial support, and Eck Finlay, to his eternal credit, moved to

8 Ten years later Hendry made *Chapman* No. 82 another Hamish Henderson issue: *Hamish Henderson's Long March*. This contained major essays by Alec Finlay and Angus Calder. In 2000, she organised Hamish's eightieth birthday celebrations at the Hub on Edinburgh's High Street and published a third volume of his works, *The Freedom Come a' Ye – An Eightieth Birthday Souvenir for Hamish Henderson* Adam McNaughton was also guest editor of a special issue of the School of Scottish Studies publication *Tocher*, featuring Hamish's life and collecting, in 1991 (*Tocher* 43).

Edinburgh determined to serve Hamish's literary needs. Their relationship began in the autumn of 1989 with this letter:

> Dear Hamish – thanks to your jovial and generous character I feel like I know you quite well; however, I had better introduce myself . . . I am Eck Finlay, Ian Hamilton Finlay's son and we met briefly last year, when I was selling 'Clamjamfrie' [a magazine created by a young student friend of Hamish's, Giles Sutherland] . . . Soon I will be visiting our mutual friend Tilda Swinton. . . Tilda's a real godsend of warmth and openness and I'm sure she will accomplish great things . . . Would you like to do a folio of your translations of Heine or Holderlin? Either would suit me, perhaps some English and Scots versions . . . my inclination is towards Holderlin . . . As for Pasolini's *L'Appennino* I do hope you feel inspired to translate it. I wish very much to publish it alongside Tom Scott and Sandy Hutchison's Scots translations of Pasolini's Friulian poems. Together these would make a very fine book . . . Carla Sassi will do an introduction, so we will have her beauty and insight – what more could anyone ask . . . I have a copy of *L'Appennino* in front of me – I'm sure you or Carla can bring out the parallels with Sorley – all in all Pasolini is a wonderful illuminator of Scottish culture.

Before their next meeting, Eck Finlay ordered a book of Hamish's essays due for publication by Polygon. When they met, Finlay asked Hamish when the essays would appear:

> And he gave me one of those twinkling looks and pointed to an old cardboard box full of photocopies and clippings, standing in the corner of the kitchen, right by the 2 bar electric fire, and said: 'There they are Eck, would you like to edit them?' So I negotiated with Polygon and started work. My fee was £150 plus the return of my original cheque![9]

Finlay occasionally also joined Hamish's band of domestic assistants.

> I used to help Hamish take a bath, as his hips were both shot by then. He would always just kneel and I'd scrub his back, a bit like a scene in the zoo; but one time he said he wanted to risk lying down properly stretched-out, knowing full well that if he got stuck then I wouldn't be able to shift his bulk. We got to chatting about the war and he talked about Karnak, and then recited the whole of one of Rilke's elegies, I think it was the tenth, in German – with tears in his eyes. It was a strange incident, above all about great art poetry,

9 Alec Finlay, email to TN, 2008.

> and *Germania*. Him being naked, the bath being wet, me sitting on the loo; all that was no more important to me than whether a tinker smelt: he entered a state of deep emotional identification, deeper than anyone I have known. He was back in the desert, and he was at one with Rilke. That is the point of the incident. His ability to transcend.[10]

Finlay soon set himself an ambitious four-part plan. First, he would publish a major collection of Hamish's prose writings; second, he would publish a selection of letters; third, he would initiate the writing of a major biography (possibly an autobiography); fourth, he would begin editing *The Complete Poems of Hamish Henderson*. Only two of these objectives were realised but what Finlay achieved was of permanent importance. In 1992 *Alias MacAlias*: *Writings on Songs, Folk and Literature,* Hamish Henderson, edited by Alec Finlay (Polygon), was published. It contained an introduction by Dr Angus Calder but lacked substantial contextualisation and, as with the *Collected Poems*, the critical response was minimal.

For Hamish the book's title *Alias MacAlias* had a philosophical importance. He had used the same the title for an article about MacDiarmid, published in *Scottish International* (No. 6) in 1969. It was the communality of life and artistic production that he wanted readers to think about. The essays are full of ideas but publication stimulated hardly a ripple of interest, and institutional rejection of the book seems to have been the order of the day. On I January 1993 Martin Green wrote from Liskeard in Cornwall: 'Dear Hamish . . . having made enquiries I learn that no library in the UK has purchased a copy!' Such wilful rejection stimulated Freddie Freeman to write an 'open letter' to the *Scotsman*:

> The silence is deafening. Why has no one fully appreciated or even taken exception to Hamish Henderson's recently published essays, *Alias MacAlias*, which so clearly mark a watershed in Scottish history? I suspect it is because his comments on social class and oral tradition sit well with no one . . . [his] arguments regarding the dynamic and resilient nature of Scottish culture are nothing short of revolutionary; his reflections on art, language and social interaction exceedingly controversial. They endeavour to counter-blast all naysaying claims, emanating from right and left, which see Scotland's history since 1603 onwards, as a process of fragmentation and loss, socially, psychologically and artistically. At a time when our thinking tends to be polarised and blinkered he risks misinterpretation for truth.[11]

10 Alec Finlay, email to TN, 2008.

11 Freddie Freeman, draft letter in Henderson archive.

In 1994 Finlay's Morning Star Press published *The Obscure Voice* – translations by Hamish of six of his favourite Italian poems. The booklet is introduced by Dr Carla Sassi and illustrated by Ian McKeever.

In 1996 Polygon published *The Armstrong Nose – Selected Letters of Hamish Henderson*, edited by Alec Finlay. This contains an impressive 45 page 'Afterword' entitled 'A River That Flows On – A critical overview of Hamish Henderson's life and work', in which Finlay addresses the totality of Hamish's intellectual and creative achievement. This was the first such evaluation and it remains the best.[12] The critical response to *The Armstrong Nose* was relatively positive and the book was shortlisted for the 1997 Ruth Michaelis–Jena Ratcliff Prize (for books on folklore).[13] Unfortunately, I was joint winner of the prize for my book *The Summer Walkers* (sharing the £4,000 prize money with Ben Buxton for *The Vatersay Raiders*). I told Hamish I would much rather have shared the prize with him.

Because Hamish had been closely involved with the creation of *The Summer Walkers* and I had used many of his photographs in the book, I sent him a cheque for a thousand pounds. To disguise the fact that my letter contained a cheque I sent it in a cheap brown envelope. Presuming it to be a bill, Hamish tore it up and flushed it down the toilet. Hearing nothing from him, I phoned to ask whether he had received the cheque. He couldn't remember. Slowly the truth dawned on him and on 30 June he wrote: 'Dear Tim . . . you should have seen the easy nonchalance with which I tore a thousand pound cheque into small pieces and chucked 'em down the toilet bowl! It was a scene that I certainly could never have foreseen, and which can well describe as a one-off. All the same, I can't deny that it was with a certain regretful nostalgia that I recollected that scene when I woke up this morning!' Three years later, Calum and Rory Macdonald, of the Gaelic band Runrig, wrote a barn-storming song entitled 'The Summer Walkers', which pays moving tribute to the Travellers, my book and Hamish's pioneering research:

Sometimes when you journey
Through the pages of a book
You're taken places beyond words
You let them speak their truth

---

12 This Afterword has now been rewritten and enlarged as the introduction to Polygon's 2004 second edition of *Alias MacAlias*.

13 Finlay has raised the question as to whether the art-poem/folksong split in Hamish's literary career echoes a split in his life's progress. When he was part of a coherent male community at school, at university, in the army, he wrote art poetry. When he returned, alone, to the incoherent and sexually repressive Scotland of the post-war period, he fell headlong in love with the communality of folksong. This Finlay suggests might explain Hamish's inability to write a second great book.

Today I've opened treasures
That my eyes could scarce believe
They're the words of confirmation
Everything that makes me sing . . .

Now your words are not of sentiment
Shallow or untrue
But wells of living water
And from their clear deep sides we drew
The songs, the tin, the horses
This country's great and ancient wilds
Your faith in God and man and nature
And the keenness of your guile . . .
For you were the summer walkers
And the fishers of the pearl.[14]

The fourth and last young publisher to shape Hamish's later years was Nicholas Johnson from North Devon. In 1992 he established the Six Towns Poetry Festival at Newcastle-under-Lyme, and in 1995 Hamish was a festival guest speaker. Johnson was already working on a collection of poetry by Hamish, Sorley MacLean and Tom Scott, and Hamish played a major part in its completion because Scott was dead and MacLean was very old. Hamish copied out most of his own poems by hand and sent them to Devon on scrappy bits of paper (as though he were a schoolboy again). But it was with Roman firmness he insisted the collection be titled *Pervigilium Scotiae*: *Scotland's Vigil* and contain this Afterword.

> Scotland has always been a multi-lingual country and its poets have usually had at least three languages at their disposal. In 1637 the Aberdeen poet Arthur Johnston edited an anthology of Scottish Latin poets entitled *Delitiae Poetarum Scotorum*; this included work by the famous humanist scholar George Buchanan (a native Gaelic speaker), whom Dr. Samuel Johnson was later to call 'a poetical genius'. In our own century native English speakers have learned and written notable poetry in Scottish Gaelic.
>
> The title of the present reader *Pervigilium Scotiae* (Scotland's Vigil) can boast therefore a formidable historical resonance; it recalls the days of the Scottish Latin poets . . . but also recalls the noble self-sacrificing devotion of the young Scottish Home Rulers who maintained a Vigil on Edinburgh's Calton Hill from 1992 until the successful Referendum result of 1997. It also recalls, of course, the

14 *Flower of the West: the Runrig Songbook* (Ridge Press, Aberdeen).

wonderful anonymous (and much anthologised) Latin song-poem *Pervigilium Veneris* (The Vigil of Venus).[15]

The collection came out as a handsome, large-format paperback of 126 pages. Its launch coincided with the penultimate Six Towns Poetry Festival. Flora MacNeil and Kenna Campbell were there and helped inspire Hamish to give an outstanding public performance that I recorded on video. Driving him back to Scotland I mentioned that I had written a poem about his death, following a dream on 24 October. 'Tim' he said, 'I want to hear this – stop the car!' Beyond Penicuik, I drew into a lay-by and read him 'Hamish Henderson's Last Goodnight' (see Appendix 3).[16]

Sometimes when I visited Hamish at home, he would ask me to read from my book *Part Seen, Part Imagined*; one piece on Originality, by a young Glasgow art student named Janet Aitken, written in 1893, visibly struck him:

> Everyone is original in the true sense of the word, but every mind has not this power of impressing itself on other minds; of forcing them to see its light and no other . . . it is the focusing of light upon one point, commonly called the concentration of energy, which alone can bring general recognition of originality. Men and women are only original because they cannot help themselves. With the original character it is always 'Here I stand I can do no other'. No man did an original thing intentionally, your true original is unconscious – it is a great matter for a man to find his own line and keep to it. . . It is not the amount of genius or moral power expended, but concentrated, that makes what the world calls a great man.[17]

One chapter heading in this book is a quotation from Maurice Maeterlinck, 'The Three Words' (the words being 'I love you', or 'God is Love'). Perhaps this and Janet Aitken's extract inspired Hamish because, one night at about this time, he suddenly scrawled out the following statement – spread over seven pages:

> The Three Words. Love: Love is the only God that I believe in.

15 Afterword, in Tom Scott, Sorley MacLean, Hamish Henderson, *Pervigilium Scotiae: Scotland's Vigil* (Etruscan Press 1997).

16 In May 1997 Hamish gave a poetry reading at a pub in Iddesleigh, North Devon. Johnson asked Hamish if he had made plans for his funeral. Hamish answered: 'No. But they always bury you well in Scotland.'

17 Quoted in Timothy Neat, *Part Seen, Part Imagined – Meaning and Symbolism in the Work of Charles Rennie Mackintosh and Margaret Macdonald* (Canongate 1994).

> The books of the Holy Bible never say but one time just exactly what love is, and in those three little words it pours out a hundred million college educations, and says, God is love. And that is the only real definitive answer to the ten thousand wild queries and questions that I my own self tossed at my bible – that is the only real sensible easy honest warm plain quick and clear answer I found – when I was too ready to throw so-called cowardly thieving poisonous religion out of my back door. It was those three words that made not only religion but also several other sorts of superstitious fears and hatreds in me meet a very quick death. God is love. God is really love. Love casts out hate. Love gets rid of all fears. Love washes all clean. Love forgives all debts. Love forgets all mistakes. Love overcomes all errors, and excuses and pardons and understands the reason why the mistake, the error, the stumble was made. Love heals all. Love operates faster and surer than time or space or both. Love does not command you, order you, dictate to you. Love asks rather for you to tell its forces what to do, and where to go, and how to build up your planet here by the blueprint plan of your heart's desire. Love can't operate on your behalf as long as your own sickly fear will not permit love to operate on your behalf. Your love commands must ever be just exactly the direct opposite of war's crazy baseless hatreds, peace, peace, and sweet peace must be the song on your tongue tip. – Peace is love. Love is peace. – Your love command must for all eternity be your peace command. [18]

Why did Hamish not write more such statements, more poetry of the kind people expect of a major poet? One famous literary 'failure' that seems to parallel Hamish's so-called failure is that of Walt Whitman. During the American Civil War, Whitman so gave himself to his fellow man that his poetry never recovered. Harold Bloom, writing in the *Guardian* on 17 December 2005, hits the nail on the head.

> Day after day, for several years, [Whitman] had exhausted himself, in the military hospitals of Washington DC, dressing wounds, reading to, and writing letters for, the ill and maimed, comforting the dying. The extraordinary vitalism and immediacy departed from his poetry. It is as if he had sacrificed his own imagination on the altar of those martyred, like Lincoln, in the fused cause of union and emancipation.

It was not so much war service as allegiance to 'the folk' that exhausted Hamish. He himself was aware of the problem as early as the 1960s,

18 HH, unpublished notes, Henderson archive.

when he noted: 'The collector grows to become owned by his subjects; if a collector cannot thole this responsibility – he shouldn't be a collector.'[19] The idea that the committed artist must lose and dissolve himself in service of the people is a recurrent motif in Hamish's writings. In 1950 he described the poet's search for 'lyric perfection – in exchange for the sacrifice of the creator', and in his 'Fourth Elegy' he writes:

> The sons of man
> grow and go down in pain: they kneel for the load
> and bow like brutes, in patience accepting the burden,
> the pain fort and dour . . .[20]

For Hamish, literature was only part of the wholeness of life and, as Charles Darwin had been thrilled to make contact with pigeon-fanciers and apple-growers, so Hamish exulted in the company of miners, pearl fishers, horse-breeders and street-crawlers – they stimulated his mind, they opened horizons; he believed everyman had his place on the great wheel of progress. He sought knowledge and found pleasure in unique qualities resident within what the unthinking would describe as the undifferentiated mass: he would conjure love where it was not, nurtured poetry where it was hidden.

Poets like MacDiarmid, hungry for 'immortal lyrics', often wilfully forget their sources. Magic realists like Gabriel Garcia Márquez use the fantastic theatre of folk-belief as the engine of their own high literary achievement. Hamish subordinated his pursuit of personal artistry in an attempt to empower and enable the folk themselves. Sir Bernard Crick in a critique of the first volume of this biography described the soldiers of the Pioneer Corps as 'the lowest of the low'; Hamish loved 'the humble lowly' and found in them a poetry rarely roused in university common rooms. He believed poetry – like the air – was fresher in a tinker tent than in a palace.

Amongst the major twentieth-century writers it was probably James Joyce who anticipated Hamish's all-inclusive philosophy most closely. His immersion in Dublin, in the life of the Liffey, in the surging oral traditions of Ireland, preceded Hamish's immersion in Scottish life, but whereas Joyce went abroad to write big books, Hamish returned from the Second World War determined to repoint and sculpt the House of Scotland. Hamish's profligacy was part of his life's philosophy.

---

19 HH, unpublished notes, Henderson archive. Marian Blythman remembers a ditty Hamish used to sing at this time that reinforces that idea:

> I would hae been a straight working fellow
> If it wisnae for the ferrograph machine:
> I was tall and I was handsome – till I got the ferrograph . . .

20 HH, Fourth *Elegy, Elegies for the Dead in Cyrenaica* (Polygon 2008).

This profligacy brings us back to the letter E.P. Thompson wrote to Hamish in 1949: 'Remember always who you are writing for: . . . you must not forget that your songs and ballads – are quite as important as the Elegies.' Few educated people believe Thompson's point to be true but this letter is doubly important because the sentiments expressed were Hamish's own. Like Burns, Hamish was a song poet who grew up knowing song to be an ingrained fact of the Scots psyche. For him, poetry could not be divorced from song. Song becomes poetry, poetry becomes people. Immortality, if it exists, must exist in the marriage of the individual with his fellows – in art, in nature. After an evening at a communist play Hamish noted: 'The search for gold: – the more I bring off and accomplish in life, for the happiness of those close to me, the longer I shall live after death.' In Hamish's archive there is a newspaper clipping headlined, 'Love Darg at Newtyle'. A love darg was a day when a whole community came together to give a day's labour in honour of a newly-wed couple. Their house, their croft, their lives would be set going with a will and with joy. Hamish saw his life as a love darg and knew such work would bring pain as well as pleasure. At the time of MacDiarmid's sixtieth birthday and the Folksong Flyting, in 1962, he put it directly:

> Scotland hates and fears its creative writers. Why is there here this conspiracy of the old against the young – which you get everywhere – but which with us is so blatantly tyrannical? It goes back to the fantastic theocratic tyranny of C17th and the attempt to divide the nation into a small, elect elite and the damned mass . . . This brings us back to MacDiarmid, for his vision of literature grows out of this tyrannical division – there is an artistic elite and there is folk culture. But Christ died for all men and Scots literature arises out of the whole Scots people.[21]

---

21 HH, unpublished notes, Henderson archive.

TWENTY-SEVEN

Per Bacco! Struggling to Hold On

Dinnae fa' cause it gets ye doon.
'a kid in Melville Terrace', HH

The last struggle of most human beings is with their own bodies: Hamish's body was large and his last struggle began early. By the time of his marriage in 1959 he was already partially dependent on alcohol and by the time I met him in 1967 he knew himself he had a problem. He had been a heavy, convivial drinker for thirty years – in the army, in revolutionary politics, on the folk scene – it was part of his life as a Scot and, whilst he knew the dangers, he believed any cure likely to be far more damaging than the disease. Drinking was for him an act of compotation, of communion – a secular laying-on of hands. Like Boswell, he believed controlled drinking 'one of the great arts of living', and he liked to quote Boswell's riposte to Johnson's refusal of a dram:

> He urged that in proportion as drinking makes a man different from what he was before he was drunk, it is bad, because it has so far affected his reason. But may it not be answered that a man might be altered by it *for the better*, that his spirits may be exhilarated without his reason being affected.

Whisky is, however, a two edged-sword. In December 1973, coming home after a session at Sandy Bell's, Hamish fell on ice outside his flat and struggled upstairs with a painful arm. Katzel describes him, 'tholing it for hours, in his chair, in the kitchen. Next morning I insisted he see a doctor. Finally he went. The bones in his right elbow were badly splintered.' In 1974 Hamish suffered a devastating attack of pneumonia that marooned him in St Mary's Hospital in Paddington for two months (as mentioned). In 1975 Katzel moved out with their daughters. In the same year he had an operation for piles and remained in hospital for almost a week. Katzel visited and found the American student/folklorist Linda Williamson with him. I happened to call in on the day on which Generalissimo Franco died so I greeted him: 'Well Hamish, we've got something to celebrate – Franco is dead!' He replied, 'Ah Tim – I wouldn't celebrate the death of any man.' In 1978, he fell again and broke his hip. After hospitalisation in Edinburgh he was sent for recuperation to the Veterans' Home at Musselburgh. He enjoyed himself there, getting visits from Lorne Maclaine Campbell VC (another Old Alleynian) and Sorley MacLean.

Living alone in a six-roomed flat, Hamish gradually began to realise that he needed some kind of home-help cum pub-companion cum personal-assistant. Consequently, he began a series of friendships with young men who offered various combinations of help. The first was Robert Hawkes (eldest son of Hamish's old friends from Dry Drayton, Leo and Violet Hawkes). In the mid seventies Robert had come to Edinburgh as a postgraduate researcher in atomic physics, and after Hamish broke his hip Robert gave him regular support. He bought food, helped him in the flat, and gave him a shoulder home from Sandy Bell's. In 1980, Robert left Edinburgh to take up a prestigious research post in the United States.

Soon, Russell Butchard, a footloose young man who enjoyed the Sandy Bell's life, took over Robert's role. A renowned womaniser, Russell was not shy about putting Hamish to bed or helping him into the bath. Russell accompanied Hamish to folk festivals, concerts, conferences and the theatre: he also smoked and sold cannabis. Travelling through Spain after a visit to Morocco in 1982, Russell was arrested for possession of hashish. He got a year in El Centro Penitenciario, Badajoz. Conditions were hard and, as usual, Hamish sprang into action – writing letters, sending books and encouraging all and sundry to do the same. On 17 February 1983 Russell wrote to Hamish:

> Thank you for your last three letters and the enclosures – the book I look forward to reading in the library – and basking in . . . The drastic liberalisation that Spain is making in the hashish laws is going to have some interesting and far reaching consequences for the whole of Europe – thus I hope to have the pleasure of your company towards the end of the month . . . Here we get no hot food and there is no heating – I am writing this with a sack on my hand.

Back in Scotland, Russell soon went his own way. Meanwhile Hamish had been to the Edinburgh Dog Pound, with his daughter Janet, to get her a puppy for her thirteenth birthday. The dog would live with Hamish but be walked and fed by Janet, which meant Janet would see a lot more of her father. They chose a black and tan collie–alsatian named Sandy. He was three-quarters grown and half-trained; within six months he was the size of a she-wolf, but remained half-trained for the rest of his life. Hamish grew very fond of Sandy, fascinated by his animality and the impact he made on those around him. For years Hamish had found pub 'closing-hours' a useful discipline on his drinking but now, as the new drinking laws opened the doors of irresponsibility, Hamish used Sandy as his 'shaper of days'. Paddy O'Neill, one of Hamish's later helpers, describes the dog: 'Sandy was Hamish's conscience. Sandy would yelp at the pub door when he wanted home or when he sensed his maister had

had more than enough!' Sandy also helped Hamish to stay close to Janet during her teens. He was an intelligent dog with a wonderful sense of humour and was devoted to all the family.

Hamish was now a senior lecturer at the University of Edinburgh, but he and Sandy became almost inseparable. Sandy became Hamish's regular companion at lectures, in Sandy Bell's bar, and at restaurants across Edinburgh. Questions would be asked, doors were closed, confrontations occurred. The idea that this man was an eccentric got a new lease of life. This irritated Hamish. He had always strongly opposed any suggestion that he or his ideas were eccentric.

For Hamish, Sandy was a manifestation of life – he was Everydog. By giving this mongrel the chance of a life, he was asserting a life principle beyond breeding, money, laws or class propriety. In the 1980s dogs were still free to wander the Meadows in Edinburgh, and Sandy did – daily with Janet and Katzel, sometimes with Hamish, sometimes alone. Taken to Leith, to be lodged for a weekend, Sandy would sometimes escape and be back at Melville Terrace within the hour! Sandy became part of the theatre of Hamish's life: as St Francis had celebrated the wolf, Hamish celebrated this city-dog.

In 1983 Hamish's elder daughter, Tina, announced that she was going to marry Charlie Marshall, a young insurance man she'd met at a dance in Edinburgh. Katzel and Hamish thought Tina was too young (at nineteen) and, as she was still at university, they wondered whether she might be sensible to wait a year or two. But the couple were keen to go ahead and a grand wedding was soon arranged. A traditional Church of Scotland ceremony was followed by a reception at the Lady Nairn Hotel by Duddingston Loch. Lizzie Higgins sang at the wedding, and friends came from near and far. Hamish made a traditional 'father-of-the-bride speech' and led the dancing with aplomb.

After the wedding, money was in short supply and, to cover his debts, Hamish sold a number of his more valuable manuscripts including letters from MacDiarmid, Jeannie Robertson, George Campbell Hay, Kathleen Raine, Fionn MacColla, Sydney Goodsir Smith and Robert Garioch, mostly to the National Library of Scotland. This represented a tiny percentage of his vast archive and, having made photocopies of the material that was sold, the historical completeness of the archive was minimally affected.

Hamish's third long-term assistant, Michael Law, came from Hawick. Michael had been unemployed for some time and was struggling to find himself after years of youthful wandering. He met Hamish at a party at the house of William Montgomerie to launch a new book of Montgomerie's poems, *Time to Time* (1985). Michael spoke to Hamish about his interest 'in poetry – poetry spoken and sung – not dead on the page'. Hamish was delighted and soon had his 'new apprentice' reciting his poems in Sandy Bell's. In 1987, after Hamish had another bad fall, Michael moved into 20 Melville Terrace to care for Hamish:

> We were walking down steps from the University library. He stumbled forward and crashed sideways. I knew he was badly hurt. I helped him across to the School. His femur was splintered. It was amazing that he walked at all. We phoned for an ambulance; then he was taken off to the Royal Infirmary. After that I moved into the flat. I stayed only about a year but remained on-call until I got married in 1989. Hamish helped me through a very difficult time. Looking back I can see he made me what I am. Poetry meant so much to Hamish. He would sit and read aloud in his chair. And he would so move himself, he'd have to stop. He would look up and raise his hand, moving it very slightly to the right, and say 'strong poetry, Michael'. And the tears would be coming down his cheeks.

On his retirement at the end of August 1987, Hamish was pleasantly surprised by his financial situation. He got a tax-free gratuity of £32,000 plus three pensions: a state pension of £96.45 per week, an Army disability pension of £91.32 per month, and a University pension of £1,032 per month (these amounts as per 1996). He retained his office and continued a close association with the School, becoming an Honorary Fellow.

On 29 June 1987 Murray Ritchie quoted Hamish in an article in the *Glasgow Herald*: 'You are a journalist and you must look the world in the eye but I am a poet and I perhaps look at the greater truth.' Ritchie continued, 'like so many of the literary leftists who became non-persons in Scotland after the war, Henderson is a Scottish republican socialist'. This recognition of Hamish as a political 'non-person' in Scotland is nicely counter-balanced by a tale told by Alasdair Gray (author of the acclaimed novel *Lanark*). Gray was staying at Hawthornden Castle, a retreat for poets and writers, with novelist Ian Rankin, and poets George MacBeth and Ruth Fainlight. One night they were discussing ballads. Ruth Fainlight spoke of her interest in 'The Ballad of the Speaking Heart': she said she thought it was French but knew nothing else about it. So Gray rang Hamish: 'Hamish, this is Alasdair Gray – I'm out at Hawthornden. Do you know a ballad called "The Ballad of the Speaking Heart"?' Hamish answered, 'Yes, I know it. Do you want me to sing it?' The four writers gathered round the phone and Hamish sang the whole ballad. Gray then asked, 'And do you know who wrote it, Hamish?' 'I did', came the reply, 'and the tune's based upon "La Chanson de Marie-des-Anges" by Jean Richepin; his dates were 1849 to 1926. Is there anything else you need to know?' The ballad remained unpublished until 1995, when it appeared in Joy Hendry's *Chapman* celebration of Norman MacCaig's eighty-fifth birthday.

One of the consequences of Edinburgh's burgeoning prosperity in the 1980s was the establishment of the Scotch Malt Whisky Society in Leith, and in 1988 Hamish was made 'Honorary Malt Whisky Drinker of the Year'. Pip Hills organised things and Hamish found himself delivered of a dozen splendid malts. In exchange Hamish gave the 'Immortal Memory' at the Society's Burns Night. In 1989 he was sent a second case of malt and another invitation to celebrate Burns Night. That year, writer Liz Lochhead and historian Michael Fry were the prime guests. Guests were surprised to see Hamish arrive accompanied by two beautiful young women – his daughters Tina and Janet. Hamish also insisted that I got a ticket, as his minder. It was another grand night. Michael Fry got drunk and, in the old Oxbridge manner, started throwing bread around the hall and shouting abuse. He was finally escorted out into the cold to await a taxi home. Perhaps it was this incident that reminded Hamish to jot down something Professor David Daiches had told him years previously: 'Gentility in Scotland was *willed*, deliberately sought for as a substitute for a lost courtliness and indeed a lost literary language.'

Hamish was now drinking himself close to oblivion most nights and, whilst he sometimes continued to sing and speak vigorously into the small hours, his powers of intellectual concentration fluctuated. In bars, searching for clarity of focus, he would suddenly exclaim, 'Ah, Tim – ma heid's in a creel!' It was a surreal and brilliant image. His reputation guaranteed that he would be bought drinks wherever he went, and he had always found it hard to refuse a well-meant offer. Seeing a bar lined up 'wi' drinks for me!' he would drink the lot and drip the dregs of each dram into a pint. It was 'bardic payment' for a lifetime's singing. Fortunately he never got indigestion and rarely a bad hangover. A typical tale of Hamish's life at this time comes from Stewart D. Brown of Newport-on-Tay. 'Hamish came to speak at the Dundee Folk Festival. Afterwards he installed himself in the bar while the ceilidh unfolded upstairs. As "The Freedom Come a' Ye" finished, a young lad rushed up to tell me: "There's an auld geezer downstairs, blootered, but he has a' the words to that ane!"'

The magazine *Cencrastus* organised celebrations for Hamish's seventieth birthday. The hall of St Paul's Episcopal Church was hired for a night of poetry, song, music and remembrance. When, at one o'clock in the morning, the Gay Gordons was called, it was Ruth Frame,[1] one of Scotland's leading auld-style dancers, who led Hamish on to the floor. He found it difficult to twirl her, so she took the man's role and started twirling him! He crashed to the floor. We got him to a bench. He lay there, white with shock. I asked: 'Hamish, are you all right?' 'Tim,' he said 'this is life, this is what life is.' He'd broken his wrist.

1991 was to be the year of the death of Sandy. The dog died of a cancerous

1 Ruth Frame is a dancer and singer (from a Plymouth Brethren background) whom Hamish had befriended and inspired: in 1985 she wrote, 'Dear Hamish, Just a wee note. Truly you are lovely and beautiful. Even if we were never to meet again, you have shared something with me, something I will treasure for the rest of my life. Thank you for the day. Love and a smile – Ruth'.

growth brought on, Hamish believed, by a fall on the stairs outside his flat. With Sandy dead, a number of people worried about Hamish's future but, although he felt Sandy's loss like a death in the family, Hamish's overwhelming commitment was to life and he moved on.

In the spring of 1991 Professor Frank Bechhofer, director of the Social Science Research Centre at Edinburgh University, put Hamish's name forward for an Honorary Degree. The proposal did not succeed in the first round but the following year Bechhofer renewed his proposal and won his case. It was he who gave the Laureation address, on 16 July 1992:

> Mr Vice-Chancellor, in the name and by the authority of the Senatus Academicus, I have the honour to present for the degree of Doctor *honoris causa* Hamish Scott Henderson. Scholar and man of the people, poet, folklorist and collector, writer and singer of songs, political activist and personification of the best form of Scottish culture which is not inward looking but confident and international . . . To hold a conversation with Hamish is to encounter anecdote, profound scholarship and erudition, humour, passion, and a deep affection for human beings and their culture . . .

On 13 September 1992 Hamish joined in the Hugh MacDiarmid Centenary celebrations in Langholm, speaking in company with Sorley MacLean, Iain Crichton Smith, Edwin Morgan and Norman MacCaig. His speech was published in Chapman's *MacDiarmid Centenary Issue*. It shows how arguments offered with the humour and irony on a public platform can look self-centred on the printed page. Good oratory can look slack in print.

Hamish now had two new helpers, Paul Fernie and Paddy O'Neill. Both were in their twenties, married, working part-time and pleased to join Hamish's circle. They didn't much like each other but Hamish established an informal system of rotation that suited them all reasonably well for almost ten years. Both came from Irish backgrounds. Paul was dark with tight curls; shy, good-natured but prone to both laziness and irresponsibility. Paddy was red-haired with frizzy curls, mild-mannered, ultra-loyal, hardworking and very much his own man. Paul did significant 'library research' for Hamish as Eck Finlay prepared the books *Alias MacAlias* and *The Armstrong Nose* for publication. Both men had to bear the stigma of being recurrently ridiculed as 'Hamish's latest bum boys'. Both were, however, contented heterosexuals, and Hamish became inordinately fond of the children of both his helpers.

Why did the rumours of Hamish's homosexuality circulate so long and so widely? Over many years various people liked to assume and spread the rumour that Hamish and I had a homosexual relationship.

We did not. Indeed, twelve years passed before I even knew people suspected Hamish of being a homosexual. This was when Cathy Mangan, the American wife of the poet Gerry Mangan, warned my wife about my relationship with Hamish: because 'everyone knows Hamish is a homosexual'. In 2007 I discussed this issue with the journalist Alan Taylor. He told me, 'if Norman MacCaig was in a bar and saw Hamish, he would look up, nod across, and announce loudly: "Do you see that man over there? He's a homo!".' MacCaig's boldness epitomises a wider social malaise: the need to pigeon-hole 'outsiders': Hamish's bohemian tastes, mysteriously English background, his gusto for what might be described as 'the Franco-Italian, Greco-Turkish life-style' singled him out as a mark for his foes. That Hamish, lifelong, publicly spoke up for gay rights was seen as clear evidence of a personal addiction to sodomy!

Naturally such suggestions were manna to those officers and agents working for British Intelligence who kept a recurrent eye on Hamish throughout his life. Even after homosexuality was decriminalised in 1967 for at least two decades it remained a sword of Damocles suspended above anyone with political ambitions. Hamish loved men and boys as he loved beautiful women, ugly women, young girls in their innocence, dogs in their dogginess, beautiful paintings, bawdy songs, dirty jokes, brilliant minds,[2] the music of the Hebrides and the view west from Morar. He had a unified cultural sensibility, he exulted in joy; William Blake more than Burns was his sexual exemplar:

> The monumental mason
> Will clip that angel's wings
> Or will he be a choir-boy
> Aloft where angels sing?[3]

As his seventy-fifth birthday approached, Hamish wrote to Canon Kenyon Wright,[4] asking him whether he would conduct his funeral service, 'when the time comes'. Kenyon Wright replied on 21 July 1994:

> Thank you for your note. I would of course be honoured to conduct the service at your – distant I trust – funeral. I hope I'll not be called

---

2 In 1992 I told him about an eccentric retired sea-captain from Newport-on-Tay, an SNP enthusiast and inventor, who had designed a new hull with a variable keel – for racing yachts – that would win the Americas Cup! At this Hamish's eyes lit up. When I added, 'Of course, I expect it's all pie-in-the-sky', he looked at me: 'Tim, if you believe that – you don't know Scotland.'

3 HH, unpublished poem (after Blake), Henderson archive.

4 A leading campaigner for a Scottish Parliament and a member, with Hamish, of the Scottish Refugee Council.

> to such a duty for a very long time – indeed you may be attending mine first! Such is life. *'Sic transit Gloria mundi'*. I hope to see you soon – I mean alive and kicking!

Kenyon Wright then put Hamish's letter in his wallet where it remained for seven years, until news of Hamish's death reached him. And it was he who conducted the funeral service at St Mary's Cathedral in Edinburgh – in white robes and with eloquent, reverent command. Hamish liked to keep death as far from his door as possible but when it loomed he addressed it with style and propriety, 'wanting', as the poet Charles Causley had told him, 'things to be done as they belong to be done'. When his friend Tom Scott went into hospital Hamish visited him like a pastor. On 24 August 1995 Heather Scott wrote to him:

> Dear Hamish, I was so happy when Tom told me that you had been to see him in hospital, and that you had given him the beautiful book on Celtic Britain which I and my family will always treasure . . . Tom was already far on his journey away from us when you saw him, but I know it meant a great deal to Tom that you and he made that meeting of friendship at the end – your appreciation and reminiscences were read at the funeral service . . . You and Tom were always on the same side really – fighting for the same cause of Freedom and Justice. Long may you continue to do so.

On 27 July 1996 Hamish attended the ninetieth birthday celebrations of Belle Stewart at Keithbank Mill, Blairgowrie. He was sporting a black eye and entered the Mill to a rousing 'tinkers' welcome': Belle, swathed in Stewart tartan, greeted him like a Prince and the two well-worn old codgers were soon chortling like lovers. They had been dear friends for forty-five years. A year later Hamish returned to Blair for Belle's funeral. Frank Bechhofer's wife Jean was his driver. Hamish led the tributes at the post-burial ceilidh but, driving back to Edinburgh, Jean reports him 'worrying all the way. Had he done Belle justice, had he said the right things? I said he'd done very well. Slowly he cheered up and when I helped him out of the car he asked me if I would drive him to Padstow for May Day!'

Sorley MacLean died in November 1996. Hamish took the train to the Kyle of Lochalsh. The artist Will Maclean drove me. When we met Hamish in Portree, I told him how we had crashed into a rutting stag in Kintail. He said: 'Tim, that was very appropriate' and he quoted from 'Hallaig':

> and when the sun goes down behind Dun Cana
> a vehement bullet will come from the gun of love;

and will strike the deer that goes dizzily,
sniffing at the grass-grown ruined homes;
his eye will freeze in the wood,
his blood will not be traced while I live.[5]

The following January Norman MacCaig died in Edinburgh. Hamish was quite frail but insisted on attending the funeral service. Leaving the church, a photograph shows him noble, patrician and calmly in charge of his faculties. However, he was medically now far from well. In a notebook he writes 'Permanent leg ulcers (treated with Hyperbaric Oxygen Therapy), recurrent bouts of gout (treated with Amoxicillin – Clav Acid 250), phlebitis and Triludan [for] catarrh.' When prescribed antibiotics he would rather proudly refrain from alcohol for a day or two, then gleefully return to a diet of beer and malt whisky. His flat had now become his castle. He slept under blankets in a narrow divan bed in the north-facing master bedroom. It had a chair, a wall-sized bookcase and house telephone. He kept a plastic basin by the bed for use as a pot and spittoon. Lacking central heating, the flat was heated by three or four moveable electric heaters. Hamish would usually rise late, make a pot of tea and boil himself two eggs (timed to four minutes precisely). He ate them with buttered bread or toast and would listen to the news. Sometimes the *Scotsman* and *Guardian* would be brought in by a helper; otherwise he would potter along the road to get them. Towards lunchtime he would check his post at the School of Scottish Studies and then wander on to Sandy Bell's. One day, Paddy O'Neill was grumbling about the 'unfairness' of things: Hamish retorted with firmness, 'Paddy, there's nothing fair in life! You'll have to get used to it, or do something about it!!' Age and alcohol seemed to keep him on the edge of a semi-permanent euphoria.

When I visited him at his flat, usually to discuss imminent events or new projects, I would arrive with an Italian loaf, parma ham and dolcelatte, perhaps a bag of tomatoes and a couple of bottles of red wine. We would talk, read poems; he would sing. He was still capable of intellectual leaps, creative excitement and sharp thrusts of criticism. If I stayed the night, I would sleep on the settee in the sitting room (in the eighties with Sandy, in the nineties alone). We also phoned and wrote regularly. I often appended a poem or song. In one letter he mentions how he had supplied Gershon Legman with Alasdair MacMhaister Alasdair's long Gaelic poem about penises, for inclusion in *The Horn Book*, then continued: 'unquestionably the most remarkable paean ever written in praise of the poet's own penis is in Burns's letter to Robert Ainslie, of 3rd March 1788 . . . ' Hamish then wrote out the whole of this Burns letter

5 Sorley MacLean, 'Hallaig', *Spring Tide and Neap Tide; Selected Poems 1932–72* (Canongate 1977).

before concluding with a reference to my original letter: '"I shall be in Edinburgh in the middle of next week . . . " (I'd forgotten for a moment whether it was Robert Burns or Tim Neat writing!)'

By this time Katzel Henderson had retired from her job as a sportswear sales assistant at Jenners department store, and her relationship with Hamish was becoming, once again, close. In April 1997, she took him to Coburg for a family reunion. He sent me a card: 'I'm just recovering from a splendid party held last night in a hotel beside the castle you can see in the distance: I had to make a speech (in my best Perthshire German) in honour of Katzel and her twin brother Viktor, both now 60 years of age! The beer here is rare and tasty.' The following June she took him to Sardinia. Their hotel opened out on to the beach. Again he sent a card: 'Am on Gramsci's island for the first time – its coastline is truly fabulous! We're looking forward to *le quatorze juillet*!' (Hamish and Katzel were both coming to the wedding of my daughter Mary, and Hamish had promised to sing 'La Marseillaise'.)

Unfortunately, Paul Fernie, Hamish's primary helper, was now beginning to become a problem. He was drinking heavily and probably involved with drugs. His wife, Gayle, was determined to leave him and, to Hamish's consternation, deny him access to the children. Disturbed and desperately short of money, Fernie began to use Hamish's credit card and bank account for his own personal needs. Hamish had reasons to be suspicious but felt a tremendous loyalty to Paul and 'his two wee bairnies'. If he knew of the problem, he certainly refused to confront it. Paul had done him good service. If he was taking a few pounds, did it matter? Paul's needs and his children's needs were the reality. Katzel, however, was very worried about 'the Paul Problem', and it cast a shadow over their Sardinian holiday. Katzel reports, 'Hamish was very quiet. I would go out for a swim. He would just sit – taking pleasure in the sea and the mountains. He was like Thomas Mann. If I asked him what he was thinking about, he would say he was thinking about Gramsci.'[6]

The wedding of *le quatorze juillet* took place under a chestnut tree at Balmerino Abbey, in Fife. Hamish and Katzel came by train from Edinburgh. Martyn Bennett was piper. The wedding feast was a Brueghelesque affair in a sheep shed on the St Fort estate. Hamish sang 'La Marseillaise' and 'Banks o' Sicily' and, the following day, he wrote to Margaret Bennett (who had been unable to attend):

> Poor Margaret! I only wish some alchemy could make those damnable problems vanish. Yesterday Katzel and I were in Fife – in the grounds of the ruined Balmerino Abbey, to be precise . . . it was a great occasion! Martyn and Kirsten did splendid service

6 Katzel Henderson, conversation with TN, 2007.

– the composition was truly spine-tingling. Tim was wearing a kilt – MacLaren tartan! He looked magnificent.

Increasingly confined to his flat, Hamish became a selective but avid watcher of television and listener to radio. One television play he particularly enjoyed was Hugh Whitmore's *Breaking the Code*, an exploration of the life of computer genius Alan Turing (hounded to suicide for his leftwing tendencies and homosexual interests). He wrote to me: 'Many thanks for telling me about the TV play about Turing – I watched it – thought it was brilliant. What a marvellous actor Derek Jacobi is.' For Hamish's seventy-eighth birthday in 1997 John Berger sent a copy of his essay *How to Live with Stones – A Letter to Subcomandante Marcos in the Mountains of Southeast Mexico.*[7] When Berger's novel *To the Wedding* was presented on radio by Théâtre de Complicité, Hamish made certain he heard it. It dealt with post-national Europe and human resilience in the face of AIDS.

For forty years Hamish had been rubbing shoulders with the fantastic underbelly of Scots life, influencing the generation that produced Irvine Welsh, Ian Rankin, *Taggart* and *Rab C. Nesbitt.* And, by the spring of 1998, Paul Fernie's personal circumstances were unravelling like a television soap opera. Social workers, childcare officers, lawyers and police officers – all got involved in what became a dramatic divorce case. As Paul peddled the story that he would never see his children again, Hamish dished out money. Paddy O'Neill reports, 'Hamish always forgave Paul his moments of weakness but things got so bad I believe Paul went very close to breaking Hamish's heart.'[8] One day Katzel found Hamish in a dreadful state; he appeared to have suffered the first of what became a series of minor strokes and remained in a confused state for many weeks. Despite this, as Mayday loomed, Hamish decided that he must go on his annual trip to Padstow, and if no one would go with him he would go alone, which he did. In July 1998 he travelled to Aberdeen to receive an Honorary Doctorate from Aberdeen University. Dr Ian Olson instigated arrangements, and Katzel and Tina went with Hamish.[9]

In May 1999 Hamish was fit enough to accept an invitation to a celebration in honour of the Stewarts of Blair, in Blairgowrie Town Hall. I

---

7 Marcos is a Marxist philosopher who left academic life to lead the indigenous resistance movement in the mountains of Mexico. By the mid 1990s he had become a living folk hero, with 'invisibility' part of his mythic power.

8 Paddy O'Neill, conversation with TN, 2008.

9 Hamish was awarded a University of Dundee LLD in 1980, an Honorary DLitt by the Open University in 1983, and the University of Edinburgh and Aberdeen degrees in 1992 and 1998. In 2001 he was offered a fifth Honorary Doctorate, by the University of Glasgow. However, Katzel felt that Hamish was not well enough and she did not want to accept the doctorate on his behalf, so he was unable to accept it.

drove him there and, as usual, being 'on the road' stimulated him. We spoke about Effie Gray and John Ruskin and the glass-blowers of Venice. Time sped by and we were in Blairgowrie Town Hall before we knew it. It was packed, the Boys of the Lough were on stage but the crowd rose as one to give Hamish a thunderous ovation.

At the end of May, my son Francis and Francesca Marubini from Milan were married in the Valle d'Aosta. Hamish and Katzel were invited but Katzel was already committed to a holiday in Germany, and Hamish was deemed unfit to travel. Whilst we were away he made a number of confused phone calls to both Coburg and Milan and appears to have suffered another minor stroke. On her return, Katzel decided that, whatever Paul Fernie was doing or not doing, she must keep a close eye on Hamish. One thing she did was to systematically feed him ginkgo biloba and, by August, Hamish had recovered sufficiently to attend the Edinburgh Book Festival. My book, *The Voice of the Bard* (Polygon 1999) featured in a 'Meet the Bard' session in the Spiegel Tent in Charlotte Square, and I chaired an event at which Hamish, Duncan Williamson, Charlotte Munro and Donald MacDonald of South Lochboisdale all spoke. Taking advantage of this window of health, Hamish went to Blair Atholl to spend a week with Dolina MacLennan in September. It became what she described as 'one long farewell ceilidh', and singers and musicians came from far and wide to say 'farewell to the master'. Hamish and Dolina went up to Loch Fascally, where Hamish had taken Tina and Janet for holidays. It was a very happy time and Dolina decided, 'this was the memory I wanted keep, and I never saw him again.'

Meantime, in Edinburgh, Katzel learned that Hamish had bank and credit card debts of £17,000. When she raised the matter with Paul Fernie, he disappeared the same day – never to be seen again by the Henderson family. Hamish refused to believe what had happened and insisted that no criminal charges be brought against Fernie. This meant that Katzel, on behalf of Hamish, was responsible for the debt. Janet Henderson and her fiancé, Olivier Hickman, came from London to help sort the matter out. The flat was re-mortgaged, and new monthly repayments agreed, but it took many years to pay off the debt. Thirty years earlier Hamish had noted:

> Psychology is interested in man as a kind of disease
> Folklore is interested in man as a kind of tragedy.[10]

Hamish now found it difficult to climb the four flights to his study in the School of Scottish Studies, so Dr Margaret Mackay arranged for his books and papers to be moved to a more accessible room, replicating their earlier location as closely as possible. Hamish was pleased with the new

10 HH, unpublished notes, Henderson archive.

arrangement and to mark the occasion they went to Sandy Bell's. 'No one there knew we were coming but when we opened the door we could hear a guitar player at the back strumming "The Freedome Come a' Ye". It set the seal on a day of change for Hamish and made it seem all right.'[11]

By this time, surprisingly, Hamish's need for alcohol had become a thing of the past. As he became unable to get to and from the pub, he virtually stopped drinking. This fact raises medical and cultural questions. For many years Hamish was heavily dependent on alcohol but his addiction seems self-evidently less physical than psychological. His real addiction was to human conviviality and the grand plans he had set himself in youth. Alcohol was a tool he used to get close to the deeps of the Scottish psyche and, as infirmity separated him from direct contact with people, his drinking fell by the wayside.

It could be claimed that Hamish also used drink as a means of keeping his 'enemies' at bay. He had long used alcohol as a shamanic tool. It brought song to the tongue and liberated unconscious forces. He knew his intellect and education could divide him from the mass and from his own powers of divination. Like Charlie Chaplin, Hamish knew himself to be a vehicle for people and forces beyond him, and the recitations he copied into his mother's recipe book as a child show how early this shamanic impulse was part of his personality. One of these recitations ends, 'The Lime-light man fell onto my head / And knocked me into the drum.' In middle age he wrote:

Tempus originates
Tempus coagulates
Tempus conflagates.

Underdog
Underground:
And we in drams
Behold the Hebrides.[12]

11 Dr Margaret Mackay, conversation with TN, 2007.
12 HH, unpublished notes, Henderson archive.

TWENTY-EIGHT

The Politics of Wisdom

The Colour Question? The biggest threat to the world. Where would Burns stand? South Africa – Mandela – Rivonia – Action.

HH (1970)[1]

Following the Devolution Referendum in 1979 a new 'Campaign for a Scottish Assembly' was soon up and running. For once, the Scottish Trades Union Congress, led by James Milne, took a lead, and Hamish was invited to join its devolution committee. Another by-product of the Referendum was the rise of Siol nan Gaidheal (Seed of the Gael), an organisation of nationalist activists with very clear ecological and anti-nuclear policies. In 1980 Hamish sent me a note: 'Here's a copy of the leaflet being handed out by Siol nan Gaidheal at the Conference [SNP] . . . Nice if something comes of it!' Siol nan Gaidheal leaders believed an Irish sense of political drama was needed in Scotland; some of them talked of armed rebellion, and parades of up to five hundred were soon organised, with Highland dress, broadswords, banners and pipers very much to the fore. The founder of Siol nan Gaidheal, Tom Moore, was a Scot who had spent his boyhood in the USA. He brought a heady mixture of rhetoric and muscle to the movement that worried the SNP leadership, which in 1982 cut off all connections. Hardliners then formed Arm nan Gaidheal (ANG: Army of the Gael), 'a secret underground army that argued that England was an aggressive imperial enemy that needed to be directly opposed'. Between November 1982 and March 1983 a number of incendiary bomb attacks were made on rural electricity substations across Lowland Scotland. ANG supporters were arrested and 'exemplary' sentences handed out. Hamish was sympathetic to the grievances of Siol nan Gaidheal but saw the movement activities as symptomatic of Scotland's problems, not a cure for her ills. He notes:

The piper is still on the parapet
But like the indomitable old whore of Nantuckett
Who went to hell in a bucket

1 HH, unpublished notebook jottings, Henderson archive.

He won't be blate when the moment comes
To offer a soldier's farewell.[2]

As a political activist, however, Hamish was now determinedly non-militant, and many within both the nationalist community and the peace movement looked to him for a new leadership appropriate to the times. On 8 December 1981 he joined twenty-seven Scots who wrote to the Ambassador of the USSR in London: 'Dear Sir, we the undersigned, mindful of Dr Andrei Sakharov's great services in the cause of Peace, earnestly request the Soviet Government to adhere to the letter and the spirit of the Helsinki Declaration of Human Rights and grant an exit visa to Miss Liza Alexeyeva [the Sakharov's daughter-in-law who wished to leave the USSR to join her husband in the West].' During the miners' strike of 1984 Hamish gave full support to the strikers and worked closely with John Holloway of the Edinburgh University Miners' Support Group. On 5 November he wrote to me: 'There's a big concert in support of the miners in the Assembly Rooms, George Street, on Sunday the 18th at 7.30 – the Boys o' the Lough, The Whistlebinkies, and several others. Why not come down and bring some students?' In December he wrote cheques for £15 for the Miners' Kids Christmas Party fund, and £40 to the Miners' Union.

In January 1985, the seventieth birthday of Ewan MacColl was celebrated at the Royal Festival Hall in London. Folklorist Vic Gammon selected the theme of the conference debate, 'Artist: Maker or Tool?' London County Council supported the event, and Hamish and Ken Livingstone (then Mayor of London) were soon getting on like blood relatives. The Dundee Hendersons had married into the shipbuilder Livingstones of Burntisland, Fife, in the early nineteenth century, and the two men found they had plenty in common. Consequently, London County Council decided that the RS *Discovery* should be returned to Dundee.

That summer the Edinburgh Festival hosted an Edinburgh–Dublin Symposium at which Hamish delivered a wide-ranging talk on the Scottish psyche:

> The Scottish working class – rural and urban – has a much better record of resistance to English influences than the bourgeoisie and the aristocracy – and there are many hopeful signs which point to a future awakening. If previous experience is anything to go by it is the Scottish working class which will, in the long run, make some sense of this tangled history . . . Meanwhile the poets and artists grapple with the story, viewing our strange Scotland with a mixture of love and loathing . . . I close with a short poem written many years ago by the late Hugh MacDiarmid: 'New light blots

2 HH, unpublished poem, Henderson archive.

> out this distinction of class. / O magical change, O miracle / I am suddenly beyond myself. / Red, white and square / Tearing the soul to rags!'[3]

The Thatcher government's determination to break the back of Britain's 'dependency culture' was now impacting strongly on higher education. Many small university departments, like the School of Scottish Studies, found themselves strapped for cash and facing demands for closure. Searching for new sources of funding the School launched a newsletter, *The Carrying Stream*. It was Hamish's title, and the first issue concludes with a verse of seasonal good wishes. It had been collected in Gaelic from Mrs Catherine Dix of Berneray; Hamish turned it into Scots:

> Gweed luck, this seely day o' Yule
> And a' the days that come ahint.
> May love and joy be yours for aye,
> And naething may ye ever wint.
> May fortune guide ye as ye gang,
> Nae slippery stane e'er gar ye fa'.
> An ashet fu', a cosie bield,
> And routh o' joy be wi ye a'!

Hamish's participation in the School of Scottish Studies' attempt to raise funds might be described as dysfunctional; he wrote to me, Sorley MacLean and Winnie Mandela! Here is his letter to Mrs Mandela:

> We in this department have huge admiration for your work in South Africa, and wish your cause every success . . . We are sure you will agree that study of International Folklore is a peaceful and humane discipline which helps to reveal the essential unity of human beings in their struggle for a better life. The basic folk tales of the world are the patrimony of the whole human race, they treasure and embody the universal. In the near future the SSS plans to publish a book containing an account of our work and a series of messages from poets like Sorley MacLean and distinguished people like yourself – about our aims and achievements. We would be most grateful if you could spare the time to write a few lines about your work and ideals . . . Finally, may I add with due respect, that it was I myself who wrote the song – 'Rivonia' – about your noble husband.

Following his retirement from the School of Scottish Studies in 1987 Hamish redoubled his efforts to prevent closure of Newbattle Abbey

---

3 HH, unpublished lecture notes, Henderson archive.

Adult Education College in Midlothian. In January 1988, in league with Raymond Ross, he organised a fund-raising concert at which thirty poets, musicians and novelists from across Scotland spoke up for the continuance of Newbattle. On 28 May he wrote to the *Scotsman*: 'The silly season has come early this year. The Right Reverend Thatcher thinks Adam Smith is her spiritual ancestor, and her local satrap Malcolm Rifkind wants us to believe that Scottish culture began with the Act of Union . . . The closing down of Newbattle would be an act of wanton educational and cultural vandalism. We must not let the rump of the Tory party in Scotland get away with it.' On 29 May Hamish attended a demonstration for 'A Nuclear Free Scotland' in Glasgow. In June he wrote to suggest I attend 'the inaugural meeting of the Adam Ferguson Club (which needless to say intends to show up the Tory distortions relating to the Scottish Enlightenment). This is certainly something you should be a member of! . . . I think I told you that old Adam Ferguson lived in Sciennes Hill House, just up the road from us. It was in that house that the young Walter Scott met Burns for the first and last time.'

Hamish's anti-Thatcherism was now reaching boiling point, and for the next three years the campaign against the poll tax became the focus of his political work. On 24 November 1988 he wrote to the *Scotsman*:

> Mr Michael Hirst, Vice Chairman of the Scottish Conservative Party, gives his opinion that the Committee of 100 against the poll-tax 'contains virtually no one of standing in Scottish life'. As I am a member of the committee myself, it is not for me to jib at such a distinguished individual's status; nevertheless, I'd like to suggest that the committee does encompass a pretty representative cross-section of the Scottish population – the 'kindly Scots' of popular parlance . . . I suppose Mr Hirst would have considered the committee's membership more impressive if it had included a bevy of well-heeled Scottish peers, or names familiar to readers of society glossies – the sort of characters Hugh MacDiarmid described as 'famous fatheads, and noted connoisseurs of bread and butter' . . .

The Dundee singer and Radio Tay DJ Sheena Wellington wrote Hamish an enthusiastic letter of support: 'How I enjoyed your letter . . . as an attack on Michael Hirst's ill-informed attack on the Committee of 100 it was masterly . . . in broadcasting we are continually having to watch our step these days. The latest nonsense – "we'll defeat terrorism by stopping people speaking and singing in support of the *aims* of the terrorists" . . . Having already ruffled the IBA's feathers by describing the death of Victor Jara as murder, and by committing a contempt of court during the Spymaster fiasco, they might well think I'm too much of an agitator to keep at Radio Tay . . . But may I ask if you will do me the honour of accepting the Golden Welly Award for 1988 for Services to Folk Music.' Sheena's contract at Radio Tay was soon terminated but she quickly established herself as one of Scotland's leading professional folksingers, most notably at the opening of the Scottish Parliament in 1999. In 2008, Sheena reminisced about Hamish:

> I was in Auchtermuchty for the Folk festival. We were lodged in a Guest House. I was tucking my son John into bed when I heard a small rumpus downstairs. I went out onto the landing and there was Hamish – playing with two dogs and, once he'd got them settled, he started to recite Burns' long poem 'The Twa Dugs'. They sat very quiet taking in every word. So I thought 'This is history' and I went back into the bedroom and got John up, and we leaned over the banister to hear Hamish go through the whole poem. Ten years later, when Hamish died, John asked me 'How old was I when Hamish recited 'The Twa Dugs' to the dogs in Auchtermuchty?'[4]

Hamish's participation in the anti-poll-tax campaign was, however, deadly serious and the notes he made for the public speeches he delivered show that his opposition, far from being self-indulgent rebelliousness, was based on a sense of common justice that the British Conservative Party itself would embrace three years down the line:

1) Ability to pay has been deemed irrelevant
2) It will prove expensive and difficult to collect
3) The tax constitutes a threat to civil liberties
4) It will create an army of bureaucrats and snoopers
5) It will increase the powers of Secretary of State at the expense of a Parliament already unrepresentative of 'the Scottish interest'.[5]

Hamish joined a group who labelled themselves 'CAN PAY, WON'T PAY!' and deliberately courted arrest. He also became part of an 'Underground Anti-Poll-Tax Defence Organisation', set up to defend any person or property assailed by poll-tax collectors, bailiffs, or the police in the Edinburgh area. On 6 May 1989 he phoned me to ask if he could send a letter, in my name, to the *Scotsman*. A recent editorial had labelled him 'an eccentric' and he wanted to Scotch the rumour! (He believed it bad form to respond to personal criticism himself.) He also wanted to promote the anti-poll-tax cause. He dictated his letter over the phone and I agreed to put my name to it. Thus Timothy Neat became perhaps the last of Hamish's many aliases.

4 Sheena Wellington, conversation with TN, 2008.
5 HH, unpublished speech notes, Henderson archive.

> Sir, – Your third leader today refers to Hamish Henderson's 'imperishable reputation as a radical academic and (some might say) eccentric.' I don't know who 'some' are supposed to be. However, if this distinguished poet and veteran campaigner for causes like CND and Newbattle – and implacable opponent of the poll tax – is to be regarded as 'eccentric', I only wish he would bite a good number of other academics, not to mention a whole gang of cultural pundits and governmental panjandrums. Indeed, I would suggest that if the Scottish nation could imbibe a goodly draught of that same 'eccentricity' it might stand a better chance of shaking off its present political malaise and recover effective control of its own affairs. Timothy Neat.[6]

On 8 September 1989 the *Scotsman* carried a letter under Hamish's own name: 'Last week, like some thousands of my fellow-citizens, I received through the post a seven-day warning regarding non-payment of the poll-tax. I need hardly say I am ignoring it. I regard this tax not only as utterly immoral but also as utterly stupid, a view increasingly shared by those on the right who initially supported it. I am resolved to fight this one out to the bitter end . . . ' The fact that Parliamentary debates about the extension of the poll tax to England and Wales coincided with passage of the 'Football Supporters Act, of 1989' stimulated Hamish to note:

> I can well believe that Mrs Thatcher is worried about the hooliganism of English football fans; their conduct reflects badly on the England she has helped to create. In many ways she has only herself to blame. By letting the genie of jingoism out of the bottle at the time of the Falklands War she stirred up dangerous atavistic elements in the body politic: furthermore her economic policies have had the inevitable consequence of creating an underclass ripe, and a target, for the National Front. In Scotland our teenage ruffians have shown themselves to belong to a superior class of hooligan: consequently, knowing that our people are highly unlikely to riot – Mrs Thatcher decided to test out her iniquitous poll-tax here.[7]

On 31 March 1990 a great demonstration was held in London against the imposition of the poll tax in England. A major riot known as the Battle of Trafalgar Square broke out. Within months opinion polls showed that support for the poll tax had fallen to 2 per cent and, in November, Mrs

---

6 Many years later I told this story to Andrew Hood, Scotsman letters editor at the time. He was a little miffed, but pleased to know that even the finest letters editor could be beguiled – when necessary!

7 HH, unpublished notes, Henderson archive.

Thatcher was hounded from office by her own Party. The new Prime Minister, John Major, then cancelled the tax. In July 1992 the Gecko Press in Edinburgh published a booklet documenting the campaign in Broughton and Inverleith: *Cause to Be Proud – a local group's struggle against the Poll Tax*. A flyer carried Hamish's words: 'It was moral instinct that brought me to the anti poll tax cause – a simple sense of unfairness. It was completely immoral, we couldn't put up with it, something had to be done.' Ian Bell reviewed the booklet in the *Herald*: 'These are ordinary people who have done extraordinary things.'

On 12 January 1990 Hamish attended an Edinburgh demonstration against the looming Gulf War. When 'Parents for Survival' asked him to become a link in their 'Chain of Peace across Scotland – Glasgow Green to Grangemouth', he joined in with a will: noting before setting off, 'I'm putting my arms around Scotland'. In July 1990 Campbell Christie of the Scottish Trades Union Congress organised a celebratory 'Day for Scotland', a mass rally-cum-folk-festival on the Falleninch Field outside Stirling. Musical groups such as Runrig, Hue and Cry, Deacon Blue were there and, at one point, folk guitarist Dick Gaughan brought Hamish forward to sing 'The Freedom Come a' Ye'. Ten thousand people sang with him, and for many it was an unforgettable moment.

Although still an MP, Norman Buchan was now dying of cancer. Courageously tidying up his affairs, he wrote to Hamish to reminisce about their folk work, about the magazine *Conflict*, about Hamish's use of the alias Robin Antrim, about blind Martin Milligan,[8] 'now retired and married for a third time!' In October Hamish sent Norman a long letter with his own copy of *Lark Rise to Candleford*. Later, he wrote a noble obituary and attended the Memorial Concert in Glasgow's New Concert Hall. Janey Buchan, in a letter of thanks to Hamish, mentioned how affronted she had felt when the City – to which Norman had given so much – charged her '£3,000 + VAT + 10% of the take!' for the use of the hall.[9]

When John Major was returned to Downing Street following the 1992 General Election, Hamish refocused his attention on the devolution issue,

8 Martin Milligan collaborated with Hamish and Norman Buchan in organising the first Edinburgh People's Festival in 1949 (see Volume 1 of this biography).

9 In 2004, Janey Buchan told me the following anecdote. On Norman's first day at St Andrews House (following his appointment as Assistant Secretary of State for Scotland) his first official meeting was with the senior civil servant. His second was with 'Security'. As he entered the room Norman decided to break the ice by announcing: 'If you're going to ask me whether I am, or ever have been . . . the answer is yes' . . . The officer responded with condescending seriousness: 'We know. And if you want to send Christmas cards to any of your old friends – we have their latest addresses!' Unfortunately, instead of ordering him out of Scotland, Buchan got down to work. And so the old order continues.

signing up with every group committed to a parliament in Scotland. On 12 December a huge pro-devolution rally took place in the Edinburgh Meadows. Knowing themselves vulnerable in a big crowd, Hamish and Margaret Bennett decided they would 'escort' each other. Margaret hired herself a powered wheelchair, and describes their day:

> We set off from the School in high spirits, Hamish saying the buggy gave him something to cling on to! I had bedecked it with saltires because the powers at the SSS did not agree with our participation – Sandy Fenton was Head of Department and twice posters advertising the Rally had been removed from the School notice board. But unafeart we were soon part of this enormous gathering crowd. Many excellent speeches were made. It was clear that a watershed had been reached. It was William McIlvanney who mounted the stage with Hamish. He made a speech, then introduced Hamish. Hamish was in his element. He spoke powerfully and splendidly. The crowd were riveted – beside me were a group of lads, workers, who had never heard of him. 'Wha's this auld fellow?' they ask – and before they got their answer – the crowd, singing 'The Freedom Come A' Ye', had them ecstatic! Twenty thousand people were there. That was the day the tectonic shift happened. As we navigated the buggy back to the School, Hamish did not say much but if he wasn't thinking backwards and forwards he wouldn't have been Hamish.[10]

Hamish also gave his support to a more radical campaign entitled 'Democracy for Scotland'. He was a founder member and signed 'The Declaration of Calton Hill on Vigil Day 100'. A camp was established and the promise was made that the Vigil would continue until a Scottish Parliament was established. In April one of the organisers, Stuart McHardy, writes:

> Dear Hamish, On the 10 April, 1993, the Vigil for a Scottish Parliament will be one year old. DESTINY MARCHES from Whithorn, Iona, Arbroath and Berwick will be arriving at the Vigil that day and will end on Calton Hill where we will be raising a 'Democracy Cairn' . . . The marchers will be bringing stones from along their routes to place on the cairn which is to be both a monument to the Vigil and a symbol of the Scottish people's ongoing commitment to democracy and freedom . . . The ceremonial laying of stones from around Scotland will follow the carrying of the brazier from the Vigil to the top of the Calton Hill at 2 p.m. on the day . . . The brazier will be

10 Margaret Bennett, e-mail to TN, 2007.

> preceded by a piper . . . Speeches will be followed by the singing of 'The Freedom Come a' Ye' . . . In the evening there will be a Ceilidh at the Unemployed Workers Centre in Broughton Street.

'We will build our cairn' is a key line in Hamish's *Elegies for the Dead in Cyrenaica* and as the youth of Scotland carried stones from every corner of the land to build their Democracy Cairn he felt a real satisfaction. Poetry was becoming people, and for the next six years Hamish made regular treks to Calton Hill to support the assembly of youngsters.

For Hamish, 9 October 1993 was a momentous day: the day when the City of Glasgow played host to Nelson Mandela when he formally accepted the 'Freedom of the City' from nine of the British cities that had awarded him 'their freedom' during his years of imprisonment. It was twenty-nine years since Hamish had written 'Rivonia' (the first of more than 200 songs written in Mandela's honour). With Bishop Trevor Huddleston, Hamish was one of the special guests invited to a reception in the City Chambers. And in the early afternoon, Hamish and Mandela went out on to the central balcony together to sing 'Rivonia' to a crowd of tens of thousands below them in George Square. When Hamish finished singing, the two men embraced and spun into a dance – a dance that inspired the singer Ian Davison to write his great song 'Mandela Danced'.[11]

Today, the Western world has appropriated Mandela as a symbol of its permanent commitment to equality, democracy and peace, but it should not be forgotten that when Hamish wrote 'Rivonia' Mandela was involved in an armed struggle defined by most Western governments as 'terrorism' and that the majority of the British people saw White South Africa as a bastion of Christian righteousness against Black communist aggression. Time has marbled our comprehension of the South African struggle. It was harsh, bloody and brutal, and Hamish's 'Rivonia' helps us remember how things actually were. In recent years 'Rivonia' has lost out to more sugary Mandela songs but it remains poetry of visceral power. In lines like 'Spear of the nation unbroken' the reference is to Hamish and Alba, as well as to Mandela and South Africa.

By the mid 1990s, many of the devolution proposals advocated by the Campaign for a Scottish Assembly were British Labour Party policy, and when Tony Blair won his crushing electoral victory in May 1997, Scottish devolution was a government priority. In September 1997 a referendum was held and, at last, an overwhelming majority of the Scottish electorate voted for major constitutional change. On 6 May 1999 the first Scottish Parliamentary elections in almost three hundred

---

11 The celebrations continued in the Royal Concert Hall, where the folksingers Arthur Johnstone, the McCluskey Brothers, the Eurydice Choir, Mara Louw and others took up what Hamish had begun.

years were held. On 12 May the new Parliament sat for the first time. Two months later on 1 July there was a formal opening by the Queen. It was a historic moment and carefully choreographed as an occasion designed to draw Scotland (and Britain) together. The great and the good were invited, children from every part of Scotland, the disabled, bankers and film stars – all were gathered. Then a great procession – led by Donald Dewar, Sean Connery, Ewan MacGregor, Michael Forsyth, Tony Blair and David Steel – walked down the High Street from the Castle. As the procession passed the Scottish Storytelling Centre, its Director, Donald Smith, suddenly recalled Hamish's words: 'Eventually, the politics follows the culture.'

> And as I watched the children passing, a poem began to form in my mind. I later entitled it 'Man and Boy' and dedicated it to Hamish. One line acts as a refrain – 'a long stride shortens the road'. That stride was Hamish's. The road? The road back to Scotland's independent nationhood; the road forward towards a new post-imperial family of nations. 'We've dragged our feet too long', Hamish had told me, years before: 'now is the time'.[12]

With the Scottish Parliament re-established, the Democracy Watch on Calton Hill was free to stand down, and on St Andrews Day, 30 November 1999, a special ceremony took place. The leaders of the Vigil asked Hamish to attend and light 'the Beacon for Democracy' – which still burns on Calton Hill. It was a small-scale but great occasion. Metalwork apprentices from Govan had welded a great metal basket in the form of a quaich and this was placed on top of a broch-like cairn, made of stones gathered from every corner of Scotland and all the countries of Europe. The day was cold and blustery; about one hundred people assembled. The ecologist Alastair McIntosh made a moving speech. When Hamish arrived he was given a seat in a bower-like tent made out of a huge saltire. Three men crouched before him to make the fire that would light the beacon. The damp made the task difficult: the spinning of the fire-stick went on and on. Suddenly, a great cry went up: 'It's hard to light the fire of democracy in Scotland!' At last, the tinder leapt to flame. A single voice called out: 'A Blessing on the Fire!' A hundred voices came back: 'A Blessing on the Fire!' A torch was then lighted and, to the beat of a bodhran, Hamish was helped forward to the cairn. There, Tawny Macleod, a five-year-old from Govan, unveiled the beacon and Hamish, with the help of Ian Thompson, slowly lifted the torch to light the beacon flame. 'The Freedom Come a' Ye' was then sung and Hamish, almost inaudibly, turned to speak these words:

---

12 Donald Smith, conversation with TN, 2007.

> Freedom. A few years back it seemed a puff of wind would blow all this out. But today, it is not a question of why but when. I will not live to see it – but I wish you all the very best.

Those four sentences ended a political career that began in a small cottage by the hump-backed bridge in Glenshee eighty years previously, a career that had unfolded as visionary, fantastical and heroic.

TWENTY-NINE

Under the Earth I Go

Ladyis . . . This is the legend of my life, though Latyne it be nane.
HH[1]

On 11 November 1999 Hamish's eightieth birthday was celebrated quietly at home with his family, but the following weekend Joy Hendry organised a magnificent two-day ceilidh at the Hub, beneath Edinburgh Castle. Alastair Clark described it in the *Scotsman*:

> It was a night of great emotion. Strong men and women wiped away tears at the end of it. Tears of joy, tears of gratitude to Hamish Henderson, the Big Yin of the traditional music revival who, more than any living Scot, had made it all happen. Like so many in the audience, like everybody on stage on Saturday night, this particular scribbler owes him more than he will ever know.
>
> How can a man live so long and do so many rebellious things? There is hope for us all. And he was there to enjoy it, greeted by an ovation as he joined the audience at the start, and a standing one after he joined the many luminaries who had come to pay tribute to him on stage.

Dozens of poets, singers, musicians and friends had assembled and performed to packed houses. The number of figures from the world of politics was small but one ageing Young Communist Leaguer, Danny Couper of Aberdeen, made up for them all when – on hearing the news that Hamish was £17,000 in debt – he sat down and wrote a cheque for £5,000. He gave it to Katzel, explaining: 'I was brought up in the fifties in poverty. It was Hamish who gave me the reason to build for the future. What Hamish did for me, for Jeannie Robertson, for the city of Aberdeen can never be repaid. I was a young communist who became a successful fish merchant. Hamish was something else!'

One of the big surprises at the Hub was a notable speech by Hamish's old *bête noire,* the poet George Bruce, aged ninety-one. He spoke at length

1 Hamish used this rubric to introduce his last publication, *Hamish Henderson: Collected Poems and Songs* (Curly Snake 2000).

and without notes. It was a performance honed like a sermon. The audience was spellbound, and Joy Hendry delighted 'at the sight of these two adversaries burying the hatchet'. Bruce certainly spoke for Hamish but, in my view, he remained his old censorious and commanding self. There he was, a lean, bronzed, well-heeled nonagenarian in absolute possession of his faculties, congratulating Hamish on reaching eighty, 'still drinking and still adding colour to Scotland's national life'! The minister's cat was playing with a mouse in the pews but Hamish took it all in good spirit and, with impeccable timing, left the hall (with Katzel) once 'The Freedom Come a' Ye' had been sung.

Hamish saw in the millennium at home at 20 Melville Terrace. Katzel was with him. Edinburgh Social Services Department now supplied a level of domestic support. The 'betrayal' by Paul Fernie had hit Hamish hard but it was now behind him, partly because, deep down, he knew Paul had behaved like most human beings – in his own short-term interest. Hamish knew he was privileged: he had a good pension, and the mortgage on his flat had long been paid. Paul had little and believed he was about to lose what he loved most in the world – his two children. Why should he not take what he believed they needed? Retribution was not Hamish's way. Indeed, he feared that Paul's sense of guilt might destroy him; and four years later Paul was dead.

The big event of Hamish's millennial year was the wedding of his daughter, Janet, to Olivier Hickman, in Provence. Janet was a copyright lawyer working as a consultant in London, Olivier a Cambridge graduate working in finance in the music industry. The wedding took place in Valréas, not far from Avignon. Katzel organised Hamish's itinerary with great care, booking him a Club Class air ticket – with extra legroom. His diary records: '17/07/00: Rise 8.20, Taxi 9.20, 10.50 plane leaves . . . Saturday 22 July, Sand – Weddin!' His old sense of military precision and youthful ecstasy remained central to his being. 'Sand' was one of his pet-names for Janet: others were 'Wee Sweetie' and 'Smallie', despite her six feet. Janet was named after his mother and she had a special place in his heart. The final entry in Hamish's last diary is her London telephone number.

Knowing he was likely to be unsteady on his feet, Hamish asked me to join the wedding party and escort Janet up the aisle where, before the altar, he would take over. I agreed and drove to France via Hull and Zeebrugge. My youngest daughter, Ishbel, and her friend Jenny came with me en route for a Mediterranean holiday. Hamish suggested that I lodge at the same boarding house as Marian Sugden, his old friend from Cambridge. Janet arranged this, and I learned some new things about Hamish from Marian. She told me that Naomi Mitchison had joked, 'lodging Hamish is like having a giraffe in the house!' and that during a holiday visit to Trinity Hall when the girls were young, Tina had exclaimed: 'Oh, it's so embarrassing when Dad starts to sing!', to which Hamish had responded with firmness: 'Then you'll have to get used to a lot of embarrassment!'

Hamish and Katzel, and her sister Elisabet, stayed in the handsome Cézannesque house of Olivier's father, Reg Hickman. After the formal civil marriage all the guests assembled at the ancient romanesque Knights' Templar church of L'église Saint-Denis, in Richerenches. An Episcopal priest had come from Marseilles. In Maclaren tartan I escorted Janet – resplendent in a full-length wedding dress – to the front of the church and gave her to Hamish. The service was traditional but included secular readings, and Hamish read two Shakespeare sonnets. In the afternoon the reception was held in the gardens of the Hickman house, and dinner served in a great open tent. Seeking the shade, Hamish pottered about under the trees. In his straw sun-hat he looked like the aged Matisse, or a Somerset parson. Katzel was supremely happy but more than pleased when Elisabet, helpful as she had always been, took Hamish off and tucked him into bed.

Next day Katzel and I discussed whether I might drive Hamish back to Scotland, as the Club Class ticket was refundable. We could have fun, and she and Elisabet would enjoy a short break. I said, 'if Hamish is happy to do a dog-leg via Ronchamp – where I need to take photos – he's more than welcome.' 'The longer the dog-leg the better,' said Hamish, and off we set into a thunderstorm. That evening we reached Besançon and found an old-fashioned hotel near the railway station. There was a single room for Hamish on the first floor, one for me on the fourth: at the top of a steep winding staircase, with a lavatory on each level – exuding that strangely erotic smell that most cheap French hotels retained until about 1970. At six thirty next morning I was awoken by a telephone call announcing something was wrong – *'avec votre papa!'* I heard Hamish's cries long before I reached him. He'd fallen out of bed and couldn't get up! He told me, 'At first I thought I would be able to get up. Then I thought you'd be coming down! After half an hour, I thought, I'd better give a shout. I called out in French. Nothing happened! Then, because we're near the German border, I thought, I'll try German! Nobody came! So then I started in English. Then I was shouting for you! I'm sorry, Tim, but here you are.'

We had a breakfast of coffee and croissants and arrived at the Chapelle de Notre Dame at Ronchamp at eleven o'clock. It was closed (it was Monday). I needed photographs of this Le Corbusier masterpiece, to illustrate the biography of Thomas Howarth[2] that I was then writing – so, planning to return next day, we drove on to Colmar to see the Isenheim altarpiece, painted by Matthias Grünewald, Hamish viewing it from a wheelchair. In the evening we drove back to Ronchamp and got lodgings

2 Thomas Neat and Gilliam MacDermott, *Thomas Howarth, Mackintosh and the Modern Movement: A Biography* (IYNX Publishing 2002).

at the youth hostel. Next morning I queued to photograph Le Corbusier's Mackintoshesque chapel and at 9.45 I rushed back to the youth hostel. It took half an hour to get Hamish dressed, then we began a race against time to catch the five o'clock ferry from Zeebrugge, 550 miles away. Twice we stopped for petrol. Then on we drove at a steady 100 miles per hour, the gendarmes parting the traffic before us! We arrived at the ferry terminal with two minutes to spare, the last car aboard. Hamish thought we were catching the Dublin boat, telling me, 'Tim! You've not met the Behans. You'll like them. We'll have a great old time.' We shared a cabin and, after I'd got him wedged in the bottom bunk, I started reading the *Elegies* aloud to him. Occasionally, he would correct my pronunciation or raise a point of interest. In two sessions, I read the whole poem and, when I finished, he said: 'Tim, though I say it myself, I think they're good – very good. And you read them very well.' He mentioned his satisfaction at the 'sound' of the second of these two lines about Alexandria: 'And here, the bay's horseshoe: / How nobly it clanged through laconic communiqués!'

Before seven o'clock next day, we were driving north from Hull. I suggested we detour west to view Hadrian's Wall, something Hamish said he'd never done. Holding his elbow, I stepped him forward to the wall. He put his hand on the top stone and, looking north into Scotland, said: 'So – this is where civilisation ended.'

On 10 August Hamish attended a party at BBC Scotland celebrating the 21st anniversary of the radio programme *Travelling Folk*, fronted since 1979 by his old friend the folksinger Archie Fisher. On 10 October he gave his last poetry reading. It was to members of the Saltire Society of Dumfries-shire, organised by May and Charles McKerrell of Lochmaben. I drove him there and, with time on our hands, stopped at Roslyn Chapel. It was drizzling, so Hamish stayed in the car but I had a quick look round. In Biggar we stopped at the Crown Inn, drank two pints of beer and lunched on venison casserole. The McKerrells were a bit surprised to see us turn up in a battered pick-up van, but when May informed Hamish that Burns had been wined and dined 'in this very room' we began to feel at home – and soon we were being treated like bards. Hamish was given a room with a splendid four-poster bed. When we went down to dinner the dining table was laid with white cloth, silver and fine glasses, and May proudly announced that she had prepared us a special Borders treat, venison casserole! Hamish tucked in like a native and said nothing about our lunch. Soon he was singing 'The Freedom Come a' Ye' and then it was on to Dumfries for 'the reading'. Hamish was now tired and he asked me to read for him. Then, with a dram, he revived and a small but deeply appreciative audience had a memorable evening. Hamish did not appear for a breakfast at which May McKerrell described the New Year and Mid Summer festivities in Lochmaben. As she did so, I realised that they were 'fertility rites' of great interest and, on the road back to Edinburgh, Hamish was soon plumbing me for every last detail.

Appropriately, Hamish's last public appearance was in Glasgow, on 24 January 2001. The burgeoning Celtic Connections Festival, which owes a great debt to Hamish· had invited him to join a panel, chaired by the broadcaster Iain Anderson. Others on the panel were Margaret Bennett, Adam McNaughtan, Norman MacLean, Brian Miller[3] and myself. As Hamish entered the room, the whole audience rose to applaud him to the platform. Afterwards Margaret Bennett, Bill Innes, Hamish and I had supper together. Hamish dozed most of the way back to Edinburgh, but insisted he climb the four flights to his flat unhindered. In March he suffered another minor stroke. Katzel found him lying cold and barely conscious in the flat. Following treatment at the Edinburgh Royal Infirmary he was moved to the Astley Ainsley convalescent hospital on the south side of Edinburgh, where he stayed for four months. Katzel visited most days, and old friends came by. Margaret Bennett was a regular. Maggie Mackay brought news of the School of Scottish Studies. On one occasion I brought two ancient 'golden' cups I'd found in the Oxfam shop in Perth, which Hamish hoped were Pictish. We poured two whiskies and toasted 'The Golden Age'.

During the summer Katzel searched for a suitable place where Hamish might end his days. She selected the Grange Care Home quite close to the Edinburgh Meadows. His room had an *en suite* bathroom and a window on to a small garden-courtyard, with a tree. Via a narrow corridor he had access to a spacious lounge and communal dining room. My first visit took place on 12 September 2001. Hamish was in the sitting room, wrapped in blankets, dozing in an armchair. Recognising me, his face beamed and he looked around the room. Old men and women were bent over newspapers, the front pages ablaze with photographs of New York and the Twin Towers burning. He looked back to me and said, with a jut of the head: 'Here we go again!'

The number of people who visited Hamish at the Grange was small but those who did visit marvellously represented the peoples and places he loved most. For example, Marc Frazzini and Alasdair Gray called in, as did James Kelman: through them he said goodbye to Italy and to Glasgow. In early October, Niall O'Murchada arrived from Ireland to speak about the *Beurla-reagaird* (the Traveller's bardic cover-tongue) and Hamish said goodbye to Ireland. Ewan McVicar, from Linlithgow, came to talk about his work with children's songs and Hamish told him, 'Ewan, you have done a great thing for Scotland'. Alison McMorland and Geordie

3 Miller is a fine folksinger who worked closely with Hamish over many years. His daughter, Siobhan, is now one of the leading singers of the new generation and, following Hamish's death, his wife, Jan, made the first sculpted bust of Hamish (now displayed above the bar in Sandy Bell's).

McIntyre came several times to sing: memorably, Ewan MacColl's 'The Joy of Living'. Storytellers Mairi MacArthur and Bob Pegg, Padraig McNeill[4] and Duncan Williamson called. Thus, he said goodbye to Highlands and Lowlands, to England, and farewell to the Travelling People. Martyn Bennett came to play and discuss his latest demo-tapes, Margaret sang him 'The Cave of Gold'. She also kept a fierce eye on how staff were treating this 'very distinguished old man'. The sitting room, like those of most care homes, occasionally became a menagerie of brayings, belchings and cries for help. Margaret remembers: 'One day we were having a struggle to make ourselves heard above the noise of the other "inmates" – so I said, "Hamish! Let's pretend we're at the Traverse!" "Yes!" he said, "In the front row!" And he roared with laughter.'[5]

In early November, I arranged to take Hamish out for a drive. By ten o'clock, he was ready – washed, shaved, spruce, seated in a wheelchair and ready to go. The care home staff were nonplussed when I turned up in my open-backed Volkswagen Caddie. 'Is it a pig-truck?' asked one young man from Eastern Europe. 'No,' I replied, 'It's a bee-truck! This is the ideal vehicle for old men; we'll be in Moscow by lunchtime!' 'Yes, it's a proper tinker truck', said Hamish. And the Caddie was soon proving its worth: the cabin was warm, the high viewpoint reminded Hamish of his Jeep, and the open back allowed us to take not just the wheelchair but a zimmer-frame, a pair of crutches, a walking stick, three blankets and a rubber exercise mat. First stop was the School of Scottish Studies in George Square. Hamish didn't get out but reminded me of how, in 1983, he thought he had seen Arthur Koestler being driven round the square, in a taxi, looking up at the buildings. This had puzzled Hamish because Koestler had committed suicide the previous week! Many months later, when it was announced that the Koestler Parapsychology Unit was to be established in Edinburgh, Hamish realised that 'he must have come up to check the place out!' One reason why Hamish continued admiring Koestler long after the great days of *Darkness at Noon* was that he seems to have recognised that they shared a weakness: Koestler writes 'I have spoilt most of my novels out of a sense of duty to some "cause"; I knew the artist should not exhort or preach, and I kept exhorting and preaching'.[6]

Having crossed the Forth Bridge we sped north, then east towards Blairgowrie. On seeing the stone bridge that crosses the Isla river, Hamish began singing: 'Busk, busk bonnie lassie and come awa' wi' me / And I'll tak ye tae Glen Isla and bonnie Glenshee . . .' We stopped in a lay-by

---

4 McNeill is a Gaelic-speaking singer and professional storyteller strongly influenced by Hamish. After his death, McNeill wrote a song 'Tae Hamish': 'Like yon Guid Man o' Ballangeich / Wi' blisters on yer haun / You split the grun and sowed the seeds / For yer vision to live on.'

5 Margaret Bennett, conversation with TN, 2008.

6 Arthur Koestler, *Arrow in the Blue* (Macmillan 1969).

beneath the great beech-hedge planted by soldiers going off to join the Rebellion of 1745, and had a picnic of oatcakes, cheese and fruit juice. Driving into Blairgowrie we passed Ramleh, the house in which Hamish was born. In Rattray, I knocked, unannounced, at the door of Sheila Stewart. She had first met Hamish, as a teenager, forty-six years earlier. She kissed him through the van window. I poured three small whiskies. Sheila said, 'I dinnae drink, Hamish, but I'll drink a dram with you the day.' After that it was on to the Spittal of Glenshee. Hamish got out and leaned against the Caddie door. He spoke of his favourite stone in the graveyard behind the cottage, carved with two words – *an duine* – the man. After a while I said, 'Well, Hamish, we've got three choices of road going back: straight home through Dundee; west to Pitlochry and down the A9; or north over the Devil's Elbow!' He said, 'Tim, o'er the Deil's Elbow.' So on we drove – to Braemar and down the Dee. I thought he would fall asleep but he didn't. We spoke about the Anglo-American 'war on terror', about Jacobitism, about the nineteenth-century poet from Glen Clova, Arabella Marie Ogilvie. Having re-crossed the Dee, darkness was falling as we arrived at the Cairnamount. I pulled in at the small car park on the south side of the pass. Half of Pictland was laid out before us: the barley-lands of Kincardineshire, the distant Red Head of Angus, the grey gleam of the North Sea, the Grampians ranging north and west behind us. Hamish said, 'It would seem unlikely, but I've never been here before. Never.'

On the M90, driving south towards Kelty, Hamish, announced, 'Tim, I'll have to get out! If I don't get out, I'll dee! I'll have to get out, now!' I pulled in by the Butterchurn Café, above Kelty. It was a cold starlit night. Within minutes, he revived and on we drove. Arriving at the Grange, I got a ticking off. 'It's half past eight. We expected you back at two thirty! You've been gone ten hours!' Two hundred and seventy miles we had done.

By January 2002 Hamish was very frail. I took him two bees-wax candles and a jar of honey as a New Year present. The great Highland storyteller Alec John Williamson had told me of how the 'old-style Travellers' would be buried with a hammer, a silver sixpence and a candle in their coffins: 'Knock on the door with the hammer, pay the ferryman with the sixpence, and light your way with a candle.' We spoke about God and how it is much more likely that He is man's creation than that we are God's. We reminisced about Janet's wedding and when I reminded him of what he'd said when we reached Hadrian's Wall, he said, 'You'll tell our story, won't you, Tim?' I said, 'I will.'

In February the Saltire Society of Dumfries-shire sent a letter requesting that Hamish do another reading. This was not possible, so on 2 March I went alone to show *The Tree of Liberty* at the Burns Centre in Dumfries. After the film, Morag Aitkenhead, wife of Hamish's old friend John Aitkenhead, asked me to take 'all the best wishes of everybody here to Hamish'. Next morning, May McKerrell said she'd give me some flowers to give to Hamish. What she gave me was a flower growing in a pot – a gerbera, from North Africa – with a single rust-orange bloom. Arriving at the care home, I found Hamish in the sitting room, asleep. I placed the flower pot on a table beside him and took his hand. He awoke. I said, 'Hamish, I'm on my way back from Dumfries. We showed *The Tree of Liberty,* and May McKerrell asked me to bring you this flower as a gift – from the Saltire Society of Dumfries-shire.' He looked at the flower, then towards the window and said: 'All the flowers in here are artificial flowers – but this is a real flower, growing out of its own earth.'

I told him how well the film had been received: that Morag Williams had said how thrilling it was, that Morag Aitkenhead had asked me to tell him how young he looked in the film and how well he'd spoken for Burns. He looked at me and said: 'Isn't it marvellous, Tim, that we've lived long enough to see such success.' I said, 'Not *we*, Hamish, *you,* Hamish!' Soon, I kissed him goodbye and left. It was Sunday 3 March, Katzel's birthday. During the afternoon she and Tina brought cream cakes, and the three of them shared a party with those around them. The next day Hamish suffered the stroke from which he died four days later.

On Wednesday 6 March I visited again. Hamish was propped up on pillows, unable to move or speak. He was on a drip but his left eye was still taking things in. The bulb in the bedside lamp had gone and the only light in the room was a bare bulb – hanging directly above the head of any visitor sitting by the bed. No replacement bulbs were available, so I switched the 'torture-light' off and lit the bees-wax candles. Hamish was calm but his breathing was very laboured. Beside the bed was a bowl of water and small swabs with which one could dampen his lips. Katzel had spent two days at his side. Tina had visited. Janet was coming from London the next day. I read him poems.

Friday 8 March was the day that the final text of *The Horseman's Word* (the last of my quintet of books on Highland life) was to be delivered to the publishers, in Edinburgh. Hamish had been part of the whole project so I took the text to him before going on to the Polygon offices in Newington Road. Janet was seated and tending him from the far side of the bed. Before lunch I returned. Verdi's 'March of the Hebrew Slaves' was playing on the radio. I then went across to the School of Scottish Studies to report that Hamish was likely to die that day. At three o'clock I returned for a third visit. I sat at his right side and talked for a while. When I rose to say *adieu,* I was uncertain what to say. I took his hand, bent towards him and said: 'James Stewart of Alford phoned me to tell you all the Travellers are out for you, Hamish.' It seemed to mean something to him so I went on: 'All Scotland's out for you, Hamish.' I bent forward to kiss him, and the tears splashed down on his face. His cheek was cold with the tears. I whispered, 'We love you Hamish.' At the door,

I looked back. His good eye seemed to fix on me as if willing me on, and Hugh MacDiarmid's words, written about the death of his father, came to me:

> The sunlicht still on me, you row'd in clood,
> We look upon each ither noo like hills
> Across a valley. I'm nae mair your son.
> It is my mind, nae son o' yours, that looks,
> And that great darkness o' your death comes up
> And equals it across the way.[7]

The funeral service took place at St Mary's Episcopal Cathedral in the West End of Edinburgh at two o'clock on Friday 15 March 2002. Hamish's coffin was carried by six bearers, informally dressed: Hamish's two sons-in-law, Charlie Marshall and Olivier Hickman; two Scots Travellers, Duncan Williamson and Ian Stewart of Blairgowrie; the folk-singer Geordie McIntyre and a neighbour of Hamish's. Allan MacDonald was piper.[8] Silhouetted against the lighted West Door – kilted, bonneted, inspired, Allan led the bearers towards the altar, the music soaring like birds up into the high vaults. It was magnificent. Fifteen hundred people stood. Canon Kenyon Wright, in white robes, led the service. Janet Henderson spoke a moving tribute (see Appendix 4) and read Hamish's First Elegy. Sheila Stewart sang 'Here's a man youse don't meet every day'. After eighty minutes, the body was returned into the sunlight – Arthur Johnstone leading the singing of 'The Freedom Come a' Ye'. Twice it was sung. The body was then taken to Leith for cremation, with just the Henderson family and Alex and Chrissie Hawkes from Dry Drayton present. The following week Hamish's ashes were delivered to Katzel in a liver-coloured urn, in a red velvet valise.

Many letters of condolence arrived for Katzel. Former communist, Anzio Beachhead commander Denis Healey wrote from the House of Lords, acknowledging the greatness of 'The D Day Dodgers' and the fact that he did not know that Hamish had been the man who wrote it. Stanley Robertson wrote from Aberdeen: 'Hamish was dearly loved by the Travelling families whom he brought out of obscurity. He will be missed by us all.' Perhaps the most moving tribute came from Mairghread Ellis of Edinburgh, a podiatrist:

> Dear Mrs Henderson – In 1993 I could hardly believe I'd met *the man*!! And what a legend. I shed a tear on Monday, not for me, not

---

7 From 'At My Father's Grave', published in the *Complete Poems* (Martin Brian and O'Keeffe 1978).

8 Hamish had originally requested, seven years earlier, that Ian Grant, an army piper, should be his piper, but he could not be contacted.

> for Hamish, but for Scotland – then I thought no don't cry: for what a legacy he has left us all, in showing us how to save and cherish our heritage . . . what a privilege it was to have him as a patient and sit at the feet (literally!) of such a great man.

Radio and television reported the news of Hamish's death and funeral, press obituaries were impressive and the Scottish Parliament, a few weeks later, devoted a full session to pay tribute to Hamish's life and achievements. No other Scot has been so honoured in the new Parliament.

On 4 May 2002, Hamish's son-in-law, Charlie Marshall, drove north to Blair with the ashes. At the Angus Hotel he met with George Gunn, the ashes bearer, Angus Calder and me, ready to go up to Ben Gulabin. George and Angus were hungry so, whilst they ate, Charlie and I decided to visit Sheila Stewart at Rattray. She invited us in, and sat down with the urn, still in its velvet sack, on her lap. She said, 'There's some weight in Hamish, yet! He was a big man!' Then she called out: 'Hamish! Come on through!' and out of the kitchen came her grandson, Hamish. She passed him the urn: 'In this sack are the ashes of Hamish Henderson, whom you are named after. They're taking him back to Glenshee. So you should remember this. My eldest son is Hamish. You are Hamish. All the Stewarts loved Hamish. And he loved us. In the old days we were treated like scum. He changed our lives. Now we are, almost, treated like ordinary people.' When she gave the ashes back to Charlie, I said: 'Sheila, you can come with us, up to Ben Gulabin'. 'No', she said, 'that's man's work.'

Driving north in a three-vehicle convoy, we parked in a small lay-by within sound of the Glenshee Water. George Gunn took charge of the ashes and on the climb to the summit would allow no one to share his task. After we'd gone about half a mile, I suddenly remembered that I'd forgotten the two 'golden cups' that I'd found in the charity shop and from which Hamish and I had drunk drams at the Astley Ainsley Hospital. The cups were safe in the dashboard. I pushed them into my rucksack and set off again. Reaching the spot where I'd left the others, I heard a tinkling sound behind me: turning round, I saw one of the cups rolling away down the steep path. I chased after it and, when I'd caught it, pushed both cups to the very bottom of the rucksack. Rejoining the group I told Angus the story of how 'one of the gold cups had tried to do a runner!' He was suffering leg cramps and asked in some irritation: 'What are these cups?' 'Pictish cups' I said, 'solid gold – they're for the grave of Hamish. I found them in the Oxfam shop in Perth!'

At the summit of Ben Gulabin, we flew 'the Gramsci banner' – the gigantic portrait of Antonio Gramsci used in *Play Me Something*, in Venice, and a strange ecstasy overtook us. I shouted, 'Now for a dram from the Pictish cups!' I held out the two golden cups – one in each hand. Angus turned them over, looking at the beaten images of the rising-sun, a sailing barque and a gigantic abstracted figure seated at the tiller; and the blood drained from his face. He had brought with him an ancient Chinese poem about ancestors and a golden cup – to read at the scattering of the ashes.

Now George Gunn had to decide where and how to scatter the ashes. Finally, he found *the* spot, overlooking the Glenshee Water, with the hump-backed bridge and Hamish's cottage in the distance. There was a natural tomb amongst the rocks and George said, 'This is the place.' Angus then spoke for Hamish, and read his Chinese poem. George spoke and read a new, very druidic poem he'd written that morning. We toasted '*an duine*', and drank again from the gold cups. George then uncapped the urn and poured the ashes of Hamish into the hollow of the granite tomb. As he did so, through fissures in the rocks, plumes of white ash shot up all around us in the heather – as though a family of dragons had woken. After the dust had drifted away on the wind, I reached into the tomb and placed the two gold cups in the remnants of the ash. George then covered the entrance to the tomb with a number of large rocks, and we began our descent. On reaching the road, the sun was shafting a marvellous orange light on to the hills to the east. We scanned the sky and, above the ridge opposite, an eagle appeared. As we watched, it closed its wings and began a stoop that it sustained for almost a mile, then opened its wings and alighted on the crags of Ben Gulabin, where we had left Hamish just an hour before.

Who doth redeem thy life, that thou
To death mayst not go down?[9]

Almost a year later I found those lines amongst Hamish's papers, and shortly afterwards I had a dream. I was walking with a band of men along a rough track – half grass, half gravel – through rolling green hills. There was a broken dry-stane dyke on our left. Two or three of us were walking ahead, the rest talking quietly in twos and threes some way behind. I turned to check whether Hamish was keeping up. Ill-clad, aged, he was slowly shambling along finding the rutted track difficult. I called out, 'Are you all right, Hamish?' He stopped, looked up and thrust his jaw forward with a double nod to suggest he was. I walked on but, realising something was wrong, looked back a second time. Hamish was now on the far side of the dyke, in a graveyard beyond which a grey stone church-tower rose amongst trees. His arms were above his head, his fists tight, his torso naked as he trod the remnants of his robes into the grass. White-skinned, he looked like El Greco's painting of the Apotheosis of St John and, as I was thinking this, his body turned to gilt-bronze and a great cry came from him, 'Oss, Oss'. The gold of his body was now oozing and dripping

9 Psalm 103, verse 4a, *The Psalms of David in Metre*, written in Hamish's hand in notes in the Henderson archive.

blood like sweat from head to foot. With head thrust back and his fists still high, a second cry came from him, 'Oss, Oss'. He then collapsed slowly, vertically, to the ground and a third cry came, 'Oss, Oss! Wee Oss!'.[10] His body was now white marble; all trace of the blood was gone. He steadied himself, head down, resting on one arm. He had become 'The Dying Gaul', silent, defiant, proud. And on the wind I heard the words he had spoken on his seventieth birthday – when he fell and broke his wrist dancing the 'Gay Gordons': 'Tim, this is life, this is what life is.'

10 'Oss, Oss, Wee Oss' is the cry of the 'Mayers' at the Padstow May Day celebrations. With it, they dance and the Obby Osses are revived from ceremonial death to life.

APPENDIX ONE

Hamish's Rewrite of the Dialogue – Collected by the Dean of Lismore – Between St Patrick and Ossian (or the Druid)

Patrick: Hamish, how can you compose folksong?

Hamish: It may seem a contradiction in terms, and many members of the old school of folk-music scholars would consider it so – so maybe I'm sticking my neck out if I claim, and I do claim, that all the songs I compose myself are folksong.

Patrick: How did you compose it?

Hamish: One at a time. At the end of the Sicilian Campaign, in the last war, I heard a tune composed by an old friend of mine – 'Farewell to the Creeks' and the words 'Fare ye well ye banks o' Sicily' fell into place whilst I listened; not a phrase that's very original – it draws on the common stock of phrases and ideas which are common in Scots folksong – and this is the way most folk poets work. They nearly always use a tune (or a variant of that tune that's known already) and sometimes a line or an idea from a previous song. In fact, the song which at birth (so to speak) is already a folksong in the making has usually got something of other songs bedded in it.[1]

This is one reason why – when other people like the song and sing it, they don't regard it as being the property of the author and feel at liberty to change it. For instance, just after the war, at a party, a man sang a song of mine. I told him. He said, 'you couldn't have composed it – I got it from so and so, and he told me he knew the author. I tell you, Patrick, I was annoyed at the start, disconcerted, but afterwards I was quite pleased – I realised that I had made it, I had composed a folksong.

---

1 [This idea can be compared to the process in architecture whereby succeeding generations of architects continue to make use of 'the Orders of Architects', and the proportions they embody, not just in the Classical tradition but in the Modernist tradition as well . . .]

Patrick: And now quite a lot of singers, apart from Artie, sing it don't they?

Hamish: Artie Trezise. Oh yes, and some of them make a proper hash – like Robin . . . Every singer alters the song a bit – that is the folk process. And whilst one doesn't want a game of Chinese whispers, it's not just a difference of interpretation that occurs – it is a creative development, and this happens to the work of all folk poets.

Patrick: The other folk poets – who are the best of them?

Hamish: Ewan MacColl, Matt McGinn, Bob Bertram, Sydney Carter, Johnny Handle, Cyril Tawney and in the United States Pete Seeger and Bob Dylan. All of them, or nearly all, use Scots traditional tunes, variations of traditional dance tunes that go rippling and jigging their way through Scottish history, many are mouth tunes, mouth music. These are familiar enough in Gaelic but there are plenty enough in Scots tae – 'Tail Toddle' for ane! . . .

Patrick: Hamish, you've used the phrase 'the folk process'; could you explain?

Hamish: The folk process is a useful shorthand phrase for what happens to folksongs when they begin to take on a life of their own – start shedding some things, accruing others – generally taking on a new and changing form . . . Some songs are not ordained to be folksongs, even if they were to live to Doomsday – others have the folk process built into them. But you still get surprises. Robert Tannahill wrote a song called 'The Braes of Balquidder' and in its original form – as Tannahill wrote it – its not a very inspiring piece. The language is stilted, but in the North of Ireland it has been turned into a really beautiful folksong. The stilted phrases have disappeared, and it has become a haunting love song called 'The Wild Mountain Thyme'.

Patrick: Finally Hamish, what is folksong?

Hamish: What is folksong? Patrick, if I could tell you that I would earn every dollar you ever spent in Minnesota – but my aim is towards the hearthstone . . . There are no 'tasks' in folk poetry: what we are dealing with here is an artistic category that is not susceptible to definition, it exists as fact and is beyond being defined.

Patrick: Thank you Mr Henderson.

Hamish: But I have not finished, the field opens before us! The great bulk of those now earning their livings as educational folklorists could be dispatched Holus Bolus up St Bollox's Lum without Scotland or the wind being any the poorer.

Patrick: I think you should go on, or back.

Hamish: I will go on. Long lists are naturally thought highly of by ministers and teachers. Lists of men, and songs, and questions. The poets are in the main, entitled to be called 'Men'. I could name 3 bakers, 7 blacksmiths, 5 bookbinders, 14 drapers, 14 factory workers, 12 gardeners, 9 grocers, 4 miners, 1 weaver, 2 umbrella manufacturers and one US consul. That's the kind of list they come up with and where does it get them? They will list songs – To a Raindrop, To an Infant, To an Iceberg: there are six songs called 'A Sprig of Heather', four to a snowdrop, four called 'The Skylark', five called 'Twilight', and over a dozen called 'Tell me – of what shall I sing?' . . .

[This dialogue owes much to Hamish's stay on the isle of Lismore but was written following a Scottish Home Service broadcast in which Douglas Young spoke in a very Victorian and literary manner about what 'he' considered 'folk' to be.]

APPENDIX TWO

Small Magazines

In music, as in everything, the disappearing moment of experience is the firmest reality.

Benjamin Boretz

Magazines fascinated Hamish from boyhood and, throughout his life, he used them as tools in his 'great cultural plan'. After 1960 he made regular contributions to both scholarly and popular magazines, such as *Scottish Studies* and the *Scots Magazine,* but his major achievement was to stimulate small magazine publishing in Scotland; this, in turn, stimulated a wider and hugely important revival of book publishing in Scotland in the late twentieth century. Brief descriptions of some of the magazines with which Hamish was closely involved are set out below.

Chapbook was set up in 1963/64 by Hamish's friend Arthur Argo. Its remit was 'folk, literature, politics and people'. Argo edited the magazine from Aberdeenshire, but production and circulation were controlled from Glasgow by Carl MacDougall, Ian Philip and James Dunnett. *Chapbook* was cheaply printed but illustrated and appeared bi-monthly for five years. It reported and listed folk events across Britain and gave full-blooded support to CND, to the anti-apartheid movement, to the anti-Vietnam war movement, the international peace movement and the Scottish republican cause. A major feature or biographical portrait of a leading folk personality appeared in each issue. For example Morris Blythman – Scotland's most prolific post-war political song-writer – was given free reign in *Chapbook* Vol. 4, No.6 (1967). Argo's editorial closeness to Hamish is clear in the list of people profiled: Ewan MacColl, Joe Corrie, Ken Goldstein, Gershon Legman, Matt McGinn, Mary Brooksbank, Jeannie Robertson, Archie Fisher, Davie Stewart, Jimmy MacBeath and William McGonagall, as well as rising stars like Dolina MacLennan, Andy Hunter, Adam McNaughtan, Sheila Douglas, Peter Hall, Billy Connolly and Hamish himself.

It was Hamish who wrote the *Chapbook* article about McGonagall. That it was the longest scholarly article he was ever to write says a great deal about Hamish's ideological 'methodology' and belief in 'the folk process'. Hamish had long been interested in McGonagall: his grandmother had bought poems from the poet's own hand in the streets of

Dundee. By the mid fifties Hamish saw McGonagall as 'a leak in the dyke-side of half-a-dozen elitist cultural theories!' In 1963 he helped resurrect the Societas McGonnalliensis at the University of Edinburgh and gave a lecture: 'MacGonagall – bard of the poetic belly-flop'. Hamish introduced 'Scotland's most popular poet' with Gramscian seriousness and compared McGonagall's 'long awkward lines' to those used by Dante. He quotes: 'He ran, he put on speed after he had turned away: / He raced, like the runners on the track at Verona: / Not like the losers though, but like him who wins the day.' He suggested that McGonagall was a product of folk traditions very similar to those Dante had adapted, and his article triggered worldwide interest. On 30 September 1966, Charles Lawson wrote from London: 'If you find the caesura, McGonagall's verse always scans – it's no use reading it to yourself, it must be spoken aloud – and it needs plenty of breath and good resonance . . . I want to trace the development of the Cockney Music Hall out of the ballad tradition and out of folksong – so no doubt I shall come to you to pick your brains.' Professor Frank Zaic of the University of Graz in Austria wrote: 'I am preparing an article on "poetic justice" so I was particularly amused by McGonagall's couplet: "No, in the theatre we see vice punished and virtue rewarded / The villain either hanged or shot, and his career retarded"! . . . It was very kind of you to answer my questions about versions of "The Ball of Kirriemuir" so generously. I found the other day a reference to "The Ball" in Hal Porter's autobiography (Australian novelist), "The Watcher from the Cast-Iron Balcony"!' Peter Sellers wrote (6 May 1966): 'Dear Mr Henderson, How very kind of you to think of sending me more news of the Great McGonagall.

As I am sure you already know,
I am one of his ardent admirers and so,
It is with great joy this very day
That I look forward to reading it
  Without delay or dismay . . . P. Sellers. Actor and Comedian.

Hamish did not think, or pretend, that McGonagall was a major artist but his bold re-estimation of McGonagall added a dimension to Pop aesthetics and literary theory.

In 1968, as *Chapbook* folded, Hamish became involved in the foundation of three new magazines – *Chapman*, *Aquarius* and *Scottish International*. A withdrawal of Scottish Arts Council funding precipitated the demise of *Scottish International* in 1973 but during the seventies the Scottish magazine scene was suddenly very strong with *Akros*, *Saltire Review*, *Northern Review*, *Aquarius*, *Calgacus*, *Free Man*, *Gairm*, *Lallans*, *Rocket*, *Literary Review*, *Modern Scot*, *New Edinburgh Review*, *Poetry Scotland*, *Scottish Art and Letters*, *Scottish Literary Journal*, *Scottish Literary News*, *Scottish Studies*, *Tocher*, *Voice of Scotland*, *Seer*,

Clamjamfrie, *Cencrastus* and *Sandy Bell's Broadsheet*. In 1970 Hamish contributed forty-two entries to volume 1 of the *Dictionary of British Folk Tales* (ed. K.M.Briggs, London), plus 20 contributions to Volume II (1971). More surprisingly he acted as a regular contributor and consultant to *Man, Myth and Magic,* published by the Reader's Digest

Calgacus appeared for just three issues in the mid seventies but Hamish regarded it as significant magazine, not least because it was named after Scotland's first known resistance hero (elected leader of the Caledonian tribes who halted the Roman advance at Mons Graupius in AD84). In 1979 Raymond Ross set up *Cencrastus*. In 1980 Hamish stimulated the relaunch of Tambimuttu's magazine *Poetry London*. It dated back to the Second World War, when Hamish was part of Tambimuttu's Fitzrovia circle. By the late 1970s Tambimuttu had become a victim of drink and soft living but Hamish's capacity to inspire is clear in this letter from Tambimuttu's partner, Claire: 'Dear Hamish, I went to Fenner Brockway's 90th birthday celebrations . . . Tambi is full of grand ideas you've inspired . . . I think the Cavafy poem with the song betwixt is for the second issue . . . He has sworn off drink utterly now and is really on the beam. His liver will not permit one more beer – which betokens well. Since you left he hasn't had one drop. Thank you again dear Hamish – fondly till soon again – Claire.' When Tambimuttu died in June 1983, Hamish was disgusted by the manner in which *Private Eye* treated his death and wrote:

> Dear sirs, . . . The non-genuine person cannot believe that the genuine (*das Echte*) exists . . . The inimitable flavour of English Philistinism, lightly and insufficiently camouflaged as a form of pseudo-satire in Private Eye, is now clearly suffering from a terminal illness. The incessant gormless facetiousness that should have long-since turned off even the most feeble-minded of your addicted readers, has not done so. Thus you need a pseudonym for all your shite-hacks – one that can do service for everyone from Lord Gnome downwards (or upwards): it is the simple and quite attractive pseudonym Phyllis Stein. You are an organ of ruthless sadism. You remind me of the SS men who loved music. It would be idle to expect conventional 'good taste' from Private Eye, but all the same to quote a paragraph from an obituary in Pseud's Corner – when many people were mourning the death of Tambimuttu – was a bit much . . .

His letter was not published. When, in 1984, *Private Eye* embarked on a campaign to damage the career of the young Gordon Brown, Hamish went back on the offensive. When *Private Eye* again refused to publish his letters he waited for his moment – then struck back, on 11 March 1985, with this letter to the *Scotsman*:

Sir, – David Steel states in a letter to The Times that Private Eye 'is intending to be a satirical magazine'. The intention may be there – let us give the rag the benefit of the doubt – but the performance is another story. Indeed, Richard Ingrams seems intent on proving, issue after issue, the truth of a statement by the great Austrian satirist Karl Kraus that the English do not know what satire is . . . For Ingrams, satire is purulent muck-raking and club-footed facetiousness.

A few months ago Private Eye printed a short 'profile' of Gordon Brown, MP (signed 'Backbiter') which was grotesquely inadequate by any standards. The hack who did this particularly blunt hatchet-job had the temerity (lurking behind anonymity) to call Gordon Brown – one of the most able MPs in the present Parliament, and a brilliant man – 'mediocre'. His pathetic piece contained the usual farrago of distortions and errors of fact (including the inevitable irrelevant sex bit) . . . I wrote a letter to the editor correcting these and added the following comment: 'Dennis Neilson [serial killer of 16 Londoners] is on record as saying that he enjoyed a "love-hate" relationship with your pestilence-breeding organ. What a pity he couldn't have invited it round for a friendly chat some evening' . . . It did not altogether surprise me that this letter – which I would suggest bears some resemblance to genuine satire – was not printed by the bold 'satirist'.

APPENDIX THREE

Timothy Neat's Poem 'Hamish Henderson's Last Goodnight', 1997

A body broke the clouds below me,
Rising Tintoretto-like an arm and man
Came up at me through space –
His left hand reaching for my right:
Half the world was spread beneath us,
His grasp not worth the name.

I am become the morning star, he whispered,
My hour in the night-sky of life falls away
The light of the morning of daybreak has found me,
This glisten of sweat is death having its way.

Life-longing imprints the palm slipping from me,
In slow-motion a life is unlocking for ever;
The voice coming up
Is now thought more than whisper:
I loved you like a father and a son,
The secret is – both One and All
As Cornishmen would say.

Hark away! The raven rolls his glossy wing – hark away!
A ladybird's alighted on the breeches by my bed! Hark away!
Ben Vorlich's there and Dublin Toon
And Auld Reekie like a lang-dried rose.

Look on me now, not as I am
But as I was – in song,
When I was young
And in the Apennines
– In Italy, in sun.

The darkest hour is moments now – and long.
My strength light-years away,
Back into the melting pot I go – I joke!
These rolling captions mark – The End –

As when I sang John Berger out – on to the Barra Strand:
Addio, Addio – it was in music those words came
Like beastings atop a milking pail:
'The first and last of life – is herding'
And that song older than all stories told.

Ah look! The sun is up!
Its shadow easing down Glas Maol
Lighting the bridge o'er the Glenshee Water –
Look – there on the road the rain lights to the hill
A piper leaning on his son:
'The Siege of Delhi', fills my ears.

'The Siege of Delhi'
Sounding out across the sands,
As it did when he went down at Anzio.

Silenzio.

The sound of oars rested, dripping water.
Fluorescent the boys who dive the Blue Grotto,
Amber the nectar in Keith and Kinross:
The Green Man and the Jew's Harp! Silenzio!

Listen – I hear it –
The tin whistle's out . . .

Euphoric I see Schiehallion illumined –
Ask Margaret sing 'The Cave of Gold'.
Ask Janet come. It was for life and love I sang –
I see Him shining in her eyes – my Champion.

APPENDIX FOUR

Janet Henderson's Eulogy Spoken at her Father's Funeral, 15 March 2002

When my father wrote the *Elegies for the Dead in Cyrenaica* between 1943 and 1947 he was in his twenties. Now in my mid thirties I am constantly astonished by the power and maturity of these poems, so evocative of the desert war and of an era that was over long before I was born.

If, as the Elegies suggest, the war was one of the defining experiences of the first half of his life, then his marriage to my mother in 1959 was another watershed. Indeed the 1948 edition of the Elegies that I will read from today contains a dedication to her, recalling fondly their chance encounter in Leith Street on a June evening in 1956.

Perhaps because he had been orphaned at an early age, my father desperately wanted a family, and this was my mother's gift to him. Twenty years to the month after he started writing the Elegies my sister Tina was born. I arrived on the scene three years later in 1966.

Although already approaching fifty before we were old enough to really know him, we soon understood that he was no ordinary dad. Just as my mum had been captivated by his charm, humour, intellect and easy-going manner, so Tina and I were fascinated but never overawed by his commanding presence – at once enigmatic and intimate.

During our childhood we learned to expect the unexpected: sometimes he was lost in thought, patrolling up and down the long hallway at 20 Melville Terrace humming to himself; sometimes he would sit in the kitchen and sing to us – or recite poetry in German, French, Italian, Scots, Latin and Greek. Then there were the impromptu Saturday tours of Edinburgh's watering holes. Tina and I would stand stoically below bar level – the forerunners to Sandy the dog, who ten years later became his more vocal companion on these occasions!

Notwithstanding his many gifts, many moods, many parts and many guises he was *our dad* and he was devoted to us. We for our part loved him unconditionally and totally.

So too did my mother, whose loyalty, support and devotion to him was unstinting during their intense and unique forty-year partnership. Thanks to my father's amazing gifts, but also to my mother's enormous capacity for love, my sister and I enjoyed a family life that was unusually rich and diverse, but also full of love, laughter and affection.

I think my father also drew tremendous strength from the secure and nurturing environment of family life and that this helped to sustain him throughout the second half of his life.

My father was strong, brave and uncompromising in life – and last Friday he was brave and dignified in the face of death. Following his last stroke he was in great discomfort and unable to speak. However, he still managed to express delight with his eyes at the sight of his three 'beautiful girls' as he liked to call us.

The First Elegy is a poem about love, death, bravery and compassion and seems a fitting tribute to this extraordinary man – my father.

First Elegy

End of a Campaign

There are many dead in the brutish desert,
who lie uneasy
among the scrub in this landscape of half-wit
stunted ill-will. For the dead land is insatiate
and necrophilous. The sand is blowing about still.
Many who for various reasons, or because
of mere unanswerable compulsion, came here
and fought among the clutching gravestones,
shivered and sweated,
cried out, suffered thirst, were stoically silent, cursed
the spittering machine-guns, were homesick for Europe
and fast embedded in quicksand of Africa
agonized and died.
And sleep now. Sleep here the sleep of the dust.
There were our own, there were the others.
Their deaths were like their lives, human and animal.
There were no gods and precious few heroes.
What they regretted when they died had nothing to do with
race and leader, realm indivisible,
laboured Augustan speeches or vague imperial heritage.
(They saw through that guff before the axe fell.)
Their longing turned to
the lost world glimpsed in the memory of letters:
an evening at the pictures in the friendly dark,
two knowing conspirators smiling and whispering secrets;
or else
a family gathering in the homely kitchen

with Mum so proud of her boys in uniform:
their thoughts trembled
between moments of estrangement, and ecstatic moments
of reconciliation: and their desire
crucified itself against the unutterable shadow of someone
whose photo was in their wallets.
Then death made his incision.
There were our own, there were the others.
Therefore, minding the great word of Glencoe's
son, that we should not disfigure ourselves
with villainy of hatred; and seeing that all
have gone down like curs into anonymous silence,
I will bear witness for I knew the others.
Seeing that littoral and interior are alike indifferent
and the birds are drawn again to our welcoming north
why should I not sing them, the dead, the innocent?

INDEX

Page numbers followed by n (as in 16n) indicate information appearing in a footnote.